Pat Cameron is a ... nglish
Language and Li ... ining
the London Univ ... taff of
the British School at Athens to catalogue material in the School's
Stratigraphical Museum at Knossós.

She spent five years on the project, and in her spare time was able to
acquire a detailed knowledge of Crete, studying its history and the way
of life of its people, and exploring the countryside by car and on foot.
She now returns regularly to the island.

*The Snake Goddess, a faience figurine from the Temple
Repositories of Knossós (Herákleion Museum, Gallery IV)*

BLUE GUIDE

CRETE

Pat Cameron

Maps and plans drawn by John Flower

A. & C. Black
London

W. W. Norton
New York

Fifth edition 1988

Published by A & C Black (Publishers) Limited
35 Bedford Row, London WC1R 4JH

Published in the United States of America by
W W Norton & Company, Inc.
500 Fifth Avenue, New York, NY 10110

Published simultaneously in Canada by
Penguin Books Canada Limited
2801 John Street, Markham, Ontario L3R 1B4

British Library Cataloguing in Publication Data
Cameron, Pat
    Crete. — 5th ed. — (Blue guide).
    1. Crete — Description and travel —
    1981 - — Guide-books
    I. Title   II. Series
    914.99'80446 DF901.C8

    ISBN 01-7136-2692-5

ISBN 0-393-30475-2   USA

Printed and bound in Great Britain by
William Clowes Limited, Beccles and London

PREFACE

The first edition of *Blue Guide Crete*, which appeared in 1974, was an expanded version of the section covering the island in *Blue Guide Greece*. This was brought up to date twice in six years, but eventually it became clear that a major revision was necessary to meet the requirements of the large number of visitors who want to explore the archaeological and art-historical aspects of Crete's past, while at the same time enjoying the island's natural beauty and ideal climate. After the untimely death of the Guide's previous author, Stuart Rossiter, I was asked to undertake this task and the fourth edition was published in 1986. I am now glad to have been given such an early opportunity to revise and expand my previous work.

I continue to be grateful to Dr Hector Catling, Director of the British School at Athens, who allowed me to make a start on the Guide whilst I was still on the staff of the School, and then encouraged and advised me on many occasions. Vronwy Hankey gave me the initial confidence to undertake the revision, and I was fortunate during further research for this edition to enjoy Vronwy and Henry Hankey's companionship on Crete, as well as to benefit from their help and advice. The archaeology in the book owes much to Sandy MacGillivray who guided my reading and patiently answered innumerable questions; I have continued to draw upon his knowledge, and am profoundly grateful that I could do so: however, the conclusions I have reached are my own responsibility.

I regret that I cannot name individually all the members of the British School who have aided me: by researching in the Athens library, by checking details while travelling on the island, or by discussing their own academic speciality. I owe a great debt to them all. Mary MacGillivray has been a constant support and source of information. Alan Peatfield and Christine Morris made me welcome on return visits to Knossós, and assisted both with answers to practical questions and with suggestions of archaeological interest. Ann Brown's recent travels on Crete have produced a wealth of information and ideas, and I am particularly grateful to her for taking so much trouble on my account when she was fully occupied with her own project.

I should also like to thank Cheli Duran and Eléni Faragoulitákis-Kouvídes who have explained many aspects of Cretan life and language; I am deeply indebted to Eléni whose meticulous scrutiny has led to many corrections and improvements.

Kerin Hope kindly checked the medieval section of the island's history, and has most generously made some of her own work available to me. Michael Durkin and Carol Lister contributed a valuable paragraph of geological information. The National Tourist Organisation of Greece gave practical help from their offices in London as well as in Herákleion and Khaniá; this help included arranging for me complimentary flights to Crete on Olympic Airways.

John Flower was consistently kind and tolerant during the preparation of maps and plans. I am grateful to all who provided or allowed me to use photographs, especially W. Müller and P.W. Warren, the Visitors of the Ashmolean Museum in Oxford, and the Archaeological and Byzantine Services of Crete.

One most regrettable omission from the 1986 preface was the name of David Smyth who for that edition generously helped me with the basis for a new plan of the surroundings of the Palace of

Knossós; this is taken from his own large-scale plan for the 1981 Archaeological Survey of the Knossós Area (Hood and Smyth). I am grateful for further advice about new plans in this edition.

Anyone who attempts to write about Crete must be indebted to many authorities and sources. I would like to acknowledge this debt, in particular to the work of G. Cadogan, P. Callaghan, N. Coldstream, S. Hood, A. Makridákis, I. Sanders, S. Spanákis, P. Warren and D. Wilson. Some of these kindly helped with specific problems in their own field. I have also drawn on the observations of earlier travellers such as the scholar Robert Pashley, and the naval surveyor Captain (later Admiral) T.A.B. Spratt in the 19C, and the Italian Guiseppe Gerola whose treatise (1905–32) on the island's Venetian monuments laid the foundations of research in this field. The most recent addition, 'Kreta' by Gallas, Wessel and Borboudákis is likely to remain the definitive work on the churches of Byzantine Crete for many years to come. Further valuable sources are listed in the Bibliography.

During work on my first revision I received much help with the final preparation of the manuscript from my brother, Christopher Cruise. Now I would like to thank Emma Bullard, who has read the revised and expanded text and made many improvements to it. Mary Laing made many constructive suggestions. I am also grateful to my editor, Tom Neville, for his patient guidance. At various stages I have been saved from a large number of errors and obscurities. All further suggestions, whether corrections or new ideas, will be welcomed.

CONTENTS

8   CONTENTS

MAPS AND PLANS

Maps

Plans

EXPLANATIONS

Type. The main routes are described in large type. Smaller type is used for branch-routes and excursions, for historical and preliminary paragraphs, and (generally speaking) for descriptions of minor importance.

Asterisks (*, **) indicate points of special interest or excellence.

Distances are given cumulatively in kilometres (the total once in miles) from the starting-point of the route or sub-route. An attempt has been made to give road distances as accurately as possible; detours are not included in the total. Sometimes the route distances start from a junction on the bypass of a large town rather than from its centre; this is noted in the text. New kilometre posts are beginning to be installed on main routes, and figures given in the Guide conform to the new system where possible.

Walking distances have been indicated as an approximate time allowance. A Cretan asked a walking distance will always give the answer as a walking *time*, which takes account of the terrain along the way.

Abbreviations. In addition to generally accepted and self-explanatory abbreviations, the following occur in this Guide:

Ay. = Ayios, Ayía, Ayii, Ayiés (Saint or Saints)
c = circa
C = century
Dr(s) = drachma(s)
EOT (NTO) = Ελληνικός Οργανισμός Τουρισμού (National Tourist Organisation)
KTEΛ (KTEL) = Κοινόν Ταμείον Εισπράξεων Λεωφορείων (Joint Pool of Bus Owners)
ΛΕΩΦ. = Leophóros (Avenue)
OTE = Οργανισμός Τηλεπικοινωνιών Ελλάδος (Greek Telecommunications Organisation); on plans = telephone and telegraph office.
Plat. = Plateía (Square)
Rte = route

Transliteration and stress accents. The chief guiding principle has been to help the reader, with or without a classical education, to pronounce the Greek words in the text, especially the place-names, in a manner recognisable to a modern Greek speaker. Absolute consistency in transliterating is difficult for a number of reasons, but especially because some well-known words already have an accepted spelling in the English language, for example Herakleion and Zeus. Moreover, pedantically strict consistency sometimes produces unnecessarily ugly words without assisting pronunciation.

The transliteration of place-names on signposts does not always follow the system used in this Guide. The transition of modern Greek from *katharévousa* (or formal) to a *demotic* (colloquial) form, most conspicuous in the grammatical endings, is nearly complete, but a process of simplification continues and many spelling variations will still be encountered: Knossós and Knosós, Lassíthi and Lasíthi.

In addition, *all* place-names decline like other nouns; this often produces a change of stress as well as of inflection. Some places have their more modern spoken form in the accusative, for example Zákro, though they appear offically on maps and signposts in the nominative, Zákros.

Street names are usually in the genitive: literally Street of 25 August, Square of Freedom. As in English, a church may be referred to by the name of its saint in the nominative or the genitive. This is particularly noticeable in Greek in the case of monasteries: Moní Arkadíou, the monastery of Arkádi.

The written accents of Modern Greek are in the process of being drastically simplified, but because correct stress is vital to the understanding of the spoken word, the transliterated versions in the text have been given an acute accent to indicate the stress. The names of Classical sites have been stressed as in Modern Greek to help the tourist enquiring for them. Upper case characters are not accented, so in unmarked words starting with a vowel (Ayios, Embaros) the initial syllable carries the stress.

Panayía Kerá, Kritsá

CRETE

Among the islands of the Mediterranean **CRETE**, in Greek KPHTH (Kríti), has always been of paramount importance both because of its position and its size; it is by far the largest of the Greek islands. Lying across the southern Aegean basin, it forms a link in the chain through Kýthera to the mainland of Greece, and through Kásos and Kárpathos to Rhodes and Turkey, while to the S the coast of Africa is only 300km away. The island, 250km long and nearly 60km at its widest point, is dominated by its great mountain backbone: in the W the White Mountains (Levká Ori, 2453m), the massif of Mount Ida (Psilorítis, 2456m) in the centre, to the E of that the Lasíthi mountains (Díkte, 2148m), and at the eastern end, beyond the narrow isthmus of Ierápetra, the Siteía range. The mountains are composed of folded rocks, ranging in age from Late Palaeozoic to Early Tertiary. These hard crystalline limestones, phyllite, schist, and occasional altered igneous rocks (such as serpentinite) were placed in their present position by Alpine earth movements. In contrast to the upland areas, the low-lying ground is formed of Late Tertiary sediments, notably cream-coloured limestones, sands, clays and gypsum, deposited after the main mountain-forming episode.

The mountains slope gently to the N and very sharply on the southern coast. This has resulted in habitation being concentrated on the N coast around and behind the great bays of Kastélli, Khaniá, Soúda, Réthymnon, Herákleion, Mirabéllo and Siteía. By contrast the southern coast cannot support much of a population and there is only one large town, Ierápetra. The fertile Mesará plain, watered by the Ieropótamos, is the only cultivable area of any size in the S, but terraced hillsides often make good use of less propitious land. An interesting geographical feature is the incidence of high upland plains enclosed by a ring of mountains, such as the Lasíthi plain, that of Nída on Mount Ida and the Omalós in the White Mountains.

Lying along and just above the 35th parallel of latitude, the island is farther S than Algiers or Tunis. Crete enjoys a typical Mediterranean climate with long hot dry summers. The winter rain, often torrential, falls as snow in the mountains, but the proximity of the sea ensures an extensive frost-free lowland zone. This climate favours the island's two main crops, the olive and the vine; it is also suitable for the fig, almond, pomegranate and quince, all of which can be found growing wild. (The Latin name of the quince is derived from Kydonía, one of Crete's ancient cities.) The carob tree too, an evergreen with distinctive elongated pods, grows well, and thrives even in relatively arid conditions. Melons and apricots are traditionally successful, and there are extensive citrus groves especially in the NW coastal belt. These include oranges, lemons and increasingly tangerines; Cretan oranges are said locally, and with some justification, to be the best in the world. Along the S coast which enjoys relatively higher winter temperatures, serried ranks of practical but unsightly plastic greenhouses produce the typical Mediterranean vegetables year-round for the Athens markets. The number of banana groves is increasing, and there are new projects for kiwi fruit and avocado pears. The Herákleion market demonstrates the quality of local produce in season. The upland plains, especially Lasíthi, grow potatoes, onions and apples, also some cereals, though Crete is no longer the granary it was in the Roman and Venetian periods.

About 20 per cent of the island's population of a little over 500,000 lives and works in Herákleion, which is the fifth largest city in

Greece, and has the highest per capita income in the whole country. The benefits of tourism are chiefly responsible for this prosperity. In addition, since Greece joined the European Economic Community the number of industrial projects on the island has grown significantly. Herákleion has a new industrial zone in the hills to the S of the airport, and many internationally recognised names appear on the factories, engineering works and bottling plants.

In the villages most of the work is still concerned with the vines and the olives, both labour-intensive operations at certain times of the year; since Minoan times olive oil has been an important source of wealth for the Cretans. This employment is now supplemented by horticulture, and there remains some local weaving, tanning and potting. An accepted way to raise money for a daughter's dowry or to build a new house has been to serve a spell 'on the ships' in Greece's merchant navy. Money has also returned to Crete from workers in the USA and West Germany, but permits for such work are now more difficult to obtain.

The climate and geographical position close to Asia are responsible for the island's astonishing variety of wild plants and flowers. The many hundreds of known species include over 130 peculiar to Crete. In particular many varieties of orchid and ophrys are to be found in the spring. Botanists will not need to be reminded of the specialised flora of Crete's mountains, gorges and coasts; many guided botanical tours are arranged from all parts of the world. However, the visitor with a more general interest can also scarcely fail to be delighted by the island's wild flowers. Sheets of *Anenome coronaria* in early spring are followed by *Ranunculus asiaticus*, most noticeable in a shining buttercup yellow. In damp ground under trees and bushes *Cyclamen creticum* flourishes. At the edge of the melting snow on Ida or the Omalós plain appear belts of Crete's special crocus, *C. sieberi var. sieberi*, often mixed with *Chionodoxa cretica*. In their season there are wild iris and scented narcissus, lupins, gladiolus and tulips. There are asphodels and mandragora or mandrake familiar from literature. In late spring the fields turn yellow with *Chrysanthemum coronaria*, and the hillsides are coloured by pink and white varieties of cistus. When the first oleanders flower in dried-up stream-beds, or planted along the roads, it is a sign that spring is over. There are autumn flowers too, as growth starts again in October after the first rains, but they are less profuse and conspicuous, a more specialised interest.

Crete's original forest cover has been exploited since Minoan times, but until the 16C cypress trees were still abundant on Mount Ida. The forests declined drastically during the Turkish occupation; that process has not been halted and, in addition, herds of goats cause damage which prevents regeneration. Large areas have been reduced to a scrub known elsewhere in the Mediterranean region as 'macchie' or 'garigue', and in Greece as 'phrýgana'. The typical vegetation can be uncomfortably spiny, but the all-pervading scent of herbs such as sage, thyme and origano will provide ample compensation, and the undergrowth shelters a great many members of the orchid family. The main archaeological sites are now sprayed with herbicides; unfortunately this has become the easiest way to protect walls and other features from invasive roots and weed cover. But many of the less well-known sites to which this Guide points have not been affected, and moreover are legally protected from cultivation and grazing, so that they are ideal refuges for all manner of plant life.

Among the wild animals now found are the Cretan ibex (known

locally as the kri-kri or the agrími, a word used in Greek for any wild animal), badger, wild cat, marten and weasel. The agrími, *Capra aegagrus cretensis*, often depicted in Minoan art, survives in the wild in very limited numbers in the remoter regions of the White Mountains, and in various reserves on off-shore islands along the N coast. Reptiles are less widespread than on the mainland, though the viper is known. Scorpions are not uncommon and there is a dangerous species of poisonous spider, the rogalída, though as it lives in underground burrows this is rarely seen.

The island's bird life is very varied. Ornithologists come to Crete to observe the spring migration. Some spectacular birds of passage are egrets, hoopoes, bee-eaters and golden orioles, also large flocks of red-footed falcons. Among the resident bird population specialists watch for Bonelli's eagle, Eleonora's falcon, and the bearded vulture or lammergeier, now a species threatened with extinction, though the Greek government has made a start on protection measures. The uninitiated visitor is likely to notice other huge vultures (usually the griffon vulture), eagles, buzzards and various falcons including perhaps the swift peregrine. A flash of vivid blue, and a voice unmistakeable once heard is the blue rock thrush. A melancholy drawn-out note, rythmically repeated at intervals, comes from the Scops owl; it is a characteristic sound of the Cretan dusk.

Crete is now very conscious of the tourist potential of climate and scenery combined with the interest in antiquities, especially the remains of the Minoan civilisation both at the archaeological sites and in museums. Increasingly the economy is geared to tourism; large holiday hotels continue to be built along the N coast and even remote areas are equipped to receive visitors. After an ambitious programme of road improvement, all the main tourist objectives can be reached without difficulty, and almost without exception on an asphalt road surface. The proposed highway to serve the length of the S coast is incomplete, but it can be argued that enough of Crete is already accessible to tourist coach traffic.

The three-and-a-half-thousand-year-old Minoan civilisation will be the primary interest for the majority of readers of this Guide, but many later antiquities are also rewarding in a variety of ways. The hilltop sites, whether an Early Iron Age refuge or the acropolis of a later city-state, have great appeal for keen walkers and nature lovers even if little has yet been excavated and only the quantity of stone hints at former occupation. Crete's surviving monasteries, though often sorely depleted as religious institutions, are now on the tourist circuit; despite much restoration made necessary by their turbulent history they retain architectural surprises, and they remain for the most part havens of tranquillity. Sunday may prove the exception for then they are popular objectives for the traditional Cretan εκδρομή or 'outing'.

At the beginning of this century the Italian scholar Guiseppe Gerola listed 809 Byzantine churches with fresco paintings on Crete, and perhaps as many as 600 still remain in sufficiently good condition to be studied by experts; the Service for Byzantine Antiquities is engaged in an admirable programme of conservation. In recent years the qualities of Cretan painting have increasingly come to be accepted by art-historians. Specialists in this field will already be aware of what they seek on the island, but for the uninitiated a number of the better-preserved and more easily accessible frescoed churches and chapels are noted in the itineraries. In other circumstances an exhibition of these paintings would attract great attention. No such exhibition could match the beauty of their native setting.

HISTORICAL BACKGROUND TO CRETAN ANTIQUITIES

Neolithic Period (c 6000–3000 BC). The earliest settlers of Crete arrived by sea from the East or South, perhaps from Anatolia (Asia Minor). Their economy was based on farming, with domesticated animals and cultivated crops, and they spun and wove cloth. They lived in villages in the open, sometimes on low hills as at Knossós and Phaistós, and perhaps for part of the year in caves. They built simple rectangular houses, at first entirely of sun-dried mudbrick and later of mudbrick on a stone socle. Their burial places, frequently in caves or rock shelters, were outside the settlements, which suggests a relatively advanced culture. Cave sanctuaries evidently played an important part all through the Neolithic period. The first inhabitants of Knossós seem to have been at an aceramic stage of development, but this was short-lived and Neolithic pottery reached a high standard in the dark burnished wares, sometimes with incised decoration of simple geometric patterns filled with white paste. Other characteristic artefacts were stone and bone tools, bone arrowheads, obsidian blades, stone vessels and maceheads. There are female figurines in both stone and clay, often of pronounced steatopygous shapes. By the end of the fourth millenium BC, settlement had spread throughout Crete, and as far as some relatively remote off-shore islands.

The Bronze Age (3000–1100 BC). Sir Arthur Evans characterised the Cretan Bronze Age as Minoan, after the legendary King Minos. He identified Early, Middle and Late Minoan periods (EM, MM, LM), and gave each period three sub-divisions (EMI, EMII, EMIII and so on). In some cases these periods were further refined to reflect archaeological evidence (eg LMIA and LMIB, even LMIIIA1 and LMIIIA2), but usually these sub-divisions can be ignored by the layman.

Evans based this system on stratigraphy and changes in pottery styles recognised during his excavations at the Palace of Knossós and correlated with work at other sites on Crete. The system has certain limitations, especially in E Crete where the pottery styles may be more conservative than at Knossós, but by and large three-quarters of a century of archaeological study has confirmed rather than refuted Evans's original interpretation.

More recently the eminent Greek archaeologist N. Pláton proposed a system of chronology based on major events now fairly well established in the time-span of the Minoan Palaces. Pláton divided the Bronze Age into four periods: Prepalatial (the approximate equivalent of Evans's Early Minoan), Protopalatial (the period of the Old Palaces), Neopalatial (the period of the New Palaces) and Postpalatial. A difficulty here is that while the majority of Minoan sites were destroyed in 1450 BC, the Palace of Knossós flourished for a further 70 years, so Postpalatial dates may be open to confusion.

Both these systems, which are not incompatible, are attempts to establish a relative chronology or intelligible sequence within the Bronze Age of Crete. For an absolute chronology, or calender dates, archaeologists beginning with Evans painstakingly built up correlations with the world outside Crete, especially Egypt, using foreign artefacts excavated in a reliable context on the island, and Cretan artefacts similarly found abroad. Absolute dating of the Egyptian sequence was possible because its hieroglyphic script had been deciphered in 1822. The scientific method of Carbon 14 dating, with an error factor at the time of the Minoan Palaces of about 100 years, is a great deal less accurate than correlation with what are in effect historical dates from Egypt.

The Prepalatial Period (3000–1900 BC), EMI–III and MMIA. The transition from Neolithic to Early Minoan c 3000 BC resulted from a gradual infiltration of new settlers, again probably from the East, bringing with them the technique of copper-working. Many new settlements date from this time. The EMI period is marked by several innovations in pottery technique and style. The pottery is handmade, but it is much more skilfully fired, and there are distinctive new shapes such as the beak-spouted jug. Pýrgos ware (named after the cave site near Nírou Kháni excavated in 1918) includes tall pedestalled chalices, and their patterned surface is achieved by burnishing. The first pottery decorated with paint also dates from this period. Ayios Onoúphrios ware has patterns composed of narrow stripes of red or brown on a buff or cream ground; these groups of stripes are arranged in a variety of designs, sometimes intersecting for a cross-hatched effect. Burial in caves continued, but the first built tombs are recorded; there was a primitive 'tholos' near Krási on the route up to Lasíthi, and a huge cemetery of pit graves at Ayía Photiá in E Crete. At Pýrgos, near Nírou Kháni, the first known interments in clay coffins or 'larnakes' were discovered.

The circular tombs of the Mesará plain appear for the first time during EMII (2600–2200). Tombs of this type, which occur elsewhere on Crete but less frequently, are large communal graves, stone-built and free-standing, with a single low entrance always facing E. They were in use for many generations during the second half of the third millenium, and some continued during the following period contemporary with the Old Palaces. The term 'tholos' (indicating a circular domed shape), which is often applied to these tombs, may be misleading, for it is thought unlikely that, in the case of the larger ones, at least, they would have been vaulted in stone.

The monochrome and painted pottery styles of EMI continued their development into EMII, but this period marked the appearance of the mottled red, orange and black ware named after the site of Vasilikí, where it was first found. The striking effect was achieved by a combination of uneven firing and the use of several different-coloured slips on the same vessel.

Two sites of this period have been thoroughly excavated. Mýrtos (Phournoú Koriphí) on the S coast is a close-knit settlement with defined living areas, kitchens, store-rooms and workrooms, but without separately defined houses. At Vasilikí in E Crete the settlement plan suggests a less communal social structure. The quality of the architecture of the so-called 'House on the Hill' at this site has long been recognised; important features were the paving of a West Court, and internal walls finished with hard red-painted plaster. Recent study has revealed that this building is not one but two houses, both dated within the second half of EMII. Vasilikí is said to foreshadow the mode of life of the Palace civilisation of the next millenium. A more centralised society was encouraging specialised craftsmen who produced the bronze daggers, gold jewellery, ivory work, seals and stone vases, often of superb refinement, which are known from the tombs of this Prepalatial period. Foreign contact increased and with it foreign influence; a Minoan colony was founded on Kýthera, an island off the southern Peloponnese.

The Old Palace or Protopalatial Period (1900–1700 BC), MMIB–MMII. The latter part of the MMI period is the conventionally accepted date for the foundation of the Middle Bronze Age Palaces at Knossós and Phaistós. There is fuller evidence of town life on the main sites, and individual villas are known at Mállia and Khamaízi. Peak sanctuaries, as on Mount Júktas above Knossós and Petsophás above Palaíkastro, began to play a part in Minoan religious life. The Early Minoan tombs continued in use, but in many places a new method of burial was introduced with the body placed in a clay storage jar (pithos), as at the cemetery at Pakhyámmos near Gourniá.

In the Palaces the EMIII/MMI style of pottery with white spiral decoration on a dark ground was succeeded by brilliant thin-walled polychrome vases, known as Kamáres ware, made possible by the introduction about that time of the potter's wheel. Great strides were made in all forms of metalwork; bronzesmiths mastered elaborate castings in two-piece moulds, and understood the lost-wax (*cire perdue*) process. Some of their best work was reserved for the daggers, other weapons and tools exemplified in finds of this period from the Mesará tombs. The superb jewellery on display in the Herákleion museum includes examples of the goldsmiths' work, showing a free use of granulation and filigree techniques, with decorative patterns in minute grains of gold, or designs using fine gold threads. The art of the seal engraver also developed rapidly; remains of a sealcutter's workshop have been found at Mállia, including tools and unfinished seals, while a deposit of nearly 7000 sealings at Phaistós has greatly enlarged the corpus of known designs. Though soft stones continued to be used and earlier shapes survived, harder stones appear in new shapes, with more vigorous and life-like designs. The so-called Hieroglyphic Deposit at Knossós (sealings, labels and tablets) testifies to the connection between seals and writing.

Foreign contacts were wide; Egyptian scarabs appear in Crete and MMII pottery in Cyprus, Egypt and the Near East, while both pottery and stone vases have been found on the Greek mainland and in the islands. In about 1700 BC a great catastrophe left the Palaces in ruins. The damage was almost certainly caused by earthquakes, and the huge blocks hurled from the S Façade at Knossós into Evans's 'House of the Fallen Blocks' are evidence of the strength of the upheaval.

The New Palace or Neopalatial Period (1700–1450 BC), MMIII–LMI. After the great disaster the Palaces were rebuilt, and to this period belong most of the Minoan buildings whose remains are now visible, including the mansions that surround the Palaces, and the country houses scattered across the island. Fresco paintings decorated the walls of their major rooms; efficient plumbing and drainage systems were installed. The extensive areas filled with great storage jars bear witness both to the economic prosperity of the age and to the sophisticated redistribution system on which it was based.

Foreign contacts were wide-ranging. Crete exercised a profound influence on the mainland of Greece from c 1600 BC onwards, and indelibly stamped its character on what came to be called Mycenaean culture. Influence on the Cycladic Islands was even more profound; it is suggested that there were Minoan colonies on some of them, for example Kéa and Mélos, and the clearest example yet excavated of a provincial Minoan town is the Akrotíri site on Théra (Santorini). Strong influence, if not actual settlement, has been noted on Rhodes and Kos, while sites in Asia Minor (e.g. Miletus and Troy)

*The Bull's Head Rhyton from the Little Palace at Knossós
(Herákleion Museum. Gallery IV)*

were well within the Minoan trading orbit. Further afield Minoan products reached the Lipari islands in the W and Cyprus, the Levant and Egypt in the E. At this point Crete commanded apparently unlimited supplies of copper and tin (copper ingots from Ayía Triáda and Zákros, Palatial hoards of bronze vessels at Knossós, Mállia and Týlissos). There is debate concerning the source of these metals; recent scientific research suggests much copper may have come from deposits in the Lávrion area in Attica, and only a small quantity from the much better-known source in Cyprus. The source of tin, a vital constituent of bronze, is even more uncertain; Cornwall, Bohemia and Sinai have all been suggested.

It is a mark of the prosperity of the times that decorated pottery was no longer the leading artistic medium (despite the excellence of the so-called 'Marine Style'). The innovative artists may have turned to fresco painting, and craftsmen were working in stone (vasemakers, gemcutters) or metal (weapons as well as vessels). Pottery ornament and shape, in many cases both based on metalwork, became highly repetitive, in marked contrast to the great diversity of the earlier polychrome Kamáres ware. Technically, however, the best pottery of the New Palace period is excellent.

The Minoans used a syllabic script (Linear A) to write an as yet undeciphered language. It appears on sun-dried clay tablets from Ayía Triáda and Khaniá, Mýrtos (Pýrgos), Palaíkastro, Týlissos and Zákros; also on large clay pithoi, on a potter's wheel and on offering tables. These last are often from sacred caves or sanctuaries and their inscriptions are doubtless of a religious nature.

Around the year 1500 BC a volcanic eruption destroyed the island of Théra and its settlements, and Crete cannot have been unaware of this catastrophe only 150km to the N. However, some other explanation must be sought for the widespread destruction on the island some 50 years later. There was a LMIB (c 1450) horizon of fire-destruction at Minoan sites right across Crete, and the type of damage is consistent with destruction by human agency rather than by natural causes such as earthquake or tidal wave.

The Final Palace Period at Knossós (1450–1380 BC), LMII–LMIIIA1. For reasons imperfectly understood, Knossós was less affected by this destruction than other sites. Its damage was soon repaired and its life continued for several generations, apparently under the direction of Mycenaean Greeks who were either responsible for or took advantage of the events that had brought low the rest of Crete. At this period archives in the Linear B (Mycenaean Greek) script which had supplanted Linear A show clearly that Knossós was the administrative centre of the island. Sometime around 1380 BC Knossós itself was completely destroyed.

The Postpalatial Period; Last Years of the Bronze Age (1380–1100 BC), LMIIIA2–LMIIIC. After the widespread destruction in the mid 15C, many of the sites were never reoccupied. In this category are the settlement at Mókhlos and the large villas at Nírou Kháni, Sklavókambos and Vathýpetro. In some cases of 14–13C reoccupation on a reduced scale, individual houses or rooms were cleared and re-used, but there were also substantial new buildings as at Ayía Triáda and Týlissos. Occasionally new settlements were established, for instance at Khóndros near Viánnos. The town at Khaniá flourished (with vases imported from Cyprus indicating foreign contacts) and it seems likely that it became the centre of power on the island.

Shrines from this Postpalatial period have been found; characteristic furnishings include snake tubes and clay female figurines with raised arms and cylindrical skirts. Examples noted in the text are at Knossós, Gourniá, Ayía Triáda and Mitrópolis near Górtyn. A new and distinct method of burial was introduced, with rectangular painted clay chests (larnakes) placed in chamber tombs.

The epics of Homer, written down about 700 BC, set events which can be dated to the 13C against the background of an heroic age. Unfortunately, tantalising hints of life in prehistoric times have to be accepted in part as the romantic embroidery of succeeding generations of story-tellers, and not as a completely reliable account of the period.

The Early Iron Age (1100–c 650 BC). Geometric and Orientalising Periods. The Subminoan period of transition was a troubled time, and there was a movement of population to inaccessible mountain refuge sites such as Karphí above Lasíthi. Knowledge about this period is still slight, but two things are noticeable: there is some continuity of cult from the Late Bronze Age to the Iron Age, as shown by deposits of objects in sacred caves, notably the Idaian Cave on Mount Ida and the Diktaian cave above Psykhró; moreover a number of Iron Age settlements have traces of LMIII occupation. Górtyn, Praisós, and Vrókastro are examples. A rich cemetery at Priniás in central Crete was in continuous use from Late Minoan times to the Greco-Roman period.

In retrospect it can be seen that a new era was beginning. The cultural traits of the Minoan and Mycenaean civilisations lost their dominance, and gradually the elements emerged which would shape Crete in the Hellenic world. Increasing familiarity with the technique of working iron, and its potential strength as opposed to bronze for agricultural tools and for weapons, were a basis for future economic development.

During the disturbed conditions early in the millenium the Dorians, a tribe of Greek speakers distinguished by their dialect, had begun to infiltrate from the Peloponnese. Homer (Odyssey, XIX, 177) speaks of a mixed population, including Dorians and Eteocretans. The latter adhered to Minoan traditions, and inscriptions show that their language was prehellenic, but gradually the Dorians spread throughout the island. At Praisós and Dréros an apparently peaceful assimilation can be traced. The Dorians are credited with the rise of the 'polis', or city-state, and the social institutions associated with it.

The chronology of this period is still based on pottery sequences largely built up from cremation urns (pithoi) and the vases which accompanied them as grave gifts (Herákleion Museum, Galleries XI and XII). There was local variation in burial practices, but cremation became the common rite, the urn containing the ashes being placed in a rock-cut or stone-built tholos family tomb which remained in use for several generations.

Pottery decoration based on increasingly elaborate arrangements of geometric patterns has given its name to the period. One Knossian workshop incorporated into its designs fan-tailed birds with raised wing, and there are rare but important portrayals of figures such as the Mistress of Animals. During the 8C, pottery styles began to reflect influences from the eastern shores of the Mediterranean, and there grew up on the island one of the earliest Orientalising cultures of the Aegean. Once again Crete's geographical position on a trade route from the Levant to the Central Mediterranean was an important factor in shaping her development.

This oriental influence is most strikingly demonstrated by the new figured relief work on beaten bronze for the votive shields from the Sanctuary of Zeus in the Idaian cave; these remarkable pieces, some of which are exhibited in the Herákleion museum, are attributed to a guild of itinerant bronze workers from the East. The same technique is used for gold jewellery from a tomb at Teké which is part of the Knossós North Cemetery. The characteristic burial urns of this period were decorated with Orientalising motifs in vivid polychrome of red and blue on a white ground.

This period saw the rise of the 'polis' or city-state. The island was divided among a great number of these small city-states, each built in an easily defendable position usually on a hill-top with a water supply and agricultural land available nearby. Territory was jealously guarded and feuds were common. The cities were ruled by the Kosmoi, a small body (less than ten) elected annually as administrators and, if necessary, as leaders in war. By the mid 8C Dréros had an agorá (or city-centre) and beside it a small temple, a sanctuary of Apollo Delphinios. In the following century an oath administered to the young men of Dréros lays down an exacting code of behaviour, with the civic virtue of loyalty to the 'polis' already pre-eminent.

Round about 750 BC a semitic script was adopted for the Greek language and from this time inscriptions are a useful aid to archaeological interpretation.

The Archaic, Classical and Hellenistic Periods (c 650–67 BC). The Daidalic style of sculpture, named after the legendary craftsman Daidalos, may have originated in Crete, and it played a leading part in the development of Archaic Greek sculpture. Daidalic figures adopt

Egyptian conventions such as the rigidly frontal posture, and wig-like hair. A statue from Elévtherna and the goddesses from above the transom of the Priniás Temple A doorway (both in Herákleion Museum, Gallery XIX) are good representative examples, as are the terracottas from Oloús and Siteía in the museums at Siteía and Ayios Nikólaos.

Politically Crete remained somewhat detached from the main-stream of Greek history, from the impact of the Persian Wars and the short-lived brilliance of 5C Athens. The traditionally conservative and aristocratic pattern of Doric society continued to prevail.

Despite this detachment, the conquests of Alexander the Great of Macedon and the imperial aspirations of his successors brought new prosperity to the island. The warlike character and traditional bravery of the Cretans became a marketable commodity; they were in demand as mercenaries, and payment for their services enriched the island. Piracy was a less reputable but well-documented source of income.

On a wider scale the extensive trade patterns of the Hellenistic world in the wake of Alexander's conquests gave added importance to control of the sea routes. On the island the petty wars and fluctuating alliances continued, as Knossós, Lýttos, Górtyn and Kydonía (Khaniá) gradually emerged as the main contenders for supremacy. But the rivalry was complicated by the involvement of foreign powers exploiting their influence on Crete in their own power struggle for control of the Aegean. Against a background of Macedonian expansionism, the Spartans intrigued in West Crete, the Egyptians gave garrison support to Itanos, Rhodes cultivated Oloús, and Eumenes of Pergamon contracted an alliance with 13 of the city-states. Gradually Rome became involved in Crete, first as a peace-maker between warring city-states, and then to reduce the menace of piracy from bases on the island.

The Greek mainland became part of the Roman Empire in the mid 2C BC. There was an abortive expedition against Crete in 71 BC, and two years later Q. Caecilius Metellus (later Creticus) invaded with three legions. It took him nearly three years to subdue the island.

The Roman and First Byzantine Periods (67 BC–AD 824). With its capital at Górtyn, Crete became, with Cyrene in N Africa, part of a joint praetorian province. It was administered by a proconsul who governed with a Provincial Council and a system of magistrates again known as Kosmoi. Knossós was made a Roman colony at a date still disputed, but not later than 27 BC. The island lay on the route which linked Rome with her Empire in the East. It shared the Eastern Mediterranean culture transmitted along the trade routes and enjoyed from the conquest until the 7C AD an unusual period of peace and prosperity, reflected in large spreading settlements in low-lying or coastal areas such as Górtyn, Knossós or Ierápytna (Ierápetra). Significantly, Lató on its almost impregnable hill near Kritsá gave way in importance to Lató pros Kamára at modern Ayios Nikólaos on the Bay of Mirabéllo. The settlement pattern came to include isolated villas and farms unknown in warlike Hellenistic times. Many sites such as Mókhlos were inhabited for the first time since the Bronze Age. It speaks volumes for the skill of the Roman Empire's colonial administration that, for perhaps the only time in Crete's history, foreign rule was not accompanied by a perpetual state of rebellion.

After AD 330 historians refer variously to a Late Roman or Early

Byzantine period. The triumph of Christianity and the foundation of Constantinople by the Emperor Constantine the Great mark the beginning of the Byzantine era in Greece. With the division of the Roman Empire in 395, it was natural for Crete to become part of the eastern sphere of influence, looking to the new imperial capital on the Bosphorus, the brightest beacon of European civilisation during the centuries when the Western Empire was in decline.

The architects of the earliest churches on Crete followed the prevailing practice by adopting the form of the basilica, a standard Roman public edifice divided into three aisles by interior colonnades; one or three apses were added at the E end to form the sanctuary, while at the W a portico (narthex) extended along the whole width of the building. The sites of some 70 of these churches are known or suspected, and the great majority are attributed to the mid 5–mid 6C. The best preserved, and architecturally the most sophisticated is Ayios Títos at Górtyn, but many other basilica sites have been excavated, for example at Pánormos on the N coast, Vizári in the Amári valley and high in the hills above Gouledifrom Vári, S of Réthymnon; the church at Vizári is interesting because it dates from the late 8C, not long before the Arab conquest.

The Arab Occupation (824–961). During the 7C the decline of the Roman Empire affected the security of the E Mediterranean, and Crete was under constant threat from Arab raiders based in N Africa. In 674 the main Arab fleet wintered on the island. In 824 a band of Arab adventurers, originally from Spain, but by then based on Alexandria in Egypt, captured the island and held it against several relief expeditions from Constantinople until 961. Sicily also was lost to Christendom at this time.

The Arabs ravaged the island, destroyed every one of the basilica churches, and left little positive evidence of their occupation apart from their coinage. The major exception is their foundation, on the site of modern Herákleion, of El Khandak (meaning ditch or moat), for a while the slave-trading capital of the E Mediterranean.

The Second Byzantine Period (961–1204). Eventually in 961 Nikephóros Phokás recaptured El Khandak, and the Arabs left Crete. Cyprus too was freed (965), and Byzantine control of the sea allowed regular communication between Crete and 'the City', as Constantinople was known to the Greek world. With the island restored to Byzantium, the main task was to reinvigorate the much-depleted Christian community. The monk Nikon the Repenter led a band of clergy to the island. Many basilica churches were built or rebuilt, some to serve as episcopal churches. Early in the 11C Ayios Ioánnis Xénos, St. John the 'Stranger', also called Ermítis, the hermit (who came from a village on the edge of the Asteroúsia Mountains), was celebrated as an evangelist all over W Crete, and is still revered today.

The castle of Témenos (Rte 3D) is all that remains of an abortive attempt to move the capital to a less vulnerable position inland, and the administrative centre was re-established on the ruins of El Khandak (thereafter Khándakas). In the twelfth century it was thought necessary to strengthen the Christian ruling class, and the tradition is that 12 noble families, the Arkhontópouli ('aristocrats') were sent out to Crete from Constantinople. Their names, such as Kallérgis, Skordílis, Khortákis, have been influential throughout subsequent Cretan history. Many of the small churches and chapels that these families built on their estates survive today, in some cases gloriously redecorated in the following centuries. Gradually prosperity seems to have returned, based on an agricultural economy rather than piracy. This, Crete's second Byzantine period, was to last until 1204.

The death of the Emperor Basil II (1025) is usually taken as the zenith of the Byzantine Empire. With benefit of hindsight the next 400 years can be seen to have been a period of slow but inevitable decline. The Great Schism of 1054 effected the final break between Rome and Constantinople. The Crusades, which began as a movement to rescue Christianity's holy places from the Moslems, ended in a thinly-veiled power struggle between the forces of the West. Venice, originally a vassal of the Byzantine Empire, became first an independent ally and then an implacable foe. In 1081 the Emperor Alexius I made trading concessions to Venice which were eventually to result in her commercial dominance in the E Mediterranean. But these concessions also caused much bitterness, which came to a head with the 'Massacre of the Latins' at Constantinople (1182). In 1204 Venice succeeded in diverting the fourth Crusade to Constantinople in order to put the young Alexius IV on the imperial throne. But his failure to fulfil his promises to Venice led to the sack of Constantinople not by Moslems, but by the forces of Christendom.

The Venetian Period (1204–1669). In the subsequent division of the Empire, Crete was apportioned to Boniface of Montferrat who, prefering mainland territory, sold the island to Venice reputedly for 1000 silver marks. Meanwhile, rival forces from Genoa landed on the island under the command of the notorious pirate, Enrico Pescatore, and, often with Cretan support, fortified isolated settlements from Canea (Khaniá) to Ayios Nikólaos. But Venice was not to be trifled with. In 1210, a Venetian Governor, Jacopo Tiepolo, was appointed to Candia (as Khándakas, and indeed the whole island came to be known), and took the title 'Duke of Crete'. The island produced grain, wood for shipbuilding, oil, hides and wine; but more important it had an unequalled strategic position for trade with the Levant. Harbours and dockyards were a priority.

Venice set about imposing a feudal administration with Venetian colonists as the ruling class. Castles were built, or strengthened, to control the countryside. But 'La Serenissima' found herself running up against the implacably independent Cretan character, and the inevitable conflict became a tale of ferocious revolts and harsh repression. The new taxes and labour obligations were a heavy burden. By 1363 even the Venetian nobility on Crete was divided. One faction, incensed by excessive demands from Venice, went so far as to declare the short-lived Republic of St. Titus. The rebellion was eventually crushed by an expedition sent from Venice, and punitive measures were applied. The plateau of Lasíthi (Rte 6), a refuge for the rebels, was forcibly depopulated and cultivation and pasturing were banned.

Throughout this period of oppression, Cretan links with a regenerated Constantinople were cemented by a common language and religion. The Venetians imported their own ecclesiastical hierarchy, and built many Latin monasteries. Pope Alexander V (1409/10) was born in the Mirabéllo district, and educated by the Franciscans in Candia before he set out for Italy. The Orthodox clergy, ordained outside the island, were officially subject to Latin bishops, but there

The church at Arkádi

was little active proselytising by Venetian Catholics. The Cretan ruling families continued to build and decorate their small (Orthodox) churches and chapels, the survivors of which are so moving today.

The Italian scholar Giuseppe Gerola, in his great work on Venetian architecture, 'Monumenti Veneti nell'Isola di Creta', published in 1905, listed more than 800 frescoed churches on Crete (the majority 14–15C). A remarkable concentration of 600 or so still retain at least fragments for specialist study. All the wall paintings are strongly conservative; against a background of foreign occupation and uncertain economic conditions they scrupulously preserve the hagiographic traditions of Byzantine art. Orthodoxy was a very strong thread in the fabric of Cretan nationalism.

Gradually an uneasy co-existence was established between Venetians and Cretans, and by the 15C there was some intermarriage (sometimes with adoption of the Orthodox faith) and much less overt hostility. With the capture of Constantinople by the Turks (1453), Crete became an important staging-post for Greeks fleeing to the West, and this gave a new impetus to Byzantine culture on the island. The larger monasteries (Arkádi, Goniá, Ayía Triáda, Angárathos) became centres of learning, and great libraries were built up. In the 16C the college in Herákleion attached to Ayía Aikateríni, a daughter foundation of the important Orthodox monastery on Mount Sinai, became renowned for its scholarship. Fresco painting continued, but Crete also produced many notable icon painters, the greatest of them being Mikhaíl Damaskinós, several of whose works hang today in the Ayía Aikateríni collection. Some of these artists left Crete to work abroad, among them Doménico Theotokópoulos, who moved to Venice probably in 1567, was in Rome in 1570 as a disciple of Titian, and then went on to Toledo in Spain, where he became famous as El Greco.

In the field of literature, poetry and drama flourished during the 16th and 17th centuries. One enormously long heroic poem, the 'Erotókritos' by Vinzétzos Kornáros, remains popular today, as much for its use of the Cretan vernacular as for its romantic sentiments. It is read, sung and quoted wherever Cretans gather.

As Venetian power declined, the Turks pressed westward. They landed on Crete in 1645 and two years later laid siege to Candia. The city held out for 22 years, making this one of the longest sieges in history. Help from the Christian world came too little and too late, and in 1669 this last bastion of Christendom in the E Mediterranean fell into Turkish hands.

The Turkish Occupation (1669–1898). This time the overlords came not from a different rite within the Christian church, but from a different faith. The island was divided into three Pashaliks, and was ruled from Herákleion, known after the long siege as Megálo Kástro, the great fortress. The 'Sublime Porte' was not at first particularly destructive, but was totally indifferent to the economic conditions of the countryside, thereby causing great hardship and deprivation. The Turkish administrators favoured urban life both for safety and because it better suited their traditions; and their mosques (without exception converted churches), fountains, and a few houses preserved in the towns along the N coast are the only visible reminders of this foreign occupation of more than 200 years.

There was ruthless discrimination against Christians, especially insofar as taxation and property were concerned; survival frequently depended on compromise, and tactical conversions to Mohammedanism were understandably frequent. There was a sharp contrast between the vulnerable lowland districts and the remote and inaccessible mountain areas where sporadic rebellion and scheming in the cause of independence became a way of life. Unfortunately the lowlanders often had to endure the reprisals when the warriors withdrew to their mountain strongholds.

In 1770 a major revolt was led by the legendary Daskaloyiánnis from the proudly independent Sphakiá district of W Crete; he was encouraged by the Russians, as part of a diversionary move to further their own strategy on the mainland. The revolt collapsed, its leader surrendered and was executed, and Sphakiá suffered accordingly.

Throughout the island leadership was provided, often covertly and in dangerous circumstances, by the monasteries. Their efforts were directed not only to protecting the Orthodox church but also to preserving through education the Greek cultural tradition, the ultimate aim being Cretan independence.

On the wider scene Crete had once again become a pawn in international power politics, this time in the world of the 'Great Powers' of post-Napoleonic Europe, at that time Britain, France, Italy and Russia. The Revolt of 1821, triggered by the outbreak of the Greek War of Independence, was crushed with Egyptian help, and when, in 1832, the Greek state was established it did not include Crete, which had to undergo the humiliation of ten years of Egyptian rule.

The Greek throne was given to Prince Otto of Wittelsbach, and placed under the protection of Britain, Russia and France; but this attempt to establish stable constitutional government was unsuccessful, and in 1862 Otto was deposed. A Danish Prince became King George I of the Hellenes, a hint of concession to the idea of a broader-based Greek state. In Crete the renewed outcry for 'enosis', union with Greece, resulted in the uprising of 1866, when the blowing-up of the Arkádi monastery attracted world-wide sympathy for Crete's plight.

Greece's attention was taken up with problems on her northern frontiers, and her relationship with the Great Powers was often strained to the point of hostility. Uprisings continued on Crete until 1898 when the Powers finally took the opportunity of peace negotiations over mainland territory between Greece and the Ottoman Empire, to impose a settlement on the island. Crete was granted autonomous status under Ottoman suzerainty, and a High Commissioner was appointed, in the person of Prince George, second son of the Greek King, who governed from Khaniá.

In a further crisis in 1906 Prince George resigned. His eight years of rule had brought 'enosis' no closer, and he was faced with the rebel Cretan Assembly, constituted as a rival government pledged to this union with Greece. One of its leaders was Elevthérios Venizélos. Born in Khaniá in 1864 (but technically a Greek subject) he had been prominent as a young man in the struggle for the island's independence, and now was an influential member of the Assembly, which first raised the Greek flag on Crete, on the hill of Prophítis Ilías on the Akrotíri overlooking Khaniá. The crisis was temporarily resolved, with the appointment of the veteran Alexander Zaïmis as High Commissioner, but two years later Venizélos was called to Athens in a climate of nationalist rebellion, and after a revision of the constitution he became Prime Minister of Greece for the first of many times.

In 1913 'enosis' was at long last achieved. At the Treaty of Bucharest, which ended the Balkan Wars, Greek sovereignty over Crete was accepted and amid scenes of wild rejoicing the island finally became an integral part of the Greek nation.

Modern History (from 1913). An understanding of the early part of this turbulent period is inextricably involved with the decline of the Ottoman Empire, which led in due course to the emergence of modern Turkey, and with Greece's struggle to come to terms with her northern neighbours in a multilateral conflict among the evolving Balkan states.

Political consciousness is essential to the Greek character, as is still evident in the passsionate arguments of day-to-day conversation, so that despite physical isolation from the zones of conflict, Crete was much involved after 1913 in the decisions and events unfolding in Athens. For much of this period constitutional issues were in one way or another crucial, with the uneasy relationship between monarchy and elected government often at the heart of the matter.

The Cretan-born statesman Elevthérios Venizélos was a force in national politics and a central figure in this constitutional controversy for a quarter of a century. Venizelos came to be respected as a master of diplomacy abroad, and as a leader with the strength of an exceptional command over public opinion at home.

During the 1914–18 war, his convictions, which led him to favour the cause of the western allies, often put him at loggerheads with King Constantine I whose wife was the sister of the German Kaiser. In September 1916 matters came to a head, and from his native Khaniá Venizelos issued a proclamation which led to his establishing a rival government in the mainland city of Salonika (Thessaloníki). After nine months of negotiations, the king left the country and was succeeded by his second son, Prince Alexander. In Athens Venizélos recalled the parliament which the king had dissolved in December 1915, and received an overwhelming vote of confidence after a speech lasting nearly nine hours. The country entered the war on the allied side and played a part in the eventual victory.

Between 1920 and 1922 Greece was involved in a disastrous campaign of expansionism on the mainland of Turkey for which Venizélos did not escape all blame. The political motives included the ancient 'Megáli Idéa', the reconstitution of the Byzantine Empire with its capital at Constantinople. The trauma of defeat and the sack of Smyrna, the Greek city on the coast of Asia Minor, by Turkish forces under Mustapha Kemal is still a painful memory in Crete today. The ensuing exchange of populations under the Treaty of Lausanne (1923) brought more than a million refugees to Greece. A considerable proportion of them (including some Armenian families) were resettled on Crete, taking over the redistributed property of Turks who had remained behind when their army departed in 1898. The upheaval caused much hardship on both sides, but in modern times it has resulted in a homogeneous population spared any risk of the tensions suffered by Cyprus.

Constitutional questions continued to dominate Greek politics; for a period the country became a republic. Venizélos was in and out of office as Leader of the Liberal party, but his lasting achievements at this time were in the field of foreign affairs. In 1932 in a climate dominated by the insoluble problems and hardship of the years of worldwide economic depression, and faced with bitter opposition to measures which were seen as an attempt to restrict the freedom of the press, Venizélos was forced to resign. The following year he survived an assassination attempt, and then in a mood of frustration at the failure of the Republic he retired to Crete. In 1935, after a last unsuccessful republican coup, he fled into exile; condemned to death in his absence, he was pardoned under an amnesty declared by King George II after the restoration of the monarchy, but died in France in 1936. He is buried on the Akrotíri outside Khaniá.

The new figure at the centre of Greek politics was the fervent monarchist, General Metáxas; his solution for constitutional stalemate was to persuade the King to dissolve Parliament (the Chamber did not sit again for ten years), and himself to assume power as a dictator. However he foresaw that war in Europe was inevitable, and he has been given due share of the credit for the fact that Greece alone among the countries of SE Europe was in a position effectively to resist aggression when it came.

Mussolini occupied Albania on Easter Monday 1939, and the threat posed by a fascist power on Greece's border led to a British and French guarantee of Greek territorial sovereignty. Metáxas reaffirmed neutrality early in August 1940. On 27 October he attended an evening reception at the Italian legation in Athens, but early next day the Italian Minister conveyed to him an ultimatum which he rejected with the single word 'No'. This legendary gesture of defiance is proudly commemorated by a national holiday ('Oxi' day) on 28 October each year. Mussolini's troops were even at the time of the ultimatum already invading Greece, which became the only country voluntarily to enter the war on the Allied side during that period when Britain stood alone against the Axis powers.

The Greek army drove back the Italians to a position of stalemate in the mountainous terrain of Albania, but the balance was to be altered by Hitler's decision to enter Greece for the protection of the southern flank of his planned Russian front.

Metáxas died unexpectedly at the end of January 1941. In March Greece accepted reinforcement by a small expeditionary force composed of British, Australian and New Zealand troops, and a frontline was established in northern Greece, but the combined forces were unable to halt Hitler's invasion, and despite Greece's proclaimed determination to fight to the last, the campaign became a series of rearguard actions. In mid April the Prime Minister committed suicide; the King turned to a Cretan, Emmanuel Tsouderós, and it was to Crete that the inevitable evacuation was to be directed.

The Battle of Crete. The withdrawal of the expeditionary force from the mainland of Greece took place during the last week of April and the first week of May 1941. King George was evacuated with his Government and Prime Minister Tsouderós. He lived briefly at the Villa Ariadne at Knossós and was then established at Khaniá. The island was defended from sea-borne invasion by the British Mediterranean Fleet.

As the campaign on the mainland ran into difficulties during 1940, Churchill had continually insisted on the strategic importance of holding Crete, but the resources of General Wavell, C-in-C Middle East, were greatly overstretched and it was not feasible to create the fortress of Churchill's vision.

The terrain of the likely battlefield presented particular problems. All the main harbours, including the huge anchorage of Soúda Bay, were on the N coast and exposed to enemy aircraft; the more protected fishing ports on the S coast were useless for supply purposes because there was then only one serviceable road across the island, and that not completed right to the S coast. There were airfields at Herákleion and at Máleme, W of Khaniá (at that time the capital of the island), and a landing-strip between them at Réthymnon, all on the narrow N coast plain that rendered communications and troop movement by day very difficult.

Historians writing with the benefit of hindsight have been critical of the lack of preparation or of any defined policy at this time; there had been six changes of command in the six months before 30 April, when Wavell appointed the eminent New Zealander General Bernard Freyberg VC as C-in-C.

Hitler's principal objective was to use Crete as an air base against British forces in the E. Mediterranean. His commander was General Student (of XI Air Corps), whose strength included a crack assault regiment of glider-borne storm troopers, a parachute division, a specialised mountain division and groups of the dreaded Stuka dive bombers. The Luftwaffe, flying from rapidly constructed forward bases in the Peloponnese and the Aegean islands, had undisputed command of the air.

Freyberg's garrison consisted of 32,000 British, Australian and New Zealand troops (including 21,000 of the expeditionary force who had been evacuated from the mainland), and 11,000 well-trained but lightly-armed Greek troops. The Cretan division, to its lasting chagrin, had been cut off on the Albanian front. It proved impossible to operate planes from the exposed airfields, so the force was severely handicapped by lack of air cover.

General Freyberg's Creforce headquarters was located to the NE of Khaniá in the Soúda sector. W of Khaniá was the New Zealand Division, with some Greek support including a unit out along the coast at Kastélli. The New Zealanders were thus responsible for the defence of the vital airfield at Máleme; this was dominated by their command position at the end of a ridge running out from the White Mountains, named Hill 107.

In the centre of the line, in the area around Réthymnon, were four Australian and two Greek battalions. The Herákleion sector was held by three British, two Australian and three Greek battalions, the airport being defended by a British force.

The airborne invasion began on 20 May. The landings concentrated as expected on the airfields and the main towns of the N coast. In the Máleme area the Germans established a toehold W of the river Tavronítis and S of Kolymbári. A detachment of parachutists attempted to land in the broad valley (nick-named Prison Valley) running S towards the Omalós and the White Mountains; their aim was to converge with the forces on the coast road to advance on Khaniá, but at the end of the first day most of the German troops in this sector were disorganised and not responding to central control. The assault (using gliders) on the Akrotíri failed entirely, and thus the threat from the rear to Khaniá and Freyberg's headquarters did not materialise.

The Réthymnon airstrip, important to the Germans for a flanking movement to capture the anchorage of Soúda, was successfully defended, despite a heavy imbalance of troops and firepower, by the Australians. Around the Herákleion airfield the Germans were in considerable disarray, and in the town their initial success had developed into heavy street-fighting with the civilian population, which led to a position of stalemate.

The first wave of landings met much stronger resistance than had been expected by German Intelligence, which had also underestimated the hostile reaction of the local Cretan population. The invading forces suffered heavy losses which were particularly critical in their command structure. It is generally agreed that this first assault was very nearly defeated, that General Student's eventual success was by a narrow margin, and that at the end of the first day the outcome hung in the balance.

However what turned out to be the crucial battle had developed to the S and W of Máleme, centred on the New Zealand position on Hill 107. With hindsight it can be seen that the position of the German assault forces was exceedingly precarious. However in the confusion of battle, which was compounded by an almost total breakdown in communications due to a shortage of vital wireless sets, essential defence reinforcements did not become available in time. On the evening of the first day of the assault, the commanding height had to be evacuated, leaving the vital airfield undefended, and thus the fragile balance altered. Some historians have said that at this point the battle for Crete was lost and won.

German forces were quick to exploit the situation, and to use the airfield to bring in troops and vital supplies. A counter-attack, organised on the second day, was carried out during that night, 21–22 May, but despite the valiant efforts of the Maori battalion, Máleme airfield remained in enemy hands. On the fourth day of the battle German fighter planes began operating from its runway.

At sea the German invasion fleet was routed on 21 and 22 May, but with appalling losses to the Royal Navy. Throughout the battle the Navy was operating in waters which could only be reached through narrow straits (c 50–60km), guarded in the W by the island of Kýthera, and in the E by Kásos and Kárpathos, all in enemy hands. Once into the Cretan sea, as the Greeks call this area S of Théra (Santorini), ships were in reach of the network of bomber airfields that crowded the islands of the Aegean. Over three days Admiral Cunningham lost two cruisers and four destroyers, and had a battleship, two cruisers and four destroyers severely damaged.

On land the Máleme position had been given up, and the weary Australian and New Zealand troops fought a series of brave rearguard actions as they fell back on Khaniá. On 26 May, with the Luftwaffe fighters at Máleme within a 20km range, Khaniá and the Soúda sector were plainly indefensible, and early next day the order reached their garrisons for the long withdrawal S across the island to Sphakiá, a coast-to coast distance of c 40km.

The retreat along this route over the E flank of the White Mountains was only possible at all because of the heroic obstinacy of a Greek regiment cut off at the S end of 'Prison Valley', in the area of the Alikianós river-crossing (on the modern road up to the Omalós plateau). For two days (24–25 May) these troops, reinforced by gendarmerie and civilians, held up crack German mountain troops who otherwise, in an outflanking move by the Mesklá and Kerítis valley route, would have cut the Sphakiá road, the only possible line of retreat for Freyberg's army. (King George and his ministers had been escorted down the Gorge of Samariá to embark at Ayiá Rouméli.)

The shambles of this march over the mountains, by the upland plain of Askýphou and the precipitous Nímbros gorge, has been described in many records, including Freyberg's own official report. However, the column was successfully protected against constant enemy harrassment by relays of rearguard troops. Some 12,000 men were involved in the retreat, and during the nights of 28–31 May the Navy evacuated about three-quarters of them from the coast between Komitádes and Khóra Sphakíon. Evelyn Waugh gives a vivid account of the retreat as (from the New Zealand viewpoint) does Geoffrey Cox (see Bibliography).

At Réthymnon the Australians denied the Germans the use of the airstrip for the whole course of the battle, until they were at last overwhelmed on 31 May. From the port of Herákleion the Royal Navy evacuated the garrison by sea through the perilous Kásos strait on the night of the 28–29, with horrific loss of men and ships; the episode symbolises the courage with which this campaign was fought. The bald figures at its conclusion were: 18,000 evacuated, 12,000 taken prisoner, 2000 killed.

A considerable number of men who had not been evacuated were hidden by the Cretans and then helped to escape from the island. There are many accounts of the Resistance movement that developed during the German occupation of Crete. The guerilla warfare, coordinated by Allied undercover agents and supplied from N Africa, affected German morale, and tied down units increasingly needed on other fronts. The civilian population suffered appallingly in the inevitable acts of retribution. One extraordinary account of the Resistance, *The Cretan Runner*, is especially recommended because its author who was part of the movement is himself Cretan. Available in translation (see Bibliography) this book throws light not only on the progress of the guerilla war, and on the involvement of idiosyncratic foreigners as seen through native eyes, but incidentally on many essentials of the Cretan character.

GLOSSARY

ABACUS, a flat block crowning the capital of a column.

AGORA, public square or market-place.

ASHLAR, square-cut stone in regular courses of masonry.

ATRIUM, forecourt of a Roman house or basilica.

AYIOS, AYIA (f.), AYII (m.pl.), AYIES (f.pl.) Saint(s).

BASILICA, originally a Roman building used for civil administration; in Christian architecture, an aisled church with a clerestory and an apse or apses, but without transepts.

BEMA, the chancel in a Greek Orthodox church.

BRECCIA, a conglomerate rock.

CELLA, central portion of a temple, enclosed within solid walls.

DEMOTIC, the vernacular Greek language, as opposed to KATHAREVOUSA, formal academic Greek.

DIMARKHEION, town-hall.

EXEDRA, semi-circular (sometimes rectangular) recess with seats.

FAIENCE, in antiquity, the product of fusing granular quartz or sand with an alkali, which was then coated with an alkaline glaze.

FIBULA, pin to fasten clothing, ornamental as well as practical.

FRESCO, painting executed on wet plaster.

GYPSUM, an easily worked white to pinkish-buff limestone.

HORNS OF CONSECRATION, stylised bull's horns, associated with Minoan shrines.

ICONOSTASIS, screen adorned with icons in Orthodox church separating the sanctuary from the main body of the church.

KERNOS, cult vessel with a number of small receptacles.

KOULOURA, Greek word meaning round and hollow, hence a pit.

KRATER, large two-handled bowl used for mixing wine and water, associated with ceremonial drinking.

LARNAX, LARNAKES (pl.), clay coffin(s).

LUSTRAL BASIN, small sunken room in Minoan architecture associated with purification and cleansing.

MEGARON, in Greek, an imposing hall. The Mycenaean megaron was rectangular with a central hearth, and a single entrance through the porch at one end.

MELTEMI, the prevailing N wind of summer in the Aegean.

NARTHEX, a shallow porch extendng the width of a church, derived from the basilica plan.

NOMARKHEION, centre of provincial administration (for the Nome or province).

OBSIDIAN, a natural glass occurring in restricted volcanic areas.

ODEION, concert-hall, usually in the shape of a Greek theatre, but roofed.

ORTHOSTAT, large stone slab set vertically.

PANAYIA, the All-Holy Virgin.

PANTOKRATOR, Christ, the Ruler of all things, portrayed in the act of blessing, and with a bible in the other hand; usually a half-figure in the painted decoration of the dome of a Byzantine church.

PERISTYLE, colonnaded court resembling a cloister.

PHYLAX, or PHYLAKAS, guardian, here of antiquities.

PITHOS, PITHOI (pl.), large pottery jar(s) for the storage of oil, wine, grain, etc.; such vessels were also used for inhumation burial. A smaller version, usually decorated, held the ashes after a cremation.

PLATYTERA, representation of the Virgin and Child as a

symbol of the Incarnation.

PRONAOS, porch in front of the cella of a temple.

PROPYLON, or PROPYLAEUM, gateway of architectural importance. Plural form, PROPYLAEA, for a multiple entrance.

PYXIS, small lidded box in pottery, stone, ivory, etc.

RHYTON, vessel designed for the pouring of libations; often a tapering shape with hole at tip, but sometimes in human or animal form.

SCARAB, beetle-shaped seal.

STEATOPYGOUS, fat-buttocked.

STIRRUP JAR, jar with a blocked central mouth, three stirrup handles connected to the false neck and a spout added to the shoulder.

STOA, porch or portico not attached to a larger building.

TEMENOS, a sacred precinct.

THOLOS, circular vaulted building.

Linear B tablet from Knossós

SELECTED BIBLIOGRAPHY

Art, Archaeology, Myth and History. K. Branigan, *The Tombs of the Mesara*; A. Brown, *Arthur Evans and the Palace of Minos*; G. Cadogan, *Palaces of Minoan Crete*; J. Chadwick, *Linear B and Related Scripts*; R. Clogg, *A Short History of Modern Greece*; C. Daváras, *Guide to Cretan Antiquities*; (Sir) A. Evans, *The Palace of Minos*; R. Graves, *The Greek Myths*; R. Higgins, *Minoan and Mycenaean Art*; S. Hood, *The Arts in Prehistoric Greece, The Home of the Heroes, The Aegean before the Greeks, The Minoans*; R.W. Hutchinson, *Prehistoric Crete*; K. Kalokýris, *The Byzantine Wall-paintings of Crete*; S. Marinátos and M. Hirmer, *Crete and Mycenae*; J.D.S. Pendlebury, *The Archaeology of Crete*; N. Pláton, *Zakros*; M. Ventris and J. Chadwick, *The Decipherment of Linear B*; R.F. Willetts, *Cretan Cults and Festivals, Ancient Crete: A Social History, Everyday Life in Ancient Crete*; C.M. Woodhouse, *Modern Greece: A Short History*; E. Zachariadou, *Trade and Crusade: Venetian Crete and the Emirates of Menteshe and Aydin (1300–1415)*.

General. C. Buckley, *Greece and Crete 1941*; A. Clark, *The Fall of Crete*; G. Cox, *A Tale of Two Battles*; X. Fielding, *The Stronghold*; A. Hopkins, *Crete—its Past, Present and People*; A. Huxley and W. Taylor, *Flowers of Greece and the Aegean*; N. Kazantzákis, *Zorba the Greek, Report to Greco, Freedom and Death, The Odyssey: A Modern Sequel, Christ Recrucified*; E. Lear, *The Cretan Journal*; M. Llewellyn Smith, *The Great Island*; R. Pashley, *Travels in Crete*; G. Psychoundákis (trans. P. Leigh Fermor), *The Cretan Runner*; D. Powell, *The Villa Ariadne*; I. McD.G. Stewart, *The Struggle for Crete*; E. Waugh, *Diaries, Officers and Gentlemen*.

Some of these books are out of print, but they should be obtainable from libraries. A number may be bought locally from bookshops or museums on Crete. A few are available as inexpensive Athens reprints, but imported books are subject to a heavy tax and are therefore expensive. In case of.difficulty, consult *Zeno's Bookshop*, 6 Denmark Street, London WC2H 8LP (off Charing Cross Road); tel. 01–836 2522, or the *Hellenic Book Service*, 122 Charing Cross Road, London WC2H 0JR; tel. 01–836 7071.

PRACTICAL INFORMATION

I Travel to Crete

Travel Information and Bookings. There is no longer the need for a stark choice between an all-inclusive 'package' holiday based on one resort hotel, and totally independent travel bookings. An increasing number of travel agents offer arrangements which combine the financial advantages of group travel with itineraries tailored to individual requirements. Much preliminary information may be obtained, in person or by post (free), from the National Tourist Organisation of Greece (NTO), 195 Regent Street, London, W1R 8DR (tel. 01–734 5997), open 9.30–17.30 (Friday 16.30); closed all day on Saturdays. The New York office is at 645 Fifth Avenue, Olympic Tower, New York, NY 10022 (tel. 212 4215 777). The organisation does not recommend hotels, nor make travel arrangements.

The London office publishes a useful booklet of tour operators specialising in travel to Greece, with a detailed section on Crete. The list is cross-indexed for destination, type of holiday and the dozen or so UK airports from which charter flights now operate to Crete. Olympic Holidays Ltd can be recommended, and Thomas Cook is a well-known and long-established firm, but a great number of smaller specialists offer an excellent individual service.

Passports are necessary for all British travellers entering Greece; a British Visitor's Passport is valid. No visa is required for Greece, but permission to stay is granted in the first instance only for a period of three months.

Comprehensive Health Insurance is strongly recommended and can easily be arranged through the travel agent making the bookings.

By Air. Olympic Airways maintains scheduled services from Athens airport (Ellinikó West) to both Herákleion and Khaniá: peak summer service Athens–Herákleion, eight flights a day, and to Khaniá, five flights, both services offering connections to and from most major cities in Europe and the USA. On scheduled services from abroad via Athens, there are advantages in travelling Olympic on both legs of the journey. You avoid the necessity to change terminals at Athens airport, and in the event of a missed connection, the airline is responsible for your onward journey (not necessarily the case when two airlines are involved). This is particularly important when leaving an island where strong winds can affect schedules.

From Herákleion Olympic Airways flies to Rhodes, Mýkonos, Santorini (Théra), Páros and Thessaloníki. An airport was opened at Siteía in 1984; it presently has flights only to Rhodes via Kásos and Kárpathos, but a direct service from Athens may be introduced in the future.

On all Olympic Airways flights, travellers are advised to pay careful attention to instructions about the reconfirming of return flights.

Charter flights are primarily intended for complete package holidays, but surplus seats are sometimes available (with a nominal charge for accommodation), and any travel agent specialising in departures to Crete will be aware of these possibilities.

By Sea. There is a Car Ferry service nightly all the year round between Piraeus (port of Athens) and Herákleion (12 hours), also between Piraeus and Soúda for Khaniá (11 hours). To Herákleion there are two sailings run by rival companies, Minoan Lines and ANEK (departures 18.30 and 19.00 respectively). For Khaniá, ANEK has a sailing every night (at 19.00) and Minoan Lines one on altern-ate nights (departing Piraeus on Monday, Wednesday and Friday at 18.30 and returning the following night at the same departure time).

Piraeus booking offices: Minoan Lines tel. (01) 411 8211; The ANEK line tel. (01) 411 8611.
    For offices on Crete, see the sections of practical information under Herákleion and Khaniá. Boat tickets are widely available at agencies through-out the island.

Accommodation on the ferries is priced in five classes: de Luxe, First, Second, Tourist and Deck. The ships are not uniform and facilities vary slightly. Prices also vary according to route and even direction because of harbour dues. An annual rise is to be expected, but in recent years this has tended to be offset for foreigners by alterations in currency exchange rates. A berth in a First Class cabin with pri-vate shower and toilet (c Drs 4500 in 1987) compared then with an air fare, Athens–Herákleion, of Drs 6600. The basic deck-class ticket covers travel in Pullman-type seats, or out on the decks in summer, and in 1987 cost Drs 2000, then about £10 sterling. Ticket prices do not include meals, but all ships have a restaurant (restricted to First and Second Class passengers) and a cafeteria. In high season it is essential to book in advance if you bring a car or want a cabin. At peak times, such as August weekends or festivals, there may be extra services by day.

Direct ferry services to Crete from abroad: in 1987 the Italian Adriatica Line ran a regular car and passenger service Venice–Piraeus–Herákleion–Alexandria, and the Greek Stability Line called at Herákleion on a route from Piraeus to Limassol and Haifa. There can be no guarantee that these services will continue to operate, but if they are of interest it is worth making enquiries about them or any similar new arrangements. Marlines has plans for a weekly service Ancona–Patras–Herákleion–Izmir.

Domestic ferry schedules around the Aegean (except for the above direct services) are liable to alter from year to year, and the new pro-gramme is not announced much before Easter, so it is essential to make careful enquiries at a tourist information office or a travel agent. In recent years a weekly boat on the Piraeus–Rhodes route has called at Ayios Nikólaos and Siteía. Also Kísamos (Kastélli-Kisámou) in W Crete has been linked by a twice-weekly service to Kýthera, and ports in the S Peloponnese (on a route terminating at Piraeus). For shipping agents see the information section under the appro-priate town.

Money. The monetary unit is the drachma (Δράχμα), abbreviated to Δρχ or Drs. There are coins of 1, 2, 5, 10, 20 and 50 drachmas, and notes of 50, 100, 500, 1000 and 5000.

Currency Regulations. There are at present no restrictions on the amount of sterling that may be taken out of the UK. However, Greek currency control is strict, and (1987) not more than Drs 3000 in notes may be brought into or taken out of Greece. There are no restrictions on foreign currency, but amounts over £300 should be declared if they are to be exported again.

Customs Regulations. Note that if you travel from mainland Greece all formalities will be attended to at the point of entry to Greece. For travellers coming from EEC member-states there are regulations that limit the value of goods which may be imported duty free (details obtainable from the NTO). In practice bona fide holiday-makers will have no trouble from the Customs authorities. 300 cigarettes and 1.5 litres of spirits are allowed. Radios and similar equipment may be entered on the owner's passport to ensure re-export (or payment of the appropriate tax), on departure.

Importation of Motor Vehicles. Consult the London office of the NTO (see above) which issues a leaflet of explicit instructions. See also 'Blue Guide Greece'. On entry to Greece the vehicle will be noted in the driver's passport, so that driver and vehicle must leave the country together. Membership of the AA or RAC is an advantage, for in case of breakdown it ensures free assistance from the Greek equivalent ELPA (ΕΛΠΑ).

Antiquities. The regulations to protect Greece's heritage are strictly and comprehensively enforced; even picking up sherds on an ancient site is prohibited. Importation of antiquities and works of art is free, but such articles should be declared on entry if they are to be re-exported. Except with special permission, it is forbidden to export antiquities and works of art (dated before 1830) which have been obtained (whether bought or found) in Greece. If a traveller's luggage contains antiquities not covered by an export permit (supplied with bona fide purchases) the articles are liable to be confiscated and prosecution may follow. Note that the use of metal detectors is prohibited throughout Greece.

II   Travelling on Crete

Tourist Information. The National Tourist Organisation of Greece (NTO, in Greek EOT) maintains a regional office in Herákleion, and information offices at Herákleion airport, and in Khaniá and Réthymnon. Municipal Information offices are a new and useful development; at present they are in operation in Ayios Nikólaos, Ierápetra and Siteía, but others will follow. For addresses and telephone numbers consult the information section for the appropriate town.

The Tourist Police is in the process of being replaced as a separate organisation by members of the ordinary police force who staff information desks in police stations.

Motoring. The majority of visitors touring Crete by car use rented vehicles. The Fly-Drive arrangement, whereby a hire car is waiting at the airport on arrival, is extremely popular, or the rental can be arranged for a selected period later in the holiday. Cars, jeeps, motor cycles and scooters may be hired from agencies in all the main towns, in the large hotels and at the airports, and a local arrangement is convenient when the vehicle is only required for occasional expeditions, but the rate per day will be higher than when the cost of car hire is part of a package arranged abroad. (In either case the rate, including any optional insurance costs, is subject to 18 per cent V.A.T.) Hertz provide an excellent service; they have more than a dozen agents across the island, including desks at both airports. (Head office: 44, Odós 25 Avgoústou, Herákleion. tel. (081) 229 802). Other firms may be less expensive but the condition of their cars and their emergency service are not always as good. A valid driving licence is required; most firms stipulate that it must have been held for at least one year. Some firms require the driver to have reached the age of 23; others set the limit at 21 provided the rental is backed by a credit card, which is in any case the best way to handle the necessary deposit. For motor bike and scooter hire the age limit is 19. In all cases it is wise to check that you have full comprehensive insurance.

Roads. There has been steady improvement in the general condition of the island's road system. All main roads, and those to the popular tourist objectives, now have an asphalt surface, and much work is being done on country roads in remote rural areas, for the benefit of isolated communities. Non-asphalt surfaces are generally noted in the text (though this information is likely to become out-of-date), but driven with reasonable caution hard-packed dirt roads need present no problems. Except on the N Coast Highway between Khaniá and Ayios Nikólaos, distances may be deceptive, and extra time should be allowed for gradients and winding roads. There are long-term plans for a S Coast Highway, but despite a recent resumption of work only some sections of this have been completed, and roads to the S coast still tend to radiate in the natural historical pattern from the capitals of the four nomes or provinces. It is customary to use the horn on blind corners; in the mountains, rock falls are a hazard, and subsidence or the torrential winter rains may produce unexpected potholes or gaps at the edge of the road. However, upkeep is generally good (except in the villages where the cost is often a burdensome charge on the inhabitants), and the road system is now more than adequate for exploring to the remotest parts of the island.

Signposts have been greatly improved in recent years in conjunction with a new system of kilometre posts that is being set up along the main routes. There are duplicate signs, 50m apart, on all the main roads, the second one helpfully transliterating the Greek alphabet. (The result does not always match exactly the transliteration used in this Guide.) On minor roads the convention is to sign the chief destination once, and then to signpost the turnings off the road without repeating the original destination. It is assumed that you continue straight ahead unless directed otherwise.

Taxis are easily available (and cheap) in the main towns, and one will be found on request in almost any village on the island (see below). A taxi is sometimes invaluable to supplement an awkward bus schedule. Hire by the day may be arranged, but both itinerary and price should be agreed beforehand. The rates to all main towns from Herákleion airport are clearly displayed in the arrival hall.

Country Bus travel on the island is efficient and inexpensive. Long-distance buses run to schedule fairly frequently between the four nome capitals (Khaniá, Réthymnon, Herákleion and Ayios Nikólaos). Because these services are operated (as they are throughout Greece) by Joint Pools of Bus Owners, KTEL, journeys via Herákleion may involve a change of bus station. Within each nome there are services between the provincial capital and the chief towns of the eparchies (districts). Villages without a formal bus service nearly always have a communal taxi with comparable prices (marked ΑΓOPAION) which acts in lieu of a bus. Tickets for inter-nome destinations are sold at an office (praktoreíon) in the bus station, and those for destinations within the nome are sold on the bus. Retain all tickets until the journey is completed; inspectors are not uncommon. Sample prices (1987): Herákleion to Khaniá, Drs 750; Herákleion to Siteía, Drs 700. At country stops, hail the bus in a clear fashion; it will not halt automatically.

Within the nome, timetables are naturally designed for the needs of villagers: for shopping in town, hospital visiting, for the school day. They are therefore often not particularly convenient for tourist excursions, but sometimes a taxi may bridge the gap to the nearest long-distance route. Note that Sunday bus schedules are usually reduced. Summer (mid April–mid October) and winter schedules differ markedly, so early or late season holiday-makers should check especially carefully, at the bus station itself if possible.

Walking. Crete offers many advantages to walkers, not least the chance to escape from the tourist scene to experience the natural beauty of the island, and to catch a glimpse of a traditional way of life which is altering fast while still retaining its own distinct character. The physical scale of the island is such that the scenery varies strikingly within the range of one day's walk. People in rural areas are friendly and helpful out of a tradition of hospitality to strangers which has not been eroded, as it sometimes has in the tourist resorts, by sheer weight of numbers. Local transport is generous with lifts.

The remote mountain areas are relatively unpopulated, and are only suitable for experienced walkers who will know how to take sensible precautions. Consult the Greek Alpine Club in Herákleion or Khaniá (see town information sections), or in case of difficulty the NTO.

Many of the better-known walks described in this Guide, for example along the S flank of the White Mountains or to archaeological sites such as Lissós or the Kamáres cave, are marked with intermittent splashes of paint. Here, obviously, you will find other foreigners. However, if desired, it should also be possible to pick up hints and suggestions in the chapters of route descriptions in order to get right off the beaten track into the Cretan countryside.

Crete's modern road system dates from the period since the end of the Second World War. Realignments have been required for motor traffic, but the age-old routes between villages remain, and are still used as footpaths. The roughly paved trackway or 'kalderími' is usually thought of as a Turkish road, and some were indeed built by the Turks to help control a rebellious countryside, but they often follow the line of the earlier Venetian or even Roman roads.

Large-scale maps showing these paths are not available for detailed advance planning; on a cross-country route it is a matter of studying the lie of the land on the road map, and then asking for directions (important to accent names correctly) to the next village, antiquity or church.

Maps may be obtained by post from Stanfords, 12–14 Long Acre, London, WC2E 9LP (tel. 01–836 1321). Telephone orders are accepted with Access or Barclaycard. The Leisure Map of Crete

(1:275,000) from Clyde Surveys is a clearly-presented road map with much useful tourist information, including large-scale town plans. There is an imported version from Freytag and Berndt; this is basically the same map on the larger scale 1:200,000. Nelles publishes an alternative, Crete (1:200,000), on which a number of country roads and tracks are indicated, and this, together with helpful contour information, may appeal to walkers.

Coastal Boats. There is a well-established boat service operating to schedule on a route along the S coast between Khóra Sphakíon and Palaiókhora (details given in Rtes 15 and 18). Its primary function is to transport from Ayiá Rouméli the great numbers of people who now walk down the gorge of Samariá to the Libyan Sea, but it offers many other opportunities to explore parts of this coast which are not accessible by road. The boats also serve the island of Gávdos.

Various examples of local initiative are noted in the following text—boats from Kolymbári to the Diktýnnaion sanctuary, a regular caique from Kastélli to the fortress of Gramboúsa—and others may be expected as a response to the needs of tourism.

It is sometimes possible to hire a boat privately, for example from Ayios Nikólaos to visit Pseíra, but with considerations such as the cost of fuel and the potential profit from the alternative of a day's fishing, this has become a relatively expensive business.

III   Post, Telephones and Banking

Postal Information. The main post office (ΤΑΧΥΔΡΟΜΕΙΟΝ; takhydromeíon) in each of the four big towns (the nome capitals) is open for normal postal business Monday–Friday 08.00–20.00; subsidiary post offices in temporary caravan accommodation are now appearing in popular tourist areas; their location is noted in the appropriate information sections. Their opening hours are as above (but also on Saturdays), and Sunday 09.00–18.00. In other towns and the larger villages the hours are Monday–Friday 07.30–15.30. Staff generally speak some English. Letter-boxes (ΓΡΑΜΜΑΤΟ-ΚΙΒΩΤΙΟΝ) and the new post office caravans are painted yellow. Postage stamps, γραμματόσημα (grammatósimo, pl. -tósima), are obtainable at kiosks and at many shops which sell postcards, but a small premium is charged for the convenience.

Correspondence marked 'Poste Restante' (to be called for) may be addressed to any post office and is handed to the addressee on proof of identity (passport preferable). A fee is charged. The surname of the addressee, especially the capital letter, should be clearly written.

Parcels are not delivered in Greece. They must be collected from a Parcels Office, where they are subject to handling fees, full customs charges, and often to delay. Dutiable goods sent by letter post are liable to double duty on examination. The bus companies operate an efficient parcels service between their own booking-halls (praktoreía).

The Post Office now operates a *Currency Exchange* for both cheques and foreign money, exactly on a par with the banking system. The hours are: in conventional post offices Monday–Friday 08.00–13.30; in the new caravans 08.00–20.00 DAILY, except Sunday 09.00–18.00.

The extra opening hours and the wide network of post offices across the island make this a particularly welcome innovation.

Telephones. The Greek telephone and telegraph services are maintained by a public corporation (quite separate from the postal authority), the Οργανισμός Τηλεπικοινωνιών Ελλάδος (OTE, always referred to by its acronym pronounced O-táy). All large towns have a central office of the company, with call-boxes and arrangements for making local and long-distance calls. The calls are metered, and payment is made to the cashier at the end, with no need for correct change. The same system works for the many instruments available to the public at kiosks (períptera, see below) and in hotels, cafés, bars, etc. throughout the island. Major OTE offices operate a 24-hour service. Most villages have an OTE centre, usually the local kapheneíon; in some cases opening hours are restricted.

Coin-operated call-boxes are gradually increasing in number. They usually take 5 and 10 drachma coins.

Area Codes on the island:
Herákleion 081
Khaniá 0821
Réthymnon 0831
Ayios Nikólaos 0841
Siteía 0843
Kísamos (Kastélli Kisámou) 0822
Ierápetra 0842

For the UK dial 0044 and drop the first 0 of the British area code. For the USA dial 001. Transferred-charge calls can be arranged through the operator (domestic 132, international 161).

Telegrams are most easily sent from OTE centres; English is accepted.

Banking Hours. At present Monday–Friday 08.00–14.00. In high season, at tourist centres such as Ayios Nikólaos, one foreign exchange till may reopen at 17.30.

These bank opening hours are now supplemented by the convenient Currency Exchange service operated by the Post Office—see above.

IV   Hotels and Restaurants

Hotels on Crete are inspected annually and graded in six categories; de Luxe to Class E. Charges are fixed by the Greek Hotel Association, and the room rate, inclusive of service and taxes, is displayed, usually on the back of the door. Other accommodation, such as pensions, rooms for rent and self-catering apartments, is also regularly inspected and graded.

The NTO issues a booklet listing all hotels on the island of Class C and above, giving category and telephone numbers (but not prices); it is an indispensable aid for anyone planning to travel around the island using this type of accommodation. (Make sure you are given the current one.) Occasionally in the route descriptions below, the existence of a hotel is mentioned where it might be useful in an out-of-the-way location. To avoid disappointment it is essential that, before firm plans are made, the NTO list is consulted.

The great majority of resort hotels are closed from the end of

October to mid March—apply to the NTO for a separate list of the few that remain open.

Hotel charges go up each spring, with an annual increase of about 15 per cent (in drachma terms) the pattern in recent years, but as a rough guide a range of 1987 prices is given in the table below.

		Single	**Double**
LUX	HB	5200–8400	7000–13,500
A	HB	2800–5200	4500–9000
B	HB	1900–3900	3300–5800
C	BB	1200–2300	1500–2800
D	RR	700–1100	950–1350
E	RR	650–950	900–1200

HB = half-board; BB = bed and breakfast; RR = room rate. There may be surcharges for short stays (less than three nights) and during the high season (July and August). A small reduction (20 per cent) can be expected for single occupancy of a double room if no single is available.

In general two levels of *prices* apply on Crete. Whereas simple food and accommodation (above all in rural areas) are still relatively cheap by European standards, charges for the smarter holiday accommodation and luxury goods in the tourist resorts are scarcely lower than anywhere else in the Mediterranean.

Whether in the main towns or at beach resorts, the *accommodation* offered by de Luxe and Class A hotels is comparable with that of their counterparts elsewhere. They have private bath (or shower), balconies, room service, and a full range of tourist facilities. Demi-pension terms are usually obligatory. Class B hotels are thus classified because of limitations of space, number of public rooms and room service. Class C hotels can be expected to provide simple, clean bedrooms, sometimes with balconies, almost always with private shower/w.c. Frequently they have no restaurant, and thus no compulsory demi-pension terms, which frees their guests to enjoy a meal in the local taverna.

Classes D and E (rare) are for the adventurous traveller, prepared to put up with spartan conditions in pursuit of economy or a bed in a chosen location.

The independent traveller will not be surprised that here, as elsewhere around the Mediterranean, many hotels near popular beaches are geared (especially in the high season) to package tours and block bookings from agencies abroad, rather than to the unexpected overnight guest.

A characteristic feature of touring on Crete is the ubiquitous *Rent Room*. In place of the traditional hospitality in family homes, inexpensive rooms (on average not much over £5 sterling for a double room in 1987) are now available for a single night or a longer period. Often they are in purpose-built modern houses, with private (if eccentric) facilities, and a communal fridge and simple kitchen where food may be kept and prepared. It is customary to make a thorough inspection before coming to a decision, and a negative one will be respected. Out-of-season, and depending on local circumstances, bargaining may lead to a mutually satisfactory reduction in the officially regulated price. In the text, rent rooms are mentioned at a few chosen points, but a large proportion of villages on the island can provide a room of some description. The English phrase is familiar, but in case of difficulty ask for 'ενα δωμάτιο' (ena domátio, a room).

Self-catering villas and flats are growing in popularity. Their prices, too, are regulated by the authorities (consult NTO). It is sometimes possible (especially out of season) to arrange a rental locally, through the agents in the big towns recommended for organised travel, but most properties are contracted on an annual basis to agencies abroad, and are obtainable only as part of a holiday package which includes flight costs. The NTO in London can supply a list of such agencies. For high-season rentals enquiries must be made well in advance.

Camping on Crete is officially restricted to recognised camping sites. A current list with telephone numbers is available at all NTO offices; in 1987 there were a dozen or so such sites, all by or near the sea.

Youth Hostels. The Greek Youth Hostel Association (4 Odós Dragatsanioú, Athens) is affiliated to the International Youth Hostels Federation. The number of hostels on Crete tends to vary from year to year but in 1987 they were to be found in all the main N coast towns, including Siteía, also in Ierápetra and near Plakiás on the S coast. The NTO compiles a list.

Restaurants. Hotel menus on Crete usually keep to a bland international cuisine with only an occasional touch of local colour, more noticeable in the name of the dish than in its flavour. Formal restaurants (ΕΣΤΙΑΤΟΡΙΑ; estiatória) are rare on the island and restricted to the main centres. Instead there is the Tavérna (TABEPNA), often family-owned and run, and characterised by a relaxed, friendly atmosphere and a strongly conservative, uncompromisingly Greek cuisine. The dishes vary according to season, using local produce when it is plentiful and keeping prices down accordingly. Cretan produce has a deservedly good reputation; even in the smart markets of Athens the cry 'fresh from Crete' is a recommendation. Most tavernas have their own inexpensive 'house' wine (χυμά, khimá). (Traditionally this is ordered not by the litre or half litre, but by the kilo—ena kiló, ena misó kiló.) In summer, taverna tables are moved outdoors.

In towns and tourist resorts a menu may be displayed near the entrance. By law this must give for each dish first the basic price and then the final charge, which includes taxes and service (15 per cent). It is customary to leave 5 per cent on the table unless you are served by the owner himself.

A ΨΗΤΑΡΙΑ (psitariá) generally provides meat (and chicken) roasted on the spit, or charcoal-grills each order. A ΖΑΧΑΡΟΠΛΑΣΤΕΙΟΝ (zakharoplasteíon) or patisserie, sells pastries and confectionary, ice-creams, coffee and drinks of all sorts; for the younger generation these are replacing the traditional Greek kapheneíon (see below). Larger establishments in the towns may serve light meals, but in general their prices are not cheap.

'Snacks' are easy to find in all the main centres, where establishments selling pizza and hamburgers probably now outnumber those offering the traditional 'souvláki', little pieces of meat grilled on a wooden skewer, or 'tirópitta', a flaky-pastry cheese pie.

The traditional Greek café (ΚΑΦΕΝΕΙΟΝ) of the villages is an austere establishment usually thronged with male patrons for whom it is both a local club and political forum. Casual customers generally feel more comfortable at the tables outside. The kapheneíon serves

Greek coffee, bottled soft drinks, ice-creams, and alcoholic drinks such as rakí or koniák (Greek brandy).

An EEOXIKON KENTPON (Exokhikón Kéntron), a 'rural centre', combines the functions of café and taverna out in the countryside or at the beach.

Food and Drink. The favourite Greek aperitif is *oúzo*, a strong aniseed-flavoured drink made from the residue left when grapes have been pressed for wine. Traditionally it is served with *mezédes*, snacks consisting of anything from a slice of cheese or tomato or an olive to pieces of salami sausage or grilled octopus. In Crete oúzo is often replaced by *rakí* (also called tzikoudiá), a stronger distillation without aniseed flavouring. Beer and lager (both locally brewed and imported) are very popular.

Cretan wine (κρασί, krasí) can be excellent. Retsína, the resinated white wine particularly characteristic of the Attica region of mainland Greece, is bottled on the island (and is still very cheap) but there is also a large variety of unresinated table wines, white (άσπρο, áspro), red (μαύρο, mávro, literally black), or rosé (κόκκινο, kókkino, literally red). At grander restaurants (and in most supermarkets) the principal mainland varieties (Cambás, Demestiká) are available, but the local bottlings are just as good and cheaper. Minós, Górtys and Lató are widely known. Relative newcomers, recommended, are Logádo and Olympiás. The Arkhánes cooperative ranks high (and has won awards) in assessments of Greek wines. Most 'house' wine in jugs is 'kókkino', the characteristically brownish rosé of Crete.

Tavernas which serve meals both at midday and in the evening (and, especially in the towns, not quite all do) usually cook their prepared dishes (étimo fayetó, literally 'ready food') at lunchtime. Depending on the size of the establishment, there may be from two to a dozen dishes ready for inspection, with a choice of meat dishes, stuffed vegetables, and pulses such as beans, lentils, or chick-peas cooked as a cross between a soup and a vegetable stew. It is possible to order grilled meat and fried potatoes, or an omelet and salad, but the traditional lunchtime dishes are prepared in advance. In the evening these dishes may still be available, but only rarely will they have been cooked afresh. If in doubt it may be wise to avoid them.

A Cretan party starts the evening meal with a variety of hors d'oeuvres (orektiká) for communal tasting, including a large mixed ('Greek') salad with olives and féta cheese. The dishes are set on the table with knives and forks and bread, but no individual plates unless these are specially requested. The subsequent orders of grilled meat or fish, or a house speciality such as 'stiffádo' (stew), will arrive in haphazard fashion as they are ready from the stove or the charcoal grill.

Menus are everywhere translated and most waiters speak a little English, but the correct way to order a taverna meal is to go to the kitchen to inspect the food. Even in the larger restaurants in Herákleion, Cretans are expected to visit the kitchen or serving counter to see what is offered. Fish should be individually selected, and will then be weighed to ascertain the eventual charge on the bill. (Prawns, a popular choice with tourists, are in season only October–May. In summer they will be frozen.) There are many specialist fish tavernas around the coast of Crete.

The traditional taverna did not serve a dessert course or coffee; for delicious pastries or ice-cream one moved on to linger in the

MENU **43**

Zakharoplasteíon. However, in places frequented by tourists, fresh fruit, ice-creams and coffee are now often available to end a taverna meal. Greek coffee is served on the grounds in small cups. It is traditionally very sweet but can be ordered 'medium' or without sugar (see below). Instant coffee (referred to as Nescafé) is also available, but more expensive.

The MENU below describes some of the more widely available dishes. Fish and vegetables are available according to season.

ΟΡΕΚΤΙΚΑ (orektiká), Hors d'oeuvres
Ταραμοσαλάτα (taramosaláta), smoked cod's roe paté
Ντολμαδάκια (dolmadákia), stuffed vine leaves served cold, or hot with egg-and-lemon sauce
Ελιές (eliés), olives
Τζατζίκι (tzatzíki), yoghurt flavoured with grated cucumber and garlic
Κολοκυθάκια τηγανιτά (kolokithákia tiganitá), fried baby marrows
Σαγανάκι κεφαλοτύρι (saganáki kefalotíri), fried cheese
Μελιτζανοσαλάτα (melidzanosaláta), aubergine salad
Γίγαντες (yígantes), butter beans in oil and lemon dressing
Καλαμαράκια (kalamarákia), fried baby squid
Μαρίδες (marídes), whitebait
Σκορδαλιά (skordaliá), garlic dip
Σαλιγκάρια (salingária), snails (a Lenten speciality)

ΣΟΥΠΕΣ (soupés), Soups
Σούπα αυγολέμονο (soúpa avgholémono), egg and lemon soup
Ψαρόσουπα (psarósoupa), fish soup
Φακές (fakés), lentil soup
Φασόλια (fasólia), haricot bean soup
Ρεβίθια (revithia), chick-pea soup

ΖΥΜΑΡΙΚΑ (zimariká) ΚΑΙ ΡΙΖΙ (rízi), Pasta and Rice dishes
Πιλάφι (piláfi), plain rice pilaf
Μακαρόνια (makarónia), spaghetti, με σάλτσα (me sáltsa) with sauce, με σάλτσα και τυρί (me sáltsa ke tirí) with sauce and cheese
Παστίτσιο (pastítsio), macaroni baked with meat and bechamel sauce

ΨΑΡΙΑ (psária), Fish
Φαγκρί (fangrí), sea bream, and Λιθρίνι (lithríni), red bream
Ξιφίας (ksifías), swordfish
Μπαρμπούνια (barboúnia), red mullet
Γαρίδες (garídes), prawns
Κταπόδι (ktapódi), octopus

ΑΥΓΑ (avgá), Eggs
Βραστά (vrastá) boiled, Αυγά μάτια (avgá mátia) fried
Ομελέτα (omeléta), omelet, ζαμπόν (jambón), with ham; πατάτες (patátes), with fried potato

ΕΝΤΡΑΔΕΣ (entrádes), Entrées
Μουσακά (mousaká), layers of aubergine, minced beef, and cheese, covered with bechamel sauce and baked in the oven
Αρνάκι φασολάκια (arnáki fasolákia), lamb with beans
Ψητό κοτόπουλο (psitó kotópoulo), roast chicken
Στιφάδο (stifádo), rich beef stew with onions
Τζουτζουκάκια (tsoutsoukákia), meat balls in tomato sauce

ΣΧΑΡΑΣ (skháras), Grills
Σουβλάκι (-ια) souvláki (-ia), kebab(s) of pork (occasionally lamb)
Μπριζόλες χοιρινές (brizóles khirinés), pork chops
Μπριζόλα μοσχαρίσια (brizóla moskharísia), veal chop
Παϊδάκια αρνί (païdákia arní), lamb cutlets (or chops)
Φιλέτο (filéto), steak
Κοκορέτσι (kokorétsi), lamb's liver, kidney, sweetbreads and heart, sliced and wrapped in intestines, then cooked on the spit
Κεφτέδες σχάρας (keftédes skháras), grilled meat balls

ΛΑΧΑΝΙΚΑ ΚΑΙ ΣΑΛΑΤΕΣ (lakhaniká ke salátes), Vegetable dishes and Salads
Γεμιστές ντομάτες (yemistés domátes), stuffed tomatoes
Γεμιστές πιπεριές (yemistés piperiés), stuffed peppers
Παπουτσάκια (papoutsákia), stuffed aubergines with cheese (literally, 'little shoes')
Μπριάμ (briám), mixed vegetables stewed in olive oil
Αγκινάρες (angináres), artichokes
Αλα πολίτα (ala políta), artichokes with potatoes, carrots, onions, and sometimes broad beans, flavoured with dill
Χόρτα (khórta), green vegetables, including wild greens
Φασολάκια φρέσκα (fasolákia fréska), green beans
Κουκιά (koukiá), broad beans
Χωριατική σαλάτα (khoriatikí saláta), mixed ('Greek') salad, literally village or country salad, with olives and féta cheese
Σαλάτα ντομάτες (saláta domátes), tomato salad
Αγγούρι (angoúri), cucumber
Μαρούλι (maroúli), lettuce
Λάχανο (lákhano), cabbage
Παντζάρια (pandzária), beetroot
Κρεμμύδι (kremídi), onion
Πατάτες τηγανιτές (patátes tiganités), fried potatoes (chips)

ΤΥΡΙΑ (tiriá), Cheeses
Φέτα (féta), soft white goat's milk cheese
Μησύθρα (misíthra), unsalted soft cheese made from sheep's milk, known in W Crete as ανθότιρος (anthótiros)
Γραβιέρα (graviéra), Gruyère-type hard cheese

ΓΛΥΚΑ (gliká), Sweets
Μπακλαβά (baklavá), layered pastry filled with honey and nuts
Καταΐφι (kataífi), pastry shredded and filled with sweetened nuts
Γαλακτομπούρεκο (galaktoboúreko), pastry filled with vanilla custard
Ρυζόγαλο (rizógalo), creamy rice pudding

MISCELLANEOUS
Γιαούρτι (yiaoúrti), yoghurt, με μέλι (me méli), with honey
Ψωμί (psomí), bread
Βούτυρο (voútiro), butter
Αλάτι (aláti), salt
Πιπέρι (pipéri), pepper
Μουστάρδα (moustárda), mustard
Λάδι (ládi), oil
Ξύδι (xídi), vinegar
Ζάχαρι (zákhari), sugar
Νερό (neró), water, παγωμένο (pagoméno), iced
Παγωτό (pagotó), ice cream
Λεμόνι (lemóni), a lemon
Λεμονάδα (lemonáda), lemonade
Πορτοκαλάδα (portokaláda), orangeade
Πεπόνι (pepóni), melon
Καρπούζι (karpoúzi), water melon
ΕΛΛΗΝΙΚΟΣ ΚΑΦΕΣ (ellinikós kafés), Greek coffee (served on the grounds) γλυκός (glikós), sweet; μέτριος (métrios), medium sweet; σκέτος (skétos), without sugar; διπλός (diplós) a double, a large cup

V   General Information

Season. Summer on Crete is generally dry and warm without extremes at sea level; summer temperatures are moderated by the often strong prevailing N wind (the meltémi). The sea is warm enough for swimming from mid April to November. Amounts of rain or snow (mostly between December and March) vary widely throughout the island, being heavy in the central mountainous areas. As a guide, the following table gives average air and sea temperatures.

	Air	Sea		Air	Sea
Jan.	12.3	17.1	**July**	26.4	24.2
Feb.	12.5	16.2	**Aug.**	26.4	24.8
March	13.8	16.9	**Sept.**	23.6	24.4
April	16.8	17.9	**Oct.**	20.3	22.5
May	20.4	20.0	**Nov.**	17.2	19.6
June	24.4	22.3	**Dec.**	13.9	17.4

Use of Time. Package holidays may be chosen for a great variety of reasons other than convenient access to the island's antiquities, but with improved road conditions the tourist can visit Herákleion Museum and the Palace of Knossós in one day from a base almost anywhere on Crete. The determined touring motorist can see the greater part of the island in two weeks. Two-centre holidays are gaining in popularity, and from comfortable hotels on the coast they can offer the chance to explore both ends of the island at a more leisurely pace. It is hoped that by following the routes of this book selectively, readers will be able to adapt the suggested itineraries to their particular interests.

At the planning stage it is worth considering the possibility of using Khaniá airport in order to start a holiday in the relative tranquillity of western Crete before embarking on the more strenuous demands of Herákleion, and the major archaeological sites.

Museums and Archaeological Sites. Ancient remains of any significance are usually signposted and the sites are enclosed, though in the case of minor sites not necessarily locked. Currently admission charges are levied only at museums (including folk museums), at the major Minoan sites, at the Venetian fortress overlooking Herákleion harbour and for the fresco paintings at the Panayía Kerá.

Opening hours are liable to alter slightly each year, and it is impossible to give accurate information ahead of the annual (early spring) announcement. Moreover, the hours differ according to season, and are not uniform at sites of varying importance throughout the island. Generally, however, there are two set periods: the 'summer' season runs from mid March to mid October and 'winter' hours are considerably reduced. State museums, but not sites, are closed on Tuesdays—except for the Herákleion Archaeological Museum which closes on MONDAYS. In the text, 1987 summer opening hours are given as a rough guide, but readers are urged to CHECK on arrival on the island, either at an NTO office or by telephoning the museum or site in question. It should be expected that both museums and guarded archaeological sites will be closed on 1 January, 25 March, Good Friday afternoon, Easter Sunday, and Christmas Day. Note that Sunday opening hours apply to other public holidays and festivals, in particular: Shrove Monday (the beginning of the Orthodox Lent), Easter Saturday and Monday, 1 May, 15 August, 28 October, Christmas Eve and New Year's Eve, and 6 January (Epiphany). To avoid disappointment visitors on the island for the Greek Easter should make particularly careful enquiries about the opening arrangements for the current year, which, at the start of a new season, are often a matter of dispute until the eleventh hour.

In general photography (hand cameras only) is free on archaeological sites, and in museums is permitted (save where unpublished material is on display) on purchase of a second ticket for the camera.

ΑΠΑΓΟΡΕΥΕΤΑΙ (apagorévetai) means forbidden. Standard fees (not cheap) are chargeable for using tripods, etc., and a permit may be required. Consult the NTO.

If directions to sites are needed beyond the detailed instructions given in the text, the following phrases may be useful: yiá or pros (towards) ta arkhaía (ancient things), to kástro (any fortified height), tis anaskaphés (excavations), to phroúrio (medieval castle), to tápho (tomb). Ask for a church by its saint's name.

A great many of the frescoed churches are nowadays kept locked. Where possible, advice is given as to the whereabouts of the key (to kleidí), and if the arrangement has been changed local help is often forthcoming. There is increasing interest in these churches, and the Service for Byzantine Antiquities is keen to make them more easily accessible. However it has to be faced that the search for a key can be a time-consuming business, and is not always successful.

In Orthodox churches women are not permitted to enter the sanctuary.

The majority of monasteries now close their gates during the afternoon (usually 14.00–17.00). Owing to the decline of monastic communities, as well as the ever-increasing number of visitors, most of them no longer offer over-night accommodation. Decorous dress is always requested; exact rules are not laid down, but shorts are particularly disliked.

Public Holidays. Official public holidays in Greece are: New Year's Day; 6 January (Epiphany); Kathará Deftéra ('Clean Monday', the Orthodox Shrove Day at the beginning of Lent); 25 March (Independence Day); 1 May; Orthodox Good Friday, Easter Sunday and Monday, also Ascension Day; 15 August (Feast of the Assumption of the Virgin); 28 October ('Okhi' day; see below); Christmas Day; and 26 December.

Carnival after three weeks' festivities reaches its peak on the last Sunday before Lent with processions and student revels; on Clean Monday families take to the countryside and fly kites. Procession of shrouded bier on Good Friday (Epitáphios) and the burning of Judas in the churchyard; at midnight preceding Easter Sunday the 'Khristós anésti' (Christ is risen) celebration, with ceremonial lighting of the Paschal Candle during mass, and release of fireworks in front of churches; roasting of Paschal lambs and cracking of red Easter eggs on the morning of Easter Day. Okhi Day, commemorating the Greek 'no' (όχι) to the Italian ultimatum of 1940 (see p 26) is celebrated with remembrance services and military processions. Additional local celebrations: in Asi Goniá the sheep-shearing festival on St. George's day (23 April unless this falls in Holy Week); in Khaniá there are festivities in late May (Anniversary of Battle of Crete); in Sphakiá on 26 May and in Ierápetra on 3 October (both for Anniversary of 1821 Revolution); and in Herákleion on 11 November the feast of her patron saint (Ayios Minás).

Shops are open on summer weekdays 08.00–13.00 (most categories of food shop 13.30), also Tuesday, Thursday and Friday, 17.00–20.00 (winter 16.00–19.30). On Monday, Wednesday and Saturday they do not reopen, but the morning session is extended to 14.00 (Saturday 15.00). Tourist 'souvenir' shops, and food shops in designated 'tourist areas' may remain open all day, including Sundays. The regulations are exceedingly complicated; butchers in particular keep different hours—enquire locally. Chemists take turns to offer a 24-hour service; the rota is posted on the shop door.

Tourists on a self-catering holiday or shopping for picnic lunches will have no difficulty in finding a supermarket (accented supermárket) selling all basic requirements; opening hours are usually as for food shops above, with less strict hours in the main resorts.

The ΠΕΡΙΠΤΕΡΟ, or pavement kiosk, developed from a French model, is a characteristic feature of Greek urban life. Selling newspapers, postcards and stationery, stamps, cigarettes, chocolate, toilet articles, film, etc., kiosks are open for about 18 hours a day.

Language. A knowledge of ancient Greek is a useful basis, but no substitute, for the study of modern Greek. Apart from the unfamiliarity of modern pronunciation, many of the commonest words (e.g. water, wine, fish) no longer come from the same roots. Those who know no language but English can get along quite comfortably anywhere on the main tourist routes. A knowledge of at least the Greek alphabet is highly desirable, however, since street names, bus destination plates, etc., may otherwise be puzzling. A phrase book such as the 'Penguin Greek Phrase Book' can be very helpful.

The Greek alphabet now as in later classical times comprises 24 letters:

A α, B β, Γ γ, Δ δ, E ε, Z ζ, H η, Θ θ, I ι, K κ, Λ λ, M μ, N ν, Ξ ξ, O o, Π π, P ρ, Σ σ ς, T τ, Y υ, Φ φ, X χ, Ψ ψ, Ω ω.

Vowels. There are five basic vowel sounds in Greek to which even combinations written as dipthongs conform: α is pronounced very short, ε and αι as e in egg (when accented more open, as in the first e in there); η, ι, υ, ει, οι, υι have the sound of ea in eat; o, ω as the o in dot; ου as English oo in pool. The combinations αυ and ευ are pronounced av and ev when followed by loud consonants, af and ef before mute consonants.

Consonants are pronounced roughly as their English equivalents with the following exceptions: β = v; γ is hard and guttural, before a and o like the English g in hag, before other vowels approaching the y in your; γγ and γκ are usually equivalent to ng; δ = th as in this; θ as th in think; before an i sound λ resembles the lli sound in million; ξ has its full value always, as in ex-king; ρ is always rolled; σ (ς) is always hard, never like z; τ is pronounced half way between t and d; φ = ph or f; χ, akin to the Scottish ch as in loch, a guttural h; ψ = ps as in lips. The English sound b is represented by the Greek double consonant μπ, d by ντ. All Greek words of two syllables or more have one accent which serves to show the stressed syllable. In the termination ov the n sound is disappearing in speech and the ν is often omitted in writing.

The above are the equivalents commonly given for the Greek language, but in fact the pronunciation of the Cretan dialect is considerably softer than that of mainland Greece. In Αγιος, for example, the γ is nearer to 'j' than to the transliterated 'y' of this Guide or the alternative 'gh' of signposts, and χ approaches the 'ch' of church, or even 'sh', rather than the 'ch' in loch.

For *transliteration* in this volume see also Explanations (p 9).

Manners and Customs. Calendar and Time: all movable festivals are governed by the fixing of Easter according to the Orthodox calendar. Greece uses Eastern European Time (in summer 3 hours ahead of GMT, in winter 2 hours). Note also that π.μ. (p.m.) = English a.m. and μ.μ. (m.m.) = English p.m.

Travellers may like to pay attention to the more formal conventions of Greeks. The handshake at meeting and parting is usual and enquiry after the health taken seriously. The correct reply to καλώς ωρίσατε (kalós orísate; welcome) is καλώς σας βρίκαμε (kalós sas vríkame; glad to see you). To the enquiry τι κάνετε (ti kánete; how do

˒you do?) or πῶς εἴστε (pos íste; how are you?) the reply should be καλά ευχαριστώ, και σεῖς (kalá efkharistó, ke sis; well thank you, and you?), or έτσι και έτσι, και σεις ; (étsi ke étsi, ke sis; so-so, and you?). General greetings are χαίρετε (khérete; greetings), or less formally γιά σας (ya sas; hello). Στο καλό (sto kaló; keep well, the equivalent of godspeed) is used when bidding farewell to one who leaves, not when one is leaving oneself. Περαστικά (perastiká) is a useful word of comfort in time of illness, meaning 'may things improve'.

It is still customary to greet shopkeepers, the company in kapheneíons, etc., with καλημέρα (kaliméra; good day) or καλησπέρα (kalispéra; good evening). Σας παρακαλώ (sas parakaló; please) is used when asking for a favour or for information, but not when ordering something which is to be paid for, when θα ήθελα (tha íthela; I should like) is more appropriate. The Greek for yes is ναι (né) or, more formally, μάλιστα (málista); for no, όχι (ókhi).

When drinking in company glasses are often touched with the toast, εις υγεία σας (your health) which is generally shortened in speech to the familiar yásas, or, to a single individual, yásou (to you), or yámas (to us).

In direct contrast to English custom, personal questions showing interest in a stranger's life, politics, and money are the basis of conversation in Greece, and travellers should not be offended at being asked in the most direct way about their movements, family, occupation, salary, and politics.

The 'Volta', or evening parade, is universal throughout Crete.

Fasting is taken seriously in Lent, and is rigorous in Holy Week.

Equipment. Binoculars greatly enhance the pleasure of travel on Crete. A pocket compass can be of help in understanding inland site plans. An electric torch is useful, especially for frescoed churches or caves. Anyone on a touring holiday in the early part of the year (March–April) should remember that in the mountains the weather may still be wet, and, at least at night, cold. Cretan hillside undergrowth is very spiny, and even in summer heat the protection of trousers and sensible shoes may be preferred. Mosquito repellent is advisable; small electrical devices (very efficient) are available locally in town chemists and all supermarkets.

Electrical voltage on Crete is 220v and the current is AC.

Newspapers. Foreign-language newspapers are obtainable in the main towns and resort hotels but (because flown in) are expensive. The London papers are on sale the day after publication.

Weights and Measures. The French metric system of weights and measures, adopted in Greece in 1958, is used with the terms substantially unaltered. Thus κιλό (kiló, pl. kilá), misó kiló (half kilo), grammária (grams), etc. Some liquids are measured by weight, not in litres.

I   HERAKLEION AND CENTRAL CRETE

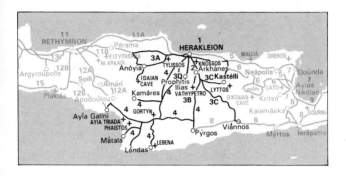

1   Herákleion

HERAKLEION or **IRAKLION** (ΗΡΑΚΛΕΙΟΝ), known also by its medieval name of *Candia*, lies midway along the N coast of Crete, and since 1971 has been the island's administrative capital. Its population of 102,000 makes it the fifth largest city in Greece, and its per capita income is the highest in the whole country. With two nightferries all the year round from Piraeus (the port of Athens), and the principal airport of the island nearby, Herákleion is for a large proportion of tourists their introduction to Crete.

The city has often been damaged by earthquake—the last major one in 1926—and historically it suffered from pirate raids, foreign occupation, and in 1941 the full horror of modern warfare. The 1941 bombing of Herákleion is strikingly illustrated by photographs in the Historical Museum. In recent years the understandable urge to modernise overnight—made possible by the advent of comparative affluence—has very often resulted in piecemeal redevelopment, usually in aesthetically unpleasing reinforced concrete. But the medieval street plan endures, the Venetian fortifications have been well restored, and other traces of the architectural past do survive to illuminate the island's history. The proximity of Knossós and the unique contents of the Archaeological Museum continue to make Herákleion one of the most important tourist objectives of the Aegean.

Tourist Information Office (NTO or in Greek EOT): 1 Odós Xanthoudídou, opposite the entrance to the Archaeological Museum. Tel. 225 636. Opening hours 08.00–18.00 (weekends and low season –14.00). Useful information (bus timetables, etc.) is posted on a board in the window. The NTO also staffs an information desk at the airport, 09.00–21.00.

Tourist Police: Leophóros Dikaiosíni, near the market.

Airport: 4km E of city on the Old Road; for details of services see Practical Information—Travel to Crete. Flight enquiries tel. 282 025. *Airport buses* run to and from Olympic Airways Terminal in Plateía Elevtherías.

Car Hire: see Practical Information—Travelling on Crete. Directions for routes from the airport are given at the end of this section.

Ferry boats from Piraeus dock at the E quay (see plan) where there is a comfortable café. Taxis meet the boats. The stop for town (and Knossós) buses is 300m W of the dock gates, by the main long-distance bus station.

Two companies operate the ferry services (see Travel to Crete). The *Minoan Lines* office is at 78 Odós 25 Avgoústou, opposite Ayios Títos (tel. 229 602); the *ANEK* line is on the same street nearer the harbour (tel. 222 481).

Accommodation is plentiful at all price levels. There are four Class A hotels in the city. There are beach hotels in both directions, at Amoudára beach (W) and at Amnisós (E), both within 15 minutes of the centre by car (also served by town buses). For a short visit without private transport, it is convenient to stay within the city walls. There is a cluster of comfortable modern Class C hotels, most without restaurant, in a central position above the Venetian harbour. They are on or near Odós Epimenídou, a one-way street running E from Odós 25 Avgoústou. For cheaper accommodation consult Tourist Information offices.

Youth Hostel: 24 Odós Khándaka.

Tour Agencies: *Candia Tours*, 51 Odós Epimenídou, (near the Lató Hotel), tel. 226 168; *Creta Travel*, 22 Odós Epimenídou, tel. 227 002; *Adamis Tours*, 23 Odós 25 Avgoústou, tel. 283 820; *Zeus of Crete*, 1 Plateía Kallergón (just out of Plateía Venizélou), tel. 221 103, and also a desk at the airport. These and many others arrange guided tours to the main archaeological sites, to the Gorge of Samariá and a number of other places of interest or natural beauty. Several *shipping agents* have offices in Odós 25 Avgoústou, and most lines are handled by Kavi Club, 2 Papalexandroú, in the little square next to the NTO, tel. 226 672.

There are one-day cruises to the islands of Santorini and Ios subject to weather conditions; in midsummer, when the 'meltémi' wind blows most strongly, it is not always possible to land on Santorini.

The Greek Alpine Club runs a refuge hut on Mount Ida. For information telephone (Herákleion) 227 609.

National Bank of Greece: Odós 25 Avgoústou near Ayios Títos, and Plateía Kornárou opposite the top of the market.

Post Offices: main office in Plateía Daskaloyiánni, open for all mailing business Monday–Friday 08.00–20.00. Foreign Exchange for cheques and currency operates here, mornings only till 13.30. Subsidiary offices in caravans have been established in El Greco (Theotocopoúlou) Park and at the main (E Crete) bus station on the harbour, open for all services, including Exchange, 08.00–20.00 daily except Sunday 09.00–18.00

OTE (telephone and telegraph office): El Greco Park. Area code 081.

Public Lavatories: in El Greco Park, and in the public gardens on the edge of Plateía Elevtherías, opposite the Venizélos statue and behind the Nikephóros Phokás memorial.

Car Parking is restricted to meters in the town centre 08.00–20.00 (except Sundays), and central Herákleion is no place for apprehensive drivers in unfamiliar vehicles. Municipal car park (Drs 100 per half-day) in the moat, immediately outside the New Gate on the right on entering the town (not on plan). Meter bays in Plateía Elevtherías convenient for the Archaeological Museum. (Space is more easily available in the afternoon 14.00–17.00, when shops are closed.) Or park near the seafront beyond the Historical Museum and walk (10 minutes to centre).

Buses on town routes are blue. Boarding is at the back, past a conductor selling tickets (and skilled at communicating with foreigners). Most useful bus routes are:

No. 1 ΣΤΡΑΤΩΝΕΣ E to its terminus 500m short of the airport, intermittently to the airport and every 30 minutes in summer to the Amnisós beaches. Bus stop in middle of Plateía Elevtherías.

No. 2 ΚΝΩΣΟΣ every 20 minutes from the harbour (main E Crete bus station, see plan), with convenient boarding points in Plateía Venizélou (Morosini fountain) and Odós 1821. On the return route, the bus stops in Plateía Elevtherías, for the Archaeological Museum, and then descends by the rampart directly to the harbour.

No. 6 for the beaches and hotels W of the city, also for Camping Herákleion. (Not all buses on this route run to the end of the line; look for signs on windscreen or check with the conductor). Bus stop outside the cinema in Plateía Elevtherías.

Country or long-distance buses are green. There are four bus stations, run by KTEΛ, the bus owners' association.

I. The main bus station (tel. 282 637) is E of the roundabout at the bottom of ΛΕΩΦ. ΔΟΥΚΑΣ ΜΠΩΦΟΡ (Doúkas Bófor) and serves E Crete: the plateau of Lasíthi, Mállia, Ayios Nikólaos and Siteía, the Ierápetra route via Ayios Nikólaos. Also for buses to Arkhánes.

II. The bus station outside the Khaniá Gate, 150m down the side street to the right (tel. 283 073), is for the SW routes: Górtyn, Phaistós, Mátala, Ayía Galíni; Zarós and Kamáres; Léndas. Also (tel. 283 287) for Phódele, Týlissos and Anóyia.

III. Oasis bus station (tel. 288 544), outside the New Gate (not on plan), serves Viánnos, for Arví and Mýrtos, and on by this route to Ierápetra. Also other destinations to the SE within the province of Herákleion, such as Thrapsanó and the Kastélli Pediádas region.

IV. Réthymnon and Khaniá buses leave from outside the Historical Museum (tel. 221 765); also one service a day through to Ayía Galíni via Réthymnon and Spíli.

British Consulate: 16, Odós Papalexandroú, in the little square next to the NTO (tel. 224 012).

General Hospital: Apollónion, between Odós Alber and Odós Márkou Mousoúrou, across the main road in front of the cathedral, Ayios Minás, and one block towards Plateía Kornárou and the market street.

Car Hire from the airport: you join (in less than 1km) the Old Road from E Crete which leads directly (another 3km) to the centre of Herákleion, Plateía Elevtherías. For the N Coast Highway (New Road), bypassing Herákleion to other destinations, join the Old Road, follow it less than 1km over the first cross-roads (traffic lights), and take the next left, an insignificant one-way street recently signposted only from the direction of the city. Very shortly there is a right turn, then a left bend, and the highway is in sight.

Rocca al Mare, the Venetian fortress built to guard the harbour of Candïa (Herákleion)

History. In the Neolithic period there was at least one settlement on the high ground above the Kaíratos stream-bed, on the E side of what is now Herákleion. Here the modern suburb of Póros lies on the site of a Minoan harbour town and cemetery. In Roman times 'Heraclium' was the harbour of Knossós (Strabo, X, 476, 7). With the Saracen conquest, c AD 824, the town was renamed 'El Khandak' from the great ditch dug round it; the Arab settlement became a centre of piracy and the principal slave market of the Mediterranean. After a number of abortive attempts to liberate the island, the army of Nikephóros Phokás, including Russian and Scandinavian mercenaries, laid siege to the town, and the Byzantine general is renowned for demoralising the defenders by catapulting over the walls the heads of his Moslem prisoners. After 10 months and much bloodshed, Crete was once again part of Christendom. During this second Byzantine period the city (now known as Khándakas) extended to what today are Khándakas and Daídalos streets.

When the Venetians eventually took control of Crete (1210) they made the city their capital, calling it and the island Candia. The impressive defences, walls, bastions and fortified gates (a circuit of 3km) were built over a long period (14–17C). Especially after the appointment in 1538 of Michele Sanmicheli, (architect of the Palazzo Grimani among other major buildings in Venice) to take charge of a new phase of construction, Candia, with its great fortress guarding the harbour, became one of the leading seaports of the E Mediterranean. It is copiously documented in the archives of Venice as a major city of the Venetian empire. The Duke of Crete governed the island from Candia, and in order to develop the city, both the Venetian nobility and the Greek aristocracy were obliged to build houses and to live here for part of the year.

But in due course the power of Venice fell into decline. In 1648 the ascendant Ottoman Empire began the great siege of the city, which was to last more than 21 years, making it one of the longest sieges in history. The Turkish camp lay on the hill of Fortétsa 4km S, from which their cannon bombarded the town. In the siege it is calculated that the Venetians and their allies lost 30,000 men, the Turks 118,000. The city was the last bastion of Christendom in the E Mediterranean, but the Christian world only watched and waited. Eventually, in 1668, Louis XIV sent a relief force under the command of the Duc de Beaufort. An heroic but ill-judged sortie resulted in the defeat of Beaufort's force, and the French withdrew. On 5 September 1669 the Venetian commander, Francesco Morosini, at last accepted defeat; he surrendered the city and the Venetians were allowed to sail away from Crete unharmed.

Under the Turks the town, known at that time as Megálo Kástro, the Great Fortress, was the seat of a Pashalik. It was renamed Herákleion after Turkish rule ended in 1898. Though Khaniá was then made the capital, Herákleion grew rapidly to become the chief commercial city. Because of this preeminence, and a central position, the administrative capital was transferred here in 1971.

A.   The Town

The quickest way to orientate yourself in Herákleion is to find the central crossroads with traffic lights at the downhill end of the market street (agorá); officially this crossroads is ΠΛΑΤ. ΝΙΚ. ΦΩΚΑ (Plateía Nikephórou Phoká, see plan). In shopping hours you will encounter here the traffic and bustle which is typical of modern Herákleion.

With the stalls of the market street behind you, and slightly right, you will be looking N, in the direction of the sea, into ΟΔΟΣ 25 ΑΥΓΟΥΣΤΟΥ (Odós 25 Avgoústou) which runs down to the harbour. Along it are banks, shipping offices and travel agents. To your left is ΛΕΩΦ. ΚΑΛΟΚΑΙΡΙΝΟΥ (Leophóros Kalokairinoú), which passes near the cathedral and ends at the Khaniá gate, the W exit from town. Immediately behind you is ΟΔΟΣ 1821 (Odós 1821), on the bus route to Knossós. Continuing anti-clockwise, next is the market street, officially ΟΔΟΣ 1866, and finally, right, ΛΕΩΦ. ΔΙΚΑΙΟΣΙΝΗ (Leophóros Dikaiosíni), traditionally known for its coffee houses, but now also for better-class shops. (50m N of the crossroads, away from the market and towards the sea, pavement cafés crowd the plateía around the Morosini fountain—see below.)

On the S side of Dikaiosínis is the NOMAPXEION (Nomarkheíon), the administrative and legal headquarters of the province (nome) of Herákleion. The offices occupy restored Turkish buildings on the site of Venetian barracks. The elegant marble *portal* of the central block, sent from Italy in 1409 by the Cretan pope, Alexander V, originally graced the Franciscan monastery which stood on the present site of the Archaeological Museum.

Just beyond this are steps, right, past the *statue of Ioánnis Daskaloyiánnis* (an 18C revolutionary leader from Sphakiá) to the plateía of the same name recently paved as a pedestrian precinct (tavernas and bars). On one side is the central *Post Office*.

Dikaiosíni ends in ΠΛΑΤ. ΕΛΕΥΘΕΡΙΑΣ (Plateía Elevtherías), a noble name in the Greek language, the Square of Freedom. The *Archaeological Museum* (see below) is in the near left-hand corner of the square.

The Morosini fountain during the period of Turkish rule (from Gerola, Monumenti Veneti nell'Isola di Creta, *1905– 32)*

A short way towards the sea from the central crossroads near the market is the paved ΠΛΑΤ. ΒΕΝΙΖΕΛΟΥ (Plateía Venizélou), readily identified by its Morosini fountain. The square has become a focus for tourists, with cafés open from breakfast-time on and bookstalls selling foreign newspapers. There are the usual souvenir shops, and one or two just out of the square specialise in antique items. Be prepared to bargain.

This area around the Plateía Venizélou was the centre of the Venetian city, the site of the Ducal Palace. The *fountain* was built in 1628 by order of the Venetian governor Francesco Morosini the elder, and was supplied by an aqueduct from Mount Júktas, 15km away. It was originally completed by a marble statue of Neptune, but this was demolished during the Turkish occupation. The lions are 14C work, probably from an earlier fountain elsewhere. Below the basins are delightful marine scenes in relief.

Across the road from the fountain stands the restored Venetian church of *Ayios Márkos*, now a hall for concerts, lectures and exhibitions; forthcoming events are advertised in the portico.

A triple-transept basilica was built here in 1239, damaged by earthquake in 1303 and again (after restoration) in 1508. There was a campanile at the SW corner and during the Great Siege (1648–69) the bells played their part in rallying the population. During the Turkish period the church became a mosque, and the campanile was replaced by a *minaret*; the lower part is preserved to the right of the façade.

Walking downhill, on the main street, Odós 25 Avgoústou, that leads towards the harbour, you can see (left) a public garden planted with orange trees; this is ΠΑΡΚΟ ΘΕΟΤΟΚΟΠΟΥΛΟΥ (Párko Theotokopoúlou), known to most foreigners as El Greco Park. There is a subsidiary *post office* here, and on the W side the central *telephone and telegraph office* (OTE).

On the right of the main street is the reconstructed Venetian **Loggia**, a careful copy of the original arcaded design (1626) which provided an elegant meeting-place for the Venetian nobility. Adjoining the Loggia, the restored Venetian *Armoury* has become the City Hall or ΔIMAPXEION (Dimarkheíon). Set in its N wall is a relief from the Sangredo fountain (1602) which originally decorated the NW corner of the Loggia; Sangredo was one of the Dukes of Crete. The sadly defaced female figure is believed to represent Crete, holding in her left hand a shield and in her right a club. In mythology the nymph Crete was the mother of Pasiphae (wife of Mínos) who gave birth to the Minotaur.

Behind the Loggia, set back from Odós 25 Avgoústou in a tree-lined square, is the church of Ayios Títos. Titus was St. Paul's apostle to Crete. The original Byzantine church, which had been converted into a mosque, was destroyed by earthquake in 1856. However, the mosque was rebuilt, and this, rededicated to Ayios Títos, is substantially what you see today. A reliquary with the saint's skull, which in 1669 the Venetians had taken with them to the safety of Christendom, was returned here in 1966.

The road ends at the *Inner Harbour*, a busy scene of fishing boats and yachts. The harbour is guarded by the **Venetian fortress** 'Rocca al Mare' or in Turkish 'Koúles'. Open to the public during the summer 08.45–15.00, admission (1987) Drs 200.

The original castle dated from the first years of the Venetian occupation, but it was destroyed by earthquake in 1303. The building was completely reconstructed in 1523 and the inscription over the northern gate bears this date. The restored interior with 26 chambers is an impressive example of its kind. A ramp leads to the upper level which in summer becomes on open-air theatre. There is a commanding view from the battlements.

On the external walls are three high-relief carvings of the *Lion of St. Mark*; the best preserved is the one to seaward. The walk out along the mole is recommended.

On the esplanade to the W of the harbour, just before the *Historical Museum* (see below—and note bus station for Réthymnon and Khaniá) are the ruined walls of the Venetian cathedral of St. Peter. More impressive, and just across the road from the Inner Harbour, are the restored 16C **Arsenals**, remains of the great dockyard which was begun soon after the Venetians took over the island. The Arsenals are now partially restored in two groups of echoing arcades. Here, on what was then a sloping shore, the Venetians built or repaired their ships, each vault holding one galley.

There is a pleasantly situated café beside the yacht moorings on the E quay of the Inner Harbour. Behind it are the Port Authority offices, and nearby on the Outer Harbour, the berths used by cruise liners. (The main *bus station*, serving E Crete, is just inland of these quays.) Beyond, further to the E, lie the regular Athens ferry boats, and further still, through the Customs barrier, the docks for international shipping.

From the roundabout E of the Arsenals ΛΕΩΦ. ΔΟΥΚΑΣ ΜΠΩΦΟΡ (Doúkas Bófor, i.e. Beaufort) sweeps up along the rampart to Plateía Elevtherías. At the entrance to the square the Archaeological Museum is to the right. On the left stood the St. George's Gate (1565); a Turkish fountain has been set in the restored city wall. Here the *Old Road* to E Crete descends through the ramparts.

Opposite the Museum entrance, around the corner, is the *Tourist*

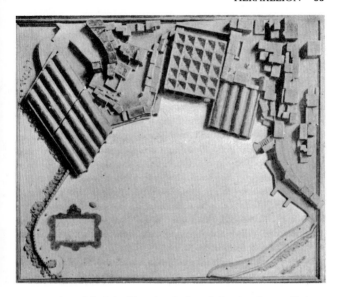

A model of the Venetian dockyard showing the vaulted Arsenals (from Gerola, Monumenti Venceti nell'Isola di Creta, 1905–32)

Information Office (NTO on plan, in Greek EOT). In the big square you can walk left along the rampart, enjoying a fine view over the harbour, to the huge *statue of Elevthérios Venizélos* (1864–1936), the respected national statesman and one of the architects of modern Greece, who was a native of Crete. Across the road from the statue are public gardens; at the far (S) end of them there is a good view of the Vituri Bastion and moated walls.

Plateía Elevtherías used to be the most popular outdoor café of Herákleion, but it has now partly succumbed to the city's ever-growing motor traffic. To complete a circular tour you could walk down Dikaiosínis, but recommended is the pedestrian precinct, parallel and one block right, ΟΔΟΣ ΔΑΙΔΑΛΟΥ (Odós Daidálou), which will bring you out exactly opposite the Morosini fountain.

A visit to the lively *market street* is a traditional feature of Herákleion life. Side streets (W) specialise in blacksmiths' work, and near the top is the fish market. At the uphill end of the street is the *Bembo fountain* (1588), composed of antique fragments, including a headless statue which the architect Zuanne Bembo brought from Ierápetra (Greco-Roman Ierápytna) in SE Crete. The fountain stands behind a polygonal kiosk, itself adapted from a Turkish fountain, and now in use as a café, convenient for a pause to observe the market scene. You will probably notice men of the older generation dressed for a day in town in the traditonal Cretan costume of breeches or baggy trousers, tall leather boots, cummerbund and the 'mavromándilo', a long black scarf knotted round the head. In the old days this was the prized symbol of manhood.

Across the open space of ΠΛΑΤ. ΚΟΡΝΑΡΟΥ (Plateía Kornárou) is the massive modern sculpture entitled 'Erotókritos and Aretoúsa'.

It was commissioned by the Municipality from the Cretan Ioánnis Parmekéllis.

To the right the main road would lead (past a taxi rank and ΟΔΟΣ Μ. ΜΟΥΣΟΥΡΟΥ (Odós M. Mousoúrou) for the new hospital, the Apollónion) to the modern cathedral of Ayios Minás, and the Icon Collection housed in the medieval church of Ayía Aikateríni (see Rte 1D below).

ΟΔΟΣ ΕΒΑΝΣ (Odós Evans) continues ahead, slightly left from the market, to pass through the walls at the reconstructed Jesus Gate (now the Kainoúria Pórta or New Gate). The walls are over 40m thick at this point (not shown on plan).

Outside the gate (right) is the entrance to the outdoor theatre which in July and August is the venue for many concerts and other events brought to Crete from the Athens Festival. In the shadow of the wall (the Jesus bastion), there is a pleasant shaded café. The large municipal Car Park uses the moat on the other side of the New Gate.

Inside the gate ΟΔΟΣ ΝΙΚ. ΠΛΑΣΤΗΡΑ (Odós Nikoláou Plastíra) leads W (5 minutes) to the Martinengo Bastion and the tomb of Níkos Kazantzákis, the eminent Cretan author of, among many other works, 'Zorba The Greek' and 'Freedom and Death'. He died in Germany in 1957. The inscription on the memorial here quotes one of Kazantzákis's more famous lines: 'I hope for nothing. I fear nothing. I am free'.

B.   The Archaeological Museum

The **Archaeological Museum**, off Plateía Elevtherías, houses a vast collection of material, amassed since 1883, from the Neolithic to Roman periods of Cretan history. The Bronze Age exhibits are outstanding and are very well displayed. Few Minoan artefacts have found their way from Crete to museums elsewhere in the world, so the collection here may justifiably be called unique.

The museum stands on the site of the Latin monastery of St. Francis which dominated this hill and the skyline of Herákleion during the Venetian period. An excavation in the garden of the entrance courtyard during 1984, under the auspices of the director of Byzantine Antiquities (M. Borboudákis), revealed part of the foundations of the monastic church, which proved to have been destroyed by Turkish bombardment during the Great Siege (1648–69).

The museum building (1937–40), designed on functional anti-seismic principles rather than aesthetic ones, provides 20 galleries on two floors, but so great is the appeal of its exhibits that in high season overcrowding is often a problem. Many people will want to make more than one visit, ideally before and after exploring some of the sites where the objects were found.

Open (summer 1987): 08.00–19.00, except Sunday 09.00–19.00. Closed Monday. Admission Drs 400. Check in advance if possible (and for public holidays) or on arrival in town. In the winter season the museum closes at 15.00.

There is a beautifully illustrated guide to the museum by its former director, the Ephor of Archaeology on Crete, J. Sakellarákis. If weight is not a problem, this is also recommended background reading during a tour of the island's sites.

The museum's Bronze Age collection is well labelled. The case numbering of the ground floor rooms has in the past been based on the principle that you start on the right of the doorway as you enter, continue round the wall anti-clockwise and then follow an anti-clockwise spiral for the central cases, usually ending down the middle of the room.

During a 10-month programme of building work in 1987 air conditioning was installed throughout the museum, with inevitable disruption as particularly fragile objects were put into storage, and cases were amalgamated to allow easier access for workmen. The installation should be complete by the start of the 1988 tourist season. It is expected that the contents of each case will then be arranged exactly as before, but the position of cases within the gallery may be altered; in particular the most outstanding exhibits, which attract the guided tours, are likely to be moved to the far end of each room where a gathering for a lecture is less of an obstruction to other museum visitors. It has not been possible to give precise information in advance of any re-arrangement, but it is hoped that this will not cause too many problems, and that careful attention to case numbers will enable the reader to understand the display. Any alterations will be incorporated in this Guide at the first opportunity.

Gallery I. Neolithic and Early Minoan (Prepalatial) Period (c 5000–2000 BC).

Cases 1 and 2 contain Neolithic and Sub-Neolithic pottery, violin-shaped and steatopygous idols, and bone and stone implements from Knossós, the cave of Eileíthyia near Amnisós, Phourní in E Crete, Phaistós and other sites. The hand-made pottery was decorated by rippling or burnishing, or with incised geometric patterns filled with a white chalky paste.

Case 3 illustrates from burial caves the various styles of 'Sub-Neolithic' or Early Minoan I (3000–2600 BC) with grey wares and pattern-burnished vases from Pártira (Central Crete) and Pýrgos (on the N coast E of Herákleion), and red-on-buff painted wares from the cave of Kyparíssi near Prophítis Ilías. Note the tall pattern-burnished cups as well as the rounded bases typical of some EMI vases.

Case 4 is devoted to Early Minoan vases from the great circular tombs at Lebéna, on the coast S of the Mesará plain: EMI red-on-buff and white-on-red wares in a great profusion of shapes. Also from Lebéna (Case 5) are jewellery, figurines and bronze daggers which illustrate the character of the society that built these communal tombs of the Mesará.

Case 6 contains distinctive EMII Vasilikí mottled ware, in particular the jugs and long-spouted teapots; these are from Vasilikí itself (upper shelves) and other E Cretan sites (bottom shelf).

In Case 7 the finest of the early stone vases come from the cemetery on the off-shore island of Mókhlos (EMII–III, 2600–2100 BC); the banded marbles and limestones are remarkably well adapted to the shapes of the vases. Breccia, chlorite and polished green serpentine, and black and creamy steatite are also used. The vases were made by hand, the inside being cut out with a reed or copper drill and an abrasive powder. There is a fine large chlorite pyxis with incised decoration (from Marónia). The pyxis lid with dog handle (Mókhlos) and the nearly complete pyxis beside it (from Zákros) are clearly by the same hand. Case 8 displays EMIII vases from Vasilikí and Mókhlos. A style with white decoration on a dark ground (black or brown) now replaces the Vasilikí mottled ware but many of the earlier shapes continue.

Case 9 contains vases from various Mesará tombs, including 'Barbotine' ware with pinched relief decoration, and a bronze basin from Kalathianá in the Asteroúsia mountains. Case 10 has EM–MMI vases from Palaíkastro in E Crete. Note the flat-bottomed boat, also the four-wheeled cart, the earliest evidence for wheeled transport on the island (c 2000 BC).

In the centre: Case 16, Early and Middle Minoan I sealstones from the Mesará, notably the ivory cylinders with designs cut at each end. See also 1098, the Babylonian haematite cylinder of the period of Hammurabi, from Tomb B at Plátanos, and 2260, the 14-sided seal with hieroglyphic symbols from Arkhánes. In Case 12, pottery and figurines from Mesará tombs; a *Bull, with tiny acrobats clinging to the horns, and the bird-shaped vases from Koumása are libation vases. Case 13 contains marble and ivory figurines and other objects, chiefly from Mesará tombs. The figurines are in the Cycladic style; a few were imported but the majority locally made.

Case 14 shows flat, leaf-shaped daggers and the longer (later) ones with a central mid-rib; most are of copper or bronze, a few of silver. In Case 15, clay figurines, including bulls, a bird and an 'agrimi' (the Cretan ibex), again from the Mesará tombs. Among fine stone vases are 'bird's nest bowls', and multiple vases known as 'kernoi', which are thought to have been used for offerings.

In the central Cases 17 and 18A are displayed elegant gold, rock crystal, and carnelian jewellery and necklaces, from Mókhlos, the Mesará tombs, and the Arkhánes cemetery (Phourní). The *Necklace in Case 18A combines gold, ivory and faience; with it are other fine ivory exhibits. Case 18 has further sealstones, including four-sided prisms, and some with signs in the hieroglyphic script.

Gallery II. Minoan Old Palace or Protopalatial Period (MMIB–II, c 1900–1700 BC), also some Prepalatial material. This room is devoted mainly to finds from Knossós and Mállia. In Case 19 are the earliest vases from the Mállia Palace and cemeteries, including Khrysólakkos; there is some mottled Vasilikí ware, also stone vases and moulds for double axes. (The much-illustrated gold bee pendant from Khrysólakkos is in Gallery VII.) Case 20 contains MMI pottery from the rectangular burial enclosures at Goúrnes, on the coast E of Herákleion, including a group of enigmatic bell-shaped objects usually referred to as 'sheep-bells', also figurines, some from the sanctuary near Týlissos. Case 21 contains a wide variety of votive offerings from peak sanctuaries (Kóphinas, Traóstalos and again Týlissos). In the corner, a pithos burial from the slopes of Aílias, over-looking Knossós, shows a typical method of interment at this period.

Case 21A and the adjacent new addition (? 21B) display material from the recent excavations at the peak sanctuary on Mount Júktas, S of Knossós. There are tables for offerings, bronze double axes, figurines, a display of jewellery and miniature objects including a gold scorpion pendant, and stone seals.

Wall Cases 22 and 23 contain pottery from houses below the West Court of Knossós, then fine polychrome Middle Minoan II vases from Knossós. The faience 'sheep-bell', the only one known in this material, comes from Póros, one of the harbours of Knossós. Between these cases are clay burial chests (larnakes) and large pithoi.

Case 24 contains MMI figurines from the peak sanctuary of Petsophás, above Palaíkastro at the eastern end of Crete. Note the elaborate head-dresses of the female figures and the daggers worn in their belts by the males. There are also three figurines from the (Prepalatial) oval house at Khamaízi in E Crete. Note the series of clay models identified as *Shrines on account of doves perched on the pillars (Knossós), or the sacral horns on the roof.

The central case nearest the entrance (25) contains the polychrome faience *Plaques found in the Palace of Knossós and known as the Town Mosaic; they are models of Minoan house façades, sometimes three storeys high. This case also contains tablets, labels and bars in the MM hieroglyphic script, which is still not fully deciphered though the numerical signs are clear. The gold-hilted dagger is from Mállia; it is shown with gold bands and bronze figurines from the peak sanctuary at Traóstalos near Zákros.

Case 26 exhibits characteristic pottery from Mállia, also bronze cauldrons; the other central cases (27–29) contain Middle Minoan seals and polychrome pottery, some in the Kamáres style, including large vessels from Knossós. Note (in 29) the pithos decorated with palm trees.

Gallery III. Minoan Old Palace or Protopalatial Period (MMIB–II, c 1900–1700 BC). Here (Case 30) are the polychrome vases from the Kamáres cave (on Mount Ida) which gave Kamáres ware its name, and the remainder of the room is devoted to the astonishing collection of *Vases and other material from the Old Palace of Phaistós.

Popular shapes are bridge-spouted jars and several forms of cup, many thin-walled and with carinated (angular) profiles imitating metal shapes. Many of these vases, and those from Knossós in the previous room, show a wonderful harmony between the design and the shape, the patterns being brilliantly adapted to the form of the vase. One example out of many is the Kamáres style jug prominent in Case 34. Some of the smaller vases are known as 'eggshell ware' because of the incredible thinness of the pottery.

Noteworthy among the larger vessels are a tall vase with attached

The Phaistós Disk (Herákleion Museum, Gallery III)

white flowers, and a fruitstand or bowl with toothed hanging rim and
elaborately painted interior (both in Case 43 at the end of the room).
Case 40 has some examples of eggshell ware, and also illustrates the
wide variety of sealings found at Phaistós. The archive, found in an
MMII deposit, consisted of over 6500 seal impressions employing
nearly 300 distinct motifs.

The central case (42) displays the contents of a shrine from a room
bordering the West Court at Phaistós. Notice the great red-
burnished clay libation table with border decoration of bulls and
spiral designs.

In Case 41 is the famous *Phaistós Disk, hand-made of clay and
stamped in a spiral with characters in an unknown script. The signs,
which are thought to constitute some form of syllabic writing, are
framed and divided up by incised lines; the inscription runs from the
outside to the centre. The disk was found in a MMIII (17C BC)
context.

Gallery IV. Neopalatial Period (MMIII–LMI, 1700–1450 BC).
Finds from the Palaces of Knossós, Phaistós and Mállia. Case 44 contains material from Knossós with examples of the Minoan Linear A
script, which is incised on an amphora shoulder and on two silver
pins, and written in cuttlefish ink inside two cups.

In Case 45 there is Knossós pottery with spiral decoration, and also
the 'Lily Vases', the white painted lilies originally on a dull lilac-
brown ground. An interesting conical rhyton decorated with horns of
consecration is from the Royal Tomb. 7741 was perhaps a lantern;
7742 was for unwinding balls of wool.

Case 46 contains material associated with the worship of the
Sacred Snake; in Minoan times this was a prominent domestic cult
associated with the concepts of immortality and reincarnation, and
the tubes have been interpreted as snake containers or shelters, with
cups for milk. *Vase in the shape of a honeycomb encircled by a
snake.

On the opposite wall, in Case 47, are bronze utensils, and terracotta and stone objects from the Palace of Mállia. *Brown schist scep-
tre, one end a leopard, the other an axe. Case 48: exhibit from the
houses in the town at Mállia.

The finds (Case 49) from the final destruction of the Palace of
Phaistós in LMIB, c 1450 BC, were not very plentiful, but notice the
graceful *Jug with an all-over pattern of grasses, and a rhyton in the
Marine Style decorated with argonauts.

Case 56 displays the skilfully restored ivory *Acrobat, perhaps a
bull-leaper (compare the fresco panel illustrated on p 74), and fragments of similar figures; there were traces of a partial covering of
gold leaf.

Also individually displayed, in Case 51, is the **Bull's Head
Rhyton (with holes in the mouth and crown of the head through
which sacred libations were poured). It was found in the Little Palace
of Knossós, and is made from serpentine, with the eyes inlaid with
jasper and rock crystal, and the nostrils outlined in white tridacna
shell; the horns (restored) were of gilded wood. Note the double axe
incised on the centre of the forehead.

Much of the material exhibited in this gallery comes from the two
sunken stone cists in a small room near the Tripartite Shrine in the
Palace of Knossós, which were named by Evans the Temple Repositories. The smaller objects from these treasure chests sealed at the
end of MMIII are displayed in Case 50; they include the two faience

Ivory acrobat from the Palace of Knossós (Herákleion Museum, Gallery IV)

figurines of the *'Snake Goddess', argonauts, flying fish and other decorative plaques (also of faience), banded limestone and marble libation vases, a rock crystal rosette for inlay, and painted shells. In Case 57 is the remarkable *Gaming Board found in a corridor at Knossós and dated c 1600 BC; the ivory frame is inlaid with rock crystal, faience, lapis lazuli, and gold and silver leaf.

Case 52 contains ceremonial swords and other weapons of Middle Minoan date from Mállia. One *Sword, nearly a metre long, has a pommel of rock crystal on an ivory hilt. On another, of rapier type, there is a pommel of bone, and on an encircling *Disk of gold leaf an acrobat is displaying his skill (see drawing). Other finds in this case include stone vase fragments with relief decoration from Knossós and Phaistós and miniature work in ivory, rock crystal, and faience. One fragment of a relief shows a procession of worshippers at a Peak Sanctuary and the offering of baskets of flowers.

A splendid series of bronzes from houses at Knossós is displayed in Case 53. These include a large saw, a tripod cauldron and bowls with chased decoration of leaves round the rims.

Case 54 contains the large vases from the Temple Repositories, including a 'bird jug', an import from the island of Mélos in the Cyclades; the birds decorating the jug have been shown to be a type of partridge. In Case 55, on one side there are bronze plates from scales, and lead and stone weights from various sites, and on the other faience reliefs from the Temple Repositories including a *Cow suckling her calf—also a marble cross. In Case 58 are the stone ritual vessels from the Temple Repositories. These are mostly rhytons in alabaster, banded limestones, and other variegated stones.

From the Central Treasury at Knossós came the *Lioness Head Rhyton made of a translucent marble-like limestone; this has Case 59 to itself. In three corners of this room are large stone vases of serpentine from Knossós.

Gallery V. The Final Palace Period at Knossós (LMII–IIIA, 1450–1380 BC). Around the walls is a series of Palace Style amphoras,

some from the Palace itself, others from the Little Palace and the
Royal Villa. It is noticeable that a formal element has entered into the
decoration, in contrast to the naturalism of the LMI vases. On the
right as you enter is a giant (unfinished) stone amphora from the
Lapidary's Workshop in the Palace with a decoration of shallow-
relief spirals; the material is banded tufa.

Case 60 contains LM material from houses by the Knossós Royal
Road. In Case 61 there are vases and architectural fragments from
the Palace, including stone friezes with split rosettes and spirals in
relief, also a large stone jug in banded limestone. and a ewer of
breccia imitating basketwork. With these are clay vases from the
Little Palace and silver vessels from the S House.

On the end wall, Case 62 exhibits several fine large stone vases
and lamps from Knossós made from a reddish marble, antico rosso,
imported from the southern Peloponnese. Above are Egyptian finds
from Knossós, including an alabaster lid with a cartouche of the
Hyksos king Khyan, a large Predynastic or early Dynastic bowl, a
carinated bowl (4th Dynasty) of diorite beside a Minoan obsidian imitation, and a diorite statuette (lower half only) of an Egyptian, perhaps an ambassador, called User (12th or early 13th Dynasty).

In the corner is a model of the LMI Royal Villa which stood on the
slope above the Kaíratos stream, and was connected to the Palace by
a paved road.

Case 63A displays vases and figurines from the grand house at
Knossós which Evans named the 'Unexplored Mansion'; it was the
subject of a detailed excavation during 1967–73. Note the oval *Pyxis
with bird decoration, three goblets of 'Ephyraean' type, and a small
clay goddess with raised arms and cylindrical skirt. In Wall Case 64
are clay and stone vases (and clay horns of consecration) from the
destruction debris of the Palace and therefore crucial to a chronological assessmant of that destruction; they have been dated to c 1400–
1380 BC. Between these two cases hangs a watercolour by the late
Piet de Jong, a reconstruction of the Tripartite Shrine beside the
Central Court at Knossós.

Turning to the central cases: in Case 69 are tablets, and some other
objects, showing inscriptions in Linear A (the still-undeciphered
script of the Minoans); they come from Ayía Triáda, Týlissos,
Phaistós, Zákros, Palaíkastro, and Gourniá. The Linear B tablets, in
an early form of Greek, are from the Knossós archives. The clay
tablets were accidentally preserved because they were baked hard
in the fires which destroyed these sites.

Case 65 displays a collection of exquisite Late Minoan sealstones.

In Case 66 are stone vases from the Palace, including a ewer of
breccia imitating basketwork, and the big flat gypsum alabastrons
found in the Throne Room, also a bull rhyton in clay. Evans conjec-
tured that the alabastrons played a part in some ritual during the last
moments before the final destruction of the Palace, a ritual perhaps
designed to avert that catastrophe.

Case 70 contains various ivories of very fine workmanship from the
houses beside the Royal Road at Knossós. Note also a group of grave
gifts including jewellery from a tomb at Póros, now a suburb of
Herákleion.

In Case 67 are two Palace-style octopus amphoras and one, earlier
and noticeably more naturalistic, of LMIB date, c 1450 BC. Case 68:
selected sherds of Knossós pottery including some Floral and Marine
Style wares.

Case 70A displays a clay *Model of a Minoan house, an important find from Arkhánes. Note the main room with a supporting pillar, the small windows for maximum insulation against both heat and cold, the small court serving as a light-well, the stepped ledge on the roof-terrace; there is evidence for timber and stone construction, and the columns characteristically taper downwards.

Gallery VI. Neopalatial and Postpalatial Cemeteries at Knossós, Arkhánes and Phaistós. Case 71 contains Late Minoan vases from the tholos tomb at Kamilári (SW of Phaistós) in use for several centuries from MMI. Three important clay models came from this tomb: one is interpreted as a *Shrine, with two pairs of seated divinities (or revered dead), and worshippers placing offerings before them; the second appears to be a banquet for the dead, the religious element emphasised by doves and horns of consecration; the third shows a ring of male dancers also in a ritual setting denoted by horns of consecration. The bird alabastron is painted in a lively style of c 1400 BC.

In Case 72 is material from the Temple Tomb at Knossós and the Royal Tomb at Isópata. From the latter came the splendid series of Egyptian 18th Dynasty alabaster *Vases and an Old Kingdom bowl in porphyry. Clay and stone vases from the Knossian cemeteries of Mávro Spélio and Zápher Papoúra follow in Case 73, with a Kouro-trophos figurine; then Case 74 for finds from a chamber tomb in the rich cemetery at Katsambás, a harbour town of Knossós. Also from this tomb group (in Case 79A between the two doors) is a remarkable ivory *Pyxis carved with a bull-catching scene akin to that on the gold cups from Vápheio (Athens, National Museum).

Next, on the end wall, is Case 75 with bronze vessels and utensils from the Tomb of the Tripod Hearth at Zápher Papoúra, and (above) comparable objects from a tholos tomb at Arkhánes. Case 75A exhibits a ritual horse-burial, exactly as it was found in a tholos tomb at Arkhánes; the horse had been sacrificed and dismembered.

The Wall Cases 76 and 77 display clay and stone vases from the Knossós cemeteries including Isópata, the Tomb of the Double Axes, and the LMII Warrior Graves excavated on the site of the Venizéleion hospital. A tomb at Ayios Ioánnis, N of Knossós, contained the ribbon-handled gold cup with embossed band of double running spirals (77). The associated bronze weapons from the Mycenaean Warrior Graves are nearby in Case 84; see also the bronze helmet with cheek pieces in Case 85.

In Case 78, from the Zápher Papoúra cemetery, is a reconstructed boar's-tusk *Helmet of a type described by Homer.

The ivory pyxis (79A) has been noted above with Case 74. The remaining wall case (79) contains stone lamps and vases including some made from Egyptian alabaster, as well as imported 18th Dynasty alabastrons, clay vases (notice the bird alabastrons), a rhyton made from a triton shell, and a glass bottle, all from the LMIII cemetery at Kalývia near Phaistós.

Case 80 dislays a libation jug with stylised argonauts and spiked decoration from a chamber tomb at Katsambás. Case 81: miniature work, jewellery, ivory toilet articles and also weapons from the cemeteries at Knossós, Katsambás and Arkhánes. Case 82 contains amphoras from the Royal Tomb at Isópata, also large stone vessels from the Katsambás cemetery, including an Egyptian alabaster vase with a cartouche of Thutmosis III (1504–1450 BC), the great king of the 18th Dynasty, and a LMII *Amphora decorated with four boar's tusk helmets like the one in Case 78. Opposite, in Case 83, are large vases from the Palace at Knossós.

Cases 86 and 87 contain jewellery and ivory toilet articles from the Phaistós and Knossós cemeteries, and from various other tombs including Kamilári; among these exhibits (see also 81 and 88) are many of the finest achievements of the Cretan goldsmiths. Particularly admired (in Case 87) are the gold *Ring, from Isópata, showing an ecststic dance with goddess and worshippers on a flower-filled ground, and earrings in the shape of bulls' heads, using the granulation technique. Case 88 displays finds from tholos tombs at Arkhánes: *Jewellery, a bronze mirror with an ivory handle, and a pyxis lid in ivory with figure-of-eight shield handles.

Gallery VII. Neopalatial Settlements and Sacred Caves of Central and South Crete (MMIII–LMI, c 1600–1450 BC). The first objects on the right are large bronze *Double Axes on restored poles and painted bases; these come from the villa of Nírou Kháni on the coast E of Herákleion. This building contained many other cult objects such as painted plaster tripod tables, and the stone horns of consecration on the right-hand wall.

Here Case 89 displays figurines, vases and stone lamps from Nírou Kháni and the villas at Týlissos, including a rhyton of dark-grey imported obsidian, extremely difficult to carve because of its hardness and liability to fracture. Among the bronze figurines of young male worshippers in the typical saluting position is a rare portrayal (from Týlissos) of an older man whose waist is released from the constriction of the customary tight belt.

In Case 90 are vases from the villas at Amnisós, Sklavókambos and Vathýpetro. Notice the fine bridge-spouted jug with zig-zag patterns and the stone conical rhyton from Sklavókambos. The stone lamps and large cup (second and lower shelves) are from Vathýpetro, the vases and head on the upper shelf from Amnisós. Beside this case, a throne from Póros made out of stone imitates a wooden prototype.

On the opposite wall, Case 91 contains vases from the two Minoan houses at Prasás, inland from Amnisós, and from a burial cave at Póros. In Case 92 are bronze figurines, both human and animal, also knives and daggers; most come from the votive deposits in the Diktaian cave, but some are from other cave sanctuaries at Patsós and Skoteinó. Case 93 displays material from Ayía Triáda, including several vases in the Marine Style and a jug with the double-axe and sacred knot motifs. Also shown are carbonised beans, barley, millet, and figs identified during the excavations at Phaistós and Palaíkastro.

Individually displayed in this room and considered among the finest examples of Minoan art are the three serpentine vases carved with relief scenes, all from Ayía Triáda: the *Chieftain Cup (95) portrays a Minoan official receiving tribute of animal hides; the much-restored *Boxer Rhyton (96) has scenes of boxing and wrestling matches, and, in the second zone from the top, of bull sports. Only the upper half of the *Harvester Vase (94) is preserved: the shoulder is carved with a procession of youths, the leader carrying a long rod, the rest pitchforks and scyths; they are accompanied by four singers, one playing the sistrum. He, like the figure in Case 89 in this room, has a dispensation from the usual tight belt. All three vases are believed to be products of a Knossós workshop (c 1550 BC).

Case 97 exhibits bronze figurines and ivory pins and inlays from Týlissos and Nírou Kháni. It also has some magnficent examples of the bronze swords and other weapons found in a votive deposit in a cave at Arkalokhóri in the centre of the island. In Case 98 a hoard of votive double axes comes from the same cave.

In Case 99 are copper talents or 'ox-hide' ingots (weight c 40kg), with incised signs, and copper hammers from Ayía Triáda. In Case 102 are human and animal votive figurines from the same site, stone vases including a beautiful dolium shell of white-spotted obsidian, and a Hittite sphinx. Case 100 shows bronze tools, utensils and jewellery, all from Ayía Triáda, two potter's wheels from Vathýpetro and seals from various sites.

Along one wall are three huge bronze cauldrons from Týlissos.

Also free-standing are various large vessels, including a stone basin from Ayía Triáda.

The central case (101) contains gold and silver jewellery from Central and E Crete. There are several examples with granulation. Here also is one of the great treasures of Minoan art, the gold *Pendant of MMI date from the Khrysólakkos cemetery at Mállia. It consists of two conjoined bees (or wasps or hornets) around a golden ball with a smaller ball within, covered with granulation.

Gallery VIII. The Zákros Room. Finds mainly from the Palace, but also from the houses in the Minoan town above it. (From Palace where not otherwise specified.) Period: almost entirely Neopalatial (1700–1450 BC) and principally from the last phase of the New Palace (LMI, c 1550–1450 BC), immediately preceding its final destruction by fire.

Case 104: vases with unusual figure-of-eight handles. Case 105 contains pottery, and stone and bronze utensils. The bronze incense burner has chased decoration of ivy leaves (see adjacent drawing).

On the opposite wall, Case 106 displays rhytons in both conical and piriform shapes, also an elegant fruit-stand with spiral and ivy-leaf decoration. Case 107 has further examples of vases from the Palace. Case 108: *Cup with double-axe decoration, stone horns of consecration and a stone capital from a votive column. The conical cup containing olives was retrieved from one of the Palace wells; the olives at first appeared perfectly preserved, but they shrivelled after only a few minutes of exposure to air.

In Case 109 is an exquisite rock crystal *Rhyton with a handle of crystal beads turned green by the bronze wire on which they are threaded. The exhibit is a tribute to the skill and dedication of the museum's conservation staff who restored this extraordinary work of art from more than 300 tiny fragments.

Case 110 contains material from the houses in the town. There are many vases in the LMIB Marine Style in the Zákros Room, but here a *Rhyton decorated with shells, tritons, seaweed, rocks and starfish is a particularly fine example. See also the amphora between Case 107 and the doorway.

Case 111 displays the *Peak Sanctuary Rhyton, a superb piece of Minoan stone-carving, and valuable evidence for an understanding of Minoan religion. It depicts in relief a mountain shrine with wild goats, plants, and flowers (drawing on wall). The material is chlorite, turned brown in parts from the effect of fire; a few traces survive of the gold leaf which once covered it.

Case 112 contains bronze weapons and tools from the Palace including a sword with gold rivets, and a ceremonial *Double axe with duplicated blades and decoration of stylised lilies (see drawing on wall). In Case 113 are bronze talents, and a complete elephant tusk found in the Palace storerooms. It is discoloured by burning in the great fire c 1450 BC. In the same case (above) is fine pottery including an elegant *Jug in the by now familiar Marine Style, decorated with argonauts.

Case 114, bridge-spouted jugs and fine stone rhytons. Case 118, further stone vases, also stone hammers and three faience animal-head rhytons. The stone vases in these two cases (114 and 118), mostly from the unplundered Treasury of the Shrine, are the finest collection of such vessels yet known from the Minoan civilisation. They comprise: conical and fluted rhytons of Egyptian alabaster and polychrome banded limestones, one also of lapis Lacedaemonius (114) (a stone imported from the only known source near Sparta); a group of chalices including examples in gabbro, white-spotted obsidian (118) and polychrome limestones; two Old Kingdom Egyptian vases in porphyritic rock (118) adapted for use by the Minoans with the addition of bridge-spout and bronze handles; several individual vases made of Egyptian alabaster and an 18th Dynasty imported alabastron; also a large multiple vase, with high curving handles, made of polychrome banded limestone (also in 118).

Case 115 has bronze objects from the Palace: large two-handled saws, two inlay plates decorated with papyrus flowers, and a circular strip, a vase mounting, with double axes.

Case 116 displays a chlorite bull's head *Rhyton; it is smaller than that from Knossós but of equally fine workmanship.

In Case 117 is miniature work from the Palace and from houses in the town: ivory double axes and a *Butterfly, all discoloured by fire in the final destruction; also a faience *Rhyton in the shape of an argonaut.

Freestanding in this room are several large painted vases, and five pithoi. One on the end wall (near Case 118) has an inscription in Linear A, including the sign for wine. It comes from the villa just outside Ano Zákros, and was found beside a wine press which can now be seen in the Siteía museum.

Gallery IX. Neopalatial Settlements of East Crete (MMIII–LMI, c 1700–1450 BC). Cases 119 and 120 on the right are devoted, in the main, to Palaíkastro. The first contains stone vases and lamps, one of antico rosso with ivy scrolls on the columns. Notice also a clay bull rhyton and bronze figurines, the large one from Praisós. Case 120 has three fine LMIB vases including an octopus *Flask and a jug with papyrus decoration, also two feline heads in clay.

Between these two cases, Case 161 displays finds from the 1970s' excavations on the Pýrgos site at Mýrtos. There are clay and stone vessels and utensils, seals and a bronze dagger. Unique is a thin-walled vase with fluted rim which contains a cluster of miniatures of the same shape.

The adjacent central case (125) has Marine Style rhytons, a gabbro rhyton and two stone libation tables from Palaíkastro.

In Case 121 (on the opposite wall) is a series of LMI vases from Gourniá; note the double vase, also a small bull's head rhyton, and a bronze figurine. The adjacent free-standing case (126) also has finds from Gourniá; there are many rhytons including a fluted stone example in antico rosso, and several very large limestone lamps. Case 127 contains a collection of bronze tools and weapons, from Gourniá and other Central and East Cretan sites. In the centre of the room (128A) the Marine Style stirrup vase from Gourniá has a case to itself.

Case 129 has material from Mókhlos, an islet off the coast E of

*A Marine Style flask from Palaíkastro (Herákleion
Museum, Gallery IX)*

Gourniá; the exhibits include clay vases, bull rhytons, a stone lamp
with foliate band decoration, and bronze vessels including a cup with
ivyleaf decoration, closely similar in shape to the gold cups from
Vapheio in the National Museum in Athens.

In Case 122 (on the wall by the door) are clay and stone vases and
lamps from the island of Pseíra, with a magnificent rhyton of breccia
and a *Basket vase decorated with double axes. The remaining wall
case (123) contains clay votive figurines, both human and animal,
from the MM–LMI sanctuary at Piskoképhalo near Siteía. The
beetles are *Rhinoceros oryctes*; sometimes they have climbed on the
human figures.

In the two remaining central cases are: (124) clay sealings from
Knossós, Ayía Triáda, Zákros and Sklavókambos, (one from Knossós
showing two figures with a hieroglyphic inscription, perhaps a title,
beside them), together with small objects, notably ivories and inlays,
from Palaíkastro and other E Cretan sites; (128) a magnificent collection of Late Minoan *Sealstones in agate, carnelian, chalcedony,
jasper, lapis Lacedaemonius, lapis lazuli, rock crystal, and other
stones, from various sites. The main seal shapes are the lentoid,
amygdaloid (almond) and flattened cylinder. Particularly noteworthy

are Nos 1656–9 from the Knossós Warrior Graves, 165–80 from the
Kalývia cemetery near Phaistós, as well as those in lapis lazuli from
Knossós.

Around the room are several large vases from E Crete including
burial pithoi from the cemetery of Pakhyámmos just E of Gourniá.

Gallery X. Postpalatial Period (LMIII, 1350–1100 BC). The decline
of the Minoan culture is reflected in the remains from the Postpalatial
age; it is noticeable that vase-painting has lost its vitality, and fine
stonework no longer occurs. Wall Case 130 (with 131) exhibits
pottery from Phinikiá, Katsambás, Phaistós, Gourniá and also from
the houses of the LMIII reoccupation in the ruins of the Palace of
Knossós. Popular shapes are the tall-stemmed kylix, tankard, ladle,

*The Poppy Goddess, a terracotta figurine from Gázi
(Herákleion Museum, Gallery X)*

krater, and stirrup vase. The earlier LM patterns, such as the octopus, have now become stylised, but the bird decoration from the first part of LMIII is of interest. See also Case 132 with pottery from the LMIII settlement at Palaíkastro, including the group of figures dancing round a musician playing the lyre.

The single wall case (133) contains large clay 'goddess' idols with raised arms from a shrine at Gázi, just W of Herákleion. The central figure has a head-dress of poppies.

Case 134 (with 136) displays (above) material from LMIII chamber tombs at Stamníi and Episkopí Pediádas, SE of Herákleion (unusual serpentine vase with five receptacles), and (below) material from Episkopí near Ierápetra, and the rich LMIII cemetery at Mouliáná in E Crete. From this Episkopí come several fine squat stirrup vases, and from Mouliáná a large flask decorated with concentric circles, also Close Style stirrup vases with octopus patterns.

In Case 135 are figurines and other cult objects from the domestic shrine of the Minoan villa or farm at Mitrópolis near Górtyn.

Case 137 displays tomb groups from Amnisós (Kárteros), Goúrnes and Pakhyámmos; the imported glass bottle is from Amnisós and the limestone horns of consecration from Póros, now an eastern suburb of Herákleion. Case 138 contains terracotta objects including life-like horses and riders.

The central cases exhibit the following objects: (139) bead necklaces, mostly of glass paste, some of semi-precious stones, from tombs at Goúrnes, Episkopí and Stamníi (Pediáda), also Mílatos near Mállia, together with stone moulds for ornaments; (140) finds from LMIII shrines at Knossós (Shrine of the Double Axes), Phaistós and Gourniá, with clay huts from the first two sites; (141) large vases, especially kraters, from Mouliáná (one with a warrior on horseback), Phaistós and Knossós; (142) contents of shrines from Gourniá, Priniás (Subminoan), Koumása in the Mesará and Kaló Khorió (the head of a large idol); (143) clay idols, animal and human, from sanctuaries at Ayía Triáda (notice especially the *Figure on a swing) and the cave of Hermes in the gorge of Patsós; (144) tools and weapons of all kinds in bronze, the main series from the two LMIIIC tombs at Mouliáná in E Crete.

Gallery XI. Subminoan, Protogeometric and Early Geometric Period (1100–800 BC). The wall cases on the right contain Protogeometric and Geometric material from sites in Central and East Crete. It is immediately apparent from the new pottery shapes and the decoration of geometric motifs that great changes are occurring on the island. During the period of the Cretan Geometric style, burial rites altered from inhumation, the habit of the Minoans and still prevalent in LMIII, to the practice of cremation; this became the rule until the end of the Late Orientalising period (c 630BC), except in extreme E Crete where the older tradition persisted. The ashes were buried in large clay vases, occasionally in a bronze vessel; the most usual pottery shape eventually became the more-or-less spherical pithos, though many variations occur and are well represented here and in the next room.

Case 145 contains vases from Phaistós (upper shelf) and from the large cemetery at Kourtés, including a kernos in the form of a ring with human figures between miniature pots. Note the rhyton in the shape of a bird (duck askos); there are several of these vessels in the following cases, each with individual character both in conformation and in the indication of plumage. Case 146 exhibits finds from

Vrókastro and Kavoúsi in E Crete including a pair of open-work basket vases (the kalathos shape), a hydria (three-handled vessel for carrying water) decorated with a chariot scene, a horse figurine and a bronze tripod. In Case 147 are Geometric vases and bronze figurines from these and other sites in Central and E Crete: Psykhró (the Diktaian cave), Ayía Triáda, Ayios Sýllas, Amnisós, Kavoúsi, and Vrókastro.

In the nearby central case (154) are clay vases and ritual objects, including little clay huts, from the earlier LMIIIC mountain refuge settlement at Karphí above Lasíthi.

The large model of a house sanctuary was found in a Protogeometric tomb at Teké, part of the Knossós North Cemetery; interesting features are the interior ledge, small high-set square windows, chimney, ventilation holes, and flat roof with course of stones near the edge, also the painted decoration on the door. (Further important material from this tomb is shown in the next gallery.)

The large clay goddess idols from the shrine at Karphí (see above) are exhibited on the end wall, in Case 148. The feet are made separately and fitted into the aperture in the cylindrical skirt. With these, also from Karphí, is a peculiar rhyton in the form of a charioteer drawn by bulls, of which only the heads are shown.

In Wall Case 149 is material from the cave sanctuary of Eileíthyia (goddess of childbirth) at Inatós near Tsoútsouros on the S coast; the votive offerings include clay figures embracing (some in coital positions) and women pregnant or giving birth. Note the model boats, also the bull figurines and many double axes in the Minoan tradition. Further important finds from this site are also on show in Case 158 near the doors (see below).

Between Cases 149 and 150 stands a majestic lidded pithos, one of the grandest examples of the new cremation urns.

Case 150 and the adjacent central Cases 155, 156 and 157 contain a series of vases from Protogeometric and Geometric tombs of the Knossós North Cemetary (Teké). Typical vase-shapes displayed in 150 are: the oinochoe (jug) in a variety of shapes and sizes including trefoil-mouthed juglets; the hydria; on the top shelf the skyphos and bell-skyphos (two-handled drinking vessels); various cups. The pithos is represented with and without a defined neck.

In Case 155 there are two bell-kraters with figured scenes. On one a hunting scene is depicted. The other has two lions attacking a man, and on the reverse side facing sphinxes, with to right a water bird; this vase too had been used as a cinerary urn before the pithos shape became customary. Note the bird askos.

Case 156 contains a fine pedestalled krater. (Another very large one, decorated with Maltese cross in concentric circles, stands beside Case 151.) Case 157 shows a globular pithos between two belly-handled amphoras, all elaborately decorated with zones of typical motifs: rosettes and chequers, hatched meander, and filled concentric circles.

In this case are finds from the rich tombs at Siderospiliá (Priniás), where a sheet-gold ornament with swastikas and a 'star of David' pendant make to the anachronistic eye a strange juxtaposition. The grave gifts included clay figurines of humans, in the Daidalic style, and of horses; the pair of galloping horses were probably harnessed to a cart, the wheels with them being part of the same model. The bronze bit from a bridle was found on the skull of a horse skeleton in a burial of ritual significance within this cemetery.

The remaining central case on this side (158) has further material from the Inatós cave, including an ivory figurine of a naked goddess, faience goddesses, scarabs, necklaces and other jewellery. The scarabs have been dated to the Saitic period in Egypt.

Case 153 (opposite) exhibits metalwork: iron and bronze tools, weapons, utensils, pins, fibulae and tweezers from various sites including Knossós, Kourtés, Kavoúsi, Vrókastro, Arkádes and Praisós. With the spread of the new skill in smelting at the necessary high temperatures, bronze was gradually replaced by iron for the manufacture of tools and weapons, though the former continued in use for figurines, bowls and ornamented pieces such as shields; unfortunately iron objects of this age on Crete are rarely well-preserved.

Gallery XII. Late Geometric and Orientalising Periods (8–7C BC), also finds (covering a long period) from the Sanctuary of Hermes Dendrites at Sými. In this room is a large series of cremation urns from tombs in the Knossós area, especially from a group near Fortétsa (now recognised as part of the Knossós North Cemetery), and also from the Arkádes cemetery near Aphráti in Central Crete. Note the distinctive polychrome decoration of the Orientalising vases, with curvilinear patterns of lotuses and rosettes. Some smaller vases from Fortétsa show Protocorinthian influence (Case 162); Crete was in touch not only with the East, but with many parts of the Greek world.

Five cases exclusively display finds, mostly pottery, from the Knossós cemetery, and others show the Knossós jewellery and precious objects beside comparable pieces from other sites on the island.

Case 159 exhibits cremation vases and gifts for the dead from Fortétsa. On the lower shelf is a bell krater with on one side facing wild goats, the Cretan agrími, and on the other a scene of boats; this early example of a vase used for a cremation burial dates from a tomb of the Protogeometric period when realistic decoration was practically unknown. The grave gifts found in it included a faience ring with a quasi-hieroglyphic design on the bezel. In contrast, above in the same case, are three polychrome Orientalising pithoi with looped feet and elaborate lids, and two examples of the lekythos with decoration of concentric circles.

Turn next to the free-standing Case 165, which displays a further three Orientalising urns, these from the tholos tomb (Khanniále Teké) which yielded the rich treasure on display in the central case in this gallery (see below). The pyxis is from the Fortétsa cemetery. Note also the bird askos with tail in the form of a hydria (also two small hydrias in this case), and the olpe with scale pattern and animal frieze which includes griffins.

Cases 166 and 167 both continue the exhibits from the Knossós cemetery. In the first, note the panels of birds in the painted decoration on the vases and their lids; one design shows a smaller bird carried on the parent's wing. In 167 are six polychrome pithoi, some with lids knobbed in the shape of miniature pots. One has a pair of human figures on the shoulder panel. There are also two lekythoi (with elongated slender neck) of the so-called Praisós type.

Wall Case 162 exhibits some of the finest clay, bronze and faience objects from these same tombs, each selected for outstanding quality. As well as exquisite small vases which include a feeding bottle and a double flask, there are unusual pieces in the form of birds and monkeys, a double horse, and trees with birds perched in their branches. One lid has Zeus before a cauldron, with birds; in one hand he holds an eagle and in the other a thunderbolt.

Cases 163 and 168 contain material from the important cemetery of Arkádes. Characteristic of this pottery are the straight-sided tub vases favoured at this site for cremation burials, the floral and plant decorative motifs influencd by eastern traditions, and the scenes of human or mythical figures incorporated in the decoration as early as the first half of the 7C BC. (The human figures often recall the style of Daidalic terracotta figurines of this period.) In Case 168 a chain of spirals terminates in feline heads (compare the pithos in the corner on the back wall). Plastic affixes are added to the vases, as on the cauldron (dinos) with griffins.

In the same case is a vessel painted in added white with a bearded man controlling a long-legged horse, one of the earliest examples (mid 7C) of man and horse depicted together. On a similar vase is a winged male figure between two sphinxes. Orientalising influence is again reflected in a scene on a situla or bucket, where the Mistress of Animals (derived from the eastern 'Potnia theron') holds aloft the tree of life between two tall birds. On the lower shelf are two vessels, one bronze the other clay, which still contain the charred bones buried in them; in each was a single aryballos, a gift for the deceased.

Case 163 has more finds from the Arkádes cemetery: a lyre player, owl figurines, an anthropomorphic hydria, a crouching lion with a dish between its paws (said to be a clay imitation of eastern faience figures), and a cylindrical cremation vessel with a grieving woman one of a pair of mourners. Notable is the oinochoe with, depicted on its neck, two figures interpreted (on slender evidence) as Theseus and Ariadne.

In the two cases (169 and 164), opposite the giant pithoi with relief decoration, there is a display of metalwork from the Knossós cemetery, and also from other sites such as the great cave sanctuary on Mount Ida. In 169 are fragments of cast bronze which once decorated tripod cauldrons; one of the better-preserved scenes shows a couple in a boat propelled by oarsmen, and it has been suggested that this too may refer to the abduction of Ariadne. The ring-handles come from tripod cauldrons. On the other side of the case are: an embossed bronze quiver with sphinxes and the 'Master of Animals' fighting lions, from Fortétsa; two 'mitrae' (body armour) with representations of a chariot; and a pair of bronze greaves from Kavóusi.

Case 164 has a bronze girdle from Fortétsa, on which three divinities in a sanctuary are protected from a chariot attack by a file of archers.

In the central case (170) is a magnificent collection of 9–7C • Jewellery, much of it from a single tomb at Teké, in the Knossós cemetery. This tholos tomb, originally constructed in the Bronze Age, was cleared out for re-use under the new rites at the height of the Protogeometric period (PGB), and remained in use until Early Orientalising times; the jewellery was found in two small plain Orientalising vases sunk into the ground just inside the tomb doorway. The treasure includes: a gold pendant with crystal and amber inlays on a plaited gold chain with snake's head terminals; a second gold pendant fashioned as a crescent ending in human heads and framing birds—strip cloissons on the crescent originally held inlays—and both it and the birds are delicately enhanced by use of the granulation technique; a gold band showing two heroes fighting lions, each panel impressed from the same matrix; a necklace of rock-crystal beads of which the string-holes are lined with gold; and two silver pins, with gold bird heads, linked by a gold loop-in-loop chain. It has been proposed that this material points to a guild of metalworkers at Knossós, originating in the Near East, and moreover that this tomb may have been their family vault.

In this same case is a series of gold, silver and electrum dumps. The near-uniformity of the gold bars looks deliberate, and they have been considered by some to be forerunners of Greek coinage. However, a more intriguing suggestion is that they were the stock-in-trade of the goldsmiths, their raw material in the form in which it was usually handled.

The case also contains other miniature gold-work from Knossós, and pieces from Arkádes and Praisós.

The five remaining cases in this gallery, starting with 160 (on the first wall), contain material from the recently excavated sanctuary at Sými near Viánnos. An inscription (3C AD) between the first two cases affirms the dedication to Hermes Dendrites. The votive offerings found at Sými range in date from the Minoan to the Hellenistic period.

In Case 160 the Minoan material includes bronze figurines of worshippers, stone vases and small altars, one with an inscription in Linear A. (See also the Minoan swords in Case 161C.) There are also offerings from the succeeding period of Mycenaean influence, and from the Early Iron Age, including a bronze figurine of a woman with spear and shield. Case 161 contains votive offerings from the later periods; note the figure of Hermes playing a lyre.

The offerings in Case 161A are in the form of open-work bronze sheets of great interest for their graphic details of the contemporary pilgrim's approach to the sanctuary.

Case 161B contains a further collection of material from the same site, mainly from the 8–5C BC: terracotta figurines and plaques, and, among the bronzes, miniature votive shields. Outstanding in Case 161C are three Minoan swords, two of them ivory-handled.

The huge relief pithoi between the doors date from Subminoan (nearest Gallery XI, from Priniás) to Archaic; the one with Orientalising motifs of sphinxes and leopard-headed spirals is from Lýttos, the others from Arkádes and Dréros.

The Gallery of the Sarcophagi (XIII). During the Bronze Age, burials were often in clay chests or larnakes. Those displayed here are of two periods: there are Middle Minoan tub-shaped examples, painted with abstract designs, from various sites including Vóri in the Mesará, and also LMIII rectangular chests on four feet, often with gabled lids. Usually the designs on these chests consist of degenerate octopuses or stylised flowers, but several examples here are more unusual; decorative elements include birds, fish, a boat (from Gázi), an animal suckling her young (Gourniá), and griffins with the sacred horns of consecration (Palaíkastro). Sometimes elliptical bathtubs with marine designs were used for burials, and examples can be seen with a plug-hole to let the water escape. From occasional remains of wood in tombs and the panelled form of the LMIII chests it is considered that this design was based on a wooden prototype.

In one corner of this room can be seen a burial, transported from an LMIIIA–B tomb at Sellópoulo, near Knossós. A second skeleton (nearer the door) is from Arkhánes; note the bronze finger-ring.

Also exhibited here is a model reconstruction of the Palace at Knossós, made (in wood) by the late master-technician, Zakharías Kanákis.

The Gallery of the Sarcophagi breaks the strict chronological sequence followed so far in the museum. A natural progression would lead from the material of the Orientalising period in the previous room (XII) to the ground-floor Gallery XIX (opposite the far end of the bookstall), which contains some important Archaic sculptures and bronzes noted in the relevant site visits elsewhere in this Guide. However, stairs from Gallery XIII lead to the museum's UPPER FLOOR, which houses the Minoan fresco display, as well as further Archaic exhibits and the Giamalákis collection, so it is convenient to leave the two remaining ground-floor rooms to the end of the visit.

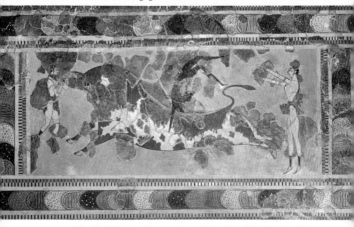

The Bull-leaper fresco from Knossós (Herákleion Museum, Gallery XIV)

Gallery XIV. Hall of the Frescoes. Here, and in Galleries XV and XVI, are displayed the Minoan Frescoes. Only fragments of the original wall-paintings remain, much restored after the collapse of walls and sometimes discoloured by the fires which destroyed the buildings they decorated. However the scenes illustrate the religious and secular life of the Minoans, including (often in the incidental details) their appreciation of the natural world around them. The artists used the true fresco technique; the paint was applied to the plaster while this was still wet, though in some cases the area of the picture seems to have been prepared by impressing with a tool or with taut string. Sometimes the plaster was moulded, before painting, into figures in very low relief, to give a three-dimensional effect.

The surviving pieces are mostly from Knossós and Ayía Triáda; Amnisós, Nírou Kháni, Pseíra, and Týlissos also contribute examples. The paintings, with few exceptions, date from the Neopalatial Period (mainly LMI, c 1550–1450 BC). Some from Knossós are LMII–IIIA, c 1450–1380 BC, and the floor with marine scenes from the shrine at Ayía Triáda is now known to belong to the Postpalatial period.

First, on the left at the top of the stairs, is a fragment of a Bull Fresco, from the Upper Hall of the Double Axes at Knossós. Next come the remains of the *Procession Fresco* with its best-preserved figure the *Cup-Bearer* (notice the seal worn as a jewel on his wrist); these frescoes adorned the Corridor of the Procession, the long ceremonial approach to the Palace and the Propylaea, a great gate where the scenes were arranged in two superimposed friezes.

Between the doors is the *Griffin Fresco* from the Palace Throne Room.

Beyond (18–24) are fragments from Ayía Triáda: a kneeling female figure, perhaps picking flowers; a seated goddess beside a building that is identified as a shrine by the horns of consecration; a cat stalking a pheasant in a landscape of rocks and plants—the cat arches its back to spring but the pheasant struts about, not suspecting danger; a fresco (very similar to one that appears on the sarcophagus in the centre of the room, and probably painted by the same artist) showing a ritual procession bearing offerings and led by a musician playing a lyre; another procession, this time of women approaching a shrine; and a woman leading a deer towards an altar. At the end of the room is a frescoed plaster floor from a LMIII (Postpalatial) shrine at Ayía Triáda. It consists of a colourful marine scene showing dolphins, an octopus and small fishes. Beyond are the remains of another floor fresco with abstract motives, from the First Palace at Phaistós (18C BC).

On the opposite wall, all except the last two frescoes are from Knossós. First is the restored *Shield Fresco* from the Upper Hall of the Colonnades; the markings on the shields represent the dappled hides of the oxen or bulls from which real shields were made. The rosette spirals are a clue to the LMII (1450–1400 BC) date of this work. A very similar Shield Fresco was found in the Palace at Tiryns on the mainland and another, more recently, at Mycenae. Next comes the familiar figure known as the Priest King or Prince of the Lilies, wearing his plumed lily head-dress and collar of fleurs-de-lis and leading an animal, perhaps a griffin, for this theme is shown on sealstones. This interpretation has recently been challenged by the theory that the figure is a boxer.

The *Charging Bull* in stucco relief is from the portico above the N Entrance Passage, the *Ladies in Blue* from the E Wing of the Palace and the Dolphins from the Queen's Megaron. There follow two colourful spiral frieze frescoes and then, from the Caravanserai S of the Palace, the frieze of partridges and hoopoes. The coloured objects are probably stones rather than eggs. Next comes the *Toreador Fresco*, the most vivid representation of bull-leaping in Minoan art. Red is the convention for male figures, white for female, and here we see both participating in this sport.

The last two frescoes on the wall are the graceful white and red Madonna lilies and irises from the LMI villa at Amnisós; such lilies are frequently seen today in Cretan gardens.

At this end of the hall there is a scale model of the Little Palace at Knossós, and a case contains fragments of a chariot and other pieces also from Knossós.

In the centre (Case 171) stands the stone **Sarcophagus** (LMIIIA, early 14C BC) from Ayía Triáda; it is carved from a single block of limestone, covered with a layer of plaster and painted, as with the wall-paintings, while the plaster was still damp. Both long sides portray funeral ceremonies: the one with processions of figures bearing offerings consists of two scenes, distinguished by background colour and the direction in which the figures are facing. On the left the female figure pouring the contents of a vase into a krater is conducting a purification rite for the deceased. The sacred surroundings are symbolised by double axes with birds perching on them. On the right the procession conveys gifts, including a model boat, towards a figure in front of a richly decorated building. This figure used to be interpreted as the spirit or personification of the deceased in front of his tomb, but considering the similarity between the long robe and the kilts in the procession, it is now thought more likely to represent a priest in charge of the rite.

On the reverse, female figures are officiating at the sacrifice of a bull, to an accompaniment on a flute. Ritual significance is seen again in the double axe with bird, the tree and the altar with sacral horns.

On the ends are shown a procession (not well preserved), and chariots driven by pairs of females and drawn by horses and griffins.

Galleries XV and XVI open off the main fresco hall. All the pieces are from Knossós except where otherwise stated.

In **Gallery XV** is the *Miniature Fresco* from rooms W of the North Entrance Passage; crowds of spectators attend some ceremony, including a dance, while another part of the picture shows a tripartite shrine with columns which have double axes attached. Next is the lady named by Evans's workmen *'La Parisienne'*; the Sacral Knot over her neck is taken to be evidence that she is a priestess. Beside her is the restored *Camp Stool fresco* with priests and priestesses sitting on stools holding chalices and goblets. 'La Parisienne' may have been associated with this group though she is on a larger scale. The Spiral Cornice Relief also came from a room W of the North Entrance Passage. Next are displayed relief fragments of athletes taking part in bull sports, then two griffins tied to a column tail to tail. (There seems to have been a whole frieze of these in high relief antithetically grouped in the E Hall of the Palace above the Corridor of the Bays.) The central case in this room contains fragments of miniature style frescoes from Knossós and Týlissos. The diagrammatic representation of a labyrinth, from Knossós, is a motif common at a later date on that city's coins.

In **Gallery XVI**, opposite, further fragments from Knossós are displayed in the central case (174); these include the *Palanquin Fresco*, part of a bull-leaping scene, pieces of the Miniature Frescoes, shrines, and dress fragments. In the corner left of the entrance from the main hall is the original restoration of the *Saffron Gatherer fresco* when the main figure was thought to be a boy. Later it was determined that it was a blue monkey, as shown in N. Pláton's adjacent restoration. Next comes the *Captain of the Blacks*, from the area of the LMI House of the Frescoes, then a dancing girl from the Queen's Megaron, a tri-columnar shrine (this fragment was found in the W Magazines of the Palace), and olive trees in relief, from the N Entrance Passage. On the opposite wall is first another olive tree in relief, then the *Blue Bird* and *Monkey Frescoes* from the House of the Frescoes; the vivid bird is a Roller. These are followed by a scene of women or goddesses in stucco relief, with elaborate dresses, from the island of Pseíra, and finally a Sacral Knot from the LMI villa at Nírou Kháni, E of Herákleion.

In recent years, owing to staff shortages, the next two rooms have, unfortunately, often been closed to the public.

*The Ayía Triáda painted sarcophagus (Herákleion
Museum, Gallery XIV)*

Gallery XVII (through XVIII). The *Giamalákis Collection. The collection
formed over a period of 40 years by the late Dr S. Giamalákis, a surgeon of
Herákleion, is now displayed in this room. There are many objects of
outstanding interest but not all are necessarily from Crete: (175) Early and
Middle Minoan pottery and a Cycladic 'Frying-pan' with incised decoration; a
steatopygous burnished Neolithic *Figurine from Apáno Khorió near Ierápetra;
(176) over 50 stone vases including some of banded marble similar to those from
Mókhlos; a case (187) of Minoan and later seals; another (188) of non-Minoan
seals, including cylinder seals and Sassanid bullas made of chalcedony; (178) a
bronze figurine of a young man bearing a ram over his shoulders; (182) Archaic
and Classical Greek terracottas and vases; (190) a bronze helmet from Axós;
(191) gold objects from the * 'Zákros Treasure' which include a diadem with the
Mistress of Animals, a cup and a bull's head; several bronzes, and in the same
case some very fine Venetian jewellery.

Gallery XVIII. Archaic and Greco-Roman Antiquities. The exhibits
in this room consist mainly of terracottas, bronzes and coins from the
Archaic, Classical, Hellenistic, and Roman cities of the island. Cases
192–194 contain: 7C to Classical clay figurines, pottery and plaques
from a votive deposit on the acropolis of Górtyn (also Case 200);
several figures with wig-like hair are in the Daidalic style; one figure
represents Athena brandishing her spear. In Case 206 the plaques
include Bellerophon fighting the Chimaera, and Klytemnestra and
Aegisthus killing Agamemnon, while others show Archaic naked or
draped goddesses wearing high polos head-dresses.—Case 195.
From Arkádes is a Daidalic head-vase (6639); from Praisós a protome
of a man with a diadem; from the sanctuary of Zeus Diktaios at
Palaíkastro a Gorgoneion (4920); also exhibited are a plaque with a
sphinx from Lýttos and several fragments of Archaic relief pithoi.
Cases 196, 197, 203 and 207A contain fine bronzes from Axós,

Dréros, the acropolis of Górtyn, the Idaian cave and Praisós. These include: mitrai (armour to protect the abdomen) from Axós, with chased decoration, one showing Pegasus, another a tripod cauldron between two lions, a third two contending athletes; a bronze corselet from Arkádes (197), a Gorgoneion and a Palladion from Dréros; numerous handle attachments from the Idaian cave; and miniature votive armour from the sanctuaries of Praisós and Górtyn. Small clay figurines of the Archaic period, human and animal, come from Amnisós, Týlissos, and the Idaian cave. In Case 198 are bronze objects of the Archaic period from Fortétsa, Axós, and the Idaian cave, including (from Axós) a splendid *Helmet with cheek pieces embossed with winged horses. A vase from Dréros, standing separately, is decorated with a wild goat and snakes in relief.

Case 205. The Classical and Hellenistic coins of Crete are mostly of bronze and silver. Rare gold coins from Lissós and Hyrtakína in SW Crete are also shown here. There are coins based on the Attic tetra-drachm with the names of Cretan archons. Greek silver coins of Athens, Aegina, Argos, Corinth, and Sikyon, and coins of Macedon and the Hellenistic monarchies are also shown. (The Roman coins of Crete are in the Study Collection.)

Case 199 is devoted to Greek black- and red-figure vases; these include a good red-figure lekythos from Kydonía (Khaniá), Classical lamps and terracottas, Attic and Boeotian vases. In cases 201 and 202, Hellenistic vases including several Gnathian examples with plant motifs on a light or dark ground, Hellenistic white marble pyxides, Greco-Roman bronzes, terracottas, lamps and glass vessels. Among these are Late Roman bronze and clay lamps with erotic relief scenes. There are also several small Greco-Roman heads in marble. Case 207, containing Classical, Hellenistic, and Roman jewellery and gems, includes a fine Victory, from Knossós, inspired by the Victory of Paionios at Olympia, ear-rings from Oloús, diadems and a series of gold and silver rings. Among the gems is one of onyx with a representation of a Centaur, another of chalcedony with Theseus and the Minotaur. Near the entrance is a life-size bronze *Statue of a boy in sandals and toga from Ierápetra. It is a most sensitive portrayal, dating from the 1C BC.

GROUND FLOOR. **Gallery XIX. Archaic Sculptures and Bronzes (700–550 BC).** Above the entrance is a 7C Gorgoneion from Dréros. In the corner to the left there is a lion head in poros from Phaistós and up on the wall to the left a *Frieze of horsemen from one of the two mid 7C temples at Priniás (ancient Rizenía). Below this frieze are two groups of Archaic sculpture from the acropolis of Górtyn, one representing a god embracing two goddesses, the other of three goddesses. Also on this side are two funerary stelai from Górtyn, a warrior and a lady spinning. Above the entrance to Gallery XX are the seated goddesses from the doorway leading into the cella of one of the Priniás temples; their thrones are placed over a frieze of lions and deer, suggesting that the divinity may be the Cretan Britomartis (Artemis), Mistress of Animals. Also exhibited on the left side of the room are an eagle and a hawk on pedestals with Ionic volutes, from the sanctuary of Zeus Thenatas at Amnisós, and the torso of an Archaic kouros from Elévtherna.

In the central Case 207 are three bronze *Statuettes (7C BC) made by the sphyrelaton technique (hammered on a wooden core and then pinned); they come from the sanctuary of Apollo Delphinios at Dréros and are believed to represent Apollo with his sister, Artemis, and his mother, Leto. Cases 208 and 209 contain the famous bronze *Shields from the Idaian cave, which have lion's head bosses and repoussé decoration showing battle and hunting scenes, an eagle gripping a sphinx, and the Cretan goddess known as the Mistress of Animals. Other shields are from Palaíkastro and Arkádes (Aphráti). A bronze tympanon from the Idaian cave shows Zeus between two Kourétes.

From Praisós (centre of the room) comes a crouching clay lion, c 600 BC. Behind the bronze statuettes are architectural fragments from the 6C temple of Zeus at Palaíkastro, with a 'sima', or water-spout, showing running chariots and a dog; also Archaic relief pithoi. Against the wall on the right of the entrance are lion's head water-spouts from the Palaíkastro temple, a head from Axós (mid-6C), a Roman copy of the Archaic Hymn to Zeus Diktaios from Palaíkastro, and a black stone stele from Dréros with a winged human figure holding a bird.

Gallery XX. Classical, Hellenistic, and Roman Sculptures. Only the most inter-esting or important pieces are listed here.

Left of the doorway are statues from *Knossós*: 273. Roman youth wearing bulla and toga praetextata; 220. Portrait head of Homer; 315. Dionysos, with wreath of ivy; 46. Bacchus pouring from a wineskin (in alabaster). Doorway of Classical house with part of the mouldings preserved. 5. Colossal statue of Hadrian with decorated corselet showing the she-wolf suckling Romulus and Remus and two Victories crowning Roma (this piece from Górtyn). 42. Torso of Aphrodite, probably a copy of a Praxitelean work. 8. (in front of Hadrian) Sarco-phagus with inscription 'Polybos'. An orator harangues the dead; below are the symbols of the Eleusinian mysteries.

On the far wall. Statues from *Górtyn*, mostly Roman copies of earlier works. 342. Torso, copy of the Doryphoros of Polykleitos. 3. Good copy of winged Pothos (Desire) by Skopas. The figure, wings missing, leans against a tree trunk. 325. Aphrodite, copy of Alkamenes's Aphrodite in the Gardens. 159. Torso of Aphrodite, probably copy of a Praxitelean work. 43. Aphrodite kneeling in a bath, copy of a work by Doidalsas. 347. Copy of the Athena Par-thenos of Pheidias, the cult statue of the Parthenon. 67, 65, 64, 66. 1C AD busts of the family of Augustus: Livia, Tiberius, Augustus, and Germanicus (?). 259, 260. Two Egyptian deities identified with Persephone, and Pluto with Cerberus; from the Temple of Isis and Serapis. 155. Fine head of Dionysos. 77. Head of Hera, copy of a Classical original. 326. Cult statue of Apollo Kitharoidos from the Temple of Apollo Pythios. 153. Pan playing the syrinx. 73. Over life-size head of the emperor Antoninus Pius (AD 131–61). 60. Bust of the emperor Septi-mius Severus (AD 193–211). 1. A bearded orator or philosopher with books at his feet, perhaps Herakleitos. 208. Artemis, indifferent copy of a Classical ori-ginal. 350, 351. Hygieia, with the sacred snakes. 349. Aphrodite, copy of a Classical original.

On the right wall. Statues from *other Cretan cities.* 2. Female figure, probably Hestia, copy of a Classical original in the severe style, from Kísamos, W Crete. 334. Roman empress, probably Julia Domna, wife of Septimius Severus and mother of Caracalla, from Khersónisos. 387. The Mállia Sarcophagus (2C AD) 265, 266. Two figures from the Death of the children of Niobe at the hands of Apollo and Artemis, poor Roman copies, from Inatós. 74. Portrayal of a eunuch, from Lýttos. 317. Fine head of Trajan (AD 98–117), from Lýttos. 336. Good copy of a Praxitelean torso of Apollo or Hermes, unknown provenance. 230. Bust of Marcus Aurelius (AD 161–180), from Lýttos. 340. Bearded head, wearing a Per-sian helmet. In front of the cult statue of Apollo is a *mosaic floor*, 2C AD, from Knossós. It is by an artist named Apollinaris (see inscription) and shows Poseidon drawn by sea-horses, accompanied by tritons and dolphins.

South Side. Classical, Hellenistic, and Roman reliefs. 378. Funeral stele showing departure of dead man, imitating the 4C BC Attic type from Herákleion. 363. Metope, late 5C BC from Knossós. It shows a labour of Her-cules, who brings the Erymanthian boar to the terrified King Eurystheus who takes refuge in a large jar. 249, 12, 10, 9. Fragments of Greco-Roman relief sarcophagi: the first, from Khersónisos, shows Atlanta's hunt of the Kalydonian boar; the others, from Górtyn, scenes of combat and Bellerophon and Pegasus; other fragments from these cities show Eros and Tantalos. 145. Attic 4C BC funeral stele, showing a hunter, a notable piece, is from the Bay of Akhláda, Herákleion.

C. The Historical Museum

The *Historical and Ethnographic Museum of Crete (opposite the Xenía Hotel) occupies the spacious neo-classical family house of Andréas Kalokairinós, a notable benefactor of Herákleion. With the help of the Kalokairinós bequest, the Society for Cretan Historical Studies built up the collection and the Museum opened in 1953.

Admission 09.00–13.00 and 15.00–17.30. Closed Sundays and public holidays. Entrance (1987) Drs 250.

This well-built house, restored and redecorated in 1903, with Doric columns and friezes (preserved in the hall) of scenes from the Iliad and the Odyssey, is a pleasant refuge from summer heat, and the wide-ranging collection is highly recommended. The major pieces are meticulously labelled in English.

In the *Entrance Hall* is a collection of photographs of the Crete of 30 years ago. Also two cannon from Venetian galleys sunk in Herákleion harbour during the Great Siege (1648–69).

Left of entrance is the *Cretan historical collection*, from Venetian armour to memorabilia of the Independent Cretan State (1898–1913) under two successive High Commissioners, Prince George up to 1906 and then Alexander Zaïmis (portrait). By the door are documents from the Turkish period, including an intriguing allegorical interpretation of Turkish rule on Crete. Much of this room is given over to exhibits connected with the long and proud struggle for independence. There are portraits of the Cretan chieftains and a lithograph of the leaders of ten revolts between 1770–1897, also a fine collection of their intimidating weapons. Foreign newspaper cuttings add contemporary comment from abroad, and there is one case of commemorative china. A recently assembled screen of historic photographs develops this theme of support from abroad for the Cretan national cause.

Right of entrance: the *Medieval collection* preserves many valuable ecclesiastical items from destroyed or abandoned Byzantine churches. Two cases display rare copper vessels, crucifixes, candlesticks and other sacred objects from the Early Christian period, found during the excavation of the 6C basilica of Ayios Títos at Górtyn. Icons from Savvathianá in the district of Malevísi include a magnificent 'Virgin as Fountain of Life' (1655). There is a carved wooden *lectern from the former monastery church of Valsamónero on the S slopes of Mount Ida, also a 17C ecclesiastical throne. *Embroidered vestments (17 and 18C) belonged to the former Asómatos monastery in the Amari Valley. A pastoral *staff is inlaid with ivory, tortoiseshell and mother-of-pearl.

Further exhibits include: two cases of glazed earthenware (16–17C); elaborate liturgical vessels; a case of Byzantine and Venetian *jewellery; gold and bronze coins.

Outstanding is a group of icons from the church of the Panayía Gouverniótissa at Potamiés on the way up to Lasíthi; also the church's painted sanctuary doors and part of the wooden iconostasis with high-quality carving (all late 16C).

In a small room off the hall, a frescoed *Byzantine chapel* is partially reconstructed.

At the foot of the stairs, the 1912 banner of a chieftain from Argyroúpolis (in the hills behind Réthymnon) proclaims 'Freedom or Death'. The stairs lead up to the *first landing* where a new display exhibits a collection of photographs recording the events of the brief period of autonomy leading up to Crete's union with Greece in 1913.

At the end of the corridor the walls are lined with photographs taken during the Battle of Crete (1941).

On the left a room is furnished as the study of *Níkos Kazantzákis* (1883–1957) with desk, library and other personal possessions from his home on the island of Aígina. Opposite, a large room has a fine collection of old maps, and also material connected with the Cretan statesman E. Tsouderós, a native of Réthymnon, who became Prime Minister of Greece on 18 April 1941, after the German invasion of Macedonia and little over a month before the Battle of Crete. The dais is furnished as his study.

The *top floor* houses a superb collection of Cretan textiles, demonstrating the wide variety of traditional handwork found on the island. In the room *left of the stairs* (on the left of the doorway) is a case of *embroidery in silk on linen including, from the former Asómatos monastery, an 18C skirt or cope border (No. 1292) with a design of mermaids, dragons and peacocks, among flowers. Opposite this case hangs a classic example of Cretan weaving, probably from W Crete (19C). In the corner, note the embroidered velvet jackets from Sphakiá and Anóyia which complement the costumes displayed outside on the landing. At the far end of this first room is an 18C dowry *chest, with painted and carved decoration; it is fitted with little jewel cases, drawers and miniature chests.

Opposite the stairhead is a fine exhibition of crochet and needlework, also further weavings. A double room (right) is fitted out as a house interior c 1900 and contains the museum's *ethnographic collection*. The two Cretan female costumes contrast the styles of Kritsá and Anóyia, villages with strong weaving traditions, the first in E Crete above Ayios Nikólaos, and the second on the slopes of Mount Ida, a little to the W of Herákleion.

In the *basement* the museum preserves a valuable collection of architectural fragments from Crete's heritage.

On the left at the bottom of the stairs a 16–17C double doorway is framed by a set of stone reliefs from the Latin monastery of St. Francis, which, until it was destroyed in the Great Siege, dominated the city of Candia from the hill where the Archaeological Museum now stands. On the far side of the doorway is a coat of arms with a lion and a Hebrew inscription; it belonged to a Jewish family living on Crete in the 16C. Between the windows stands an elegant 16–17C fountain from a Venetian nobleman's house in Candia.

Among a collection of coats of arms, one with castle, cross and griffin and an inscription in Latin and Armenian (13–14C) was carved on a tombstone from the Armenian church in Candia. In the centre of the wall, a vigorous St. George medallion, in high relief, came from the St. George's or Lazzaretto Gate (1565) in the Candia ramparts. Along the opposite wall is part of the frieze from the original Venetian Loggia (1626), including some fine sculptures. The Loggia is now rebuilt.

A second double doorway with carved stone arches and lintel leads to a small room of Byzantine exhibits: three stone well heads, the central one with elaborate carved decoration; the pulpit from the post-Arab reconstruction of the basilica of Ayios Títos at Górtyn; and a collection of capitals and impost blocks.

Across the corridor is a room of the Turkish period, with inscriptions, tombstones of governors and other notable citizens; the walls are hung with glazed porcelain tiles from an 18C mosque in the city. In this corridor are charming frescoes from a Turkish house showing the city Megálo Kástro, the great fortress (Herákleion), in an idealised landscape.

D.   The Icon Collection in Ayía Aikateríni

Open: Monday–Saturday 09.30–13.00, and Tuesday, Thursday and Saturday 17.00–19.00 (winter 16.00–18.00). Closed Sunday and public holidays. Small admission fee.

A collection of icons, old manuscripts and liturgical objects is housed in the former church of *Ayía Aikateríni of Sinai*, across a plateía at the NE corner of the modern cathedral of Ayios Minás. (The old church of Ayios Minás—the medieval predecessor—stands alongside the terrace at the cathedral's West Front.)

From Plateía Nikephórou Phoká, at the bottom of the market, a main shopping street, Kalokairinoú (once the Venetian 'Via Imperiale'), runs W to the Khaniá gate (built c 1570, now restored). A short distance along Kalokairinoú, the fifth lane to the left is a pedestrian way which leads to Plateía Ayía Aikateríni.

   The church dates from 1555, with 17C alterations. It was a dependency of the monastery of the same name on Mount Sinai, and in the 16 and 17C its college here became a renowned centre of the arts and learning, and played an important part both in preserving and disseminating Byzantine culture after the fall of Constantinople.

The first portable icons documented on Crete (1025) were brought to the island from Constantinople. There is evidence of painters travelling (in both directions) between Crete and Constantinople before the Byzantine capital fell to the Turks in 1453, but it is after this date that Crete's particular political and social circumstances (as a fervently Orthodox community within the Venetian Empire) gave the island a special importance in the field of icon painting. Production is known to have been organised in workshops staffed by large numbers of apprentices, and there are records of substantial orders to satisfy demand from Western Europe as well as from the remaining Hellenic world. The painters working on Crete at this time inherited the iconographical traditions and strict conservative technique of the style that was revived under the Palaiologan emperors (1261–1453), the last Christian rulers of Constantinople. However the Venetian regime on Crete facilitated contact with the large Greek community in Venice, and the Cretan painters were therefore open to the influence of the art of Renaissance Italy. There was in any case a demand at this time from members of the Latin church for icons 'in the Latin style'. The versatility of the 15–16C Cretan icon painters is conspicuous.
   Only a small proportion of the icons of this period have survived, and very few indeed remain on Crete. It was not customary for artists to sign their work, but one who did so is Mikhaíl Damaskinós.

Damaskinós, an older contemporary of El Greco, is recognised as one of the major icon painters of the period. He studied at Ayía Aikateríni and then, like so many other Cretan artists at that time, sought employment abroad. He is known to have worked in 'Venice 1577–82. Though many of his icons show the influence of Italian art, his most-admired paintings are those which adhere most strictly to the Byzantine tradition. Today his work is widely dispersed.

The six Damaskinós icons exhibited in this collection are paintings of

*The Council of Nicaea, an icon by Mikhaíl Damaskinós
(Ayía Aikateríni, Herákleion)*

his mature period (late 16C) after his return from Venice. They hung
in the Vrondísi monastery on the S slopes of Ida until 1800, when
they were brought for safety to Ayios Minás in Herákleion. Now they
are displayed in the main body of the Ayía Aikateríni nave, scattered
among other exhibits. The collection is not numbered, but counting
from the left behind the ticket desk (i.e. starting on the W wall of the
church) the Damaskinós icons are:

2. Η Προσκύνηση των Μάγων. The Adoration of the Magi, showing
most clearly the influence of western art.

5. Ο Μυστικός Δείπνος. The Last Supper.

8. Η Θεοτόκος η Βάτος. The Virgin with the Burning Bush, showing
Moses on Mount Horeb, and the bush which burned but was not
consumed, a symbol of the virginity of the Mother of God.

9. Μη μου άπτου. 'Noli me tangere', Christ appearing to the Holy
Women.

12.Η Οικουμενική Σύνοδος. The Ecumenical Council at Nicaea (AD

325) at which the Emperor Constantine conferred with his bishops to settle the Aryan Controversy. This work was painted in 1591.
15. Η Θεία Λειτουργία. The Divine Liturgy, with Christ celebrating mass, in the midst of the encircling hosts of angels.

The church of *Ayios Matthéos* contains a number of interesting icons, including two narrow panels which were exhibited in London (1987) in the Royal Academy exhibition 'Byzantium to El Greco'. Ayios Symeós Theodókhos (Receiver of God), St. Simeon with the Christ child in his arms, conveys the message of the Presentation in the Temple. Ayios Ioánnis Prodrómos (the Baptist) is portrayed in the iconographical tradition of the Palaiologan style (wearing a sheep-skin, and with one hand raised in the act of blessing, the other holding an open scroll); however, the wings are an innovation, and the scene lacks the traditional severed head. Both these icons, though unsigned, are now attributed to Damaskinós.
The church is less than 10 minutes on foot from Ayía Aikateríni. Cross the paved plateía to the main road opposite the W Front of the cathedral. On the far side of the road a narrow street half-left (named after a bishop martyred in 1821) opens after 20m into ΟΔΟΣ ΤΑΞΙΑΡΧΟΥ ΜΑΡΚΟΠΟΥΛΟΥ (Odós Taxiárkhou Markopoúlou); the church of Ayios Matthéos is on the right of the street after 200m.

2   Knossós

The Minoan Palace of Knossós is 5km (3 miles) from the centre of Herákleion. The site is open daily: 08.00–19.00 (Sundays–18.00); winter 10.00–sunset.

Bus No. 2 (ΚΝΩΣΟΣ) leaves the harbour terminus (near the main bus station, see Herákleion plan and town bus information, p 50) every 15 minutes; journey time 20–30 minutes. Convenient stops in town at Plateía Venizélou (Morosíni fountain) and in Odós 1821. The Palace site is at the end of the line.

There are guided coach excursions to the Palace from agents in all tourist centres including Herákleion.

By car: leave Plateía Elevtherías with the public gardens on your right. The road is a dual-carriageway as far as the cemetery church (right) of Ayios Konstantínos. Here keep left and at the next fork bear left again. (Straight ahead at this fork would lead you onto the North Coast Highway.) Away to the left of the road was the site of the Royal Tomb at Isópata, destroyed in 1942. Soon you pass under the highway, just after a slip-road from it which is the best approach from other parts of the island. At 3.5km a road (signed Ayios Sýllas) diverges for Fortétsa, on a ridge (right) from which the Turks bombarded Herákleion during the Great Siege. Opposite this turning is the Science Faculty of the University of Crete.

In 1978, an excavation in advance of building undertaken by the British School for the Greek Archaeological Service uncovered a cemetery of more than 300 tombs, dating from the Subminoan to the Early Christian period. In this necro-polis, now known as the *Knossós North Cemetery*, the richest tombs were from the Geometric and Orientalising periods; grave offerings included quantities of pottery, many bronze and iron weapons and ornaments, a little gold jewellery, and luxury items of faience from the E Mediterranean. Among the pottery, imports were identified from Athens, the Cyclades, E Greece and Cyprus.
A small group of Geometric tombs just to the N (dug in 1975–76) is part of the same great cemetery; of outstanding interest is a bronze bowl (10C) from one of

these tombs with what is perhaps the earliest Phoenician inscription yet found in Greek lands (Herákleion Museum, Gallery XI, Case 155).

150m beyond the Fortétsa turn is the Venizéleion Hospital (on the site of a former Sanatorium). Excavated here in 1952 were LMII warrior graves, with finds characteristic of the first Mycenaean influence at Knossós.

The road is now entering the settlement area which spread out around the Palace of Knossós in the Bronze Age.

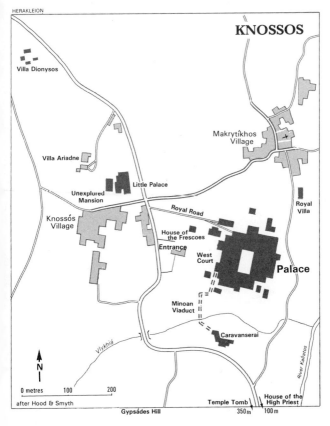

The latest thinking envisages a densely occupied central zone, and then, since there is no evidence that the Minoan town was at any time surrounded by defence walls, a gradual merging of town with countryside, with the houses on the outskirts separated by gardens or cultivated ground. The area of intensive settlement at the most flourishing period of the Minoan civilisation was approximately 750,000m², a little smaller than that of medieval Candia (Herákleion), and though calculations differ wildly—Evans's being among the more extravagant—a conservative modern estimate puts the population of the Minoan town at about 12,000.

The road to Knossós also passes through the centre of the Roman city, which occupied roughly 1km² between the modern hospital and the Bronze Age Palace. Almost nothing is now visible above ground. The road cuts through the site of the Roman theatre; at 400m beyond the hospital, just before a track, right, to a cemetery church, a slight curve in the right bank of the road shows its position. In the next field across the road, stones and column fragments lying among the vines indicate the site of the Roman Civil Basilica. Where the stone wall begins, right, there are steps up to the excavated Hadrianic *Villa Dionysos*, so called because of the subjects portrayed on its high-quality 2C mosaic floors. The site is not open to the public.

At the end of the wall a short drive leads to the *Villa Ariadne*, built by Sir Arthur Evans as his dig-house. From 1926–52 the villa belonged to the British School at Athens, but then, in a rearrangement of responsibility for the Palace site, it became the property of the Greek government. During the war the villa sheltered King Paul for a brief period after the evacuation of mainland Greece in 1941, and was the residence of the German Military Commandant during the Occupation.

At 5km cafés and tavernas, car parks, coaches and other paraphernalia of tourism mark the approach to *Knossós* (see area plan, p 85).

In Greek *mythology* Knossós was known as the palace of King Minos, one of the three offspring of Zeus and Europa, who was married to Pasiphae, daughter of the nymph Crete. Central to the legend was the Minotaur (half man, half bull), the monstrous result of Pasiphae's infatuation with a white bull sent by the god Poseidon. The Minotaur was incarcerated in the labyrinth built for Minos by his renowned architect Daidalos, and at regular intervals seven youths and seven maidens, tribute owed to Minos from Athens, were devoured by the monster. Eventually Theseus, son of the Athenian king, Aegeus, determined to kill the Minotaur and volunteered as one of the seven youths. Minos's daughter Ariadne fell passionately in love with him; she gave him a sword and a ball of woollen thread to unwind so that, after the killing, he was able to retrace his steps out of the labyrinth. The lovers sailed triumphantly from Crete, departing from the harbour of Knossós, but Theseus soon abandoned Ariadne on Naxos. His punishment was swift. On his return to Athens he neglected to hoist the pre-arranged signal of success, the white sail, and his father watching from the cliffs threw himself into the sea in despair. Thus the Aegean sea got its name.

The **PALACE OF KNOSSOS** with its surrounding town and cemeteries, was thoroughly explored at the beginning of this century thanks to the initiative of Sir Arthur Evans. After inconclusive probes had been made by the Cretan Mínos Kalokairinós in the 1880s, the site excited the imagination of Heinrich Schliemann (discoverer of ancient Troy), and he attempted to purchase the land with a view to excavating. Schliemann sensed the site's importance but failed to agree with the owner, and it was left to Evans to buy a large parcel of land and begin the great work (1900).

A major part of the site was exposed by 1906 but supplementary work, first with Duncan Mackenzie and later with J.D.S. Pendlebury, continued until the excavation of the Temple Tomb in 1924. The work is enshrined in Evans's massive four-volume 'Palace of Minos'. Sir Arthur's interest in the site was transferred to the British School at Athens, which continued exploration on a small scale until 1939, and resumed a series of fruitful research excavations in 1951 under the leadership of M.S.F. Hood.

History. There was a Neolithic village here on a low hill on the bank of the River Kaíratos, which according to radiocarbon dates was founded by 6000 BC or even earlier. The first known phase of habitation seems to have pre-dated the use of pottery. Gradually through the Neolithic period the mound of occupation debris accumulated, so that by the beginning of the Bronze Age, c 3000 BC, the Neolithic strata were up to 7m deep.

Occupation continued through the Early Minoan period. The settlement expanded and the buildings became more substantial until in EMIII, c 2200 BC, there is evidence for a forerunner of the subsequent Bronze Age Palaces, on the same alignment but of less massive construction.

The first Middle Bronze Age Palace, known at Knossós as the Old Palace, was built during MMIB, soon after 1900 BC, and was destroyed by a mighty earthquake at the close of MMII, c 1700. These two centuries equate with Pláton's Protopalatial period. When foundations for the Palace were being levelled the top of the existing mound was in effect sliced off, and much of the earlier material, including demolished buildings, was dumped to raise and extend the NW part of the site. From this unstratified Prepalatial material have come fragments of Predynastic and early Dynastic Egyptian stone vessels, important for demonstrating Minoan links with Egypt before the foundation of the Palace. Evans suggested that the Old Palace began as a series of blocks, or 'insulae', with rounded corners. One such corner can be seen at the NE of the Throne Room complex, but this hypothesis is not universally accepted.

Certainly by the close of MMII there was considerable architectural unity. The North Entrance Passage and the Throne Room had been constructed, as had the Royal Pottery Stores, the West Magazines (as Evans named this extensive storeroom complex), and the Magazines of the Giant Pithoi. A great cutting had been made in the E side of the site in which were rooms later remodelled into the Domestic Quarter.

After the earthquake destruction of c 1700 BC, the Palace was rebuilt during the following period, MMIII. The reconstructed remains visible today are largely of this New Palace. The Domestic Quarter took its final shape, the North Entrance Passage was narrowed and the North East Pillar Hall built onto it. The storage space in the W Magazines was increased by sinking rectangular cists or coffers into many of the storeroom floor spaces, as well as below the Long Corridor beside them. The capacity for storage and redistribution of commodities, and the administrative techniques to handle this operation, were the economic basis of Minoan prosperity.

Towards the close of MMIII (c 1600–1580 BC), another destruction, also probably by earthquake, necessitated some rebuilding and restoration of the West Façade and South Propylaea, and at this time the West Porch was rebuilt.

At the same time there began the building of a series of great houses around the Palace, such as the Royal Villa, the North-West Treasure House, the House of the Frescoes, the South House, the House of the Chancel Screen and the South-East House. The Temple Tomb dates to this period, as does the Little Palace, and a fine mansion adjacent and connected to it by a bridge. This Evans dubbed the Unexplored Mansion, but it has in fact since been excavated (1967–73). This Neopalatial phase of building is mirrored in the MMIII/LMI excavated town and country houses spread across Crete. The tantalising fragments of fresco decoration preserved in the Herákleion museum date from this period, which marked the artistic climax of the Minoan civilisation.

At the end of LMI, c 1450 BC, there seems to have been a major break in the history of Knossós, contemporary with a horizon of fire destruction at excavated sites throughout Crete. Explanations for this destruction have included volcanic activity on the island of Théra (Santorini), internal warfare on Crete, and conquest by invaders from the other great Bronze Age civilisation of the region, from Mycenae in the Peloponnese. At Knossós, however, there was no wholesale fire destruction at this time, either of the Palace or of the great dependent buildings, although there was a certain amount of damage. To the LMII period, after 1450 BC, belongs the Palace Throne Room complex as it now appears, and the Palace and the main dependent buildings were not finally destroyed until a great conflagration c 1380 BC in LMIIIA.

From the debris of this final fire destruction came large numbers of clay tablets in the script known as Linear B, accidentally baked and thus preserved for posterity. In contrast to the Minoan Linear A language, still undeciphered, this B script is an early form of Greek. Linear B tablets are well known from Pylos and Mycenae on the mainland, though in Late Helladic IIIB contexts, c 1200 BC.

The second half of the 15C BC at Knossós saw a development in pottery decoration referred to as the Palace Style. The naturalistic LMI vase painting, which is the epitome of Minoan art, is replaced by a strikingly formalised handling often of the same motifs, in a style which is akin to mainland decoration of this period.

The combination of Linear B tablets and this abrupt change in the pottery has led most archaeologists to accept that in its final phase, LMII/IIIA, c 1450–1380

BC, Knossós was inhabited by mainland Greeks, and became the administrative centre of Mycenaean Crete.

After the destruction of the Palace there seems to have been limited reoccupation in LMIIIB, c 1200 BC. This is attested by the Shrine of the Double Axes and the remains of massive walls along the South Front of the Palace, and also by evidence in the Little Palace and the 'Unexplored' Mansion a short distance away. Near the staircase of the Palace Propylaea Evans found what he thought was a small Classical temple. But after the end of the Bronze Age the great Palace was never again inhabited. Later remains lie thick all over the Knossós region, but it seems that a tradition of sacred ground grew up around the Palace site, possibly fostered by the myth of the Minotaur and the Labyrinth. This word may derive from the Greek 'labrys' meaning double axe. Both the Bull and the Labyrinth became standard symbols on the coins of later Knossós.

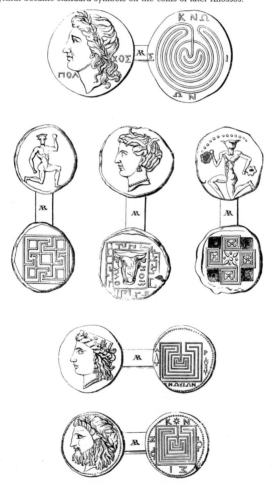

COINS OF CNOSSOS.

Coins of Greco-Roman Knossós (from Pashley, Travels in Crete, *1837)*

The *cemeteries* for the great settlement seem to have lain outside the inhabited area, on the hillsides that surround the site. Those so far known do not cover the entire Minoan history of Knossós for the earliest is a MMIA tomb on the acropolis hill to the W. Other MM graves were excavated on the Aílias slope to the E across the Kaíratos. Whereas, in common with the rest of Crete, few LMI tombs have come to light, rich LMII–LMIII graves have been excavated (from Evans's time on) to the N at Ayios Ioánnis, the 'Hospital site', Zápher Papoúra and Sellópoulo, in some cases containing splendidly furnished burials of warriors. Some of these may have been the Mycenaean successors of the Minoan rulers who vanished at the time of the destruction of the Palace c 1450. Similar but poorer groups of tombs have been found S of the settlement at various points on the Gypsádes hill. These scattered LM cemeteries might represent family burial plots on individual estates in the immediate vicinity of the town.

The *Palace site* was deserted before the end of the Bronze Age. There was settlement along the Royal Road in the Early Iron Age and the focus of the Geometric town seems to have moved to this N and W side of the Palace. The best evidence so far revealed for a flourishing settlement at this time comes from the sometimes richly endowed burials of the Knossós North Cemetery, where chamber tombs were in use for several generations.

The Palace site seems to have become a sanctuary area. Near Evans's Classical temple there is now evidence for a possible hero cult dating from as early as the Protogeometric period (10C BC). The Spring Chamber near the Minoan Caravanserai (see area plan, p 85) was frequented for cult purposes in the Subminoan period, and finds include a goddess with raised arms and a hut-urn, but the votive offerings ceased when the water from the spring dried up. On the lower slope of Gypsádes hill (just across the modern road from the Caravanserai), the Sanctuary of Demeter, goddess of the fruits of the earth, was an important place of worship from the late 8C down to the 2C AD. The sanctuary, with a huge deposit of terracottas, was excavated by the British School under N. Coldstream (1957–60); the dedication to Demeter was established by an inscription on an Early Hellenistic silver ring.

The use of chamber tombs, characteristic of the Geometric and Orientalising periods, ended abruptly around 600 BC. The vicissitudes of the period are not completely understood, and Dorian Knossós may have suffered a temporary eclipse, but it certainly emerged as one of the leading Greco-Roman city-states, vying with Lýttos and Górtyn for domination of the centre of the island.

In the 3C BC Knossós was a member of the loose federation of Cretan cities known as the Koinon. The Greek city, like its Roman successor, lay to the N of the Palace site, and there is no evidence that it ever had defensive walls, as did many of its contemporaries.

The Roman Conquest (67 BC) must have been a mixed blessing for Knossós. The Pax Romana brought stability and prosperity to the island, but Knossós had to yield pride of place to its old rival Górtyn, now the capital city of Crete and Cyrenaica. Some 40 years after the conquest Knossós became the only Roman colony on Crete, with the title Colonia Julia Nobilis Cnossus, and this would have involved adjustment to a new ruling class. Little of the Roman city has been excavated and almost nothing remains above ground, but the usual large public buildings are recorded; also temples, including an Asklepieion, and an aqueduct bringing water from the hills to the S. There were many fine houses embellished with mosaic floors and statues. The excavated Villa Dionysos, with pavements of a quality unusual on Crete, is unfortunately not open to public view. A new type of rock-cut chamber tomb with three side-niches for burials may have been introduced from Italy by the Roman colonists.

Christian churches were built at Knossós. Two basilicas have been excavated to the N of the Roman city, one a large mortuary church (5C) and the other a martyrion (early 6C) built over Christian graves. The Bishop of Knossós was present at early Councils of the Church in 431, 451 and 787. As the threat of Arab raids increased, the city's undefended position near the sea probably contributed to a decline in importance. After the Arab Conquest c 824, fortified El Khandak (Herakleion) became the capital of the island and henceforth dominated the Knossós area.

Tour of the Palace.

Open daily: 1987 08.00–19.00 (Sundays –18.00); winter 10.00–sunset. Admission Drs 400. Admission is only to the Palace and the Minoan houses in the immediate vicinity. Outside the fence all the main dependent sites, the Little Palace, the Royal Villa, the Temple Tomb (see below) are CLOSED to the public.

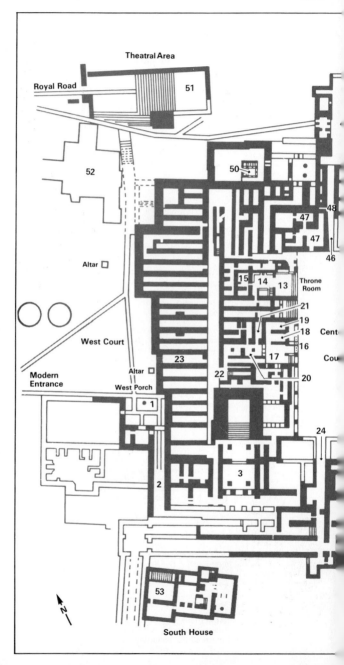

Theatral Area

Royal Road

51

52

50

48

47

47

46

Altar □

15 14 13   Throne Room

21

19

18

16

Cent

West Court

Altar □

23

17   Cou

22

20

Modern Entrance

West Porch

1

24

2

3

53

South House

N

PALACE OF KNOSSOS

0 metres   10   20   30   40

Evans's reconstructions at Knossós sometimes provoke controversy among professional archaeologists, but they give the lay visitor an immediate impression of the vast size and lavish conception of a Minoan palace-headquarters. Ideally Knossós should be the first palace site a visitor explores, because its partial reconstruction helps an understanding of the excavations at Phaistós, Mállia and Zákros.

The modern approach to the Palace leads by a trellissed path to the paved **West Court** (see main plan). The last stretch of the Minoan *ramp* is visible in the cutting to the right of the path. The bust of Sir Arthur Evans (the gift of the municipality of Herákleion) surveys his formidable achievement, and many visitors may feel that a nod of gratitude does not come amiss.

The paving of the West Court is crossed by *raised walks*, part original stone, part restored. The right hand walk directs you to the West Entrance. But notice first (left) three circular walled pits known from their shape as *kouloúras*, which may have been designed as granaries. When the court was extended at the end of the Old Palace period they were filled with rubbish including much broken pottery of high quality, and were paved over. At the bottom of the central pit you can see some remains of a house of MMIA date (2050–1900 BC), the period immediately before the construction of the Old Palace, so this feature is one of the earliest now visible on the site. A flight of steps leads down to the foundations of a room. Both the floor surfaces and the walls were found rendered with red plaster.

The Court runs up to the *West Façade*. Behind the *altar base*, a recess in the façade would have held a window in the storey above. The massive wall rests on a levelling course, and is faced with gypsum blocks now severely weathered. There are Minoan gypsum quarries on the appropriately named hill of Gypsádes to the S of the Palace. The signs of burning on the façade indicate that at the time of the great fire c 1380 BC the wind was from the S.

In the corner of the Court is the *West Entrance and Porch* (1 on plan), preserving the massive gypsum base of its single column, and an inner room with a red plaster floor. To the right (W) are the excavated remains of later houses. From the Porch, huge wooden doors opened into the *Corridor of the Procession Fresco* (2). The sockets for the doorposts remain, and between them is a small hole for a central bolt. The Corridor was paved with gypsum flagstones (the remaining fragments now very worn) which were flanked by blue schist set in red plaster. Unfortunately, part of this imposing processional way is lost owing to the erosion of the hillside, but originally the Corridor of the Procession Fresco led S before turning left and left again, describing three sides of a rectangle to reach either the main ceremonial rooms of the Palace, or the Central Court.

Where the coloured floor of the Corridor now falls away (at a modern flight of steps), the *South House* (53) can be seen in the valley below.

Unable to follow the original route, you pass through a reconstructed doorway beside a restored column. The downward taper is a typical feature of Minoan architecture. One branch of the Corridor of the Procession Fresco would have turned left to enter the *South Propylaea* (3), a monumental roofed gateway supported by four huge columns. One corner has been restored and column bases indicate the ground plan. The fresco copy is a detail from the Procession Fresco, including the so-called 'Cup-bearer' (original fragments restored in Herákleion Museum, Gallery XIV). The figures strikingly resemble those of the Keftiu (Minoans) bearing offerings to the Pharoah on the walls of 18th Dynasty Egyptian tombs. The large restored *horns of consecration*, right, originally crowned the S façade of the Palace.

A monumental staircase ascends to the *Upper Propylaea* (4 on plan of Upper Floor). To the right was a small temple of the Classical period, but in the course of excavation this was removed. The staircase leads to Evans's 'Piano Nobile', where the grand state apartments and reception halls probably lay. Evans restored this Upper Floor on the evidence of architectural elements such as column bases, door jambs, paving slabs and steps, which had collapsed into the floor below. Moreover, the thickness of the walls of the lower storey helped to indicate where the upper walls should be. A *Porticoed Vestibule* leads to a *Tri-columnar Hall* (5), off which a small room (6), Evans's *Central Treasury*, held a great collection of stone rhytons (including the Lioness Head rhyton) and other ritual vessels now exhibited in the Herákleion museum.

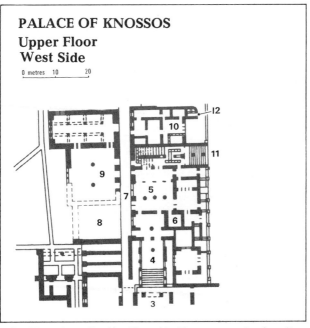

PALACE OF KNOSSOS
Upper Floor
West Side

0 metres 10 20

The *Upper Long Corridor* (7) ran N with rooms opening from it on both sides. In the reconstruction, a gap allows you to look down into the impressive *storeroom block* (8) below. The so-called 'Long Corridor of the Magazines' has 18 storerooms opening off it (22 and 23 on the main plan). The large jars, or pithoi, indicate the Palace's storage capacity for such commodities as grain, oil and wine; the blackening of the gypsum slabs at the entrance to some of the storerooms is a reminder of how fiercely the oil must have burnt at the time of the destruction. For increased storage capacity during the life of the New Palace, cists or chests were sunk in the floor. The pyramidal stone stands in the Corridor would have held double axes on poles, as portrayed on the Ayía Triáda stone sarcophagus in Herákleion Museum, Gallery XIV.

From the columnar *Hall* (5) a staircase (11) leads down to the Central Court, but keep to the Upper Long Corridor (7). On the left was a large hall (9) with two central columns, opening N into a smaller hall with six columns. Opposite this, across the Corridor, is a series of rooms in one of which (10) are hung modern copies of some of the Palace frescoes.

From the left inside the door:
1. Two panels of the Miniature Fresco. Note the tripartite shrine portrayed on the upper panel.
2. The 'Ladies in Blue'.
3. The Bull-leaper.
4. The 'Captain of the Blacks'.
5, 6, 7 and 8 are from the 'House of the Frescoes': scenes from the Blue Monkey fresco and the much-illustrated 'Blue Bird'.

You are now above the Throne Room, and can look down into the Lustral Basin beside it. Outside (left) a small private staircase (12) descends to the Central Court near the Throne Room complex. The rounded corner, left at the bottom of the stairs, is one of the surviving elements of the Old Palace ground plan.

The area for the **Central Court** was levelled at the time of the construction of the Old Palace in MMIB, c 1900 BC. The Court, c 50m by 25m and aligned NNE and SSW as at Phaistós and Mállia, was originally paved. A section of its drainage system is exposed in the NW angle of the court, where you are now standing. In this same area the excavators found an inscribed fragment of an Egyptian diorite statuette; its Middle Kingdom date was one of the pieces of evidence that helped Evans to establish the absolute chronology of Minoan Crete. The inscription gives the name of the figure represented as User, who must have been an eminent visitor to Knossós, possibly an ambassador from Egypt.

In front of the Throne Room is the Antechamber (13) (with replica throne). The fine purple limestone basin was found in the passage immediately to the N. The **Throne Room** (14) is fenced off, but from the threshold you can see the original gypsum *throne* flanked by benches and guarded by painted griffins (remains of original fresco in Herákleion Museum, Gallery XIV). The floor is crazy paving bordered by regular gypsum flagstones. Opposite the throne is the *Lustral Basin*, with steps leading down into it, that you saw from the floor above. On the Throne Room floor Evans found overturned jars, and large flat gypsum alabastrons, evidence for him of a dramatic scene during the final moments of the Palace. Behind the Throne Room, and accessible only from it, was a small shrine (15). Modern thinking tends to emphasise the religious aspects of this suite of rooms, rather than the ceremonial and regal associations of the throne.

S from the Throne Room, past the staircase (11) which you noted from above, was a *tripartite shrine* (16) similar to the one portrayed on the Miniature Frescoes (original in the Herákleion museum, copy in exhibition here above Throne Room). Pairs of columns flanked a block supporting a single column, all shielding the sanctuary behind.

Next is the Lobby of the Stone Seat (17), which leads right to the Room of the Tall Pithos (18), and the *Temple Repositories* (19). Two large cists were sunk under the floor here in the early days of the New Palace. (The smaller box between them is from a later date.)

Note the careful tight construction of the Repositories, suitable for precious objects. Peg holes show how they were fitted with slots or shelves, and they also had lids.

When this room was first excavated the chests were not found, and only when the floor began to sag the following year was their presence suspected. In the Repository nearer the Court Evans found the well-known faience figurines of the Snake Goddesses, with other furnishings of a shrine on display with them in Herákleion Museum, Gallery IV. The other large chest had been robbed, but traces of gold leaf remained and Evans put forward the theory that its precious objects had been taken to the mainland, perhaps to find their way into the Mycenae shaft graves; much of their contents has long been considered to be of Cretan workmanship.

From the Lobby of the Stone Seat (17) you can look into the outer of the two Pillar Crypts (20). Double-axe incisions on the pillars suggest religious significance, and troughs in the floor were thought to be for liquid offerings. Pillar crypts, dark and mysterious, seem to play an important part in the ritual connected with shrines and sacred treasuries. S of the Lobby of the Stone Seat ritual vessels were found fallen through from the Central Treasury above. In the Vat Room (21) off the E (nearer) Crypt, Evans found a further small treasure hoard (MMIA, 2050–1900 BC). He deduced that the Vat Room deposit pointed to the early sanctity of this area.

The passage on the S side of the crypts is now a dead end, but through a gate you can see the 'Long Corridor of the Magazines', and the storeroom block (22 and 23) which you looked down on from above. At the S end of the Court (24) a replica of the well-known Priest-King figure from the Procession Fresco stands poised to lead the procession into the Central Court. (A recent academic article puts forward the iconoclastic suggestion that this figure should be interpreted as a boxer.) Fragments of the floor pattern noticed at the start of the Procession Corridor are preserved also here at the end of it.

You now cross the angle of the court to descend the *Grand Staircase (25) to the Domestic Quarter. (The gypsum block that you pass in the court is the base of an observation tower used during the excavation.)

The gypsum staircase is one of the masterpieces of Minoan architecture. Four gentle flights are preserved, with the landings, and there is evidence for a fifth flight. This side of the Palace is built into the slope of the hill, which had partially retained the staircase and buildings as they collapsed. The Shield Fresco on the first balcony depicts the oxhides stretched and sewn on a figure-of-eight frame which Evans thought hung in the Hall of the Double Axes below. The Upper E–W Corridor leads past the fresco into the Upper Hall of the Double Axes, where only the ground plan is restored. A LMII fresco fragment, part of a larger-than-life leg and foot of a bull, was found here (now in the Herákleion museum).

The Grand Staircase descends again, to the level of the suite of rooms which from their scale and elegance seem designed for the ruler or rulers of the Palace. At the bottom of the staircase you turn right into the Hall of the Colonnades (26). Continuing ahead along the Lower E–W Corridor (27) a second right turn takes you into the King's Megaron or Hall of the Double Axes (28), so called from the masons' marks on the ashlar blocks of the adjacent light-well. The Hall is a large double room opening off the light-well, and at the far end is a broad L-shaped portico, well sheltered from Crete's prevailing winds. The double doors give great flexibility to this room space, and the balance of pillars and columns is architecturally effective. Remnants are preserved of what may be a plaster-backed throne.

From the SW corner of this Hall you pass by a dogleg passage to the *Queen's Megaron* (29) with its Dolphin and LMII rosette frescoe (original in Herákleion Museum, Gallery XIV). Stone benches line the portico walls and a verandah gives on to a light-well. Below the floor, near the LMI jar, part of the irregular paving of the Old Palace floor can be seen. Alongside the Queen's Megaron is a *bathroom*, with clay tub. Beside the bathroom a narrow corridor leads to a *toilet* (30) with a drainage system to allow flushing. Light is provided from the adjacent Court of the Distaffs (31), again named for the masons' marks on its wall.

Return to the Queen's Room (29) and leave the 'Domestic Quarter' by the Queen's Verandah. There is an alternative staircase up from the Hall of the Colonnades; at very busy periods you may have to follow a circular one-way route.

To the S of the Domestic Quarter the SE area of the Palace can be visited. Take the staircase, right, from the Queen's Verandah to find the tiny *Shrine of the Double Axes* (32), of Late Minoan IIIB date (13C, Postpalatial), in which were found, on a ledge at the back, terracotta figurines with drum-shaped bases and miniature horns of consecration. On a pebble floor in front of them was a series of clay vases. The small corridor immediately W of the shrine was called the *Corridor of the Sword Tablets*, since Linear B tablets of this class were found here. Before leaving this part of the Palace you may visit the *House of the Chancel Screen* (33), the *South-East House* (34) (see below), both MMIII–LMI buildings, the MMIA Monolithic Pillar basement (35) and a Minoan (LMI–II) kiln (36).

The **South-East House** is reached down a double flight of stairs. On the N side of the house is a *pillar room* with two double-axe stands and a niche in the E wall, also a cist let into the floor. The main rooms in the S open off a *peristyle court*, or miniature cloister, its covered walk paved with gypsum, the open centre with more weather-resistant stone. Note an interior wall of gypsum slabs laid on end.

For a shorter visit keep left (N) from the Queen's Verandah, past the broad porticoed *terrace* of the King's Megaron. The terrace was visible from the interior of the King's Megaron (Hall of the Double Axes). Behind the *East Portico* (37), find the corridor parallel to it (W) which passes a small storeroom (38) with blocks of Spartan basalt (lapis Lacedaemonius), raw material for stone vases and seals imported from the sole source near Sparta in the Peloponnese. The corridor opens into Evans's 'School Room' (with a bench along the wall) which was probably a craftsman's workshop (39), and you cross this to the *Court of the Stone Spout* (40). Ahead are the *Magazines of the Giant Pithoi* (41), with mighty vases dating from the Old Palace, (MMII c 1800 BC), and beyond them to the N were the Royal Pottery Stores, also MMII.

A staircase descends to the *East Bastion* (42) above the E Entrance. A stone water channel descends beside the steps, in a series of parabolic curves and small settling basins to break the flow of storm water and debris down the steep slope.

Ascending the stairway past the Giant Pithoi and an area which may have been stalls for animals, you reach the *Corridor of the Draught-Board* (43) where the magnificent inlaid gaming board was found (Herákleion Museum, Gallery IV). Below the corridor the clay pipes of the Palace's elaborate drainage system are visible: notice how they taper (to produce a greater head of water). From the corridor you pass a stone drain (which runs into the Court of the Stone

Spout) to enter the Magazine of the Medallion Pithoi (44). A similar pithos in stone was found in the Tomb of Klytemnestra at Mycenae. From here you could return to the Grand Staircase along the *Corridor of the Bays* (45), the thick walls of which must have supported spacious rooms above, but a staircase (before the corridor, right) leads back up to the Central Court.

Cross the Court diagonally to leave it by the North Entrance Passage (46). To the left was a complex of rooms (47) in which the Saffron Gatherer Fresco and Miniature Frescoes were found. Below these rooms were MMI stone-lined pits, perhaps granaries, or dungeons as Evans thought; on account of its massive construction he called this area the North Keep. The *North Entrance* is overlooked by the intimidating stucco relief of a charging bull (48) (remains of original in Herákleion Museum, Gallery XIV). For the New Palace this entrance was narrowed, and the North Pillar Hall (49), with double row of gypsum pillars, was added outside it. Turn left, past the North Portico to the *North Lustral Basin* (50), which is restored to give a clear picture of the Minoan original. Signs of burning on the gypsum facing, and the oil jars found in the MMIII destruction material suggest a ritual of cleansing and annointing before entry to the Palace. Near the Lustral Basin was found the alabaster lid with a cartouche of the Egyptian Hyksos King Khyan—an important clue to dating the construction of the New Palace.

The stepped *Theatral Area* (51) is superimposed on the *Royal Road* and looks W along it; it has been suggested that the area was connected with the welcoming of visitors. The road's central flags are bordered by drains. It continues W into the Minoan town of Knossós and a branch turns N to the Little Palace. A further stretch was picked up 200m W of the modern road.

The Royal Road was lined with houses, perhaps similar to those portrayed on the faience plaques of the 'Town Mosaic' (see Herákleion Museum, Gallery II) found in Middle Minoan levels in the Palace. On the left was the *House of the Frescoes* (MMIII, c 1600 BC); here Evans found the stack of fragile slabs of painted plaster now pieced together in the Herákleion museum, including the striking 'Blue Bird' scene. On the right of the road was the site of the Arsenal or Armoury.

Beside the Armoury further excavations in 1957–61 produced pottery deposits from EMII to LMIII, as well as a fine series of ivories of LMIB, dating from c 1500–1450 BC. Excavations (1971–73) along the left of the road have revealed building remains from EMII (c 2600 BC) to the 4C AD, and at the far end (left) traces of another similar road leading off S. Built at the same time as the Old Palace, soon after 1900 BC, these Knossós examples are among the earliest urban roads in Europe.

You can return to the West Court past the broken horns of consecration (gypsum), and the scant remains of the North-West Treasure House (52), where a rich hoard of bronze vessels was found.

The South House (53) merits a visit, as do the House of the Sacrificed Oxen (54) and the House of the Fallen Blocks (55), named after the massive blocks of masonry hurled into it from the Palace South Façade during the violent earthquake which destroyed the Old Palace. The *South House*, reached by steps beside the Corridor of the Procession Fresco, is partially restored on three levels.

Across the valley (S) is the Caravanserai reached by the Stepped Portico, the remains of the Minoan viaduct, but, sadly, this area is now closed to the public, as are all the other great dependent buildings listed below. In some cases a little can be seen from outside the fences. The following notes are allowed to stand as background information, and also in case the position changes during the life of this edition of the Guide. (See area plan, p 85.)

A path leads down from the main road to the *Caravanserai* with its partridge and hoopoe fresco (original in the Herákleion museum) and to the adjacent *Spring Chamber*. This was the stopping-place for those arriving from the S before they went across the great viaduct, dating from MMI, and up the ramp and stepped portico to the Palace. Along the main road to the S is the *House of the High Priest* (below the road on the left), with a stone altar, set behind a columnar balustrade, between stands for double axes. Further along the main road on the right is the partly reconstructed *Temple Tomb*, built in MMIII but remaining in use until the final destruction of the Palace. An open paved court leads to the Inner Hall and Pillar Crypt, beyond which is the Sepulchral Chamber. From the Inner Hall a small stairway leads to the upper floor which consisted of a two-columned room. The masonry of the lower rooms is excellently preserved.

NE of the Palace is the *Royal Villa*, built in MMIII (c 1600 BC). The main hall, fronted by a portico with two columns, has a gypsum balustrade at its inner end and a throne set in the wall behind the balustrade. A fine purple stone lamp stood in the opening. To the N of the megaron is a *Pillar Crypt* in which the slots in the masonry for the roof beams are visible. From here a stairway leads to the upper floor. To the S of the megaron is another ascending staircase. On its landing was found a magnificent LMII Palace Style jar (Herákleion Museum) with papyrus in relief.

The *Little Palace* lies to the right of the main Herákleion road just before Knossós is reached. This building (unfortunately always closed to the public), the largest explored at Knossós after the main Palace, consists of a series of stately halls on the E side, including a *peristyle hall* or court (comparable to that at Phaistós). The East Façade seems to have had a columned portico. To the W is a complex of smaller rooms and a staircase with two flights preserved. N of this is a Lustral Area, later (in LMIII) used as a shrine with rough stones as images (the *Fetish Shrine*). In this reoccupation phase the columned balustrade was walled up, and this had preserved the impression of the convex flutings of the earlier columns. At the N end of the building is a paved lavatory served by a drain behind it running East–West. The S end of the Palace consists of a series of *Pillar Crypts*. That in the SW corner has a tiny walled recess on its N side in which were found the famous *Bull's Head Rhyton* (Herákleion Museum, Gallery IV), a double-axe stand, and other ritual objects. The Little Palace was built in MMIII and finally destroyed at the same time as the main Palace; as in the main Palace, Linear B tablets were found in the debris.

Immediately to the W Evans uncovered the façade of another great building, which he named the *'Unexplored Mansion'*. Linked to the Little Palace by a masonry bridge, its well-planned complex of rooms, pillar basement, staircases and storerooms was uncovered by the British School (M. Popham and H. Sackett, 1967–73). Though the poorly preserved N half had been reoccupied in LMIII, the S half had never been cleared after a great fire destruction in LMII (c 1400–1380). This half of the building was filled with fine-quality painted pottery, stone vases, stone and clay tools and implements. Much scrap bronze, with a number of clay crucibles, suggested a bronze foundry located in the building.

W of the Palace, further excavations (P. Warren, 1978–82) revealed a continuation of the Minoan *town* of Knossós, dating from the first period of urban expansion (MMIA) before the founding of the Old Palace, and with uninterrupted occupation through the Middle and Late Minoan periods. Most important is the discovery of a LMI house (destroyed in 1450 BC) which, to judge from its contents of fine ritual pottery, was used as a cult centre. In a basement room of this house were found the bones of at least three children; ten per cent of these (unburnt) bones show knife-cut marks which indicate that the flesh had been deliberately cut away. The excavator suggests that in this context the most likely explanation is connected with some form of offering to the gods, possibly even preparations for a ritual meal.

As was the case with the remains of the Little Palace and 'Unexplored Mansion', Minoan levels at this town site were in places much disturbed by overlying Dark Age, Hellenistic and Roman building belonging to the later phases in the history of Knossós.

3   Excursions from Herákleion

A.   To Týlissos, Anóyia and the Idaian Cave

A quiet country road, 13.5km to the Minoan villas at Týlissos, and on to 33km (20.5 miles) Anóyia on the N flank of Mount Ida.
  You can continue via the Greco-Roman site of Axós to join the Réthymnon–Herákleion road (Rte 11B in the W Crete section of this Guide) for a round trip from Herákleion of c 100km (63 miles).
  From Anóyia up to the Nída plain (c 1400m) and the Idaian cave it is 20km on a mountain road—conditions variable according to season.

Buses: five daily to Anóyia, from the bus station outside the Khaniá gate. Reduced Sunday service.

Leave Herákleion to the W by the Khaniá gate on the Old Road to Réthymnon (Rte 11B), passing the junction with the North Coast Highway. At 10.5km branch left off the Réthymnon road towards Týlissos. This is the Malevísi district, famous at least from Venetian times for the strong sweet wine known as Malmsey which found its way to western Europe. These same fertile slopes must also have contributed to the prosperity of prehistoric Týlissos, which lay on the route from Knossós to W Crete by the northern foothills of Mount Ida.

13.5km The pleasant village of **Týlissos** preserves its prehellenic name, which occurs on Linear B tablets as tu-ri-so. The Minoan villas are on the edge of the modern village, signposted from the main street left and left again. They were excavated (1902–13) by J. Khatzidákis after the chance find of the great bronze cauldrons now on display in Herákleion Museum, Gallery VII. More recently N. Pláton reinvestigated the site. (1987 opening hours: 08.45–15.00, Sunday 09.30–14.30; closed Monday. Admission Drs 200.)

Týlissos was inhabited in the Early Bronze Age, and there are traces of MMI occupation (c 2000 BC), but of the excavated remains interest centres on three large MMIII–LMI houses contemporary with the New Palace at Knossós. Probably these should be thought of not as an isolated group of country houses but as part of the wealthy area of a prosperous town (comparable to Palaíkastro in E Crete) flourishing at the height of the Minoan civilisation. The LMI finds were numerous and of the same high quality as material from the Palaces; many are on show in Herákleion Museum, Gallery VII, including a bronze statuette of an older man in the typical votary position, hand to forehead. A number of large clay storage jars had survived.
  After the destruction of the Minoan villas (c 1450 BC) there was considerable reoccupation of the site in the LMIII period, including the building of a big circular cistern at the NE corner. There was also later Greek (Classical period) occupation and Týlissos at this time was an independent city-state with its own coins. Thus the excavated remains of the three Minoan buildings (solid black on the plan) are complicated by vestiges of earlier and later construction.

House A is the most easily intelligible of the three. Its plan (max. dimensions 35m by 18m) consists of two blocks or wings, linked by a partially covered court.
  You can walk round the S edge of the site to appreciate the finely

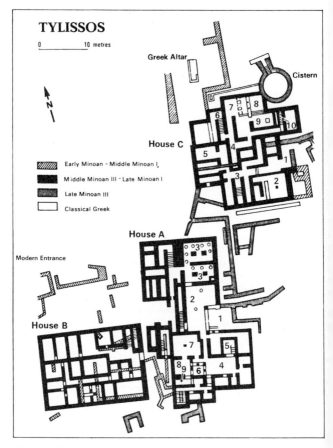

TYLISSOS

0   10 metres

Greek Altar

Cistern

House C

	Early Minoan – Middle Minoan I
	Middle Minoan III – Late Minoan I
	Late Minoan III
	Classical Greek

House A

Modern Entrance

House B

dressed ashlar masonry, and to reach House A's *entrance*, an angled passage leading into a small paved court (1 on plan). The passage, now restored, had been cut into by LMIII reoccupation walls. On the W and N sides of the court was an L-shaped *peristyle* (2); note the central column base, pithos stand, and a window lighting the staircase on the W side. N of the peristyle are two large *storerooms* (3). The pillars would have supported the upper floor, from which fallen painted plaster fragments indicated important rooms; by analogy with the Palace at Mállia it has been suggested that here was the Banqueting Hall. Food could have been prepared in the small ground floor rooms W of the storerooms, where there is a convenient second staircase. Some of the *storage jars* still in situ (3) have holes near their bases and are set on stone slabs for tapping the liquid contents, presumably oil.

A *passage* S from the peristyle court leads to the heart of the S wing. Here the main room (4) has a *lustral basin* (5) beside it. The hall (4) has an irregularly paved floor, and the typical pattern of double doors opening onto a colonnaded *light-well* (6) which also has a window in its W wall. The drain at the SW corner of the light-well can be followed on the other side of the wall. The portico to the N of the light-well leads to a *pillar crypt* (7), where the excavator found a pyramidal stand for a double axe, similar to those in the 'Corridor of the Magazines' in the Palace of Knossós. Reached from the pillar crypt are two small rooms (8 and 9), which may have been treasuries. From hereabouts came the three huge bronze cauldrons, the chance find which led to the discovery of the site. The storerooms also held Linear A tablets and a bronze ingot similar to those found at Ayía Triáda.

The lay-out of the small rooms in the SW corner, with a short passage from the central room and the proximity of a private stair-case, has suggested parallels with the presumed women's quarters in the Palaces.

House B, set on traces of earlier walls, is a notably rectangular building with few recognisable architectural features except a stair-case in the NE corner.

House C is basically square but with a characteristic irregular out-line. The Minoan walls are preserved almost to the second storey in places. The villa was cut into and overlaid by later buildings; left in situ above the Minoan levels is evidence for the LMIII house (which resembled the LMIII period building at Ayía Triáda), and the cistern complex which is contemporary with it. There are also bases for columns or statues, and an altar stone from the Classical levels.

The *entrance*, as in House A partly destroyed by later walls, is on the E side (1), and a clear system of *corridors* connects the various parts of the house. On the left (S) as you enter is a supposed *cult area* including a room with central pillar (2). Then, at the staircase (3) the corridor turns right (4), under the paving of a later floor. On the W side of the house is a block of storerooms (5); the raised *column base* here is from the LMIII reoccupation level. Off the corridor is a *staircase* (6); the lower flight dates from the original MMIII/LMI house, and the upper from the later Classical period building. Across the corridor from the staircase, at the N end of the house, is the *residential quarter*, where a main room with paved floor (7) opens E through a pier-and-door arrangement onto a large porticoed *light-well* (8). The big window, now restored, lit the room to the S (9). A corridor ran E–W outside this room to reach a staircase (10) to an upper floor, and a toilet equipped with a drain through the outer wall. To the NE of the house and built over its corner is a circular *cistern* of LMIII date entered by a staircase from the N. The water reached the cistern by a *stone channel* on the W side, having first been decanted in a basin or trap at the W end of this channel. N of the channel are remains of a large early structure (EM–MMI), and also an altar stone from the Classical period. A paved *Minoan road* runs along the W façade of House C.

After the village of Týlissos the road climbs steadily away from the coast, and the landscape becomes wilder. Beyond a war memorial you pass through a rocky defile, above a stream bed, and into a long valley with the village of Goniés spread out across the head of it. Soon (19.5km) the road cuts across the façade of the large **Minoan villa of Sklavókambos**, the excavated remains of which suffered further damage during the last war.

This substantial country house did not have the architectural refinements noticed at Týlissos. It is more crudely built, of partly worked boulders, and the floors were apparently unpaved. But the quality of the pottery, and the number of seal impressions found here show that the life of the occupants was far from crude. The main façade was along the line of the modern road with a *pillared verandah* at the Goniés end looking N across the valley. Behind this was a small open *court* with three pillars to support the peristyle roof. The *main entrance* to the house was from the E behind the façade, and in the entrance passage were found several clay sealings with bull-leaping scenes. The same seal has been recognised at Zákros, Gourniá and Ayía Triáda, which suggests a system of travelling merchants, or middlemen, in an extensive trading system.

26km Goniés (or Goniai) stands on a hill of chloritic and serpentine rock. The road, dominated by the Psilorítis mountain range ahead, reaches a crest at the nome boundary.

32km **Anóyia** (ΑΝΩΓΕΙΑ), a mountain village occupying a commanding position along a saddle (730m), has a long tradition as a centre of resistance and revolt. The village was burnt by the Turks in 1822, and flattened by the Germans in 1944 as a reprisal for its part in sheltering the captors of General Kreipe (see Rte 3B).

Anóyia is noted for its traditional brightly coloured weaving, and many of the houses have their own looms. There are two distinct village centres, one on the saddle, and the other at the little plateía on the slope below. There are tavernas and bars, two modest hotels, and rooms for rent.

At the Herákleion end of the village a road (surfaced but still rough in places after bad weather) sets off S into the mountains for (20km) the upland plain of *Nída* on Mount Ida (or Psilorítis, the high one), at 2456m the highest mountain on Crete. A little above the plain is the **Idaian cave** (Ἰδαίον Ἄντρον); a major excavation over a period of years is in progress here so the cave is fenced off and locked.

According to the myth (see also Mount Dikte, Rte 6) the infant Zeus was hidden from his jealous father, Kronos, in a remote cave in the mountains. He was nursed by the goat-nymph Amaltheia, and guarded by the nine Kouretes, the sons of 'Earth', who danced and clashed their weapons to cover the sound of the baby's cries. The most widely accepted tradition links this upbringing with the Idaian cave. The Cretan Zeus died and was reborn, and this recognisably Minoan concept was central to a cult of Zeus here on Mount Ida which was held in repute throughout the Classical world. The sacred cave was thus a place of pilgrimage in historical times; Pythagoras visited the sanctuary, with the Cretan religious teacher Epimenídes.

The mountain road up to the cave is recommended in late spring and early summer to wild-flower enthusiasts. There is intensive use of the high summer pastures for great flocks of sheep, and you will notice the 'mitáta', round stone-built huts where the shepherd make their sheep- and goat's-milk cheeses. The traditional method of roofing in stone with a true corbelled vault has been cited in connection with the roofing problem of the circular Bronze Age tombs of the Mesará, none of which was found intact.

After 15km a rough road is signposted left, W through the hills to Krousónas. Here, right of the road, a large *Minoan villa* (LMI) was recently discovered. The area is known as Zóminthos, a prehellenic name. In Minoan times the villa would have stood at the junction of major routes on these N slopes of Ida.

At last amid magnificent scenery the *Nída plain* (c 1400m) is in view ahead. On the far side of the plain the road divides. Above the track to the right, as the snow recedes in late spring, are predictable sheets of mountain flowers including crocus and chionodoxa.

The left fork leads to an unexpected café, convenient parking for the walk (15 minutes) up a track to the **Idaian cave**.

The cave was first investigated in 1885 by the Italian Mission, and was recognised as a highly important Iron Age Sanctuary. In front of the cave mouth stood a pedestal which would have held a larger-than-lifesize statue of Zeus. The votive offerings were then thought to date back to the 9C BC, and continued down to lamps and inscriptions from the Roman period. There was a wide range of terracotta and bronze figurines, wine jugs and basins, and also offerings in precious metals (Herákleion Museum, Gallery XII).

Outstanding are the ceremonial bronze *shields from the Orientalising period c 750–650 BC (Gallery XIX); these are convex, with relief decoration which includes bosses of lions and eagles. There is also a bronze drum portraying Zeus between two Kouretes figures. It has been argued that a guild of metalworkers from the Near East, established on Crete, was responsible for these high-quality pieces.

Since 1982 a new excavation under the direction of I. Sakellarákis has added to this wealth of superb finds. Some of the new material dates back to the Minoan period; the cave was in use from EM times (and there are even some Late Neolithic sherds) but the first evidence for cult practices dates from the MM period.

In the new programme of study, previously disturbed earth has been cleared and re-examined, and undisturbed deposits have been isolated. 1400 cubic metres of debris were moved in 1984, with the help of trucks running on rails. A few strictly limited tests in the undisturbed deposits led to the discovery of a complete bronze shield (similar to those described above) decorated with sphinxes and griffins; this is particularly important because for the first time the exact find place of one of these shields has been recorded.

Many fragments were found of 8–7C BC ivory objects from the Near East, among them some N Syrian material. Cretan ivories include a superb pin, its head carved in a Janus-arrangement of two women's heads, and part of a plaque with the figure of a woman in the Daidalic style, perhaps a Mistress of Beasts. From the Geometric period (c 750 BC) there were ivory block seals carved with a design of man and horse. There were also fragments of large statues in both bronze and terracotta; one painted terracotta head had an inlaid faience eye. Jewellery includes a gold pendant in the shape of a woman's head, and many rings including Roman examples with engraved bezels.

From Anóyia the road descends, but **Axós** is another beautifully situated village clinging to a high ridge. At 41.5km on the last bend before the village is a ruined *chapel* (dedicated to the saints Elevthérios and Módestos), dated 10–12C by pottery let in above the door. The building incorporates older material including fragments of columns. Only tantalising traces of wall paintings remain.

As you enter the village three roads meet by the tiny cruciform church of Ayía Eiríne (14–15C). Beyond the church a track (signposted) leads uphill to the left for 400m to the site of *ancient Axós*, which flourished in the Archaic and Hellenistic periods. The magnificent Axós bronze *helmet, with cheek-pieces in the form of winged horses, is in Herákleion Museum, Gallery XVIII. A N–S saddle connects two hills with the steep *acropolis* to the S (to the right as you approach); occupation extended down the NE slope. Little of the city survives above ground, but the extensive view makes the 5-minute walk worthwhile.

On the saddle the cemetery church of Ayios Ioánnis is built into the central nave and apse of an earlier basilica. The church has remains of late 14C–early 15C frescoes; the key is kept in the village.

On the extreme top of the acropolis, a *temple* of the Archaic period, possibly dedicated to Apollo or Athena, was excavated by the Italians at the end of the last century. The massive *temple platform* can be distinguished most easily at the extreme S of the summit of the hill, now overlooking the many circular threshing floors of the modern village in the valley below.

In the middle of the village, by a fountain, are the ruins of the double-naved Byzantine church of Ayios Mikkaíl Arkhángelos.

The road descends through Garázo to join (53km) the Old Réthymnon–Herákleion road (Rte 11B). (The oblique T-junction may be unmarked from this direction.) Turn right for the return (a further 45km) to Herákleion.

B.   To Arkhánes and Vathýpetro

15km (c 10 miles) from Herákleion to Arkhánes.

Buses approximately hourly (except Sundays) from the main bus station by the harbour, with a convenient stop in Plateía Venizélou.

20km to the Minoan villa of Vathýpetro. Unsurfaced roads in the beautiful country S of Arkhánes are being widened and improved. This easily accessible region is also strongly recommended to walkers.

A phýlakas, official custodian of the archaeological sites described below, is based in Arkhánes. It may be possible to arrange for him to unlock closed sites or to open the wine-press storeroom at Vathýpetro. Make enquiries locally at one of the kapheneíons in the plateía at the top of the village where the bus turns, or ask in advance at the NTO in Herákleion.

Take the Knossós road (Rte 2) out of Herákleion. 2km beyond the Palace a fine *aqueduct* supported by two tiers of arches spans a ravine; it was built during the brief interregnum of Egyptian rule (1832–40) to improve the Herákleion water supply. This aqueduct had a Roman predecessor.

The road climbs through *Spiliá*, and passes the turning (left) for Skaláni. After 9.5km keep right where the main road bends left signed Arkalokhóri and Viánnos. At 10.5km there is an acute right turn at a T-junction where in April 1944 Patrick Leigh Fermor and W. Stanley Moss, with their Cretan band, kidnapped the German General Kreipe while he was being driven from his HQ in Arkhánes to his residence in the Villa Ariadne at Knossós; after 18 days in hiding as they crossed the mountains, the party was picked up by a Royal Navy submarine from a cove (Rodákino) on the S coast. (The story is told by Moss in his book 'Ill Met by Moonlight' which was later filmed.)

The road runs through Káto (lower) Arkhánes before you reach the small town (pop. 3700) of Epáno (upper) Arkhánes, usually referred to simply as **Arkhánes**.

Sir Arthur Evans was the first to uncover Minoan remains here. He excavated a monumental *well-head* or reservoir of massive ashlar masonry, from which water may have been led to the Palace at Knossós. He also noticed that Minoan walls had been incorporated in some of the neighbouring houses. Since the early 1960s the Greek Archaeological Society has been excavating here each year under the direction of I. and E. Sakellarákis. Three major sites have been investigated: Turkogeitoniá, a Palatial-style complex overlaid by the buildings of the modern town; Phourní, a cemetery which produced an exceptional series of rich burial offerings including jewellery and ivory work, now among the most outstanding exhibits in the Herákleion museum; and Anemóspilia, a Minoan Sanctuary site with dramatic suggestions of human sacrifice. None of the three excavations is at present open to the public, but directions are given for those interested in assessing them through the fences (see also *phýlakas*, above).

Approach the Palace site (5 minutes on foot) from the clock-tower near the

Panayía Vatiótissa, the three-aisled church right of the road into town, and just before the one-way street system begins. Start up the left fork, against the traffic flow, but immediately take the narrow street left. At the end turn left, and follow the bend to the right, and 50m further turn right again where the gate of the *Turkogeitoniá* site is in view.

Minoan Palatial-style buildings were first located in 1965, and an intensive programme of excavations since then has gradually uncovered a site of exceptional interest. Both the architecture and the contents of the buildings so far investigated have confirmed the original hypothesis that the site is comparable with the known Minoan Palaces. Wall decoration included miniature frescoes and painted shallow reliefs. Many examples of the minor art of the Minoans included fragments of ivory statuettes from a group similar to the bull-leaper from Knossós. A large rectangular altar, familiar from numerous artistic representations, is the first to be found complete in an excavation. There was evidence for two distinct destruction levels, in LMIA and LMIB; Mycenaean artefacts were also known.

The LMIA building had been destroyed by an intense fire. From a study of fragments of frescoes in the debris it was clear that walls on both the ground and the upper floor of this building had been decorated. One particular area is cited as an example of the architectural sophistication of the building: a propylon gave access along a corridor to a L-shaped peristyle from which a monumental staircase led to an upper floor. The peristyle was paved with irregular slabs (in varying colours) which were pointed with red and yellow plaster. The colonnade of the peristyle was repeated, on a smaller scale, on the upper floor. The masonry was a combination of poros ashlar blocks and courses of bricks. At the time of the fire the upper floor collapsed, but the excavators were able to obtain such a clear understanding of the original building that it is felt that an attempt at reconstruction will be justified.

Excavations in 1966–67 brought to light a *Minoan cemetery* on the hill of *Phourní* just to the NW of the town. The principal discoveries were an *ossuary* of c 2500 BC and three well-preserved *tholos tombs* of c 1400 BC, one containing the first unplundered royal burial found in Crete. The sealed *larnax* held 140 pieces of gold jewellery, now displayed in Herákleion Museum, Gallery VI. A splendid group of white marble idols of Cycladic type are among more recent finds. In 1971, at a short distance N of Tholos A, a Mycenaean-type *grave circle* was uncovered. It comprised seven shaft graves, each of which contained an empty larnax, and had a pit for cult purposes. Bronze vases and stelai were found but no bones, suggesting that the bodies had been deliberately exhumed at a later date in antiquity.

To find the site again from the three-aisled church. On its Herákleion side is a large neo-classic school building (ΣΧΟΛΕΙΟΝ); beside this (N) is a wide turning which narrows to a rough road, negotiable by car 400m to the last group of houses. Then a rocky track follows the flank of the hill. After 200m, on a left bend, a roughly paved path (kalderími) leads straight ahead between two walls; it is 5 minutes to the site fence. Keep left along the fence, and after 150 paces strike right on a trodden path for vantage points on the uphill side of the excavation. In April the hillside is a wild garden. The kalderími leads on temptingly to a crest with a fine view over the Bay of Herákleion.

The sanctuary of *Anemóspilia* (discovered in 1979) is across the deep valley to the W of Phourní, 3km NW of Arkhánes on the N flank of Mount Júktas.

From the three-aisled church continue into the town along the one-way traffic system. 100m from the start of it take the first turning right, a dirt road along the stream; after 300m bear left. The road climbs (past a municipal rubbish dump); it is surfaced but may be rough in places after bad weather. The excavation, behind a wire fence, is on the left of the road 3km from the turning out of the town. (*View to the coast, with the Knossós valley away to the right.)

The *Minoan shrine*, within an enclosure wall, had three rooms preserved along the uphill side of a central corridor; two of them contained a great quantity of fine pottery including a chalice, ritual vases and a large stone basin, as well as pithoi for storage. In the central room life-size clay feet probably belonged to a wooden idol, and in the W room there was a free-standing altar. The shrine was destroyed by the great earthquake c 1700 BC which destroyed the Old Palaces. In the destruction debris, evidence for ritual at first pointed to animal sacrifice, but the bones found on the altar with a long bronze knife were those of a young man. Two other human skeletons were found nearby; a gold ring and an agate seal were associated with one of them. Taking account of forensic evidence, the excavators concluded that the youth on the altar had been sacrificed minutes before the building was destroyed by the earthquake disaster which the ritual was perhaps designed to avert.

South from Arkhánes a minor road leads to (5km) the excavated Minoan villa at Vathýpetro. Just off this road is the frescoed *church of Ayios Mikhaíl Arkhángelos* (at *Asómatos*). The key used to be held in Arkhánes at the Taverna Miriophitó (in the plateía at the end of the town by the bus terminus), but this arrangement has been discontinued; consult the phýlakas (see above).

Just over 1km from the plateía is a turning left to Mikhaíl Arkhángelos. (There has been an OTE notice at the turn.) After a curve right the track runs between vineyards for 1.5km. When you come to a sharp bend across a stream-bed, the trees down to the left hide the little church, all that remains of the Venetian settlement of Asómatos. The frescoes (1315–16) include a remarkable Crucifixion, and a Fall of Jericho. On the W wall (bottom left) the donor Mikhaíl Patsidiótis, with his wife, reverently offers a model of his church to his patron saint the Archangel.
  Below the church a water source was until recently a main part of the Herákleion supply.

The Vathýpetro road runs beneath **Mount Júktas** with the chapel of Aphéndis Khristós (Christ the Lord—great festival on 6 August) conspicuous on the summit (811m). Griffon vultures are a fairly common sight around the peak. A good road climbs the hill, or you can walk from the turn (30 minutes, *View). There is a direct path from Arkhánes which is shorter but very steep.

On the last bend before the church a path leads right along the flank of the hill to the telecommunications relay station; beside it is the Minoan *peak sanctuary* first investigated by Evans, who found a substantial structure with a massive temenos wall. The site is fenced but you get a good view of the excavation from the hillside above it. The sanctuary would have been visible from a great distance, and certainly from the Minoan centres at Knossós and Arkhánes.
  Recent excavations, under the direction of A. Karétsou of the Greek Archaeological Service, have explored this 400m by 400m enclosure near the summit of Γιούχτας (transliterated by the excavator Iúktas) which was in use as a place of cult at least from MMI to the Late Geometric period (c 2000–700 BC). At the S end of the enclosure two successive altars, dating from the Old and New Palace periods, both faced E. A large number of votives (that included some EMII–III material such as 'sheep bells' and Pýrgos ware) were cleared from a natural fissure in the rock around which the sanctuary seems to have been built. This chasm clearly had an important ritual function and it differentiates Júktas from other peak sanctuaries. Finds from the site are on show in Herákleion Museum, Gallery II.

The road below continues to the LMI villa of **Vathýpetro** (5km from Arkhánes), signposted 200m right of the road at a fountain. The site has recently been fenced, but is not locked. The villa, contemporary with the New Palaces, destroyed c 1450 BC, was excavated by S. Marinátos (1949–52), but his findings have not been fully published. Interesting evidence was discovered for the self-sufficiency of this large country house; as well as weaving equipment, there were both wine and olive-oil presses and probably also a potter's workshop.
  The main *SE entrance* to the house is along a corridor (1 on the plan). On the left are storerooms (2) (roofed and locked for protection,

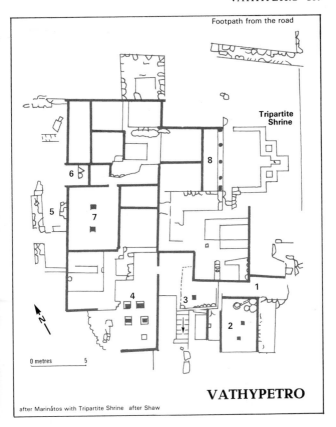

Footpath from the road

Tripartite Shrine

8

6

5

7

4

3

1

2

0 metres 5

N

VATHYPETRO

after Marinátos with Tripartite Shrine after Shaw

but see phýlakas above), where elaborate *wine-making equipment* is in a good state of preservation. At the end of the corridor the staircase (3) led to an upper floor over the storerooms. The main room (4) has four pillars and a paved floor. The site commands a superb *view to the W across the N–S route through to the Mesará plain; in the middle distance to the NW you can distinguish the twin-peaked hill of Prophítis Ilías (Castle of Témenos, Rte 3D). Along the W façade is a miniature paved *W court* (5) with drains running out of the villa wall. The *oil press* with basin was found here. The W façade has a deep recess (6) which may have held a small shrine. The roofed area (7) is another pillar basement where 16 giant *pithoi* are still in situ. To the N is a set of rooms (poorly preserved and complicated by two periods of building) which are thought to have been the private living quarters. The E entrance to this part of the house was through a *three-columned portico* (8); to the E of it, across a small court the excavator identified a **tripartite shrine** with a central recess flanked by two square niches, recalling both the shrine in the Miniature Frescoes found at Knossós and the sanctuary carved on the Mountain Shrine Rhyton from Zákros. A grander version, but on the same principle, is the Tripartite Shrine beside the Central Court of the Knossós

Palace; this is reconstructed in P. de Jong's watercolour in Herákleion Museum, Gallery V.

The road continues from Vathýpetro to Khoudétsi on the main Herákleion–Pýrgos road (see Rtes 3C, 4 and 8). A circular tour could include Moní Epanosíphis (p 140).

C. The Pediáda District

This itinerary is a circular drive from Herákleion of c 80km (50 miles) through richly-cultivated upland landscape, with opportunities to visit (22km) the Kazantzákis museum, (23km) the Angárathos monastery, (25km) the potting village of Thrapsanó, (c 40km) the site of ancient Lýttos, as well as a number of frescoed churches of the Pediáda district.

Also described (diverging after 19km) is the main road SE from Herákleion to (63km, c 40 miles) Viánnos; this can be used for a day's expedition to the S coast at Arví or Mýrtos, or as the first stage of the journey to E Crete by the route S of Lasíthi.

Buses from Herákleion to Kastélli Pediádas, also one service daily to Ierápetra (via Viánnos), from the Oasis Bus Station outside the New Gate. The long-distance Lýttos walk uses the Lasíthi bus for the return trip.

Leave Herákleion as for Rte 3B by the Knossós road, towards Arkhánes. After 8km you pass the Skaláni turning where an alternative cross-country route is signposted (left) to the Kazantzákis museum. At 9.5km the main road turns left, signed Arkalokhóri and Viánnos.

17km *Pezá* is the centre of a prosperous wine-growing area, and new plant has been installed by wine co-operatives in a determined effort to control quality and expand trade, including the export of Cretan wine. (A consistently reliable wine from this region is marketed as Logádo.) The grape harvest begins soon after the great holiday for the Feast of the Assumption (15 August). One of the largest processing plants for the green Cretan olive oil is also in Pezá.

At the fork just beyond the village, one main road S is signposted, right, for the villages at the E end of the Mesará plain, Pýrgos and Khárakas. (See Rtes 3B, 4 and 8; see also the Epanosíphis monastery 13km from this junction.) However, the recommended itinerary keeps straight on to (19km) *Ayiés Paraskiés* and then left into this village when another main road to the S curves sharply right, signed for Arkalokhóri (13km) and Viánnos (45km) (see Rte introduction and p 113).

For Thrapsanó and Kastélli you proceed E from Ayiés Paraskiés through the fertile and heavily-cultivated Pediáda countryside.

22km from Herákleion, a left turn is signposted to the village of Mirtiá, and also has a notice for the KAZANTZAKH Museum at Varvári; this is the same village's previous name.

Recommended detour (2.5km) to the museum, opened in 1983 to honour the distinguished Cretan writer Níkos Kazantzákis (1883–1957). On the Mirtiá road, pass the fork right to Astráki, and at the beginning of the village bend left, following the main street until, at the church, it turns right into the plateía in front of the museum.

Varvári, as it was then known, was the home village of Níkos Kazantzákis's father.

The museum is open (March–October): Monday, Wednesday, Saturday and Sunday, 09.00–13.00 and 16.00–20.00; Tuesday and Friday, mornings only; Thursday closed. Admission (1987) Drs 150.

The **museum** is very well arranged to illustrate Kazantzákis's personal, literary and political life in Greece and abroad, with extensive background notes in both Greek and English in a case near the door of each room. The author of 'Zorba the Greek' was born on Crete in 1883; he took a degree in law at the University of Athens, and afterwards continued his literary and philosophical studies in France, Germany and Italy. Between the two world wars he worked from his home on the island of Aíyina. Briefly in 1945 he was Minister of Education in the Greek Government.

Among Kazantzákis's best-known books are 'Freedom and Death', 'Christ Recrucified' and 'The Odyssey: A Modern Sequel'; some have been made into films and plays, but he also wrote specifically for the theatre. On display are contemporary photographs and documents, personal articles, and copies of all his books, including a great number in translation. There are also theatrical memorabilia, and one room is devoted to the character of Zorba. Kazantzákis died in Germany in 1957; in line with his somewhat unconventional views was his request for burial on the Martinengo Bastion of the Herákleion city walls.

Mirtiá is a well-tended village which welcomes tourists. The easiest way to leave it by car is to keep straight on out of the plateía, and at the end of the village to make an acute turn right to complete a triangle; at the sharp turn the road ahead would take you back to Herákleion via Skaláni (see above).

At 25km on the main Pediada route (3km beyond the museum detour) there is a by-road, left, which leads in 4km to the tranquil *Angárathos monastery, formerly one of the most important religious houses on the island. After a glimpse of the monastery ahead in trees below the skyline, you descend 1.5km to a stream-bed, and from just beyond the bridge the buildings are again in view. Here walkers may be tempted by the short-cut along field tracks, for recent road-building has not increased the romance of the approach to the Venetian monastery.

The exact date of the monastery's foundation is not known, but it is mentioned in 16C manuscripts in the British Museum and St. Mark's Library, Venice, and the records of its abbots go back to 1520. After the fall of Constantinople, Angárathos rivalled the Sinai college in Herákleion as a seat of learning, and a number of abbots went on to distinguish themselves elsewhere in the Christian world as churchmen and academics. The monastery flourished during the first half of the 17C, but at the time of the Turkish invasion of 1645 its precious objects and documents were taken for safety to the island of Kýthera, where the abbot's family had property. These valuables included a treasured icon of the Panayía (Virgin Mary); the name Angárathos enshrines the belief that the original church was built on the spot where this icon had been found, under a bush of the tall herb αγκαραθιά (Jerusalem sage).

The present church, dedicated to the Assumption of the Virgin (Feast Day 15 August), dates only from 1894, but it is surrounded by a triangular courtyard of picturesque buildings which preserve many early features. Several of these are dated by inscription: the gateways at the N and S entrances (1583 and 1565 respectively), a sarcophagus built into the N side of the court (1554), and a lofty barrel-vaulted storeroom opposite the W end of the church (1628). The old N gate is to the left of the modern approach.

Back on the Kastélli road, a turning is almost immediately (300m) signposted right to *Thrapsanó*. This village is known for its pottery, in particular the plain earthenware which includes the traditional large jars or 'pithária', little changed from the storage jars of Minoan times. A Cretan monk, Agápios Lándos, whose work was published in Venice in 1642, commented even then that all the men of Thrapsanó were potters. You can continue straight ahead to Kastélli, but the recommended route takes the right turn.

31km **Thrapsanó** is a long village set on a hillside. Pots are for sale on the main street, but most of the workshops, especially those for the very large jars, are down the hill to the left. From the little triangular plateía, you can walk downhill, but with a car it is easier to go on through the village, turning left towards Kastélli in front of the big church at the end. Out of Thrapsanó, the first track to the left leads past a prominent modern church, and along a stream-bed until it bends right and crosses it; the *pottery kilns* and workshops are in the fields on either side of this track. You can ask for the potters specialising in the large pithária.

Potting is a seasonal occupation. As soon as weather permits (April/May) the potters work a seven-day week. A primitive production line obtains, through potting, drying and firing; each pot may take up to a week from start to finish. Most of the potteries welcome visitors.

The road to Kastélli continues past (34.5km) *Evangelísmos* and (37km) *Arkhángelos.*

In the middle of the first of these villages, the domed cruciform church of Ayios Evangelísmos has unusual (14C) frescoes. Uncovered in 1981 on part of the W arm of the cross, they include Old Testament scenes, rare on Crete, of the Creation of Adam and Eve, the Garden of Eden, and the Expulsion from Paradise.

The church key is kept at the blue-painted kapheneíon across the street; ask for Kyría Katerína.

At 37.5km, in *Sklaverokhóri*, is the church of Eisódia Theotókon (The Presentation of the Virgin), with particularly well-preserved *frescoes (graffito date 1481). For a single example, during this excursion, of the widely-admired Byzantine wall-painting of Crete, these frescoes would be a good choice. Turn right in the village before a left bend, and the church is at the end of the short street. Ask for the key (for the Panayía) at one of the houses on the right, just before it.

In the customary position in the apse is portrayed the Panayía 'Platytéra', the Virgin Mary 'wider than the heavens' in Orthodox iconography, framed by angels, hierarchs and deacons; and on the arch above, the Ancient of Days. In the nave: the birth of Mary and the presentation in the temple (vault), as well as scenes from the life of Christ, including a baptism with male and female river gods; on the S wall, St. George slaying the dragon, and rescuing a princess (the daughter of the King of Alassia), with her parents on the city walls and God's hand outstretched from above. The figures opposite (N side) include St. Francis, one of only three examples on Crete of the portrayal of this subject derived from the Latin hagiography.

If you continue past the church, you almost immediately rejoin (turning right) the direct Ayiés Paraskiés–Kastélli road.

39km **Kastélli** (pop. 1300), the traditional centre of the Pediáda district, is named after its Venetian castle which survived until the early years of this century.

In the middle of Kastélli the circular route keeps left following signs for Khersónisos and Herákleion.

A detour right, on the Arkalokhóri road, takes you in 2km to Ayios Ioánnis, Lilianó, a picturesque church of considerable architectural interest (no frescoes). Halfway up the hill out of town keep right opposite a tree. After 2km there is a sign for Lilianó (right), and 100m before this turn to the village, opposite a guardhouse a metalled road runs straight to a military airfield. Between these two parallel side-roads the church is in view among olive trees.

The material in the walls re-used from older buildings is particularly noticeable in the lower courses on the N and S sides; the block serving as a bench outside the W wall has an ancient Greek inscription, and a fragment of an Early Christian altar is let into the threshold at the church door. (The ancient city of Lýttos, not far away, was still flourishing in the First Byzantine period.) The ground-plan of Ayios Ioánnis (its floor now c 1m below the present level of the cemetery) consists of a triple-aisled nave ending in three apses, with across the W end a barrel-vaulted narthex. The aisles, covered by a saddle roof of wooden construction, are divided internally by two pairs of columns (Ionic and plain abacus capitals). On the S wall, near a low window, five stone steps and part of a column are probably the remains of a pulpit; this may indicate the practice of the Latin rite.

The architectural history of Ayios Ioánnis is a conundrum: the ground-plan points to a basilica, but the short, square nave is not typical; it has been suggested that in an older phase it was covered by a dome. The basilica plan and the antiquity of the building material suggest an early date, but the roof construction, other architectural details such as corbels, and the narthex (reminiscent of the barrel-vaulted storerooms at Angárathos) all show unquestionable Venetian influence, which puts the final adaptation of this church at least no earlier than the 13C.

From the centre of Kastélli, take the Herákleion road, and then (still in the town), when it turns left, keep straight on for (3.5km) Xidás and the site of the historically important city-state of Lýttos.

Approaching (43km) *Xidás*, the modern church is visible for some distance. Across the valley to the left is the tiny (frescoed) chapel of *Ayios Yeóryios*, set among cypresses and orange trees.

To visit Ayios Yeóryios stop by the war memorial, below the modern church. From the terrace of the kapheneíon opposite, the chapel is in sight in the valley, and steps lead down to a path which passes within 50m of it. Indistinct remains of frescoes (dated by inscription 1321) are preserved in the apse and on the S wall.

Beyond Xidás the road climbs for 2km to **Lýttos.** There is little above ground of the Greco-Roman city, but the ascent is recommended for the site's majestic *position against the wall of the Lasíthi massif, overloking the Pediáda plain. Homer speaks of 'broad Lýttos' and the exploits of the Lýttian force under Idomeneus, leader of the Cretan contingent (in 'eighty black ships') at Troy. Before the crest, two *churches* on the skyline (right) mark the site, and the path (5 minutes to the top) starts directly below the N or left-hand of these two, which is dedicated to Tímios Stavrós (the Holy Cross). If you miss the path, the road bends right and, 300m further, a field-track offers an easier route with the churches almost in line ahead along the ridge.

Lýttos was one of the most powerful and warlike of the city-states, and a deadly rival of Knossós, at least from the 4C BC. Its territory reached from the N to the S coast, and included the Lasíthi plateau; its port was at Khersónisos. In the war of 221–219 BC Lýttos resisted the alliance between Knossós and Górtyn which aimed to control the whole island. The Lýttian army embarked on an expedition against Ierápytna (modern Ierápetra on the S coast), unwisely leaving the city unguarded, and Knossós seized the opportunity to destroy Lýttos utterly. In due course the city was rebuilt and put up strong resistance against Quintus Metellus in 67 BC, but survived to flourish under Roman rule and into the First

Byzantine period. Statue inscriptions dedicated to Trajan and Hadrian are particularly numerous.

Archaeological investigation is only just beginning at this huge site, so understanding depends largely on inscriptions and chance finds. The church of Tímios Stavrós (see above) is built above the foundations of a large 5C basilica; the area around it was apparently the agorá or centre of the ancient city. The second church, Ayios Yeóryios on the southern peak, which lies on a 2C AD building in which painted wall plaster was found, has architectural fragments built into its SE corner. These come from ornate piers, with crosses set in delicately carved acanthus foliage.

The relatively small hilltop area between the two churches was enclosed by a massive wall which can still be traced in places, most easily along its outer face. It is of rubble faced with squared stones in the Roman style, and has been compared to the fortifications of the acropolis at Górtyn. Its probable dating is 7C AD. A theatre, the largest recorded on Crete, was planned by the Italian, O. Belli, in the 16C, but its exact location is now uncertain. Crossing the narrow valley to the SE are remains of the massive walls of an *aqueduct* which brought Lasíthi water to Lýttos.

The panoramic view may be enjoyed without exploring the site of Lýttos by continuing 500m up the road to the watershed. Away to the left (N), the car road (see Rte 6) climbs past the Kerá convent into the mountains, and straight ahead, directly across the valley, a mule track or kalderími, one of the eight ancient ways up to the Lasíthi plateau, starts towards the Tsoúli Mníma pass. (A bulldozer has recently been set to work on the Lasíthi side of this pass.) In the opposite direction you can distinguish on a clear day the Levká Ori, or White Mountains, near the western extremity of the island.

Beyond the watershed the road soon deteriorates sharply, and in a car it is better to return from Lýttos to Kastélli.

Walkers who have made the stiff 6km ascent, and are planning to continue 12km to the main Lasíthi road (and bus route) at Avdoú, can now look forward to a gradual descent in this beautiful landscape along the country roads and tracks which connect the villages in the valley below. Turn left after 2.5km in Aski; there are signs all the way for Avdoú.

Back in Kastélli on the circular route, turn right for Herákleion. Less than 1km outside the town, a dirt road (right) leads in 2km to the beautiful old church of *Ayios Pandeleímon dating to the Second Byzantine period, (frescoes transitional 13–14C).

Passing (right) a stretch of well-preserved ancient paved road, the track keeps straight ahead at a fork, and bends left when joined by another track from the right. Soon the church almost blocks the way, shaded by two spreading oak trees, in an area made green by the nearby copious spring. In the summer months there is a simple taverna (ΕΞΟΧΙΚΟΝ ΚΕΝΤΡΟΝ) delightfully situated on the slope below the church, and the key is kept here; if the taverna is closed, ask in Piyí (see p 113).

The church stands on the foundations of an Early Christian basilica, and the Hellenistic inscriptions as well as architectural fragments suggest a previous sanctuary. Ayios Pandeleímon is the patron saint of medicine, and this, together with the health-giving waters of the spring nearby, makes it likely that there is continuity on the site from an Asklepieion.

Almost a ruin when Gerola saw it at the beginning of this century, Ayios Pandeleímon was carefully restored in 1962. The three-aisled church is a structure without parallel, incorporating many re-used architectural fragments and decorated blocks, as well as inscriptions of Hellenistic and Roman date. The partially restored blind-arcading in the S wall is thought to relate to a previous building phase, perhaps a larger cruciform domed church. One of the interior columns consists of four superimposed Corinthian capitals resting on a square abacus plate.

Frescoes are preserved in the apse and on the walls of the nave, dated stylistically to the late 13–early 14C. As well as the full-length figures of the soldier saints on the N wall, there is an unusual scene of Ayía Anna nursing the infant Mary.

You can continue along the track (1km) to rejoin the road at the nearby village, known until recently as Bizarianó, now renamed *Piyí*, which means a 'spring'. This water source fed the Roman aqueduct which supplied ancient Khersónisos.

From Piyí it is 8km till you reach the Lasíthi road (Rte 6) to turn left for another 5.5km to the North Coast Highway, and the return (23km) to Herákleion.

To Viannos

The main road runs S from Ayiés Paraskiés (see p 108) through extensive vineyards, where the vines for the 'rosákia' table grapes are laboriously trained on wire trellises.

32.5km from Herákleion is *Arkalokhóri* (pop. 2500), a busy agricultural centre. The nearby sacred cave of *Prophítis Ilías*, first explored by J. Khatzidákis, was fully excavated in 1932 by the Greek archaeologists S. Marinátos and N. Pláton.

The cave had been a place of worship from the Early Minoan period to the time of the New Palaces. Among the rich series of votive offerings was a large number of bronze rapier blades (MMIII/LMI) recalling weapons in Grave Circles A and B at Mycenae, also many small double axes in bronze, silver and gold, some decorated with traced ornament; one has a vertical inscription in Linear A. (See Herákleion Museum, Gallery VII.)

The main road turns left near the end of Arkalokhóri, and runs towards the Lasíthi range, where *Mount Díkte* is often snow-capped till May.

38km At a meeting of five roads turn right for Viánnos.

45km *Afráti.* The hill to the right is the site of the Classical city-state of Arkádes. The city was destroyed during the war between Knossós and Lýttos (221 BC), and again at the time of the Roman invasion. Nothing remains above ground today.

The Italian Archaeological Mission under D. Levi, excavated an important Geometric and Orientalising cemetery here, and from the latter period some particularly fine cremation urns with rare figurative scenes are exhibited in Herákleion Museum, Gallery XII.

49km *Embaros*, where the church of Ayios Yeóryios has frescoes by Manuel Phokás (1436–37); compare Avdoú (Rte 6) and Epáno Sými (Rte 8). Tracks lead from the village into the Lasíthi mountains.

At 58km there is a right fork for a 3km detour to *Khóndros*. A Bronze Age site here is one of the few excavated settlements known to have been founded in LMIIIA–B, after the widespread destruction in 1450 BC.

The excavation comes into view on a low double-peaked hill immediately above the village. Round a sharp bend at the first group of houses, two tracks diverge right. Take the left of these, at an acute angle to the road ahead. After 800m this track forks, and here the site is 3 minutes away, uphill to the left.

The settlement is divided into two complexes linked by double walls, and each complex consists of a number of house units rather than one large building. The architecture is said to exemplify that of LMIII: walls up to a metre thick, stone-flagged floors, low benches and fixed box-shaped hearths. The W complex (away from the modern village) had a weaving area, and a group of ritual objects suggested a shrine on an upper floor. In early spring the orchids around the site may prove a distraction.

63km Ano (upper) **Viánnos**, on the site of the classical city-state of the same name, is a large and picturesque village (pop. 1400) with several interesting churches, notably *Ayía Pelayía* which has well-preserved frescoes dating from 1360. From the huge plane tree on the left of the main street at the far end of the village, you can make your way up the stepped side-streets. The key for Ayía Pelayía is kept at the priest's house on the third or fourth level, and the church itself is on a terrace near the top of this part of the village. On the way up is the 14–15C church of *Ayios Yeóryios* with fine doorways and bellcote.

For the road ahead to Arví, Mýrtos and Ierápetra (respectively c 20, 24 and 40km from Viánnos), see Rte 8.

D.   To Prophítis Ilías and the Castle of Témenos

This is a short drive, 19km (12miles), in beautiful country behind Herákleion, recommended after a morning's sightseeing, or for a leisurely half day between strenuous excursions.

Leave Herákleion by the Khaniá gate. Immediately outside the walls, at the traffic lights, turn left uphill. The road crosses above the N Coast Highway, and (c 7km) passes a turning for *Phinikiá*, centre of a famed Venetian vineyard, and still a wine-producing area. At first you follow a fertile river valley which must always have contributed to Herákleion's prosperity, and was one of the main routes from the N coast through to the plain of the *Mesará*. Then the road climbs through (15km) *Tsagaráki*; you look across to the dramatic scenery of the rocky SW slopes of *Mount Júktas* before the final stretch where the village of *Prophítis Ilías*, and the fortification wall round the hilltop above it, come into view ahead. Note the white chapel dedicated to the Panayía immediately above the village.

Prophítis Ilías was until recently known as Kanlí Kastélli ('bloody castle'), because of a battle here in 1647 when the Venetians inflicted a great defeat on the Turks. The modern name is taken from the dedication of the principal village church.

Above the village is a twin-peaked hill. After the Byzantine general Nikephóros Phokás had driven the Saracens from the island in 961, he built a great castle on this hill and called it **Témenos**. His plan was to establish a new capital inland, less exposed to the danger of pirate raids, and to transfer there the population of Khándakas, as Herákleion was then called. But the move lacked popular support, and in 968 when Phokás was recalled to Constantinople as Emperor, only the castle had been completed.

In the early 13C the Genoese, under Enrico Pescatore, occupied Témenos but they were soon expelled by the Venetians; in their documents the castle is referred to as 'oppidum fortissimum'. The first Venetian Duke of Crete, Jacopo Tiepolo, took refuge here at a time of rebellion in Candia. The fortifications were restored after an earthquake in 1303, and again in the 16C when the Turks began to threaten the island.

Cars may be left at the top of the village near the church of Prophítis Ilías where the chapel of the Panayía, no longer in sight, is directly above you. From here an easy track runs left along the N flank of the double hill, but if you ask for the path to the Panayía, it will bring you (10 minutes) to the main W summit (see Gerola's sketch-plan). This hill, called *Rocca*, is where Nikephóros Phokás built his castle.

More than 1000 years earlier this was the site of the Greco-Roman city-state of Lýkastos and near the chapel of the Panayía is a well-preserved double *cistern*, probably Roman in date.

On the summit nothing is preserved except traces of rock cutting. The view is extensive, with an angle of Mount Júktas unfamiliar from the N coast, and the Minoan villa at Vathýpetro (Rte 3B) discernible below the quarry scar across the valley to the E. From the Rocca summit you can make your way down to the saddle to reach the E height, *Apáno Kastélli*. To the S is a fine stretch of curtain walling. N

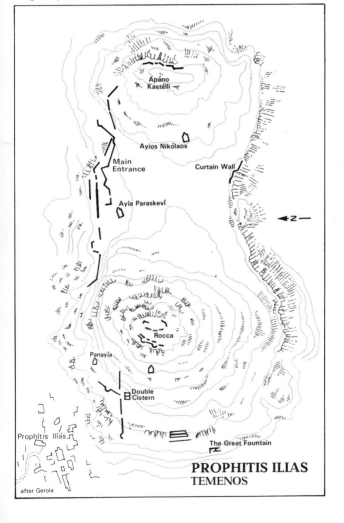

PROPHITIS ILIAS
TEMENOS

after Gerola

of the church of Ayios Nikólaos (rebuilt on old foundations) are the remains of substantial buildings, probably Venetian. The protected saddle, designed as a haven in times of trouble in the surrounding countryside, slopes down to the main *N entrance* where formidable overlapping defence walls are excellently preserved. In places the walls reuse Hellenistic material, most probably from Lýkastos.

Ayía Paraskeví has only the tantalising remains of the frescoes which the Italian scholar Guiseppe Gerola admired at the beginning of this century. It is possible to walk here directly (avoiding the scramble to the summit) by the track which will now lead you back from the church round the flank of the hill to the village (10 minutes).

It is worth walking S into the village round the foot of the hill to the Venetian *fountain* known locally as Η Μεγάλη Πηγή (megáli piyí), the great fountain. There is a precipitous path or stairway up the steep rock face above it, and remains of the guard houses; the brick courses in their walling are typical of Byzantine construction.

You can continue c 6km to Veneráto on the busy Phaistós road (Rte 4). Alternatively return through Tsagaráki, and c 2km beyond this hamlet turn right on a quiet by-road for *Ayios Sýllas* and *Vasiliés*. Through Fortétsa, this emerges on the Knossós road (Rte 2) opposite the University buildings, and you turn left for Herákleion or the N Coast Highway.

4 Herákleion to the Mesará and the Palace of Phaistós

Direct route 64km (40 miles) to the major Minoan sites of Phaistós and Ayía Triáda. 30km Ayía Varvára; 46km Górtyn, the capital of Roman Crete. Continue to the S coast at (75km) Mátala or (84km) Ayía Galíni.

A number of alternative routes branch off this direct road: a 65km round trip from Herákleion through Ayía Varvára taking in the Archaic site of Priniás; a branch road from Ayía Varvára through the S foothills of Psilorítis (Mount Ida) to (57km) Kamáres, which passes two important frescoed churches; an alternative return route to Herákleion from Ayii Déka along the Mesará plain and then N through the Témenos countryside; a road through the Asteroúsia mountains to the S coast at Léndas, site of ancient Lebéna (78km from Herákleion). These alternatives are noted at the appropriate junctions on the way to Phaistós, but are described separately at the end of the direct route.

There are buses to all these destinations from the bus station ouside the Khaniá gate in Herákleion. Frequent services to Phaistós.

The road leaves Herákleion to the W by the Khaniá gate, becomes a dual-carriageway and (2.5km) turns left (signposted Míres and Phaistós). This is also the junction for the North Coast Highway (New Road), but keep straight ahead under the bridge. From other N coast bases you can join the route here, in which case you should deduct c 3km from distances given below (and on the new kilometre posts along the road which are measured from central Herákleion).

5km A minor road (signed for Ayios Mýron and Asítes) turns right and runs parallel to the main route which it rejoins (after c 30km) at Ayía Varvára. This alternative route, slower but relatively free of traffic, is described as part of a leisurely excursion to Ayios Mýron and the Archaic site of Priniás (see p 137).

The main road climbs gently through a valley planted with vines and olives, the cypress trees scattered with dramatic effect. Occasional glimpses of hills are a foretaste of mountain views in store. At 13km you pass the turning for Daphnés, a village with a reputation for its good wine. Continue through (19km) *Sivá*. At 20.5km, in the middle of *Veneráto*, a detour left leads in 2km to the Paliani monastery.

400m after leaving the main road, turn right where the monastery sign is painted on a wall, and almost immediately at a fork keep right downhill. Since the road was given an asphalt surface during the winter of 1986, there is an alternative (signed) approach to this fork. Across the valley the road then climbs to the monastery, with the reward at the top of a wide retrospective view. The village on the hill away to the N is Ayios Mýron.

Moní Palianí is an ancient foundation, documented as an antiquity (palaiá) even in 668. Nowadays a nunnery, this is a flourishing self-supporting community. The nuns are hospitable and will point out interesting features of the old buildings; their fine handwork is for sale.

The 13C church (the narthex a 15–16C addition) retained the plan of the underlying three-aisled 6C basilica, but in the last century it was much restored after Turkish destruction and earthquake damage. Some Early Byzantine (6C) capitals and impost blocks are preserved; two capitals are in situ, four support the altar, and others lie outside in the courtyard.

In the 14C, authority over the wealthy monastery was disputed at great length between the powers of the Orthodox and Latin Churches, in the shape of the Patriarch of Constantinople and the Latin Archbishop acting under instruction from Pope Clement IV.

21km *Avyenikí*, after which the road climbs through olive groves to a less cultivated level, dominated to the right by a chapel on a craggy outcrop. Here, in the Archaic period, was the acropolis of the city-state of *Rizenía*; some important Daidalic-style sculptures from its temples can be seen in the Herákleion museum. The site is immediately to the N of the modern village of Priniás, by which name it is now usually known.

The circular rock formations in the valley below are a strong erosion feature; locally they are called 'the old lady's cheeses'. The Phaistós bus will put you down at the start of the roughly paved 'Turkish' road or kalderími, for the cross-country walk (c 1 hour) to the ancient site; ask for Priniás 'me ta pódia' (on foot), and for the kalderími, which is the second of two tracks, 200m before the 27km post.

30km *Ayía Varvára*, where the little church of Prophítis Ilías, perched high on a rock called Omphalos (navel), is said to mark the centre of Crete. In the middle of this long village the minor road from Priniás and Ayios Mýron joins the main road (5km from this junction to the start of the path to the archaeological site—see p 137).

At the end of Ayía Varvára is a turning (right) for the Valsamóneros monastery and Kamáres; this route too is described among alternative excursions below (p 138).

Shortly after Ayía Varvára on the main road to Phaistós, the *Mesará plain* comes suddenly into view, spread out below to the left; beyond it to the S are the Asteroúsia mountains which separate it from the Libyan sea. The plain which, from the foothills of the Díkte range to the Bay of Mesará, lies parallel to the S coast, is an alluvial basin of the Quaternary period. It is watered by the Ieropótamos (ancient Lethaíos, Lethe) and its tributaries. The rich soil and benign climate in the shelter of the island's central spine of mountains have favoured settlement through the ages, and this is still an area of great agricultural prosperity.

First occupied at the end of the Neolithic period, the Mesará experienced rapid population growth during the Early Bronze Age, with many settlements along the slopes of the Asteroúsia chain, and the first appearance of the monumental collective tombs, on a circular plan with entrance from the E, which have become known as the Mesará type. By the beginning of the second millenium, Phaistós had begun to emerge as the great palatial centre and economic focus of the region. At a later period the city of Górtyn on the N edge of the plain became the capital of Roman Crete, and retained a position of power until the second half of the 7C.

The road winds down from the hills and in summer the temperature increases at every bend. The wild flowers of the Mesará are strikingly larger and taller than anywhere else on Crete.

43km An acute left turn signposted for *Pýrgos* offers an alternative return drive (c 63km) to Herákleion, E along the Mesará plain, and then N through Khoudétsi and Pezá, entering Herákleion by the Knossós road. Details are given on p 140. From Pýrgos you can continue E (on an unfinished section of the projected S Coast Highway) towards Viánnos and SE Crete (Rte 8).

44km *Ayii Déka*, the Holy Ten, is named after ten Christian martyrs of the Persecution of Decius (AD 250). The church is signposted left of the through road, in the older part of the village.

This much-restored 13–14C *church* incorporates re-used material from the neighbouring city of Górtyn. In the nave an icon portrays the martyrdom, and below in a glass case is a stone on which the ten are supposed to have knelt to be executed. Many of the old buildings in the streets off the pleasant tree-shaded square in front of the church also incorporate ancient fragments from Górtyn.

A path leads (5 minutes) to the SW outskirts of the village, and to a crypt beside the portico of a modern chapel where six tile graves are venerated as the tombs of the martyrs.

46km **GORTYN** (the English rendering of Γόρτυς) was the most powerful Greco-Roman city on the island, and capital of the Roman province of Crete and Cyrenaica. The city, still largely unexcavated, lies in the olive groves where the foothills of Mount Ida meet the Mesará plain (see plan), and on either side of the Mitropolianós, a tributary of the Ieropótamos, the ancient Lethe. The main road cuts through the middle of the site, with the ruins of the basilica of Ayios Títos a convenient stopping-place on the right. You can spend a whole day at Górtyn or make a brief stop to see the *basilica* and the 5C BC *law code*, both of which are within the fenced area of the Greek-period agora.

Summer opening hours: 08.00–19.00, otherwise closed at 15.00; admission (1987) Drs 200. The rest of the huge site may be explored at will, though one or two of the individual excavations have to be viewed from vantage points outside a protective fence.

The site was first explored in the 1880s by the Italian archaeologist, Federico Halbherr; with his primary interest in epigraphy, he was drawn here by earlier travellers' tales of fragments of inscribed blocks. Almost immediately he was able to locate the major part of the Law Code inscription, still one of the most important known in the Greek world. The Italian Institute returned to the site during the early part of this century, and again from 1954–61 when the acropolis was investigated, and work has continued in recent years. The whole area of the city is littered with ploughed-out architectural fragments and pottery, and only a number of major buildings at the centre, and some cemeteries, have been systematically excavated. A recent topographical survey resulted in a plan incorporating the most up-to-date understanding of ancient Górtyn; a large-scale version is now displayed at strategic positions around the site.

History. There was a settlement on the *acropolis hill* from the end of the Bronze Age (Subminoan, c 1000 BC) until the 7C BC, during which time it became a place of religious and military significance. The acropolis was fortified in the

Geometric period and parts of the *bastioned wall* still stand. The city spread onto the plain below and was flourishing by the first half of the 5C BC, the date of the Law Code. By the time of the defeat of Phaistós (2C BC), Górtyn extended S to modern Mitrópolis and E beyond the temple of Apollo Pythios and, with the additional strength of two harbours (Mátala and Lebéna), was intermittently at war with either Knossós or Lýttos. The Carthaginian general Hannibal visited Górtyn (189 BC) after the Battle of Magnesia.

At the time of the Roman invasion (65 BC) the city put up no resistance to Quintus Metellus, and while Knossós was destroyed, Górtyn went on to flourish as the capital of the new Roman province. Many of the great public buildings date from the Imperial period, particularly from the 2C AD. St. Titus, commissioned by St. Paul to convert the island, was installed here as the first Bishop of Crete. The Byzantine city spread over the plain to the S in a great period of expansion; six basilicas and smaller churches are known to have existed contemporaneously in one small area (100m long) between Mitrópolis and the River Lethaíos. The region suffered a number of severe earthquakes, and at last, towards the end of the 7C, Górtyn was destroyed by Arab raiders. The basilica of Ayios Títos was rededicated in the 10C and there was a Venetian monastery on the Praetorium site, but the great city was never rebuilt.

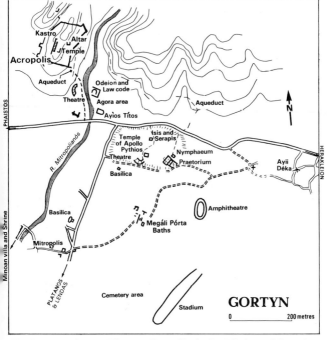

GORTYN

0 _____ 200 metres

The **Basilica of Ayios Títos**, traditionally the burial place of the saint, is by far the best-preserved Early Christian church on Crete. Its foundation is tentatively attributed to the Justinianic period (early 6C), but it underwent many reconstructions. Originally it was an imposing church, built of unusually large limestone blocks; the three-aisled basilica with narthex (see ground plan) was elaborated by the addition of a cross-dome, reflecting the influence of Eastern architecture. The ruins of the *bema* are still impressive.

After a study by the Italian Guiseppe Gerola in 1900, the church was excavated by Greek archaeologists in 1902 and again in 1920. The ground plan remains

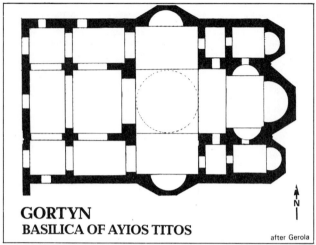

GORTYN
BASILICA OF AYIOS TITOS

after Gerola

intelligible: narthex, nave with side-aisles, central cross with side-arms which end in apses. Around the central dome, the nave and the arms of the cross were barrel-vaulted. In the triconch chancel each side-chapel has an anteroom. Architectural fragments dating from the 2C suggest a previous building, probably a temple, on the site or nearby.

The Historical Museum in Herákleion preserves stone carvings and liturgical furnishings from Ayios Titos.

The basilica stands in the unexcavated *Agora* or *Forum* area (see area plan). A path leads NW to the *Odeion*, a theatre used for musical performances or contests; the excavated remains are those of a 1C BC structure restored under Trajan after earthquake damage in the early 2C AD. This is the site of an earlier circular building of Hellenistic date, the foundations of which re-used stone blocks inscribed with the famous **Law Code of Górtyn**. The code, now displayed beyond the Roman Odeion, is in a form of the Dorian dialect and dates to the first half of the 5C BC.

The *inscription* is divided into 12 columns, 600 lines in all, 17,000 letters. It is written 'boustrophedon': this word describes the pattern of oxen ploughing a field, so alternately one line reads from left to right, the next from right to left. The inscription codifies in great detail the laws relating to property in respect of marriage and divorce, the sale and mortgage of property, the rights of heirs and the division of property among children, including adopted children. It includes procedure for adoption. It covers cases of seduction, rape and adultery, as well as general assault; also the position of slaves, and much else besides. In the history of law, the Code of Górtyn, the earliest Greek law code yet known, is of the highest importance.

Across the stream from the Odeion the outline can be detected of the *Larger Theatre* planned by the Italian O. Belli in the 16C; it is cut into the lower slope of the acropolis hill. In Roman times the stream ran through a culvert.

The **acropolis** is reached by a track from the road along the W bank of the Mitropolianós stream. Beyond the theatre, a gate marks the start of the path, and the easiest route gains height across the S slope, to reach the flat summit at its SW corner (10 minutes from the gate, a recommended climb if only for the view).

On the S brow of the hill are the excavated foundations (fenced) of the 7C BC *temple of Athena* (a rectangular building with cella and central bothros or circular pit), which continued in use, restored on several occasions but not basically altered, into early Roman times. Below the temple, terraced into the E slope, was an associated *altar of sacrifice* (8–3C BC), which stood on a wide platform suported by a massive ashlar wall. The cult statue from the temple, remains of decoration including the naked feminine triad in relief, and Geometric and Archaic finds from the rich votive deposit at the altar site, are in Herakleion Museum, Galleries XVIII and XIX; they include notable exhibits in the Daidalic style.

In the 6C the temple was succeeded on the same site by a Christian basilica.

These fenced remains are over-shadowed by an unexcavated but well-preserved Roman building known as the *Kástro*, which consists of a spacious hall sunk up to 6m into the rock. Its function, probably as some offical building, is uncertain.

The acropolis was fortified as early as the Geometric period; the Hellenistic circuit was restored in Byzantine times, and parts of this *bastioned wall* of concrete with good stone facing can still be traced.

On either side of the stream archaeologists have found branches of the great *aqueduct* that brought water to the city from Zarós on the slopes of Mount Ida.

The rest of the site of interest to visitors lies across the main road, E of the turning to Plátanos and Léndas. Paths are signposted (see area plan).

The *Temple of Isis and Serapis* is a simple rectangular cella with a crypt complex, probably for initiation ceremonies, to the S. The cella has a tripartite podium in the E wall for the statues of the Egyptian divinities; the third was possibly Hermes Anubis. A stylobate of six Ionic columns fronted the W façade. This temple is dated 1–2C AD from the dedication of Flavia Philyra and her two sons.

To the S is the **Temple of Apollo Pythios**, the main sanctuary of pre-Roman Górtyn. The original 7C temple was a simple cella with rectangular bothros just inside the doorway (right). In the Hellenistic period a pronaos was added with six half-engaged columns of the Doric order. Between the columns, four inscribed stelai displayed Górtyn's 2C BC treaties with other Cretan cities and with Eumenes II of Pergamon. The stepped *monumental altar* in front of the temple and the small *heróon* just to the NE were built at this period. During the Empire (2C AD) the temple was converted, with the addition of an apse and arcaded Corinthian columns, into a three-aisled *Christian basilica*, which continued as the religious centre of the city until c 600 when Ayios Títos was built.

Just to the SW are the remains of the *'Smaller Theatre'*, the best-preserved Roman theatre on Crete. It is built in brick-faced concrete with a double-tiered 'cavea' or seating arrangement.

To the E along the track (or it can also be reached on a signed path off the main road) is the **Praetorium**, the grand palace complex of the Roman governor of the Province; it can be viewed from outside the N fence, which follows a fine stretch of Roman (and medieval) road. Excavations have revealed several phases of building. The early 2C AD construction, contemporary with the rebuilt Odeion of the Trajanic period, probably replaced an Augustan Palace, and then was itself enlarged and rebuilt in the 4C after earthquake damage. The architectural fragments on the site include marble columns, and capitals of both the Ionic and Corinthian orders. The 4C reconstruction created the large *basilica audience hall* (27m by 12m) in the NW corner of the site; it was built of concrete, faced in this case with stone, and the floor was paved. Along the outer wall the dedicatory bases intended for statues of prominent citizens of the Roman world are preserved. E of this was the bath suite. The 2C *Nymphaeum* to the N was supplied by a branch of the city's main aqueduct (see above). The Praetorium building survived in part as a monastery during the Second Byzantine period, and the Nymphaeum became a public fountain.

SE of the Praetorium (c 150m) are the remains of the almost unexcavated *Amphitheatre* (late 2C AD). Further S the *Stadium* or Circus is scarcely discernible under cultivation.

To the W of the Amphitheatre are the remains of the Roman building which was given the name 'Megáli Pórta' or Great Gate. This has not been excavated but is believed to be a 2C AD *public baths* complex, with the arch being part of a large hall.

The museum near Ayios Títos had not been opened in 1987; finds from Górtyn are in the Herákleion museum.

Almost opposite Ayios Títos is the turning S for Plátanos and Léndas. This route is described below (see p 141); included is the detour to the Minoan villa or farm near Kanniá, less than 2km from Mitrópolis.

52km from Herákleion on the main road is *Míres* (pop. 3500), not an attractive town but the thriving centre of this agricultural region. A minor road to the left is the direct way (18km) to Mátala (see below), but for Phaistós keep straight on through the town. There is a colourful Saturday morning market in the wide main street.

About 3km beyond Míres, Phaistós comes into view ahead slightly to the left of the road, at the end of a low ridge jutting into the Mesará plain. On the slopes to the right of the road, the rich Kalývia cemetery, dating from the Postpalatial period of Mycenaean control of the island, was excavated at the turn of the century (finds in Herákleion Museum, Gallery VI).

57km Moní Kalyvianí is today one of the most flourishing ecclesiastical establishments on the island. The nuns run an orphanage and school, as well as other charitable projects. An avenue of clipped bougainvillea leads to the big modern church with Italianate campanile; behind it is the 14C frescoed chapel of the Panayía Kalivianís.

59.5km Turn left to cross the Ieropótamos and climb to (61km)
**PHAISTOS.
The Palace occupies a superb position overlooking the Mesará plain. To the N is Mount Ida, snow-capped for half the year, and to the S the Asteroúsia range hides the sea. The nearby Minoan site known as *Ayía Triáda*, at the W end of the same ridge, looks out over the Bay of Mesará. The relationship between the two sites is still uncertain, and is a matter of great interest to archaeologists working in this field.

Note that opening hours for the two sites are not identical. Summer 1987: Phaistós 08.00–19.00, Sunday 09.00–18.00; winter 10.00–16.00. Admission Drs 250.
   Ayía Triáda 08.45–15.00, Sunday 09.30–14.30, CLOSED Fridays. Admission Drs 200. If possible check with NTO or telephone Phaistós (0892 22 615) in advance.

From the bus stop and car park, a paved path leads up to the Palace site and a Tourist Pavilion (café and simple accommodation March–October).

The Palace of Phaistós and the surrounding area were excavated by the Italian Archaeological Mission on Crete. Work began in 1900 and continued for nearly a decade, with L. Pernier as director, and the results were published in the 1930s. From 1950–66 Doro Levi (for the Italian School of Archaeology at Athens, which had absorbed the Mission) conducted further extensive excavations on the S and W sides, revealing a considerable area of the Old Palace (First Palace in the Italian terminology) and of the surrounding Minoan town. Exploration and study still continue.

The site was inhabited in Neolithic and Early Minoan times; pottery deposits of these periods are found beneath the earliest palace floors, and Prepalatial structures have been uncovered W of the area of the later W Court. The Middle Minoan Palace was built in MMIB (c 1900 BC). Levi's excavations revealed three distinct phases for this building before it was destroyed, like Knossós, c 1700 BC. Over the ruins of the Old Palace a thick cement-like fill was laid and upon this was built the New Palace (excavators' Second Palace) which is mainly what visitors see today. The New Palace was destroyed, like many other major sites on the island, c 1450 BC, in LMIB. There was some reoccupation in LMIII at the end of the Bronze Age, and in the Geometric period (8C BC). Of the Classical-Hellenistic era are remains of a temple and some substantial houses. The city, mentioned in Linear B tablets and by Homer ('Iliad', II, 648, where it is described as 'well inhabited'), was important in the later periods and minted its own coins, until it was destroyed by Górtyn in the 2C BC.

As at Knossós, Mállia and Zákros, the Palace was built around a large Central Court (SE area eroded away), and has a Grand Entrance, with an elegant staircase from a West Court (see plan). The main reception rooms are immediately to the N of the Central Court, and beyond them, on the N edge of the Palace with an uninterrupted view of the mountains, are the main living quarters, comparable to the Domestic Quarter at Knossós. Also as at Knossós, the W side of the Central Court has a religious area next to storerooms, and Palace workshops tucked away to the NE. Features distinctive to Phaistós are the Grand Staircase, the Peristyle Hall and the formal N façade of the Central Court.

From the modern entrance to the site, you cross the *Upper Court* diagonally to a flight of stairs. (On your right are the remains of Hellenistic buildings.) You descend a staircase to the *Theatral Area* (1 on the plan) and the **West Court**. On your right, to the N of the West Court, is a retaining wall for the Upper Court, and below it tiered rows provided seats for the events and ceremonies that took place here.

From the West Court two successive Palace façades are still visible. When the New Palace was built (c 1650 BC) its façade was set back about 8m behind that of its predecessor, and the level of the new West Court was raised accordingly. Its new paving was laid above more than a metre of cement-like fill, in the process covering the lower tiers of the Theatral Area. During excavation this paving and fill were removed, leaving the Old Palace West Court that you now see, with its *raised paths* a distinctive Minoan feature, and (outside the fence) *kouloúras* similar to those at Knossós and Mállia.

To the S and W of the Theatral Area, beyond a fine Minoan *paved road* (also outside fence), lies part of the *Minoan town*. This, the principal area that the Italians have been excavating since 1966, includes important houses that were destroyed at the same time as the Old Palace (c 1700 BC). From this complex has come an astonishing number of polychrome vases in the *Kamáres ware* thought to have been made only at the Palace workshops of Knossós and Phaistós.

Its distinctive decoration is in white, red, orange and yellow on a black ground, the curvilinear motifs flowing over the whole surface of the pot. Kamáres ware provides some of the finest examples of the Minoan potter's art, rarely equalled in prehistoric times; a superb collection of these vases from both Palace and town at Phaistós is displayed in Herákleion Museum, Gallery III.

At the NE corner of the West Court, a group of small rooms (2 on plan) is a *Shrine complex* of the Old Palace; two adjoining areas have benches round the walls. These rooms contained a large clay 'table for offerings', stone vases, a triton shell and other cult objects now forming the central exhibit of Gallery III (see above). In a sacrificial pit to the N of the main room, charred animal bones suggested burnt offerings.

To the S of the shrine is the *Old Palace West Façade* (3), recessed, as was the later version, for the windows of the storey above. Behind this the excavated Old Palace rooms, MMIIA (Levi's phase 1B), have been covered over to form a level surface in front of the *New Palace façade*. They ended (S angle) at a corridor which provided a monumental W entrance for the Old Palace. Down the hill S of the corridor (and fenced off) work continues on the wing where the New Palace

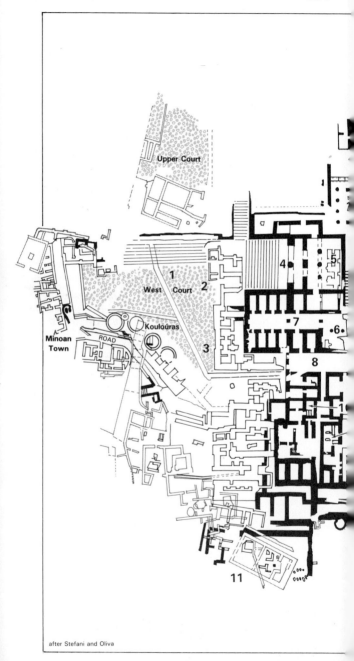

after Stefani and Oliva

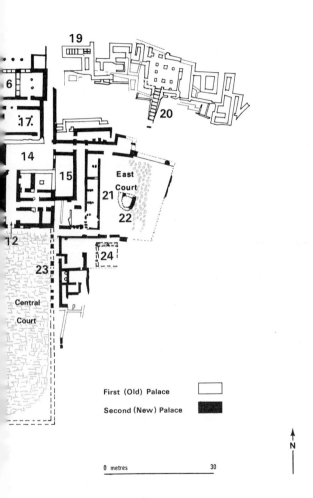

First (Old) Palace

Second (New) Palace

0 metres 30

N

PALACE OF PHAISTOS

did not extend over the ruins of its MMI–II predecessor. This has allowed archaeologists a unique opportunity to investigate Old Palace remains.

From the Theatral area of the West Court, the monumental * *Grand Staircase** into the Palace, walled in fine ashlar masonry, leads up to the *Propylon* (4). This was a porch with a massive central column, in front of a pair of double doors leading to a narrow anteroom and a large colonnaded *light-well* (5). This imposing entrance changes character at this point, for from the light-well only small unimposing exits led left by a roundabout route to the Reception Rooms, or right to the Central Court. Take the staircase which descends to the right to the level of the Court.

On the right, at the foot of the stairs and under the Propylon light-well, are *storerooms* of the Old Palace where large pithoi with painted decoration have been left in position on their stands.

The square *Hall* (6) was built with two internal columns, and there is an oval column base (very unusual in Minoan architecture) on the same line and between two pillars in the colonnade on the court; massive doors closed from both sides onto the column that rested on this oval base. The hall seems to have been associated in an administrative capacity with the double row of storerooms behind it; beneath the floor of the building and dating to the earlier Palace, were discovered in 1955 tablets in the Linear A script, and an extensive archive of *clay sealings*. From over 6500 seal-impressions on small lumps of clay, nearly 300 different motifs have been identified; a display in Herakleion Museum, Gallery III, illustrates the wide variety of subjects. Study of the material, including the impressions on the backs of the clay lumps, suggests that many of the objects sealed were not as had been thought vessels or containers but wooden door-handles, a discovery with interesting implications about the administration of storage.

Behind the columned hall, the *storeroom block* (7) is a tangible reminder of the importance of storage and redistribution to the Minoan Palace economy; the solid construction and the central pillars would have supported an upper floor, and the gypsum slabs, dadoes and column bases found in the storerooms had fallen from it. At the end of the row (right) *giant pithoi* of the New Palace period are visible behind a grille.

To the S of the Storeroom complex was a corridor (8), walled with massive stone blocks; it formed an impressive entrance on this W side of the court, and could be closed at both ends by double doors. The area S of this is poorly preserved, and is now partly fenced off. Several of the rooms here seem to have had religious purposes: there is a *pillar crypt* (9) with a bench round it as at Knossós, and behind this a *lustral basin* (10).

Down the slope at the SW corner of the site, at an oblique angle to the Minoan remains, are the lower courses of the walls of a *Temple* (11) of the Classical period (on 8C foundations), perhaps dedicated to the Great Mother, Rhea.

The Palace buildings to the S and E have been lost owing to the erosion of the hillside; however, part of the *drainage system* survives in the SW angle of the Court and is exposed near the site fence.

Looking N at this point, up the great paved **Central Court** (51.50m by 22.50m), the view is dominated by the distant mass of Mount Ida. One of its S bluffs has distinctive twin peaks with a shallow saddle between them, and a little below the right-hand peak a large dark spot, especially dramatic when there is snow on the mountain, marks the Minoan sanctuary, the *sacred cave* of Kamáres.

Both long sides of the Central Court had *porticoes* along their frontage, and some of the stone bases for wooden columns or pillars still survive; those on the W side, and at a lower level, belong to the portico of the earlier palace. The buildings on the E side of the court are preserved only at the NE end (described below).

The *N façade* of ashlar blocks has a *central doorway* designed with a formality known only at Phaistós. This is framed by half-engaged columns (originally wood) and by recesses which are considered to be *sentry boxes*. The plaster which lined them was decorated with a lozenge-pattern fresco, dark lozenges on light ground. Sockets can be seen in the threshold block for the double doors which opened into a passage (12). Just inside the passage is a further recess for a sentry, also showing the remains of lozenge-pattern fresco. Next to this is a *staircase* (with a pithos under it) which would have given access to important reception rooms on the upper floor. Perhaps, as has been suggested in similar positions at Mállia and Zákros, these included a Dining Hall.

The staircase was one of the routes to the important Peristyle Hall which could also be reached from an anteroom of the Propylon, or by the staircase from the Central Court, as well as from the grand private quarters to the N (identified by their protective cover). If you take the stairs from the NW corner of the Central Court, you pass two LMIIIB (reoccupation period) pithoi, and a stone block with double-axe masons' mark, which may have been the base of an altar. At the top of the stairs an anteroom leads into the *Peristyle Hall* (13). Part of the foundations of an earlier (Prepalatial) building have been left uncovered in the centre, but the colonnade of the hall would have produced an effect similar to a cloister, with the N side open to the mountain view from an elaborately paved verandah.

Return down the staircase noted above which leads directly to the sentry boxes guarding the entrance to the N wing of the Palace (12). A drain running down the centre of the paved passage suggests that this was unroofed and took rainwater from the buildings on either side. It leads to the *N court* (14) which lies between the main block of reception rooms facing back onto the Central Court, and the grand private quarters ahead (N). To the E is a large open area (15), its well-preserved *ashlar masonry* similar to that of the N Court; it may have been a walled garden.

The (fenced and roofed) *Private Quarters* can be viewed from their E and N sides. Here the most luxurious room of the block (16), nearest the edge of the hill, has an elaborate plan similar to that of the Hall of the Double Axes (King's Megaron) at Knossós. Pier-and-door arrangements on two sides of the main inner area (the SW angle) allowed this space to be securely enclosed or to be thrown open to the *verandah* with mountain views to the N, or to the portico giving on to a sheltered *light-well* to the E. This light-well has a drain for rainwater through the wall at its NE corner. Across a staircase to the S, the room with four columns, gypsum bench and dado (17), has been compared to the Queen's Megaron at Knossós.

From the SW corner of the larger Hall, a dogleg passage leads to a *lustral basin* (18) which has been newly lined with gypsum slabs from nearby quarries at Ayía Triáda. (View from W side.) W of the lustral basin, the outer of two small rooms was a lavatory, with a hollowed stone connected to a drain.

Proceeding E round the flank of the hill you come to a series of chests (19) built of mudbrick and originally faced with plaster. In one of them was found (1903) the mysterious **Phaistós disk**.

The disk, of baked clay c 16cm in diameter, is inscribed on both sides in an unknown ideographic script. The signs (241 in all) are set in a spiral thought to run from circumference to centre. Despite many attempts to decipher the script and various suggested solutions, the disk (prominently displayed in Herákleion Museum, Gallery III) remains an enigma.

On the NE edge of the hill lies a further complex of rooms reached by a long staircase (20). The underlying levels visible here date from the Old Palace, and the area with columns at the foot of the staircase may have been a *peristyle* anticipating the plan of the Peristyle Hall (13, above).

Returning, by the stairs, towards the centre of the site, you pass craftsmen's workshops (21) along one side of the E Court. In the middle of it (fenced), are the remains of a large *furnace* for metal-working (22); scraps of copper and bronze were found still adhering to its walls.

A ramp connected the E Court to the NE corner of the Central Court. S of this are the foundations of a set of rooms known as the *East Wing* (23). This self-contained suite demonstrates all the most delightful embellishments of Minoan domestic architecture: a versa-tile main hall, a peristyle court, a bath, even a bench outside the door to the Central Court. The finds here included LMI vases, a table for offerings and several bronze double axes. The *colonnaded court* (24) was surely designed to benefit from the uninterrupted prospect of the Mesará plain to the Asteroúsia mountains and the distant Lasíthi range, and three and a half thousand years ago this would have been, as it remains, a magnificent sight.

To *Ayía Triáda.

Leave the Phaistós car park at the far end towards the picturesque ruined church, all that remains of the monastery of Ayios Yeóryios Phalándras. Opposite it the footpath (marked) strikes off to the right around the N flank of the hill, with views of Mount Ida, and ap-proaches the site through groves of orange trees (c 30 minutes). In a car (3km) keep right at the fork by the church along the S-facing slope, which in April is a hillside garden densely covered with pink Cretan ebony.

Ayía Triáda is beautifully situated, overlooking the plain at the mouth of the Ieropótamos river and the Bay of Mesará; in the Bronze Age the sea may have come right up to the foot of the hill. The ancient name of the site is unknown though tentatively identified with the 'da-wo' of a Knossós Linear B tablet but archaeologists named it after the double-naved Venetian church (in view from the car park) which lies 250m SW towards the sea.

The site was excavated by the Italian Mission (1902–14), under the personal supervision of its director, Federico Halbherr, but for various reasons the full results were not made available at that time; the recent definitive publication of the structures and material of the New Palace period (chiefly the work of L. Banti), happily coinciding with the centenary of Italian archaeology on Crete, has gone a long way to fill this gap. New excavations to re-examine the strati-graphy with the benefit of modern methods were begun in 1977.

There is evidence of continuous occupation dating from the Neolithic period to the 13C BC, but the chief interest of Ayía Triáda is focused on the LMI and LMIII (New Palace and Postpalatial) phases, and especially on the relationship between the Minoan structures, the so-called *Royal Villa*, an the contemporary New (Second) Palace at Phaistós. The quantity and quality of the LMI finds, which included alabaster facings, inscribed tablets, carved stone vases and fresco paintings, marked this site as exceptional. There was extensive LMIII reoccupation after the 1450 BC destruction of the Palaces and other main sites on Crete; the megaron-type building here is the oldest known on the island, and the area of the lower town was reconstructed at this time. In the Geometric period part of the villa site seems to have had cult associations, for clay and bronze figurines of this date were found here. Later there was a Hellenistic shrine dedicated to Zeus Velkhanós. The little Byzantine church above the excavation, Ayios Yeóryios Galatás, has remains of *frescoes* (1302) including a rare scene in the apse with the Christ child representing the elements of the Eucharist. (Key with site guards.)

You can get a preliminary understanding of the site from the mound beside the apse of this church (see plan), from which you are looking out across the excavation to the broad river valley and Mount Ida away to the N.

The irregular remains of paving immediately in front of you indicate the position of the *Upper Court*, and the Palatial-style Minoan buildings (contemporary with the New Palace at Phaistós) occupied an L-shape along the N and W of it; there was evidence for an upper storey. Beyond (N) is the *Lower Court* with its surrounding buildings, reached by a (later) staircase, and beyond that the excavated remains of the settlement or town.

At the E end of the L-shape (under the plastic roof) is a set of rooms where the quality of the architecture suggests an important residential or reception area, with, adjoining to the W, its own storerooms. The grandest residential apartments, with the best view of the sea, named the 'signorile' quarter by the Italian excavators, lay in the NW corner (the angle of the L). Between these two areas was the main storeroom block of the Minoan complex, with many large clay pithoi. Finally to the S of the 'signorile' quarter (beyond the W end of the church) was a more modest block, perhaps for servants or attendants, which included storerooms and a kitchen.

The Minoan buildings of Ayía Triáda have traditionally been known as the *Royal Villa*, perhaps a summer palace of the rulers of Phaistós. Now the excavation report points out that these structures divide themselves into separate sectors, linked together but distinct according to their function. A peculiarity of the Minoan levels is that each quarter, whether grand or modest, had its own storage area, not for merchandise or provisions which were held in the main N storeroom block, but for valued possessions such as articles of pottery, stone and bronze. Each quarter had an independent entrance, and its own staircase to an upper floor; moreover it seems that none of the existing entrances was a principal one for the whole villa complex.

Recently it has been argued that in the distinct E and W wings we are dealing with the remains of not one but two villas, comparable with those for example at Týlissos, and part of the recognised network of estates playing a crucial role in the system of collection and distribution that was the basis of the Minoan economy.

Over part of the Minoan wing on the N side of the Upper Court there were erected, in the later (LMIII) phase, two large rectangular buildings (unshaded on plan) on different axes from the LMI construction; architecturally they resemble the megaron of mainland Mycenaean type. Abutting the first of these 'reoccupation' buildings and associated with it is a 'loggia' (facing onto the Upper Court) with rectangular flagstones and a column base.

Near the E end of the Upper Court two short flights of a narrow *staircase* (1) lead down into the **East Wing** of the L-shape described above. In the Minoan period this wing, which opened onto the E forecourt, consisted of a set of rooms (2) with windows onto light-wells,

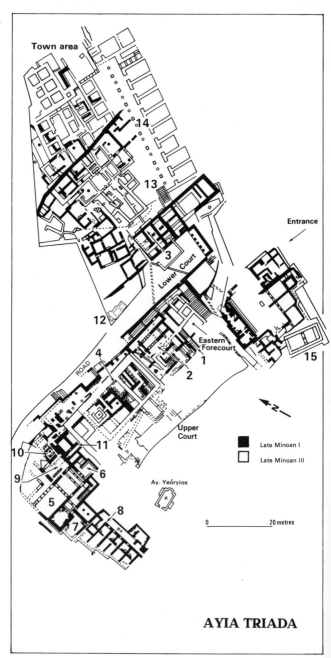

Town area

14

13

Entrance

3

Lower Court

12

Eastern Forecourt

1

2

ROAD

4

Upper Court

Late Minoan I

Late Minoan III

10

11

9

6

5

Ay. Yeóryios

8

7

15

0   20 metres

AYIA TRIADA

gypsum stairs, dadoes, benches, and a drainage system; the remains hint at the refinement of the architecture. (The upper levels of the drainage system belong to the LMIII reoccupation period.)

Originally the Lower Court was a private open space; the broad staircase now leading down to it was a later adaptation. The court was bounded to the E by a five-columned portico, and to the N by a massively built structure (3) known as the *Bastion*. A recent suggestion is that this may have been a warehouse. The paved *Minoan road* to the sea, the Rampa al Mare, led out of this court, along the N façade of the villa buildings. (The stepped section of the road is a LMIII alteration.)

The main *storerooms* (4) still contain a number of pithoi, and one, up stone steps, has five gypsum pithos stands, all severely burnt, as is the threshold itself; here is a vivid reminder of the fire which destroyed this phase of Ayía Triáda c 1450 BC.

At the point where the 'Rampa al Mare' is no longer exposed, turn left up into the **West Wing** where the grandest residential apartments of the LMI period, in what was surely a matter of deliberate choice, enjoyed the sea view. Another paved road runs along the W façade below the retaining wall.

The largest room in the villa (c 6m by 9m) is the *hall* (5) with pier-and-door arrangement on two sides. The E doors lead into two columned porticos (a scheme unusual in Minoan architecture), with breccia column bases, and black and white pebble floor with sunk rectangular basin; then across a narrow lightwell to a small *inner chamber* (6) with benches round the walls. These were covered with a gypsum facing (now restored), with red stucco filling between the slabs; note the recesses for wooden beams. This room leads on the left to a smaller chamber which originally also opened onto the lightwell. The huge, slightly raised *gypsum slab* in the paved floor has been interpreted as a divan base, and it is now suggested that it could have held a wooden bed similar to one found in the excavation at Théra. Both rooms were lit by tall pedestalled stone lamps (originals in the Herákleion museum).

It is considered that this suite provided the public rooms for entertaining guests, and alongside it (N, see below) were those for business affairs. There was an upper floor, over both sets of rooms, which could have been used for official receptions. It certainly contained valuable artefacts, among which, to judge from the scattered pieces found fallen from above in the destruction debris, were the well-known Harvester Vase and the Boxer Rhyton (fragment also in Upper Court); both these vases are of serpentine carved in relief.

The conical beaker known as the Chieftain Cup came from an upper room in the block to the S of this; the scene carved on that vessel is now interpreted as showing a Minoan official receiving tribute of animal hides. All three vases, believed to be products of a Knossós workshop, are prominently displayed in Herákleion Museum, Gallery VII.

The S block adjacent to the reception rooms is seen as servants' quarters and storerooms. The paved area (7) has been plausibly interpreted as a kitchen. with the built-in platforms with circular depressions serving as mortars for the preparation of food. Six pairs of rooms open onto a long N–S corridor (8) which leads in from the S entrance; one storeroom held pithoi and other coarse-ware vessels, clay sealings and loomweights.

N of the reception rooms, in the suite of private or business apartments, is the *archives room* (9). Here, in a gypsum chest, was found a

The Harvester Vase (Herákleion Museum, Gallery VII)

deposit of over 200 clay sealings (bearing impressions of numerous sealstones) thought to have been used to secure bundles of documents. The walls of the inner part of this room were covered with exquisite frescoes (Herákleion Museum, Gallery XIV), including a lady seated in a garden and a cat stalking a pheasant. There are stairs N to a small porticoed lightwell (10) which had a central bowl for rain-water; on the stucco plaster of the walls were scored graffiti in the Linear A script.

Behind this group of rooms and not apparently connecting with it is the small narrow Treasury (11) from which came the 19 bronze 'talents' or ox-hide ingots (raw material of a metalworking industry) now exhibited in the Herákleion museum in the same gallery as the stone vases.

The 'Rampa al Mare' leads back to the Lower Court, passing on the left (N) the remains (12) of MMIA buildings (c 2000 BC). Beyond the Bastion a LMIII stairway (13) descends to the excavated **Town**. Much of this is of LMIII date (14–13C BC), a number of houses being built over or adapted from LMI Minoan buildings. On the right at the foot of the staircase, opposite the town houses, was what seems to have been a row of *shops*, fronted by a columned portico (14) on the same principle as the design of later stoas. The shops are of a regular size, and all have large threshold blocks. This *agorá* is the only such complex so far recognised in Bronze Age excavations on Crete.

Finally, returning across the Lower Court and up the broad staircase out of it, you pass near the *Shrine* (15), subject of an important reassessment as a result of the 1978 stratigraphical examination of the foundations. The building used to be tentatively dated to MMIII– LMI, the New Palace period, though the shrine furnishings, belonging to LMIII, were thought to indicate reuse at that time. It is now clear that the structure (cella and vestibule) is purely LMIII (probably IIIA2, early 14C BC), including the frescoed floor with a seascape of octopus and dolphins, remains of which are now in Herákleion Museum, Gallery XIV. The New Palace period walls which caused the confusion are remains of a substantial Minoan house.

To reach the *cemetery area* turn left outside the site gate and follow the path which hugs the fence. This leads to the scant remains of the two circular stone-built tombs of Ayía Triáda. The better-preserved (eastern) one, Tomb A, was in use EMII–MMI, mid third to early second millenium, and had annexes outside it used as ossuaries and for offerings. The chamber and annexes held in all about 150 individuals; the grave goods included bronze daggers as well as many small clay and stone vases. Tomb B, approximately contemporary, was cleared out and reused in the Postpalatial (LMIII) period. Above this tomb was a rectangular chamber-tomb that contained the famous painted limestone sarcophagus (dated to LMIII), which is now the centrepiece of the main fresco room in Herákleion Museum (Gallery XIV). A tomb nearby with four compartments like rooms cut out of the rock produced an Egyptian seal of Queen Tyi (1411– 1375 BC), wife of Amenhotep III, and also a Hittite sphinx.
  A little way further along the path through the olive grove, (NE of Tomb A), remains of Early Minoan buildings have been uncovered during the last decade, with pottery in the Ayios Onoúphrios style; they are likely to be part of the settlement for which the great round tombs were the cemetery.

From Ayía Triáda a rough road descends to join the main Míres– Timbáki road c 1km W of the Phaistós turn, but as it involves fording the river, it is not always a viable alternative. By returning to Phaistós, you have the choice of going back down the hill to the main road to turn left for (c 20km) *Ayía Galíni* (Rte 12B), or continuing S past the ruined church on the minor road, 11km to the coast at *Mátala* (also possible by bus).

1km from Phaistós the Mátala road bears right on the edge of the village of *Ayios Ioánnis* (rent rooms and tavernas). Just past the corner the little church of *Ayios Pávlos*, hidden behind cypresses in a cemetery surrounded by an old wall, reflects in its architecture a long period of Cretan history.

Ayios Pávlos (restored 1972) is the product of three building phases. The oldest part, which now serves as the bema, is thought to be pre-Christian in date; originally it consisted of no more than a cupola supported by four massive piers between open arches, on a square ground plan. This design recalls the Spring Chambers of Late Roman times, and it may be significant that there is still a well immediately behind the cemetery. In due course the nave was added, with dome resting on a drum, and the open arches under the cupola were blocked where necessary to form the bema as we see it today. (The narthex, with open pointed arches in the Venetian style is a later addition, 15/16C.)
  A frieze round the dome above the nave carries a painted inscription; it is dated 1303–04 but it is not clear whether this refers to a time of construction or of subsequent redecoration. The inscription describes the church as: 'dedicated to the Apostle Paul in a village called Baptistiras [taken to mean the village of St. John], restored and surrounded by a wall', and further states that 'the decoration of a venerable historic building was at the command of the Emperor Andronicos II Palaiologos (1283–1328), his Empress Irene (Yolanda Montferrat) and their son Michael'. The dedication to St. Paul may have been inspired by the legend of his brief stay at Kalí Liménes, on the coast less than 10km away, when he commissioned Titus for the conversion of Crete.
  If a Spring Chamber of antiquity came to serve in due course as a Christian baptistery, that would make this 'venerable historic building' one of the earliest ecclesiastical buildings on the island still in existence.

There are remains of *frescoes* dated by the inscription (1303–04): best preserved are the Punishments of Hell on the W wall, and on the pendentives the Evangelists Matthew (SW) and Luke (NW).

Immediately opposite Ayios Pávlos, a dirt road offers a detour through the olive groves to (3.5km) the Minoan vaulted tomb of *Kamilári, one of the best preserved of this Mesará tomb type. The nearby village of the same name has several pension and simple rent-room establishments, and can be recommended as a base for exploring this part of the island.

After c 2km on the side-road you reach a crossroads near houses, and continue on the track ahead. (The village is to the left.) Pass the rutted cart-track (right) but take the first field track after it (right, c 200m from the crossroads), follow it c 1.5km to a T-junction and turn left. (If this track is boggy after rain, the next one parallel curves round to join it on the higher ground.) 100m from the T-junction the site is on top of the low hill left, fenced (landmark) but not locked.

Built at the beginning of the Palatial era, in MMIB (c 2000 BC), this large communal tomb was in use for several centuries. Its thick stone walls still stand 2m high, and the evidence from the excavation (under the direction of the Italian archaeologist, D. Levi) suggested a roof structure of wooden beams supporting masonry. A complex of five small rooms, beside a paved area outside the entrance to the circular tomb, was used for funerary cult purposes, and in the later periods also for burials.

The Kamilári tomb was robbed in antiquity, but three important clay models found by the excavators are now in Herákleion Museum, Gallery VI. Tentatively dated to the Late Minoan period, these illustrate different aspects of a precise funerary rite. Two are connected with banquets or ritual offerings for the dead; on one of them offerings are being placed on small altars in front of four figures seated in a shrine. The third model shows a group of dancers in a circle, reminiscent of Cretan dance today. The addition of horns of consecration and doves emphasises the ritual setting of the events.

From Ayios Ioánnis the asphalt road continues towards the coast. After 2km you reach the direct Míres–Mátala road and turn right onto it; the village of Síva is hidden in trees across the road (S), and this is the junction described below at the start of the excursion to the Odiyítria monastery and the Ayiophárango.

7.5km from Phaistós you pass through *Pitsídia* (rent rooms and tavernas). Just over 1km beyond the village, at the crest of a hill, is a track to the right for the site of *Kómmos*. An important excavation has been in progress here each summer since 1976, directed by J. Shaw (University of Toronto) under the auspices of the American School of Classical Studies.

After 500m the track forks. On foot you can take the right fork and the site is in view down by the sea (guardian's hut). In a car keep left at the fork; the track deteriorates near a chapel (1km) just above the beach, and from the level area beyond there is a steep path down to the shore for the 5-minute walk (N) through the tamarisk trees to the excavation. This is not open to the public but it can be viewed quite well from outside the fence.

The site consists of a Minoan town (MMIII–LMIII) on the hill at the N end of the excavation. Below, down by the shore, there is a monumental courtyard building (LMI), using Palatial-style ashlar masonry and enormous orthostats; this presumed administrative complex seems to support Evans's original assumption that Kómmos was an important Minoan harbour with a customs post. Along the N side of the building is a paved road which presumably led to Phaistós.

During the Greek period a series of temples (10–1C BC) was built above this LM complex, of which only the latest sanctuary (4–1C BC) is now visible. There is a temple, a hall thought to be a dining-hall, and ancillary buildings grouped around a courtyard containing four altars; abundant evidence was found for sacrifice and feasting. The 10C temple is one of the earliest known in Greece and fragments of Phoenician pottery associated with its foundation may suggest eastern religious influence.

The W-facing bay has one of the finest beaches on Crete; swimmers may notice ancient remains under the sea.

11km from Phaistós (75km from Herákleion) is *Mátala*. The cove around which the village has grown up offers good swimming under cliffs honeycombed with rock-cut Roman tombs (1–2C AD). There are a number of excellent waterfront tavernas, and also accommodation (rent rooms and C/D-class hotels), but Mátala, partly because of its proximity to Phaistós, has been taken over by organised (and disorganised) tourism, and in high season the noisy result may be unappealing. Rooms in the villages back from the coast, mentioned above, are suggested as more tranquil alternatives.

To the Odiyítria Monastery and the Ayiophárango.

This detour from the Phaistós–Mátala road uses unsurfaced roads, rough in places: c 8km to the monastery, 4km further towards the bay of Kalí Liménes for the recommended walk (1 hour to the sea) down the Ayiophárango, or 'holy gorge'. In high summer the number of campers in the gorge may spoil the sense of remoteness which, for the rest of the year, is one of the principal attractions of these W slopes of the Asteroúsia mountains.

2km on the Mátala side of Ayios Ioánnis (see above), at the junction with the road from Míres, a track (S) is signposted in Greek for *Síva* (Σίβας). This cuts off an awkward corner to join the surfaced road, and you proceed uphill into the village where you turn left, cross the plateía with the church on your left, and keep straight on. The dirt road, rough in places, winds through olive groves interspersed with cypresses, and climbs steadily into the foothills of the Asteroúsia mountains, the range which rises from the Mesará plain to drop steeply to the sea along the S coast. After about 3km the White Mountains of W Crete (60–70km away) are in view on a clear day, with in the foreground the distinctive angular Mount Kédros, and the Paximádia islands in the Bay of Mesará. At 4km from the main road, in *Lístaros*, turn right downhill in front of the church. The recently constructed road climbs to a less fertile level, technically garigue (in Greek phrýgana), the scrubby upland typical of so much of the island's landscape; many groups of beehives are scattered about the hillside.

At 8km the monastery of the Panayía Odiyítrias (Our Lady Guide) commands a ridge high above a tributary of the River Ayía Kyriakí which flows to the sea through the Ayiophárango. The position set back from the sea afforded some protection from the pirate raids which plagued this coast in medieval times. The rambling monastery buildings, whitewashed and only partly surrounded by a wall, are dominated by a massive rectangular stone-built tower.

Gerola came here at the turn of the century, and remarked on the familiar pattern: quadrangular enclosure, a large courtyard around a church, but the enclosing wall substantial only on the N and W sides where it bordered on the road. He noted the three gates, a gravestone with an inscription of 1564, the kitchen garden, and was much impressed by the tower of Xopatéras. This was the nickname, meaning ex-priest, of a disgraced monk who achieved fame as leader of a local band of warriors in the 1828 Revolution. The avenging Turks pursued him to the refuge of the tower where, after a heroic struggle against hopeless odds, he perished with all his family.

Legend has it that the attackers had to contend with beehives hurled from the roof of the tower. You may be offered a giant key to unlock the door for the climb to the roof by an internal staircase; the medieval atmosphere is not much disturbed.

In the church the remains of frescoes have been uncovered on the vault of the nave, with scenes from the life of the Virgin. The Odiyítria has a highly regarded collection of icons; the depiction of Christ with the twelve apostles in the branches of a vine is by the 15C painter Angelos, one of the few artists of this date who signed his work. A 15C icon of Ayios Phanoúrios has been removed to hang (No. 4) in the collection in Ayía Aikateríni in Herákleion.

For the Ayiophárango take the fork left just beyond the monastery, towards Kalí Liménes. The road descends for 2.5km, until (immediately after crossing the river-bed) you come to a farm on the right; a large flock of sheep winters here. 1km further, before a bend, a track at an acute angle (right) drops down to the river, leading (after 500m) to the start of the walk down the gorge. (If walking from the monastery you can get down to the river-bed sooner, at the farm.)

At first there is a clear path, but nearer the sea it is necessary to follow the stream-bed, so this expedition is not advisable in the spring, or after heavy rain.

Gradually the valley narrows, and after about 30 minutes the vertical walls of the gorge loom ahead—up to 100m high for a length of 600m. At the far end, with the sea almost in sight, the substantial domed church of Ayios Antónias is built into the rock wall (left), enclosing the grotto chapel asociated with Ayios Ioánnis Xénos, the 11C evangelist.

Once back on the road, it is possible for the adventurous to continue (4km) to the coast, though the surface is exceedingly rough in places. The beautiful bay of *Kalí Liménes* has one of the very few extensive beaches on the S coast of the island. It has been used since antiquity as a sheltered anchorage for ships of passage, 'secure for 10 galleys' according to a Venetian document, and was the Fair Havens of St. Paul, (Acts 27,12). Paul knew that 'the harbour was unsuitable for wintering', but in the strong S winds that are a feature of the weather along this coast there is some shelter in the lee of the two off-shore islands, Megalónisi and Ayios Pávlos. The idyllic view has been radically altered by the building of an oil bunkering station on the latter, but as there is very little associated shore activity, the installation is not necessarily a deterrent. The double-naved chapel on the western headland is dedicated to St. Paul. (Limited accommodation, and tavernas, at scattered points on the long bay.)

In the Greco-Roman period the anchorage was controlled by the city-state of Lasaía. The centre of the city was on the cliffs above an islet 100m off-shore at the E end of the beach. Nothing has been excavated, but a survey of the headland has identified the site of a temple and a probable basilica church, as well as house walls, cisterns and an aqueduct. An unusual feature is the breakwater, built of loosely piled stone blocks, running out from the shore to the islet; a narrow channel was left at the S end, allowing boats to be moved to sheltered water according to changes of wind. It is known that this coast was relatively deserted from medieval times, so the breakwater is likely to be an ancient structure.

A dirt road continues along the coast 10km to Léndas. The main road strikes inland to (c 25km) Míres, via Pigaidákia and Pómbia; some sections were very rough in 1987, but road-works were in progress.

To Ayios Mýron and Priniás.

A round trip from Herákleion of c 60km.

Leave Herákleion as for Phaistós (see start of Rte 4), but at 4.5km turn right for Ayios Mýron; distances are from this junction. The road crosses the stream (keep right at the fork after 1.5km), and winds through a valley densely planted with vines, gaining height gradually. After 7.5km you pass through *Voútes*, and at c 10km there is a fine view back to the sea, and over the main valley running inland from Herákleion, the central line of communication across the island from coast to coast. At 11.5km pass a turn for Kitharída to climb up to (13.5km) *Ayios Mýron*. This attractive village, built on the site of ancient Rávkos, is named after the 3C martyr saint who was born here, and became bishop of Knossós; keep right, on the lower road, to pass his grotto. Steps from it lead up to the big 13–14C church, cross-domed in plan with the later addition of a domed narthex; the drum supporting the main dome is designed with eight linked arches framing slender windows. (The village priest has the church key. Enquire at the kapheneíon opposite.)

At 15.5km *Pirgoú* has a view W across to the lower slopes of Mount Ida and the villages strung along its E flank at the limit of the cultivable land. 19km *Káto Asítes*.

Here a recommended detour leads in 2km to the Gorgolaíni convent. At the beginning of the village fork right and after 150m turn right at the end of the little plateía. The road climbs steeply to the nunnery which enjoys from its terrace a *view unsurpassed on this route. Except for the church of Ayios Yeóryios, the buildings of *Moní Gorgolaíni* are of no great age, but the well-tended nunnery garden is shaded and airy even in the heat of summer.

200m below the main gate on the way back to the village, at a sharp bend right, a rough track diverges left. It is worthwhile for walkers to negotiate a most disagreeable rubbish dump, because the track then crosses a valley through olive groves, and climbs W into the high pastures of the Ida foothills.

Very soon after Káto Asítes is (19.5km) *Ano Asítes* (lower and upper), and just beyond the village a glimpse of an angular hill ahead. At c 22km, the distinctive flat-topped rock formation dominates the view, with the white chapel of Ayios Pandeleímon perched on the E brow, overlooking the N–S valley route. This, the Patéla hill of **Priniás,** was the acropolis of the ancient city of *Rizenía*. The path to the hilltop starts at the crest at 23.5km; it is 10 minutes to the summit (686m, *view).

500m before this you pass the site of the cemetery of Siderospiliá, on a slope facing SE across to the acropolis. Its 680 excavated tombs yielded a continuous sequence of material and of burial rites (late 13–mid 6C BC), its development being contemporary with that of the settlement on the Patéla. The sequence consisted of pit-graves, inhumation in tholos tombs, and cremation burials.

A number of crouch-burials, without grave gifts, were probably associated with the nearby Prepalatial settlement. Roman tombs were also found.

The Italians excavated on the Patéla (1906–08) and returned here in 1969. They identified a refuge site dating from the end of the Bronze Age (LMIII), comparable to Karphí or Vrókastro. From the sanctuary near the E edge of the plateau came a goddess figurine with cylindrical skirt and raised hands similar to those from Gázi and Karphí on display in the Herákleion museum, also numerous votive terracottas including snakes and curious tubes with columns of loop handles. The sanctuary continued in use till the Archaic period.

At the W end of the hill are the ruins of a square Hellenistic fortress with corner bastions, but the most important remains on the acropolis are the excavated foundations of two 7C *temples* (fenced in the middle of the plateau).

The earlier, and better preserved, *Temple A*, is said to show Minoan influence on the Archaic Greek 'templum in antis' plan; instead of the expected two columns at the front of the porch (pronaos) between the 'antae', or side-posts, Temple A had one central pillar. In line with this inside the temple, on the long axis of the cella, there were (as at Dréros, Rte 7) two wooden columns on low stone bases with a hearth between them. Some of the sculptures which decorated the entrance to the temple were retrieved, and are well displayed in Herákleion Museum, Gallery XIX. They include two seated female figurines in the Daidalic style, from above the doorway into the cella, and fragments in low relief from friezes depicting lions and a procession of mounted spearmen.

The road continues through the village of *Priniás*, and, 5km from the site, rejoins the main Phaistós route in Ayía Varvára (p 117).

From Ayía Varvára to Valsamónero and Kamáres.

At the end of the long village of Ayía Varvára (p 117), a road branches off right, signposted Yérgeri and Kamáres, to run along the S foothills of the *Ida* massif. This recommended route (c 26km from Ayía Varvára) is scenically most rewarding driven from E to W. At the first bend out of the village there is a glimpse of the Libyan sea ahead. Beyond (10km) Yérgeri is a fine view of the *Paximádia islands* in the Bay of Mesará.

At 15km *Zarós* is a large village (pop. 2000) with abundant water; the spring here used to feed the aqueduct that supplied the numerous fountains of the great city of Górtyn. Just above the village there is a Class C hotel in a tranquil situation beside a stream.

To the NW of Zarós is the Monastery of Ayios Nikólaos where a curious little church has frescoes of two periods (14C and 15C).

You can reach the monastery by car: 500m beyond the end of the village take a track right that climbs 2km up a valley. On foot there is a shorter path: 200m before the end of the village a narrow street to the right (the first after the turning signed for the hotel) leads, past a chapel set back from the road, to the old route (c 20 minutes) between village and monastery.

This is a flourishing monastic community. The N aisle of Ayios Nikólaos was the original church, and has the earlier (14C) paintings, including a tender scene, on the N side of the bema, of the birth of the Virgin. The monastery lies at the bottom of a gorge. You can ask for directions to the cave church, also painted, of Ayios Evtímios (c 45 minutes up the hillside), or follow the path up the gorge, a walk of a little under 2 hours to the chapel of Ayios Ioánnis at the top.

At 21km from Ayía Varvára, the ***Monastery of Vrondísi** is signposted (right, 2km). Outside the monastery, shaded by two great plane trees, is a 15C Venetian *fountain* with figures (damaged) of Adam and Eve. The terrace enjoys an extensive view across foothills to the Mesará plain.

In the courtyard is the two-aisled church with bellcote. The older S aisle, dedicated to Ayios Antónios, preserves the remains of some greatly-admired frescoes dating from the first half of the 14C; these are early examples of the widely-diffused style known as *The Cretan School*, a specific trend in Palaiologan painting. In the vaulting of the apse is painted the Last Supper, a scene that occurs in this position at no other church on Crete; below it is the Apostle Communion. Also unique on Crete (in wall-painting) is the figure, on the right of the Hierarchs, of Simeon holding the Christ child.

By the end of the Venetian period Vrondísi was one of the most influential monastic communities on the island; the inscription dated 1630–36 (over one of the cell doors) came from the main gateway destroyed in 1913. The six icons by Damaskinós, now in Ayía Aikateríni in Herákleion, hung in this monastery church.

Back on the road it is 3km to the village of *Vorízia*. On the way you can see across the valley the red roof and triangular gable of the bellcote of the *church of Ayios Phanoúrios, which contains some of the finest examples of the Cretan frescoes.

A turn-off to the left at the end of the village is signposted Valsamónero. 200m downhill is the house (left, opposite a kapheneíon) of the 'phýlakas' or guardian. The arrangement is that he opens the church 08.00–13.00, but if necessary you can return here and make enquiries; avoid the siesta hours in summer. Continue 2.5km along the track keeping left at the fork just outside the village.

The church of **Ayios Phanoúrios** (a Rhodian saint) is all that remains of the once influential *Valsamónero* monastery. Its exterior is one of the best examples on the island of Venetian influence on Byzantine church architecture; on the S façade the main doorway has carved rosette decoration and over the door into the narthex is a Venetian coat-of-arms with a wreath and interwoven leaf motif. As a result of several building phases Ayios Phanoúrios has acquired a highly unusual ground plan: there are two parallel *naves* or *aisles* on the usual E–W axis, and a third at right-angles across their W end forming a *transept*. Alongside this, there is also a *narthex*.

The original nave along the N wall, erected in 1328, is dedicated to the Panayía (Virgin Mary). She was depicted in the bema above the Apostle Communion, and on the barrel vaulting of the nave there is the most complete set of scenes from her life (the *Hymns to the Mother of God*) known in Cretan fresco painting.

The S aisle (just inside the main door) is dedicated to Ayios Ioánnis Prodrómos (the forerunner, St. John the Baptist). The new building was completed by 1406–07 but was not decorated until 1428. The frescoes include a scene of St. John in the desert, where the elongated figures have been compared to the work of El Greco.

The transept honours Ayios Phanoúrios. The frescoes were painted by Konstantínos Ríkos in 1431 (inscription next to the doorway through to the narthex). In the E wall at the S end of the transept there is a miniature apse, with the Pantokrátor in the vaulting, and below this the Communion of the Angels, with Christ as high-priest offering communion to the richly-clad angels in heaven. This rarely-found scene here replaces its counterpart in the theme of the Divine Liturgy, the Communion of the Apostles. Scenes of the miracles of Ayios Phanoúrios are preserved on the E wall, and on the pillar he is depicted as a soldier-saint.

From Vorízia it is 3.5km on along the road to *Kamáres*. Just out of Vorízia the track into the mountains has been widened by bulldozers, at the start of the old route round the flank of Mount Ida to the Nída plain above Anóyia (Rte 3A). From the village of Kamáres a very steep path climbs (4–5 hours) to the **Kamáres cave** which gave its name to some of the finest polychrome pottery of the prehistoric world (Herákleion Museum, Gallery III, and see p 125).

The cave, at 1524m, was discovered by a shepherd only in 1890. It was investigated in 1904 by the Italians (under L. Mariani) who found the first examples of 'Kamáres ware' dating from the period of the Old Palaces (c 1900–1700 BC). In 1913 the site was fully excavated by the British. There was evidence for occupation during the Neolithic period, after which the cave became a sanctuary.

The climb to the cave is definitely an expedition only for experienced walkers; the route is marked rather erratically with orange paint, but these splashes are not always easy to see on the descent. Guides are sometimes available; enquire at the kapheneíon by the church (just left of the through road). There is simple overnight accommodation in the village.

At the Herákleion end of Kamáres, the walk to the cave starts up a side-street almost opposite the cemetery; after 200m, leave the track (before it is blocked by a new building) and up the bank (right) look for the first of the paint splashes. The path climbs steeply up the watercourse following a pipeline. The first landmark (after about 1 hour), is a group of water troughs. Then you strike E to the edge of the trees, looking for marked rocks which lead up to a second water point: troughs and a spring. From here it is a further hour's climb to the *cave* which is soon in view. For many years the cave-mouth has been the home of a noisy colony of Alpine choughs.

There are time-honoured paths NW to the summit of Psilorítis, and N around the shoulder to the other great sanctuary on the mountain, the Idaian cave (see Rte 3A), but for these expeditions a guide is advisable. Consult the Greek Alpine Club in Herákleion, tel. 227 609.

From the village of Kamáres a minor road runs down to Vóri and (20km) Phaistós. Alternatively you can continue (c 12km) to Apodoúlou at the S end of the Amári valley (Rte 12A).

Ayii Déka to Pýrgos and Herákleion (63km). The road also contin-ues E from Pýrgos, unfinished (1987) and very rough for c 10km, to Skiniás and Viánnos, on the way to E Crete by the route S of Lasíthi (see Rte 8). This is a section of the projected S Coast Highway.

The well-surfaced road branches off the main Herákleion–Phaistós route 1km on the Herákleion side of Ayii Déka (p 118), and runs E along the intensively-cultivated Mesará plain. You pass (4km) *Gagáles*, and at (8km) *Stóli* keep right (ignoring a left turn to Ayios Thomás that cuts back to the main Herákleion road). Continue through (12km) *Asími*. At 19.5km you reach a T-junction with the main Pýrgos–Herákleion road: turn right for (5km) Pýrgos, Viánnos and the SE coast of the island (p 180); for Herákleion turn left.

The road N climbs out of the fertile plain to (23.5km) *Ligórtinos* and (26km) *Tephéli*, and winds through the vineyards and olive groves of the upland valleys of central Crete. At 35km there is a turn left for (c 3km) *Moní Epanosíphi*. From the high point at the turning the view to the N includes Júktas, the isolated peak behind Herákleion, and Prophítis Ilías, site of the Castle of Témenos (Rte 3D).

The Epanosíphis monastery is thought to have been founded towards the end of the period of Venetian rule, c 1600; the original church, dedicated to Ayios Yeóryios, was destroyed in an earthquake in 1856. This was a particularly wealthy monastery with valuable land and property, and the community still flourishes, now under the jurisdiction of the cathedral in Herákleion. During the Turkish period it was a centre of learning, and, like so many other monasteries on the island, gave constant support to the cause of Cretan nationalism, for which it suffered severely.

There are great celebrations here on the feast of Ayios Yeóryios (23 April unless this falls in Holy Week). At other times it is a tranquil, well-tended place with a beautiful view from the terrace below the church over fertile but sparsely-populated countryside. The 19C traveller Robert Pashley remembered the cypresses and palm trees of this 'retreat from the busy hum of men'.

The road across the island continues through (43.5km) *Khoudétsi*—at 440m the highest village on this route—and then descends to join in 2km the main Herákleion–Viánnos road (Rte 3C) just outside Pezá. At 58km there is (ahead) one of the less familiar views of the Palace of Knossós, and shortly afterwards (see Rte 2) you reach the outskirts of Herákleion.

From Górtyn to Léndas (Lebéna), c 30km (18 miles).

On the main Herákleion–Phaistós road, just before the basilica of Ayios Títos (see p 122), is the left turn for Léndas on the S coast. (Distances from this junction.) After 500m, in *Mitrópolis*, you pass (right) the excavated remains of one of Górtyn's basilicas, with an unusual tri-conch plan. The 5C building was perhaps a martyrion. The polychrome mosaic floor (using some 15 colours) in the S apse is among the finest mosaics on the island; a border of bands and guilloche frames a free design of birds among flowers.

From Mitrópolis there is a recommended detour to (1.5km) the remains of a *Minoan villa* or farm near Kanniá. 750m from the main road, the Léndas road widens slightly at a small plateía. Take an unsigned narrow street to the right. By the big red-domed church at the end bear right and left, cross a stream (Mitropolianós, see Górtyn), and turn left along it. After 600m you pass (left) a white chapel (Ayios Phanoúrios) and 500m beyond it take the first track to the right. Stop after 150m where the track bears right and the (roofed) excavation is in view ahead. The site is fenced but there is a good vantage point on the far side.

This was a LMI farmhouse with a large number of storerooms containing pithoi (many still in situ). It was destroyed (like so many other Cretan sites) c 1450 BC but was reinhabited in LMIII. A household *shrine* from this period (contents in Herákleion Museum, Gallery X) had clay goddesses in the typical posture with raised arms.

The road now crosses the Mesará plain, watered by the Ieropótamos river (ancient Lethaíos or Lethe), to (5km) *Plátanos*.

On the edge of the village are the excavated remains of two Early–Middle Minoan *tombs*, circular stone-built communal burial chambers in use over a long period. They are signposted to the right in the village, and after 300m you turn right again. There are many of these tombs throughout the Mesará, and a few elsewhere on Crete, but Tombs A and B at Plátanos are the largest known; the internal diameter of Tomb A is 13m, and its wall is nearly 3m thick. These tombs are always free-standing, with a single low entrance on the E side. For the smaller ones the vault may have been completed in stone, but these Plátanos tombs were probably roofed in a lighter material: mudbrick or small stones on a framework of wooden beams, brushwood and thatch have all been suggested.

A walled trench outside Tomb A (the first you come to on the site) contained a very large number of small stone vases, presumably for ritual use. In Tomb B was found the Babylonian haematite cylinder seal of the period of Hammurabi, 1792–1750 BC (Herákleion Museum, Gallery I, Case 11).

The Léndas road continues 2km to *Plóra*, and on the far side of the village keeps left at a fork towards Apesokári. The right fork leads in 10km to the isolated monastery, **Moní Apezanón**, founded in the Venetian period. At the turn of the century G. Gerola, in his survey of Crete's Venetian monuments, described the impressive pentagonal wall enclosing the monastic buildings, with towers, a defended gateway, turreted and loop-holed battlements, and enough still remains (despite modern additions and restoration) to convey some of the original effect. There is an active community, with eight monks in residence.

From Plóra (asphalt surface for 4km, improvements under way) you climb to a less cultivated level with rewarding views across the foothills of the Asteroúsia range. Continue 6km, through *Ayios Kýrillos*, and just above the village fork right (sign). 2km further on, fork right again beside a red-roofed chapel; from a long way off a line of cypresses marks the Apezanés monastery buildings. The original N entrance is a little beyond the modern gate.

The Léndas road (from Plóra) arrives at an oblique T-junction just short of Apesokári, and you turn sharp right for the steep climb S into the *Asteroúsia* mountains. On the left of this next stretch of road, on the hill just SW of the village of Apesokári, is one of the best-preserved tombs of the Mesará type, with circular chamber standing to over 1m high, and ancillary ossuary chambers.

At 12km, on a spur, the road has cut through an unexcavated MMIII site. The cliffs to the left of the road are often of interest to bird-watchers. Looking back you can distinguish the Palace of Phaistós on its ridge jutting out into the Mesará plain; in Minoan times it must have been an impressive sight on this approach to the plain from the coves of the S coast.

18.5km *Miamoú*, where a cave site (now under the houses of the village) was excavated by the Italian A. Taramelli in 1895; the finds dating back to the Neolithic period included hearths and food debris, including shellfish remains. The evidence pointed to human occupation from the Final Neolithic to early in the EMII period (c 2500 BC), when the cave became a burial place.

The road descends, with fine coastal views. The conspicuous conical hill to the E is *Kóphinas*; on the precipitous summit the Minoans established a peak sanctuary.

29km **Léndas**, site of ancient Lebéna. Therapeutic springs made this a renowned sanctuary for healing, with a *temple of Asklepios* dating from the 4C BC and still important in Roman times; it was restored in the 2C AD, the great building period at Górtyn, of which this settlement was a harbour. The Hellenistic sanctuary was superimposed on a preceding cult of water deities. At the beginning of the century the Italian Mission excavated here.

The sanctuary site (fenced but not locked) lies on the left of the road at the beginning of the modern village. The temple, on an artificial terrace, consisted of a simple *cella* (12m by 13m) with a *podium* for the statue of the god against the W (inner) wall. Two *granite columns* still stand in front of the podium area. In the Hellenistic period the walls were of stone, but in the Roman restoration they were given a lining of brick. Near the statue base dedicated by Xenion (inscription on loose fragment) is a scrap of Roman mosaic. At the NE corner of the temple was the *Treasury*, which has a Hellenistic (3C BC) pebble mosaic floor executed in black, white and red, depicting a sea-horse framed in a scroll of waves, with two delicate palmettes. The floor was damaged in antiquity by the sinking of a shaft to hold offerings (see dedicatory inscriptions). Leading N from the Treasury was a colonnaded *Stoa*, and all along the E side a broad flight of marble steps (traces preserved) gave access to the raised level of the stoa and temple. 15m to the E of the steps the excavators uncovered a *tiled arch*, part of the building above the Asklepieion's therapeutic spring. (On the hillside a little below the temple were two great basins, perhaps for the total immersion of the sick.)

The sanctuary complex included a hostel to lodge the pilgrims; the excavation uncovered texts inscribed on the walls of this building. The ritual included the reading of votive tablets in a local Doric dialect. The therapeutic powers of the god are vividly described: one sufferer from sciatica was cured whilst he slept.

Bounding the Bay of Lebéna on the W is Cape Léndas (lion) and on the hill above was a Minoan settlement. In the vicinity of Léndas the eminent Greek archaeologist S. Alexíou excavated five large Early–Middle Minoan *tombs* of the circular Mesará type (see Plátanos, above). One lies E at Zervoús, two just W of Léndas at Papoúra, and two others c 2km to the W at Xerókambos. One of these last two produced a great deposit of vases of EMI date, and out of the whole group of tombs came three Egyptian scarabs (11th Dynasty).

In the village there is a local *phýlakas*, a guardian for the archaeological sites, who will help with directions; ask at the *kapheneíon* set back from the beach. Léndas is little more than a cluster of tavernas on a cove. It has simple rooms to rent, and two long beaches, one a 15-minute walk over the promontory to the W.

A fair dirt road leads W along the coast 10km to *Kali Liménes* (see p 136).

II EASTERN CRETE

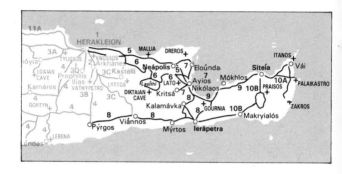

5   Herákleion to Mállia and Ayios Nikólaos

Direct route to Ayios Nikólaos by North Coast Highway (New Road) 70km (43 miles). 7km Amnisós—26km Khersónisos—37km Palace of Mállia.

The first stretch of the Old Road serves the archaeological sites of Amnisós and Nírou Kháni, as well as the airport, beaches and tourist hotels, and therefore is described below as an alternative exit from Herákleion. The detour to the Cave of Skoteinó could make an easy half-day excursion (round trip c 50km).

Frequent bus service to Mállia and Ayios Nikólaos from the main bus station near the harbour, using both the New and Old Road routes. For the Palace of Mállia, which is beyond the town, take a bus going on to Ayios Nikólaos and get off at the Palace turning.

In summer, a blue 'town' bus (No. 1) runs every 20 minutes from the centre of Herákleion, Plateía Elevtherías, to the Amnisós beaches (see Rte 1 bus information). Out of season, long-distance buses on the Old Road will stop.

Join the N Coast Highway from the Knossós road (Rte 2). Distances along the New Road route are from this highway junction. (The new kilometre posts are calculated from Khaniá). Soon the airport is in view below left, and beyond it the off-shore island of Día.

It is 7km to the exit for *Amnisós* and the Old Road.

The Old Road léaves the centre of Herákleion from Plateía Elevtherías below the Archaeological Museum, and runs through the unattractive modern suburb of *Póros*, in Minoan times one of the harbour areas of Knossós.

Here the Greek archaeologist S. Alexíou excavated a Late Neolithic settlement, and also an important Minoan cemetery contemporary with the last years of the Palace of Knossós (c 1450–1380). At Póros, in 1971, in a LMIIIB floor deposit, was found a scarab of Ankhesenamun, wife of Tutankhamun, significant in determining the absolute chronology of Late Minoan Crete.

After 2km the road crosses the bed of the Kaíratos, the stream which runs down the Knossós valley. This suburb, now the edge of town, is Néa Alikarnássos. 300m beyond the bridge, an insignificant right turn is signed for the New Road. The Old Road continues past this turning and at 3km takes the right fork signposted Ayios Nikólaos. (The spur straight ahead ends at the airport.) You bend left round a military establishment and run parallel to the highway before descending, beyond the airport, to the Bay of Amnisós.

At 6km a small cave church (right) is dedicated to Ayios Ioánnis Prodrómos (the Baptist; feast day 29 August).

7km The *municipal beach*, Karterós, is signposted. There is a token charge for simple facilities: cabins, chairs, umbrellas. A bar serves light refreshments. There are also some beach hotels along this bay, otherwise the bathing is unrestricted, and very popular in high summer with both local people and tourists. There are several access points between a track opposite the cave church (see above) and the extreme E end of the bay, surprisingly named *Tobrouk* (good fish tavernas). Far out in this bay the currents can sometimes be treacherous and even strong swimmers should take care.

For some years there has been a Riding Centre opposite the turning for the municipal beach; rides are organised up the Karterós valley and into the hills (tel. 081 282 005. English spoken).

8km **Amnisós**, mentioned in Linear B tablets, was another of the harbours of Minoan Knossós. From here Idomeneus set sail for the Trojan War. A turning right for Episkopí is also the junction with the North Coast Highway.

To visit the Amnisós antiquities turn left towards the sea, just beyond the highway junction, on a track marked Plaz Amnisós. The low hill which rises from the sea-shore has Minoan remains around its base; the ruins on the summit are of a 16C Venetian village.

Under the E side of the hill, now an insalubrious spot behind the Go-Kart track, is the excavated site of a *Minoan villa* built c 1600 BC and contemporary with the New Palace at Knossós. This is known as the *House of the Lilies*, from the graceful floral frescoes that decorated its walls (now in Herákleion Museum, Gallery XIV).

The site is fenced, but the best vantage point is on the seaward side where the villa's flagged *terrace* is immediately in front of you. This had a fine view out to sea, and behind it a spacious room which, with six sets of folding doors, could be a cool retreat open to the terrace, or an enclosed hall protected from winter storms. The *frescoes* were found in the SW area of the house, the main room with bases for two columns. The *W façade* was built of massive ashlar blocks, some of which have been toppled out of place, presumably by earthquake action. Burnt patches on the stones are a reminder of the fierce fire that destroyed the villa c 1450 BC.

The site was excavated in the 1930s by the Greek archaeologist S. Marinátos and re-examined in 1983 by a team from Heidelberg University. This was one of the sites where Marinátos found a quantity of the laval by-product pumice, which led him to relate the 1450 BC destruction level here and at many other sites on Crete to an eruption on the volcanic island of Théra (Santorini) only c 100km to the N. The relationship has been questioned, partly because pottery styles suggest that the destruction on Crete was later than the eruption which engulfed the Bronze Age sites on Santorini. Two learned sessions of the 'Thera Congress' (1971 and 1978) attended by archaeologists and a wide range of interested scientists have shown only that there is no simple, generally agreed correlation.

You can walk along the beach under the hill. On its W side, and also excavated by Marinátos, is the Archaic (6C BC) *Sanctuary of Zeus Thénatas*. The site is fenced but you can look down on it. Associated with a large round open-air altar were two life-size eagles in stone (Herákleion Museum, Gallery XIX). The massive foundation wall re-uses blocks from a Late Bronze Age building. A little further W where the rocks run down into the sea are the remains of substantial constructions below the shore line. These are thought to be LMI harbour works from the ancient port of Knossós.

On the hill-side above Amnisós is a *cave* sacred to Eileíthyia, goddess of fertility and childbirth. This was an important place of worship from Late Neolithic (see Herákleion Museum, Gallery I, Case 1) to Roman times, and was known to Homer (Od. XIX 188). The cave entrance is closed. Most people will probably be content to identify the sanctuary site, but for those who wish to explore the cave, the Archaeological Service guardian at the Minoan villa site of Nírou Kháni has the key (see below).

At the Amnisós junction with the New Road follow signs, leading under the highway, for Episkopí. The road climbs, at first W across the hill, but after a sharp bend the drop to seaward is on the left, and (1.5km from the highway) the cave is signed (left), just before a gully which the road crosses on a culvert. The cave entrance is 30 paces below the road under a fig tree. Walkers can approach straight up the gully, from which the tree is also visible.

The cave, first investigated early this century by J. Khatzidákis, was fully excavated by S. Marinátos (1920s). It has stalagmites, round one of which was a

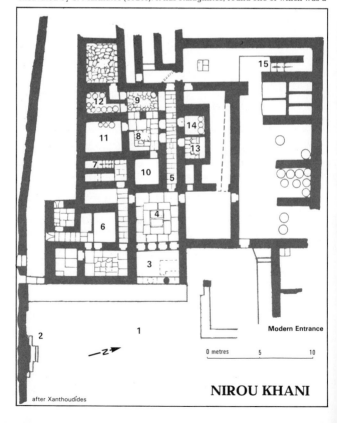

NIROU KHANI

after Xanthoudídes

0 metres   5   10

Modern Entrance

low wall suggesting that it played a part in the worship of Eileíthyia; the small terrace in front of the cave mouth also showed signs of ritual activity.

From Amnisós the Old Road follows the coast to the next sandy bay. At the far end of it, below a large hotel, stands the chapel of Ayii Theódori. A Minoan harbour and dockyard were investigated here in the 1920s; swimmers may notice traces of the installations under water.

At 13km a bridge crosses a gully just before (right) the villa of **Nírou Kháni** (sign on left). Open (summer 1987) 09.00–15.00; Sunday –14.30; closed Monday. Admission free.

This was a large Minoan country house of at least two storeys (LMIA, contemporary with the New Palaces), and the remains are among the best preserved of their kind on the island. The interior of the house is railed off, but all points of interest can be viewed from outside it.

See Plan: 1. paved courtyard with *raised paths* across it;
2. stepped platform where part of *horns of consecration* was found;
3. *main entrance* between two columns, and then through a typically Minoan pillar-and-door scheme to 4., a *hall* with gypsum dado and decorative floor paving;
5. *corridor*, originally frescoed, leading W to the central block of the house;
6. a room where four large, thin and therefore presumably ceremonial double axes were found, along with a heap of ashes, possible evidence for a *shrine* with a hearth for burnt offerings.

The main rooms are best seen from the far end by area 9. On the way round the S front you pass (7) the foundations of the *staircase* and its return. At the centre of the house is the *Room of the Benches* (8) with its integral light-well (9). There was a room above, also with benches, and also opening onto the light-well, thus creating a sheltered environment here at all seasons. Behind the Room of the Benches, and accessible only from it, is room 10, where four stone lamps were found. Rooms 11 and 12 contained about 40 tripod *tables for offerings*, stacked in piles. In 13 there is a built seat, and 14 contained a further three tables for offerings. In the light of these curious finds suggestions have been made about possible missionary activity, or the export of ritual paraphernalia from the harbour of Ayii Theódori (see above). The religious element is recognised in the name given to the site, the 'House of the High Priest'.
On the way out you will notice five storage bins (15) built of mud-brick, with steps up to them, and to the S a deposit of large storage jars.
Finds from the villa are in Herákleion Museum, Gallery VII, where the double axes are strikingly displayed on (reconstructed) poles and bases.

The road continues past a large American Air Force Base. Soon afterwards The Old Road joins the N Coast Highway below a prominent hill crowned by a radar station (16.5km from Herákleion by the highway).

At 17.5km (New Road distances) a.turning to the right is signposted for *Goúves*, for (8.5km) the sacred **Cave of Skoteinó**. This detour is also recommended as a walk; buses stop at the turning on the highway.

The road climbs gently to (1.5km) *Goúves*. There are seats provided along the way and the village has several kapheneíons in the plateía. At 3.5km is a sign-posted turn right to (4.5km) the village of *Skoteinó*. Keep left through the village and at 6km, on a corner, a track branches off to the right, signposted for the last 2.5km to the cave. At the final rise the sea is in view (right) and Mount Díkte is behind you to the E. Ahead, on bare upland, a white church (Ayía Paraskeví, dating from the period of the Venetian occupation) marks the mouth of the cave. From the crest beyond the church there is a fine view across the centre of the island.

The huge cave of Skoteinó (the name means dark) is one of the most important sanctuary sites on Crete. 160m deep, with four levels and steeply sloping galleries, it was first investigated by Sir A. Evans and has been thoroughly studied by the French speleologist P. Faure. In 1962 the Greek archaeologist C. Daváras excavated here; the finds ranged from MMI (c 2000 BC) to the Roman period, and included three important bronze statuettes, LMI male votaries. Dating from the last great flowering of the Minoan culture, these figures wear only the loincloth and stand in the typical position, right hand raised to forehead (Herákleion Museum, Gallery III).

At 23km on the highway is the turn for the Plateau of Lasíthi (Rte 6).

26km. The flourishing holiday resort of **Khersónisos** is strictly Limín Khersónisou (port of Khersónisos), because the village of that name now lies a short distance inland. On the way into the town there is a signed turning for a minor road that climbs inland 2km to *Piskopianó*, (folk museum). The main road runs straight through Khersónisos, and is lined with souvenir shops, banks, motor bikes for hire and other trappings of tourism; a turning left signed to the *port* leads down to the waterfront lined with tavernas.

Khersónisos was an important Greco-Roman harbour town, its anchorage sheltered and defended by the rocky headland to the N called Kastrí. This was the port of Lýttos c 15km inland, but must have been autonomous at least by the 4C when it issued its own coinage. Ancient Khersónisos had a famous temple dedicated to Britomartis, which was mentioned by the 1C BC Greek historian, Strabo. The city continued to flourish in the Roman period, during which a great aqueduct was built to bring water from the Kastélli Pediádas region, probably from the spring near Ayios Pandeleímon (Rte 3C). Ruins of the aqueduct (1–2C AD) can be seen beside the road up to Lasíthi (Rte 6).

Halfway along the waterfront (see plan) the road narrows, and bends around a much restored Roman *fountain*, in the form of a pyramid with an elaborate channelling system and remains of mosaics (2–3C AD) which include a fishing scene. Though the sea level has risen about 1 metre since the Roman period, vestiges of ancient harbour works can be seen in the water off the little point here. At right-angles to the shore is the southerly *mole*, its surface awash. With a second, L-shaped, quay on the line of the modern one jutting out from the Kastrí, this formed the Roman *harbour*, the safest anchorage on the N Coast between Herákleion and Oloús (Eloúnda). Breakwaters of large boulders outside the moles gave increased protection. To the left, N of the same point by the fountain, are remains of the Roman concrete *quay* along the shore. This is preserved for 30m or so above the water and the N section has a line of rectangular bollards 8–9m apart on its seaward edge; it has been estimated that the Roman harbour provided 330m of wharfage. Along the shore, just to the right (S) of the point, large dressed stone blocks are the remnants of earlier Hellenistic harbour works.

The rocky headland of *Kastrí* marked by the white chapel of Ayía Paraskeví was fortified in the Late Roman period. On its top (reached from the steps to the left of the large modern café) are the excavated remains (A. Orlandos, 1959) of an early 6C triple-aisled basilica *church*. This is one of the largest basilicas known on Crete and was probably the seat of the local bishop. Its spectacular position must have made it an impressive landmark for shipping. The mosaic floors are not well preserved but note a 2C AD Attic sarcophogus lid re-used as the altar base. The apse is unusual in being included in a rectangle. On the seaward side of the basilica, the headland meets the sea in a flat rock-shelf, and at the E end of the shelf, just submerged, are three rock-cut rectangular compartments (the largest 4m by 3m) which are thought to be Roman *fish-tanks*. These were

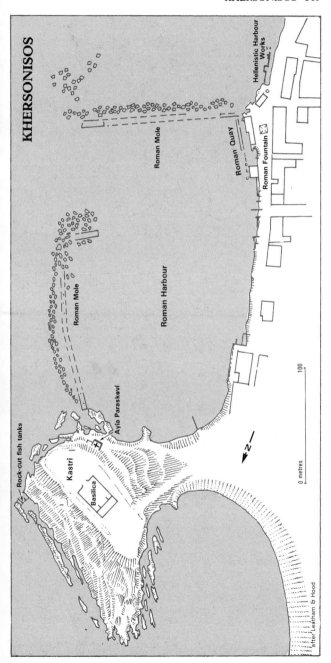

KHERSONISOS

Rock-cut fish tanks

Kastri

Basilica

Ayia Paraskevi

Roman Mole

Roman Harbour

Roman Mole

Roman Quay

Roman Fountain

Hellenistic Harbour Works

0 metres   100

after Leatham & Hood

walled and had a system of cut channels for a constant supply of fresh sea-water.

30km *Stalís* is a nebulous area of inexpensive holiday accommodation. A minor road climbs by zigzags, 9km to *Mokhós*, a village round a large shady plateía.

At 34km you reach modern *Mállia*; there is a fine long sandy beach (sign in the centre of the town) but the atmosphere of the resort is typified by the road down to the sea: a kilometre of bars, pubs and discotheques.

The archaeological site is to the E, 2km beyond the modern town. The turning from the highway is signposted (500m to the entrance gate). The walk along the beach, longer but more pleasant than the busy main road, has not been improved by an unsightly pipeline carrying water to Sísi. (No refreshments at the site.)

The Minoan Palace and town of **MALLIA** (ancient name unknown) lie on the narrow coastal plain just inland from the sea, on the route between Central and E Crete that passed to the N of the Lasíthi plateau and its girdle of mountains. Rising steeply behind the little church of Prophítis Ilías is *Mount Seléna* (1559m), which dominates this N side of the Lasíthi range.

Open (1987) 08.45–13.00; Sunday 09.30–14.30. Admission Drs 200.

The site was first explored by the Greeks under J. Hatzidákis, but since 1922 it has been systematically excavated by the French School at Athens which published the excellent 'Guide des fouilles françaises en Crète' (1966, updated 1978), available from the Herákleion and Ayios Nikólaos museums, but not at the site itself. (The site plans of Mállia distinguish areas by the Greek alphabet.) The Old Palace, like those at Knossós and Phaistós, was founded c 1900 BC in MMIB, and suffered a great destruction, as they did, c 1700 BC. After rebuilding, the New Palace flourished until LMIB when c 1450 BC both it and the main dependent buildings were destroyed. A few parts of the site, notably House E, were reoccupied in LMIII.

The remains on the site now open to the public are principally those of the New Palace period, MMIII–LMI, c 1700–1450 BC.

The Palace is approached from the paved *West Court*; note the flagstone paths forming raised walks, a typical Minoan device. One of these paths serves the N Entrance (see below), and another runs along, though not exactly parallel to, the W front. At the S end of this façade, and dating from the Old Palace, is a double row of circular structures (1), eight in all, each 5m in diameter. These pits were probably used as silos or granaries, and from the presence of the central pillars it is deduced that they were roofed.

It is possible to follow the *S front* of the (New) Palace, just inside the wire fence on your right, past the narrow opening to a Shrine, to the *Main Entrance* (2). The flagged passage of the Entrance was probably cut off from the Central Court by an extension of the wall at its N end, so that entry was effected indirectly, by turning left through a door into an antechamber (3), which gave onto a paved terrace (4) from which two steps led to the Court. Set in the terrace floor is a circular limestone table known as the Mállia *kernos*, with a large hollow at its centre and 34 smaller ones round the circumference. This has been interpreted as an *offering table* for rituals associated with harvested first fruits, or the fertility of seed, but many other explanations are also possible. Just to the N are the lower steps of a monumental Staircase (5).

The **Central Court**, more than twice as long as it is wide (48m by 22m) lies on the same NNE–SSW axis as those at Knossós and

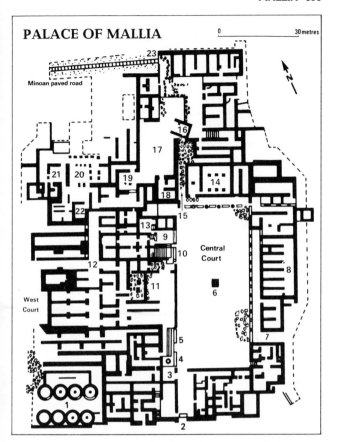

PALACE OF MALLIA

0   30 metres

Minoan paved road

23

16

17

N

21 20   19   14

22   18

15

13   8

9

12   10   Central
                  Court

11   6

West
Court

5   7

4

3

1

2

Phaistós. It is not certain whether the surface was paved all over, or only in certain areas. In the exact centre is a shallow *pit* (6) lined with mud-brick, and with four mud-brick stands in it. This may have been an altar, perhaps associated with the cult of the Pillar Crypt in the W Wing, as it is aligned between the pillars of that room (see below). It has also been suggested that its exact central position was of significance in the original laying out of the Court and its surrounding buildings. Along the E side of the Central Court was a gallery or portico supported by alternate columns and pillars, a stylistic arrangement much favoured by the Minoans, presumably for decorative reasons. Pairs of round post-holes between each pillar and column base may indicate a balustrade.

Behind the portico, at its S end, is the *E Entrance Corridor* (7) and N of it a *storeroom block* (8). The equipment in these storerooms (now for security reasons inside a locked shed) would have held oil and wine. There are raised platforms for storage vessels with spouts for drainage near their bases, also separating tubs for oil and channels for collecting spilt liquid.

A more imposing complex lay on the W side of the Court: a raised platform (9) known as the *Loggia*, perhaps for ceremonial purposes, and beside this the *Grand Staircase* (10), which would have led up to a set of large rooms above. The central part of the ground floor of this W wing is occupied by the *Hall* (11) and its interconnecting rooms. It opens to the W into a flagged *Pillar Crypt* (paved area on the plan). This would have been a dark enclosed room remarkably like those near the Temple Repositories at Knossós. There are double axes carved on the pillars. Behind this cult area are storerooms, indicating a juxtaposition of functions found also at Knossós and Phaistós. By the long W Corridor (12) you can return past a huge pithos to the area of the loggia. Here (13), on a floor dating from the Old Palace, were found the ceremonial stone axe in the shape of a leopard, and a great bronze sword with rock crystal hilt; both these outstanding examples of Minoan craftsmanship are on display in Herákleion Museum, Gallery IV.

The N Wing lay behind a colonnaded *portico*, of which the column bases are preserved. The large *Hall* (14) has six rectangular pillars in it, presumably to support a grand room on the floor above. Cooking pots were found in the small room to the W and by analogy with pots and food debris found in a comparable position at Zákros, it has been suggested that the upper storey was a Dining Hall. Part of a staircase to this upper storey remains to the E, and there is another further N.

The paved *corridor* (15) leading to the N Court is partly obstructed by a later building on an oblique alignment (16). This is thought to be a shrine, but its dating is uncertain. This corridor led to the N Entrance passing (left) the *N Court* (17).

At the S end of the N Court, up three steps, is the solidly built structure known as the Keep (18). W of this is a small court (19) with a portico to the S from which a dogleg passage leads W to the so-called *Royal Apartments*, the main private quarters of the Palace. The *Megaron* (20) has a broad verandah to the N which may have looked onto a garden; the excavated walls now visible here belong to the Old Palace. On its E and S sides the megaron gave onto *light-wells*, which could be shut off when necessary by means of a pier-and-door arrangement. To the W is a smaller paved hall (21) (usually compared to the 'Queen's Room' at Knossós), and off this (S) is a lustral basin or bath. W of these rooms was found the famous 'Acrobat's sword' (also in Herákleion Museum, Gallery IV), with the figure of an acrobat arched across a gold disk on the pommel. The Archive Room (22) yielded *tablets* in hieroglyphic script as well as in Linear A.

From the light-well E of the main megaron (20) a passage leads back to the N Court (17) and from here you can leave the Palace by its N Entrance (23), near which stand two giant *pithoi*; the one inside the entrance shows dramatic evidence of burning. A fine Minoan paved way leads W from here into the town.

Immediately to the N lies the *Agora*, a walled area c 29m by 40m, with a plaster floor. Excavated in the 1960s, it was found to be contemporary with the Old Palace. Nearer the French School's dighouse is the so-called *Hypostyle Crypt* below ground level and approached by a staircase. The building consists of a series of storerooms and two interconnected halls with benches round three sides. The puzzling lack of finds from these halls has led to the suggestion that they served as a kind of council chamber.

Around the Palace is a series of large houses, part of a *Minoan town* of considerable size which is being systematically investigated by French archaeologists.

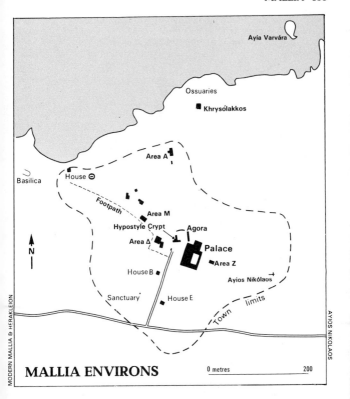

MALLIA ENVIRONS

0 metres   200

Behind the dig-house (W) is Area Δ (kept covered and closed to the public). This is a series of houses with a paved road between them. House Δα is a particularly well-preserved example of Minoan domestic architecture; it has a main hall opening on to a light-well with single column, a lustral basin with white plaster walls and red dado, and a toilet, as well as the usual storerooms.

Also roofed and fenced off is Area M (adjacent to Area Δ), where a large building of Old Palace date has been excavated. Here in 1968 a further hieroglyphic archive deposit came to light. The building has the earliest sunken lustral basin yet known. Work continues on Area M, where the refined architecture and high-quality finds make this an excavation of special value for an understanding of the Old Palace period.

A track (dotted on plan) starts almost opposite the Palace entrance gate, passes Area M and runs out to the sea (10 minutes on foot). The ruins of an Early Christian basilica (6–7C) are built over a tomb which contained an imported Attic sarcophagus of the Antonine period (2C AD, probably in re-use), now in Herákleion Museum, Gallery XX.

If you follow the coastal path E for a further 10 minutes, to a rise where the islet of Ayía Varvára comes into sight, on the right is **Khrysólakkos** (pit of gold), a large rectangular burial enclosure with

several compartments, contemporary with the Old Palace. It may
have been a royal burial-place for it is elaborately built, and from it
came the famous gold pendant of two conjoined bees (Herákleion
Museum, Gallery VII). It has been suggested that the 'Aegina treas-

*Gold bee pendant from Khrysólakkos (Herákleion
Museum, Gallery VII)*

ure' now in the British Museum was actually plundered from here
during the latter part of the 19C. The presence of clay idols indicates
that some of the rooms on the E side were for cult purposes. (The
water-pipe—see above—is presumably a temporary hindrance, but
reported plans to build a hotel near Khrysólakkos would lead to more
drastic changes.)

On the rocky bluff to the N of Khrysólakkos are natural caves
which were used as ossuaries during MMI, while to the E around the
bay of the Ayía Varvára islet are further remains, including
workshops, dating from the period of the Old Palace.

To the E of the Palace is Area Z. To find it walk from the Palace entrance gate,
outside the fence, until you are level with the E Entrance (7 on Palace plan).
Here three houses have been excavated; that to the left of the paved road shows
the best construction. Note its paved hall with column base and door jambs.

Two further excavated areas may be visited on the way back to the main
road. On the E side of the Palace approach road is the large *House* E, of MMIII–
LMI date, but reoccupied during LMIII, after the 1450 BC destruction of the
Palace. Off the W side of the approach road remains of another building have
been found. It had horns of consecration incorporated in its construction and
may therefore have been a shrine.

1.5km after you rejoin the main road there is a left turn for a detour to
(3km) Sísi. A section of the Old Road to Ayios Nikólaos (by Vrakhási)
briefly runs parallel to the highway. After 2km turn left. (Very soon
you pass to the right a by-road signposted for Mílatos.) *Sísi* grew up
round a rocky inlet where there are still agreeable tavernas, but the
village behind the harbour is changing rapidly as it develops its
tourist potential. (Good swimming from the bays to the E, signposted
in the village.)

You can continue the detour to *Mílatos* (see above) c 6km E along
the coast, where a cave is a place of modern Cretan pilgrimage on

account of a Turkish atrocity against the Christian populace committed there in 1823.

There was a Bronze Age settlement here, and important LMIII tholos tombs have been excavated (finds in the Ayios Nikólaos museum). Mílatos was a city-state in the Classical period, a contemporary of neighbouring Dréros, but was destroyed by Lýttos in the 3C BC. According to legend the great Ionian city of Miletus in Asia Minor was founded from here, and in fact Minoan influence has been identified in the archaeological record of that city.

After the Sísi turning the New Road strikes inland through the gorge of Selenári where the holy icon of Ayios Yeóryios is said to exert a benign influence on travellers. The foothills of the Lasíthi mountains (right) provide a grand scenic background.

At 49km the highway bypasses *Neápolis*, a market town (pop. 3500) that is the administrative centre of the eparchy (district) of Mirabéllo and seat of the district law court.

Near present-day Neápolis is the birthplace of Pétros Phílargos, born 1340 and, as an orphan, brought up by the Catholic friars of Ayios Antónios. He went on to study at the renowned friary of St. Francis in Candia (on the hill where the Herákleion archaeological museum now stands), and took orders in 1357. A career as an academic and theologian led him to many European universities including Oxford. He travelled as an evangelist to Lithuania, and was appointed ambassador to the court of the Duke of Milan, Giovanni Visconti. On 26 June, 1409, in the city of Pisa, he was proclaimed Pope as Alexander V, but the following year, before he had reached Rome, he died and was buried in Bologna. There were rumours of poison.

Derelict windmills enhance the landscape before a tunnel brings the road out above the Bay of Mirabéllo.

At 70km on the outskirts of *Ayios Nikólaos*, a wide crossroads offers (left) the Eloúnda road (avoiding the centre of town), and (right) the bypass leading on to East Crete. Ahead, in Ayios Nikólaos, a one-way system now operates so it helps to be familiar with the town plan. (You will be diverted right leaving the hospital on your left, and then bear left and right to Odós Plastíra high above the town's lake.) On a short visit you may prefer to park where you are diverted right, and walk downhill against the traffic flow, past the Archaeological Museum, 5 minutes to the harbour front.

6   The Lasíthi Plain and the Cave of Zeus

57km (34 miles) to Tzermiádo, principal village of the upland plateau of Lasíthi, continuing to (70km) Psykhró for the Diktaian cave.

The excursion is recommended both for the dramatic climb to the top of the pass which cuts through the girdle of mountains round the Lasíthi plain, and for the plain itself, irrigated in the dry season by thousands of white-sailed wind pumps. The Diktaian cave, a traditional birthplace of Zeus, has become one of the principal tourist attractions of the island. (Suitable shoes and a sweater advised, and a torch is useful.) There is simple accommodation on the plain in the villages of Tzermiádo, Ayios Yeóryios and Psykhró.

Bus service, twice daily from Herákleion to Psykhró. Also once a day from Ayios Nikólaos.

Take the N Coast Highway from Herákleion in the direction of Ayios Nikólaos (see Rte 5) until at 23km you turn inland for the Lasíthi plateau. At 29km a road branches off right to Kastélli Pediádas (Rte

3C). Shortly after this, in the ravine below the road (right) are the ruined piers of a Roman *aqueduct* which supplied ancient Khersónisos from springs at Piyí near Kastélli. At 32km before the village of Potamiés, a large sign indicates the track left up to the frescoed Byzantine *church of the Panayía, all that remains of the Gouverniótissa monastery. Passing almost immediately the chapel of Sotíros Khristós (Our Saviour Christ), also frescoed, you climb 1.5km to the monastery church which looks out over the Langáda Valley from the hillside above.

The church used to be open 09.00 (Sundays 10.00)–12.30, and 13.30–18.30, but in 1987 the arrangement had lapsed. If necessary, enquire at the kapheneíon in Potamiés.

The cruciform church of the Panayía (dedicated to the Assumption of the Virgin; festival 15 August) has cross-arms of equal length and a central dome resting on a drum lit by blind-arcaded windows. The *frescoes* date from the second half of the 14C. The paintings are best preserved in the W arm of the cross, with a double tier of gospel scenes above the worshipping saints. The church is dominated by the Pantokrátor in the dome, above the four evangelists on the pendentives.

Beyond Potamiés the road levels out as it approaches the dramatic wall of the Lasíthi mountains. The knob shape conspicuous on the skyline is Karphí, meaning the Nail. Clinging to its precipitous slopes are the remains of a refuge settlement (see below) built at the very end of the Bronze Age by a community still adhering to Minoan religious traditions 300 years after the collapse of Minoan power.

39km *Avdoú* is an unspoilt village with several interesting churches.

Ayios Konstantinos, 1.5km from the village, has frescoes by the brothers Mánuel and Ioánnis Phokás, dated by the donor's inscription to 1445 (compare frescoes by Mánuel dated 1436–37 at Embaros, Rte 3C, and Epáno Sými, Rte 8).
   The owner of the first kapheneíon on the right will direct you, across the road into the village to find the keyholder.
   Right of the road as you enter Avdoú (50m before the kapheneíon) is the track to the church. Bear right and continue (along a stretch of old paved road) to a bridge; 500m beyond it is a fork, where the church precinct is in view among the trees right.
   The church of *Ayios Antónios* lies in the village (signed, opposite the above kapheneíon, left and immediately left again). Its 14C frescoes of gospel scenes are interesting for their powerful draughtsmanship executed largely in tones of brown paint.
   The little cruciform church of *Ayios Yeóryios* stands in a cemetery on the N edge of the village. Little remains of its frescoes, but a visit to the church is an excuse to explore the village on foot. Turn off the main thoroughfare as for Ayios Antónios but follow this street (without turning left again) as it winds through the village. The main plateía is to the right.

From *Goniés* the climb begins in earnest. At 41.5km a road diverges downhill to *Mokhós*, scene of an animated festival on 15 August. (This would also be the route up to Lasíthi from the coastal region around Mállia.) At 44.5km a loop (left) off the main road takes you through the delightful village of *Krási*. On one side of the plateía is a copious supply of spring water harnessed through vaulted draw basins, and, opposite, an enormous ancient plane tree which 12 people cannnot girdle (well-sited cafés).

Nearby, one of the earliest known examples of a circular stone-built tholos tomb (EMI, c 3000 BC), originally noticed by Evans, was excavated in 1929 by S. Marinátos.

48.5km Just below the road (right), at *Kerá*, is the Convent of the Panayía Kardiótissa, dedicated to the Virgin Mary. (Festival for the Birth of the Virgin, 8 September.)

Open 08.00–13.00 and 15.00–19.00. *View from the terrace, and a well-tended garden that benefits from the mountain climate.

The highly unusual ground plan of the church is the result of four successive building phases, though it is interesting that care was taken with windows, stonework and decorative tiling in order to achieve a homogeneous exterior. The original three-apsed chapel serves as the bema of the present convent church. To enlarge this chapel an extended narthex was added, forming a short three-aisled nave or triple transept, with steps to adjust to the slope of the hillside on which the convent is built. Parallel to this is a conventional narthex which is now the entrance to the church. A further addition is a small chapel to the N of the original one. The frescoes in the bema are dated to the early 14C; those elsewhere in the church were painted later in the same century, and show the influence of the Macedonian school.

Beyond the hamlet of Kerá, the road climbs to (52.5km) the *Selí Ambélou pass* (900m), marked by a row of stone-built windmills which continued to grind corn until early this century. (The windmills have recently been joined by less romantic modern buildings.) The *view from the pass extends back to the coast and forward to Mount Díkte, the highest peak (2148m) in the range.

The excavated Subminoan refuge of *Karphí* is on a summit to the left (E) of the pass. To reach it, it is possible to follow the crest of the ridge from the windmills, or take a very steep path from Kerá, but the recommended route is a walk of less than an hour up from the plain (see Tzermiádo).

Below, at 817–850m lies the **Lasíthi plateau** (Oropédio Lasithíou). There are several of these fertile upland plains on Crete but Lasíthi is the only area above 800m that is inhabited all the year round. There is a strong sense of community among the 20 or so villages around the edge of the plain. In winter the passes may be blocked by snow, so preparations in autumn are still a serious business.

The plateau's fertility is a result of the rich alluvial soil brought down from the mountains by the melting snows which drain into a swallow hole at the western end near Káto Metokhí. Severe flooding in spring was always a problem, and drainage was improved by a grid of ditches (known as 'linies') giving much of the plain the appearance of a chess-board. Recent research has made it possible to date the construction of this system very precisely to 1631–33, at a time when the plain grew wheat, and the success of the crop was of importance to the rulers of the Venetian Empire. The fertile plain is irrigated by countless picturesque windpumps, each with four to eight triangular sails of white cloth that, from early summer, revolve anti-clockwise to draw water to the surface.

Lasíthi lies above the olive-tree line, but its apples and potatoes are valued in the markets of Athens as well as throughout Crete. Some cereals are still grown, also other fruit crops and an abundance of almonds. The plain is a splendid sight at blossom time.

There is evidence for Neolithic occupation with an important sanctuary at the Cave of Trapéza. The great cave at Psykhró was a place of pilgrimage from Middle Minoan times to the 7C BC, a period of a thousand years. In Hellenistic times the area was under the control of Lýttos (Rte 3C), a powerful city-state to the W just outside the girdle of mountains, and there is plenty of evidence for Roman settlement presumably exploiting the rich soil.

The Lasíthi plain, with only eight natural passes through the encircling mountains, has always been an easily defended refuge, and hence at many

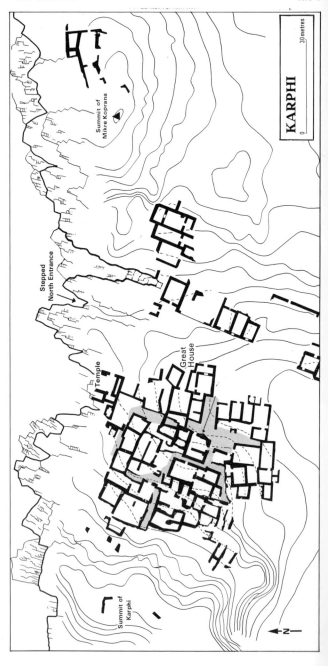

periods the chief base in E Crete for rebellion and revolt. During the early part of the Venetian Occupation the situation was so critical that in 1263 the authorities forcibly cleared the plain and forbade tillage or pasturage for nearly two centuries, a desparate decision considering that Crete made a considerable contribution to the granaries of Venice.

Descending 1.5km from the Selí Ambélou pass, you come to the road which makes a circuit of the plain. To the right, on the newly-improved road, it is 8km to the Diktaian cave at Psykhró; you pass after 3km the ruins of the Vidianí monastery. The following route circles the plain in the opposite (clockwise) direction. Turn left and continue through *Lagoú* to *Tzermiádo* (4km from the pass, 56.5km from Herákleion), the principal village (pop. 1200) of the eparchy or district of Lasíthi. (Pension and rent-room accommodation available.) On the edge of the village is the start of the walk into the mountains to the excavated Subminoan site of **Karphí**.

Just before you enter the village you pass, left, large modern buildings, the ΚΕΝΤΡΟ ΥΓΕΙΑΣ or district health centre. On the village side of this complex a stony track leads N into the mountains, at the start of the walk to Karphí. You climb gently for about 20 minutes to the *Níssimos plateau*, a small fertile area probably also cultivated in ancient times. In April and May the wet gullies in the surrounding hills still shelter the creamy white peony indigenous to Crete, *P. clusii*.

The track would take you straight across the Níssimos plain to a paved kalderími through the hills towards the N coast, but your destination, a saddle between two peaks at the top of a conspicuous long narrowing gully, is now visible to your left. Leave the track and keep left along the edge of the plateau, to pick up a path which gains height up the left incline of this gully. You pass the Astivideró spring. The path ascends in a fairly straight line until it crosses the gully near the top, before leading you between outcrops of rock up the slope from which the ancient buildings are in view. The concrete survey post should crown the peak to your right. There are two groups of small tholos tombs along this path, with a circular vault usually covering an approximately rectangular chamber.

There was a Middle Minoan Peak Sanctuary on the knob at Karphí but the settlement, excavated (1937–39) by the British School under J. Pendlebury, dates from the very end of the Bronze Age (11C BC) and continues into the Protogeometric period. This desolate site, presumably chosen for defensive purposes, was occupied for perhaps 150 years and then peacefully evacuated, limiting the excavator to a partial view of the Minoans who built this remote refuge. They certainly worshipped Cretan gods some 3–400 years after the destruction of the political power of the Minoan Palace civilisation, and the many ritual features revealed by the excavation may mean the site was of particular religious significance.

The settlement clings to the SE slopes of 'the Nail' and spreads across the saddle between the two peaks (see plan). The houses were roughly built of stone without plaster, and only thresholds and doorjambs were of well-cut blocks. Pendlebury's *Great House* can be identified by its superior construction; a series of bronze finds confirmed the relative importance of this building. The paved streets (shaded on plan) give shape to the town, though individual house plans, where clusters of rooms are huddled together in agglomerative fashion, are not so easy to make out. There was a stepped N entrance from the steep ascent. The *Temple* or civic shrine was also at the edge of this precipice and part of it has been eroded away. The largest room with remains of an altar was entered from the E and had two small adjoining rooms opposite this doorway. Among the furnishings left behind in the shrine when the settlement was abandoned were clay goddesses with the traditional cylindrical skirt and hands raised in a gesture of blessing. One, nearly a metre high, has birds perching in her crown. A unique rhyton is in the form of a chariot drawn by three oxen represented only by their heads (all in Herákleion Museum, Gallery XI).

There is an alternative return route to the Lasíthi plain. Follow the ridge W, passing a second water supply, Vitsilóvrisis, the Fountain of the Eagles. (The modern inscription commemorates the British archaeological team which excavated Karphí.) You can see a white chapel on the outer slope of the hills. A little beyond this you meet a path crossing the ridge, and turning left onto it you very soon start the descent to Lasíthi on a stepped stone-built kalderími, another of the eight ancient ways through the girdle of hills. You reach the Tzermiádo road 500m W of the Lasíthi Health Centre and the track at the start of the ascent.

In the middle of Tzermiádo an acute left turn is signed for the *Trapéza cave*, but by car it is better to continue through the village in the direction of Psykhró, for soon a new road leads off to the left, and 300m along it the path (10 minutes) is signposted (*Krónio*). *View from terrace in front of cave mouth. The site was frequented from the Neolithic period (5th millenium BC). It is disputed whether the earliest levels show evidence for occupation, but the cave was certainly used for Neolithic burials, and later as a sanctuary. In the Middle Minoan period it seems to have been abandoned in favour of the Diktaian cave at Psykhró. The nearby hill of Kástellos to the E was the site of a Middle Minoan settlement.

The road turns S, passing (61.5km) *Moní Kroustalenías* at the junction with the road down to Ayios Nikólaos (see below), and follows the E edge of the plain through *Ayios Konstantínos* to (65.5km) the village of *Ayios Yeóryios* (good tavernas and simple accommodation). The very well-arranged *Folklore Museum is open daily, 10.00—16.00; admission (1987) Drs 100.

At 70km you reach *Psykhró* (pension and rent rooms). At the end of the village, a turning (left, signposted 'Spileon') leads up to a Tourist Pavilion and car park, from which there is a superb *view over the plain. A stepped path ascends (15 minutes) to the **Cave of Psykhró**.

Open 08.00—17.00; tickets (Drs 150) at cave entrance. Guides are available but not essential. Donkeys may be hired for the ascent from the Tourist Pavilion—return ride (1987) Drs 700.

There are many rival stories but according to one tradition, this is the Diktaian cave where the Hymn of the Kouretes says Zeus was born. Many thousands of visitors are drawn to the cave each year on this account, though some scholars dispute the location.

An oracle had decreed that Kronos, the youngest of the Titans, would be dethroned by his son, so his wife Rhea contrived to give birth in a cave deep in the mountains of Crete (hence the title Zeus Kretagenes, Cretan-born). In Hesiod's version, Kronos had swallowed his five previous offspring, but in this case he was duped with a stone wrapped in swaddling clothes; meanwhile the infant Zeus was spirited away, traditionally to the cave on Mount Ida, to be raised by the goat-nymph, Amaltheia. (See also Rte 6.) All six children proved to be immortal, and in due course Kronos was to give way to Zeus.

The cave (1025m above sea level and 150m above the village of Psykhró) attracted the interest of a number of archaeologists (including Evans) at the end of the last century, and enough material was brought to light to suggest that the site was rich in votive deposits and a cult centre of antiquity. The cave was excavated (1899—1900) by D.G. Hogarth for the British School, and yielded remains from Middle Minoan to Late Geometric times. Notable are libation tables, most in serpentine or limestone, one (purchased by Evans, now in the Ashmolean Museum, Oxford) inscribed with Linear A signs, and a series of small bronzes: human and animal figurines, and models including a chariot, as well as double axes, rings, pins and blades (all these in Herákleion Museum).

The descent into the cave is steep and slippery, and the lower depths are chilly. The upper part of the cave (the NW area to the right of the entrance) contained pottery and animal bones consistent with sacrificial offerings, and there was an *altar*, roughly built and about 1m high, round which most of the fragments of libation tables were discovered. The innermost recess, against the cave wall, was a *temenos*, or sacred precinct, defined by a wall and roughly paved. To the S (ahead) is the entrance to the main cavern which descends 65m; at the bottom water now lies for most of the year. Bronze votives were found in great numbers in the pool, in the vertical crevices formed by the fine stalactites, and sometimes embedded in the stalactites themselves. Almost all the finds from this lowest level were of LM date. This was the main period of use, but there was a lesser revival of ritual activity in the 8–7C when open-work bronze plaques were the characteristic votive offerings.

The improved road now completes in a further 8km the circuit of the plain, to the deserted *Vidianí monastery* (19C foundation), and the junction below the windmills on the road back to Herákleion.

About 4km from Psykhró, just beyond *Káto Metokhí*, you pass the swallow hole that drains the plateau; this is frequently a rewarding area for bird-watchers. Here, by the fine new bridge, is the start of the old kalderími over the girdle of mountains by the Tsoúli Mníma pass towards Lýttos. Recently a bulldozer has worked on a track up to the high pastures, and the mule path was obstructed in places. Allow about an hour to the pass from which the kalderími snakes down by a circuitous route to Tíkhos, where the ancient aqueduct carried Lasíthi water to Lýttos. From the pass there is a magnificent view over the Pediáda countryside (Rte 3C).

From the Plateau of Lasíthi to Ayios Nikólaos, 40km (25 miles).

From the junction by the Kroustalénia monastery take the road (E) signposted for Ayios Nikólaos. Through *Mésa Lasíthi*, you climb steeply out of the plain ('view) to a high pass, *Patéra ta Seliá* (1100m), and then descend to (10km) *Mésa Potamí*. The road continues along the river valley among holm-oaks and fruit trees below Mount Seléna to (13.5km) *Exo Potamí*. A second col with the derelict stone-built windmills of Katakaloú marks the boundary between the provinces of Lasíthi and Mirabéllo. The road runs between Makhairá (1486m) to the N and Katharó (1664m) to the S.

Beyond (17km) *Zénia* there is a sharp descent. At c 26km you pass a turning left for (6km) Neápolis and the N Coast Highway. For the direct route to Ayios Nikólaos on minor roads, keep right here, and then keep right again through *Exo Lakónia* and *Phlamourianá* to cross the Ayios Nikólaos bypass at the junction with the road to Kritsá (Rte 7).

7 Ayios Nikólaos and Excursions in the Locality

AYIOS NIKOLAOS, a little harbour town beautifully situated on the W side of the *Bay of Mirabéllo*, has developed into the most popular tourist resort of Crete without losing its charm. The modern town has grown up only since the second half of the last century, and is now the administrative centre of the province of Lasíthi, which comprises the whole of E Crete. (See plan at end of book.)

The short tree-lined avenue, ΛΕΩΦ. ΚΟΥΝΔΟΥΡΟΥ (Leophóros Koundoúrou), more often referred to as the 'main street', descends from ΠΛΑΤ. ΗΡΩΩΝ (Plateia Iróon) to the crowded *harbour*, the social centre of the town. To the left a channel dug in 1867–71, and crossed by a bridge, links the harbour with the small picturesque *Lake Voulisméni*; there was a tradition that this was bottomless, but it is now known to be funnel-shaped to a depth of 64m. The backdrop is a steep cliff; to enjoy the *view from the top, take ΟΔΟΣ Ν. ΠΛΑΣΤΙΡΑ (N. Plastíra) W from the main street (see above). The combination of lake and harbour is Ayios Nikólaos's particular attraction.

The town is one of the best shopping centres on Crete, and among the ubiquitous souvenir shops can be found some better-quality establishments for clothes, rugs, leather goods and jewellery. The broad esplanade running N from the harbour offers a stroll by the sea past the sheltered anchorage to the promontory looking back on the town; this is also the road to Eloúnda.

From Herákleion airport to Ayios Nikólaos, one hour by road; taxi fare (1987) Drs 3000. Frequent buses from the Herákleion main bus station near the harbour (New Road route for Express).

Tourist Information: the new Municipal Information Office is on the waterfront, at the N end of the bridge between the lake and the harbour; it occupies the ground floor of the Port Authority building (see town plan). Opening hours: 08.00–21.00, tel. 22 357. *Area code* 0841.

Olympic Airways office: 20 Nik. Plastíra (tel. 22 033), on the cliff above the lake.

Boat connections: in recent years there has been at least one weekly service through Ayios Nikólaos on the Athens–Rhodes route, with intermediate calls at various Cycladic islands to the N, and Siteía, Kásos, Kárpathos and Kos to the E, but note that domestic (inter-island) boat schedules are liable to alter every year. All NTO offices have current timetables. Shipping agent in Ayios Nikólaos: Massarós Travel, 29 R. Koundoúrou, on the left half-way down the main street, tel. 22 267.

Hotels: in 1987 the NTO listed some 70 hotels and pensions between de Luxe and Class C, the majority geared to package holidays arranged from abroad; in high season the best in any price bracket are liable to be fully booked with tours from all parts of the world. Ayios Nikólaos, above all places in Crete, is to be preferred outside the high season. The luxury hotels (with bungalows) are all beautifully situated on the bay and can be recommended. If you need medium-priced accommodation for a few nights during a touring holiday, look along the sea front in the direction of Eloúnda, ΑΚΤΗ Σ. ΚΟΥΝΔΟΥΡΟΥ (Aktí S. Koundoúrou), around the lake, or out on the bay between the ferry quay and Kitroplateía. In case of difficulty consult the Municipal Information Office. For longer periods consider also Eloúnda and Pláka (see below), or Istro, formerly Kaló Khorió (Rte 9).

Youth Hostel: 3 Stratigoú Koraká.

Restaurants: prices may be higher than comparable establishments elsewhere on Crete, and more geared to international notions of eating; sample menus are displayed outside most premises. Recommended: the Kitroplateía area.

Tourist Police now occupy an office in the regular Police Station, ΟΔΟΣ Κ. ΠΑΛΑΙΟΛΟΓΟΥ (Odós K. Palaiológou), on the left before the museum (see town plan).

Tourist agencies abound. Creta Tours, Odós Palaiológou, across from the lake, runs coach tours to all the main tourist attractions on the island.

Motor boat excursions around the Mirabéllo bay are organised by Buzz Travel, Nostos and K Tours, now amalgamated under one management but retaining three offices: near the ferry quay, in the main street, and on the seafront towards Eloúnda.

Bus Station: by the sea, down the hill S of the central Plateía Iróon (see town plan). Tel. 22 234. Services to Mállia and Herákleion approximately hourly until early evening; to Eloúnda and to Kritsá frequently; to Siteía and to Ierápetra five or six times daily. Detailed information is displayed in the office.

Swimming. Ayios Nikólaos did not become famous because of its bathing beaches. From the SW corner of the harbour ΟΔΟΣ ΣΦΑΚΙΑΝΗ (Odós Sphakianí) leads over the promontory to the small pebbly beach, called Kitroplateía because of its traditional association with the shipping of citrus fruits. There is also a long beach stretching S from the bus station, and another, attractively reed-fringed, is 10 minutes further on foot, just outside the town at the start of the road to Siteía (Rte 9).

In the early Hellenistic period the settlement here on the bay was the harbour of Lató (Λατώ η Ετέρα), the city-state in the hills near modern Kritsá. The harbour town was known as Lató 'pros Kamára' ('towards the arch') and it has been suggested that the arch in question is the cliff which overhangs the lake at Ayios Nikólaos. This coastal settlement flourished in Roman times, on the low hill jutting into the bay between the modern port and the Kitroplateía.

In later times, a cove a short way along the bay NW towards Eloúnda became the Venetian harbour; almost completely sheltered from the prevailing winds, it still provides a safe winter anchorage for small boats. The harbour was named the Porto di San Nicolo after the little Byzantine church overlooking it. (The recently restored church contains some of the earliest frescoes on Crete—see below.) To protect this Porto di San Nicolo, there was the medieval Castle of Mirabéllo, which had been built by the Genoese during their brief stay on the island after 1204; it occupied the height now to the E of Plateía Iróon, but nothing remains today. The castle was sacked by a Turkish raiding party in 1537, more than a century before the Turks finally captured Crete. When the Turkish threat became more serious, the Venetians assigned the defence of the Mirabéllo bay to the almost impregnable fortress of Spinalónga.

The Byzantine church of ***Ayios Nikólaos** is in sight from the Eloúnda road on a headland next to the Minos Palace hotel. (Enquire about the key at the Municipal Information office on the harbour.) This is a single-nave church with three bays, the central one supporting a dome. The building is difficult to date architecturally, but restoration work in 1968 uncovered frescoes which go back at least to the early years of the Second Byzantine period (late 10—early 11C), not long after the island had been reclaimed for Christendom from the Arabs. Two layers of paintings were found: there are remains of 14C work, including fragments of the Pantokrátor in the dome, but unique on Crete (and rare in Greece) is the evidence for the earlier frescoes. These can be seen to have consisted of formal designs of geometric motifs such as interlocking circles, quatrefoils and blossoms, consistent with the principles advanced in the 8–9C by the Iconoclasts, who banned the representation of the divine or saintly form in religious art.

On the road uphill from the bridge by the lake (Odós Palaiológou) is the ***Archaeological Museum.**

Open (1987) 08.45–15.00, Sundays and holidays 09.30–14.30. Closed Tuesdays. Admission: Drs 200.

Built in the early 1970s with eight rooms around a central court, the museum houses finds from sites all over E Crete. The clearly-labelled cases are arranged in roughly chronological order, and the first three rooms contain Bronze Age material of exceptional quality. For visitors with a particular interest the official publication, by the eminent Greek archaeologist, C. Daváras, describes the major exhibits and sets them in context; it is also beautifully illustrated. (On sale by the same author is 'Guide to Cretan Antiquities', recommended in the Bibliography.)

Room I. Neolithic and Early Minoan. The first case you come to contains a stone idol from Pelekitá, a remote cave with Neolithic material on the seaward side of Mount Traóstalos, N of Zákros.

Four cases are devoted to finds from the huge Early Minoan cemetery (first half of the third millenium BC) at Ayía Photiá on the coast just E of Siteía; characteristic is the pottery's burnished surface and incised decoration, often with white clay filling. Typical shapes include the 'chalice' and 'frying pan'. Note the *Biconical bird-shaped jar in the central case near the window, and left of the window a lidded *Double vase on a tall foot. In this case there is also a series of bronze weapons, one deliberately bent to render it harmless.

The Mýrtos site (Phournoú Koriphí) W of Ierápetra is a settlement of the EMII period (c 2600–2150); in the centre case are disks from the potter's workshop, a primitive form of slow wheel. The distinctively mottled pottery with a slightly lustrous surface, here and in the next room, is Vasilikí ware, named after the type-site on the isthmus of Ierápetra; the effect is thought to have been achieved by uneven firing and perhaps by the use of different coloured slips on the same vessel. The 'teapot' with exaggerated spout is a common shape.

The Goddess of Mýrtos, an Early Minoan rhyton (Ayios Nikólaos Museum)

Room II, Early and Middle Minoan (c 2600–1700 BC). The highly unusual *'Goddess of Mýrtos', an EMII libation vase, deservedly has a case to itself. On the left wall are finds from EMII burials at Mókhlos, a tiny off-shore island halfway between Ayios Nikólaos and Siteía. Note especially the gold jewellery, also the stone vases with the veining of the material superbly exploited. *Diadem decorated with three Cretan ibexes in dot-repoussé technique; 'teapot' vase in brecchia.

In the next case are Linear A inscriptions on stone libation tables from Petsophás, the Peak Sanctuary of Palaíkastro. The cases between giant pithoi from the Palace of Zákros contain grave groups from the Myrsíni tholos (the first tomb of Mesará type to be excavated in E Crete), and from the MM burial enclosures at Zákros. The central case displays bronze tools and weapons, and below them a potter's wheel from a tomb at Kritsá; the wheel was introduced in Crete c 1900 BC. The remaining corner has two cases of votive offerings from Peak Sanctuaries, which were places of pilgrimage in Minoan times. The terracotta figurines throw interesting light on the physical appearance of the worshippers, and on their needs and desires. Note the quadruple horns of consecration, symbol of Minoan religion.

Room III, Late Minoan. The 1970s' excavation of the LMI villa at Makryialós, on the Libyan sea E of Ierápetra, produced finds which vividly illustrate the quality of life in the large Minoan country houses and estates contemporary with the New Palaces (c 1550–1450 BC). The Marine Style pottery (wall case, left) is thought to come from the Knossós workshop, and the marble *Chalice (centre) from Zákros. In the case to the right of the door are further votive offerings from Petsophás which, unlike many other Peak Sanctuaries, was still frequented in Neopalatial times.

In the next-door case is one of the museum's outstanding exhibits. The steatite *Triton, a rare and extraordinary piece of Minoan workmanship, was found (1981) in an excavation near the NE corner of the Palace of Mállia. The relief carving is a scene of two facing genii, one pouring a libation from a double-spouted vase into the outstretched hands of his companion. In the same case are a tiny ivory crocodile and a sphinx from the LMIII cemetery at Mílatos, about 5km E of Mállia.

This room displays a fine collection of Minoan clay sarcophagi. These were of two types: chests (larnakes) with low feet and gabled lids, and the oval 'bath-tub' shape, often with drainage holes suggesting that they had functioned as bath tubs. The decoration includes birds, fish and the stylised octopus.

The central case displays seals, ivory work and jewellery. Note the superbly decorated gold pin with an inscription of 18 Linear A signs; this was presented to the museum by the Belgian archaeologist J-P. Olivier, who had purchased it in Brussels.

Three wall cases at the far end of the room contain tomb groups from the LMIII cemetery at Myrsíni near Siteía. The pottery includes several conical clay rhytons pierced at the tip for use as libation vases. Note also the incense burners. From the same cemetery comes (central case) the female figurine on drum base with hands joined perhaps in an attitude of worship.

Room IV, Late Minoan III (Postpalatial) and Early Iron Age. The infant burial (centre) is displayed exactly as found in the transitional LMIII–Protogeometric cemetery at Kryá, S of Siteía. The wall cases (left) exhibit material from the last phases of the Bronze Age, chiefly from the cemeteries at Myrsíni and Kritsá (14–13C BC). The new straight-sided cremation urns are characteristic, but the typically Minoan horns of consecration motif still occurs in the decoration.

The Early Iron Age covers the Subminoan, Geometric and Orientalising periods. During this time the pottery from this part of the island is relatively uninspired and rustic, and by contrast accentuates the quality of contemporary pieces from central Crete (cf. Herákleion Museum, Galleries XI and XII).

Room V. Terracotta Collection; finds of the Archaic and Classical periods (7–5C BC), mainly from the city-state of Oloús near Eloúnda, and from a rich deposit, presumably associated with a shrine, discovered near the centre of modern Siteía. Many of the female figurines, heads and plaques are fine examples of the Daidalic style; some retain traces of the paint which originally adorned them. *Archaic head from Siteía, separately displayed. Note the clay animals from Oloús, and various types of lamp.

The anteroom (VI) continues the display of terracottas from Oloús, with some contemporary vases.

Room VII. Greco-Roman material, much of it from an important Roman cemetery on the edge of Ayios Nikólaos, the Lató pros Kamára of the Roman period. At the far end of the room is an outstanding exhibit, a skull still adorned with a gold wreath; the nearby bronze aryballos came from the same burial which is dated by the silver coin of Polyrrhénia to the early 1C AD.

To Spinalónga.

There are excursions by caique every afternoon in summer (sea conditions permitting) from Ayios Nikólaos harbour to the ruined Venetian fortress of **Spinalónga**, built on a rock at the NW corner of the Bay of Mirabéllo.

Duration of trip approximately 4 hours, usually including a stop for swimming. Price c Drs 1000. (The fortress can also be reached by small boat from Eloúnda or Pláka.)

The caiques pass close to Ayii Pántes (All Saints), the island reserve for the 'agrími' or Cretan ibex. The protected herd has grown to some 200 animals, and the adult male is a fine sight. The route follows the coast N to the peninsula of Spinalónga; on the neck of land now joining it to the mainland was the ancient city of Oloús (see p 173).

The Spinalónga *fortress* controlled the entrance to the anchorage of Eloúnda as well as defending all the Mirabéllo bay. Built in 1579, it remained in Venetian hands till 1715. The Turks then held it until 1903. From 1903–55 the fortress was a leper colony.

The guided visit includes a tour of the fortifications both from the sea and from the battlements within, and a sympathetic account of the leper colony. Most of the buildings within the enceinte, including the lepers' village, are in an advanced state of decay, and for reasons of safety independent exploration is discouraged.

Across from the islet on the NE shore of the peninsula is the quarry from which came blocks for the Venetian ramparts.

*To Kritsá and Lató.

A round trip of less than 30km (c 16 miles); 9km to the frescoed church of the Panayía Kerá outside the attractive weaving village of Kritsá, and on to Lató, an excavated example of a city-state of the Greek period beautifully situated in the hills.

Above Kritsá, 16km W into the Lasíthi mountains, is the Katheró plain.
Frequent bus service to Kritsá. From Kritsá to Lató on foot, one hour. Also morning bus to Kroústas, E of Kritsá.

From the central Plateía Iróon follow the signs for Siteía as far as the bypass, but then continue straight across the main road clearly signed to (9km) Kritsá. After 100m a road to the right sets off for the plateau of Lasíthi (see Rte 6). The Kritsá road climbs through landscape scarred by quarrying, and then levels out among olive groves, with the village of Kritsá clinging to the wall of the Lasíthi mountains ahead. 7km from the bypass, clearly signed on the right of the road is the **·** **·**church of the **Panayía Kerá** (Our Lady of Kerá).

Open: 09.00–15.00 (Sunday –14.00), closed Friday. Winter hours reduced. (Check first with Tourist Information if possible.) Small admission fee.

On sale at the church: 'Panaghia Kera: Byzantine wall-paintings at Kritsa' by M. Borboudákis is a knowledgeable and well-illustrated commentary; the author is Ephor (director) of Byzantine Antiquities on Crete.
  The church dates from the early years of the Venetian occupation and its frescoes are among the finest and most complete on the island. Recent restoration work afforded an opportunity for a chronological reassessment.

The domed three-aisled church is dedicated to the Assumption of the Virgin, as is its CENTRAL AISLE or nave which is now considered the original structure (mid 13C). Two phases of painting have been identified in this aisle, both dated stylistically within the 13C. Remnants of the earlier decoration are preserved only in the apse and on the flat surfaces of the arches supporting the dome. On the *S arch* is the figure of a female saint, but better preserved, in the *apse*, is the Ascension above four Hierarchs holding open scrolls and dressed in chasubles decorated with crosses; on the jambs the two deacons, Stéphanos and Romanós.
  The *dome* and the *nave* are decorated in the later style. Instead of the conventional Christ Pantokrátor in the dome, there are four gospel scenes (an arrangement perhaps dictated by the quadrating effect of the reinforcing ribs), but some expected elements are preserved: four angels in the apex triangles, the twelve prophets round the cylinder of the vault, and the four evangelists on the pendentives. The four gospel scenes in chronological order and anti-clockwise from the W are: the Presentation, the Baptism, the Raising of Lazarus and the Entry into Jerusalem. Further scenes from the gospel cycle also occupy their usual place on the *vault* of the nave. In the handling of these scenes there is a noticeable observation of detail charmingly rendered in contemporary medieval terms, for example the Venetian glass and pottery on the tables laid for the Last Supper and Herod's Feast. On the side walls are the worshipping Saints, among them (on the NW pillar) a rare St. Francis, or Frantzískos, showing the strength of the influence of the Western Church.
  On the *W wall* are the remains of a portrayal of the Crucifixion; the Centurion's soldiers wear 13C armour. Below are gruesome scenes of the Punishment of the Damned.
  The SOUTH AISLE (early 14C) is dedicated to the Virgin's mother, Ayía Anna, who looks down from the quadrant of the *apse*. The *vault* of the aisle is decorated with a robust series of scenes narrating, with much human tenderness, the life of the Virgin; they are largely inspired by the Apocrypha. The scenes are arranged in pairs on either side of the vault, beginning at the E end with the House of Joachim (the husband of St. Anne), and the angel's answer to Joachim's prayers for his barren wife. After the rejoicing the story

*The Embrace of Joachim and Anna, from the frescoes in
the Panayía Kerá, Kritsá*

continues through Mary's birth, her presentation to Zacharias in the
temple, Joseph's Sorrow (his early misunderstanding of his wife's
pregnancy) and 'the Water of Trial', a test of the Virgin's chastity.
Finally there is the Journey to Bethlehem, and Mary triumphant with
the Infant Christ encircled above a closed gate that, as in the vision of
Ezekiel (with arms raised in prayer), would not exclude the Lord God
of Israel.

On the W wall is an inscription naming the donor, Antónios
Lámeras, and the village of 'Kritzea'. The date here is now worn
away but is recorded as 'the century beginning 1292'.

The NORTH AISLE is dedicated to Ayios Antónios, and the frescoes
(dated to the mid 14C) proclaim Christ's Second Coming. This is the
most ambitious treatment of this theme known from Crete. Below the
Pantokrátor (damaged) in the bema, are the Hierarchs with the text
of the Second Coming. Towards the E end of the vault are the

enthroned apostles, and the massed ranks of angels, with below them the Saints, all in prayerful readiness for the salvation of the world. On the arch the angel holds a scroll of stars (Book of Revelation). Next (N) in the vault is the depiction of Paradise, a walled garden with fruit trees and birds—the four rivers of Paradise (Tigris, Euphrates, Geon and Phison) named only by their initial letters; beside the enthroned Virgin, the Patriarchs, Abraham, Isaac and Jacob, protect the souls of the just. The gate of Paradise is guarded by St. Peter who admits the righteous thief. Opposite: the dance of the martyrs and saints entering Paradise. Two panels of the wise and foolish virgins, candles lit and extinguished, are unusual in this context.

High up on the W wall the Archangel Michael sounds the last trumpet call which proclaims the Second Coming, above the recording angel supervising the scales of judgement. Adjacent on the vault are scenes of the Earth (with snake) and Sea (with boat) delivering up their dead for judgement.

Of exceptional interest in the NW corner (wall) is the period detail of the *portrait of the donor, Yeóryios Mazizánis, with his wife and child.

There are a number of other frescoed churches in this region of interest to specialists: the cemetery church of Ayios Ioánnis (dated 1370 by an inscription which also records a financial contribution by the Skordílis family); Ayios Yeóryios Kavousiótis on the Kroústas road out of Kritsá, which has remains of frescoes by two painters (late 13C and mid 14C); and Ayios Konstantínos (1354–55). These churches are locked and not always accessible, but consult the head guard at the Panayía Kerá about the current arrangements.

At the entrance to the village you pass the turn (right) for Lató (see below).

The large village of **Kritsá** (pop. c 2000) is renowned for its weaving, considered by many the finest on Crete. The most characteristic pieces are either in natural wool colours of cream, grey and brown, or in a strong red. The village streets are terraced up the hillside, with extensive views down to the coast, and cafés and tavernas from which to enjoy the outlook. (Some rooms to rent.) The old streets are narrow, so for a visit it is best to leave a vehicle in the signed car-park and walk.

In the village a road forks left (past Ayios Yeóryios—see above) to *Kroústas*. 1.5km along it, *Ayios Ioánnis Theológos* (Evangelist) is superbly situated at the head of a valley. The triple-aisled church dating back to the Second Byzantine period became an annexe of the monastery of Toploú at the eastern tip of the island (key held at next-door house).

There are convenient buses up to Kroústas from Ayios Nikólaos, and the walk (5.5km) back to Kritsá, past this church, is recommended. Alternatively, serious walkers will enjoy the old route, now part track, part kalderími, N from Kroústas c 2 hours to Kaló Khorió. (Frequent N coast buses for the return to Ayios Nikólaos.)

From the top of Kritsá village street a dirt road sets off for (16km) the **Katharó plain**, 1100m up in the Díkte range of mountains, under Mount Lázaros, and on the route to one of the eight traditional passes into the plateau of Lasíthi. The plain is only inhabited during the summer months. The track, until recently very rough, has now been levelled by the bulldozer (and the scars will take some time to heal). The improvements have resulted in easy access to empty hills, and the drive is recommended for wide views, for the wooded area and (in spring and autumn) the alpine flowers. In April the yellow *Arum creticum* is a striking sight along the way.

To Lató.

At the beginning of Kritsá, 10km from Ayios Nikólaos, a one-way traffic system begins. 300m after this, beside a chapel, is the dirt road, right, for (3.5km) Lató. After 400m bend right, and then at two unsigned forks in the road keep right again. The track ends at the site, known locally as *Goulás*, which covers two acropolis peaks and the saddle between them where the centre of the ancient city lay.

The city-state of Lató (Λατώ η Ετέρα) was founded in the Archaic period (7C BC) and flourished down to Early Hellenistic times, but as there is hardly any evidence of Roman occupation, it is known to have declined in importance by then in favour of its harbour 'Lató pros Kamára' (see Ayios Nikólaos). Recent study has shown that this hilltop city was destroyed c 200 BC.

Though securely identified by an inscription during the French School's exploration of 1899–1900, Lató was largely ignored in favour of Minoan remains until excavations were begun again in 1967; it is now the most extensively excavated site of its period on the island. The principal interest lies in the detailed evidence of the town plan, and the light it throws on the character and organisation of the city. Lató can also be enjoyed for the dramatic beauty of its position, which offers from the N acropolis a panoramic view of E Crete.

The road to the site now ends somewhat above the original entrance and approach. It is worth walking 100m downhill (to a path to the right) to find the *city gate* in the fortification wall (see plan). The gateway, designed for easy defence, leads through two inner doorways into a small square court from which a long stepped *street* leaves at right angles. The street is bordered on the right by shops and workshops, which open from the steps and back on to the defensive wall itself. On the left a stout wall ascends the steep slope; it is interrupted by several narrow doorways leading into the N sector of the town. This wall is given added strength by two *towers*, which were found to serve in a dual capacity as houses. The street bends right and then left to reach the *agorá*, a pentagonal area with in the centre a deep square cistern and a shrine. From the shrine (probably an open-air structure) came many figurines dated to the 6C BC.

The agorá in its present form dates to the beginning of the Hellenistic era, 4–3C. The W side is bounded by a *stoa* that has stone benches round three walls behind a Doric colonnade. (The S end is cut by a modern threshing floor.) On the S side of the shrine, set at an angle, is an *exédra*, a rectangular shelter open to the court.

On the N, flanked by two towers, is an elaborate staircase, in the form of a triple flight of broad steps separated by narrow ones for easier ascent. The towers buttressed the building above, and contributed to the monumental effect of the design, which suggests both the Minoan 'theatrical area' that is so characteristic a feature at Knossós and Phaistós, and the seating arrangement of a Greek theatre. The staircase gives access to an upper terrace on which stood the Hellenistic *prytaneíon* (a civic building, often compared to a town hall and essential to the administration of the city-state). On the E side is a peristyle court which leads W into the main hall with benches and a central hearth. The small rooms to the N are thought to have held the city's archives. An inscription found here, recording a treaty between Górtyn and Lató, was important for the identification of the prytaneíon.

Across the agorá above its SE corner, is a terrace supported by a well-preserved retaining wall of rustic polygonal masonry; on the terrace there remain four courses of a *temple*, dated late 4–early 3C, approximately contemporary with the major civic buildings. The temple was rectangular, with pronaos and cella, and without columns; outside the entrance (E) stood a stepped altar. Further E,

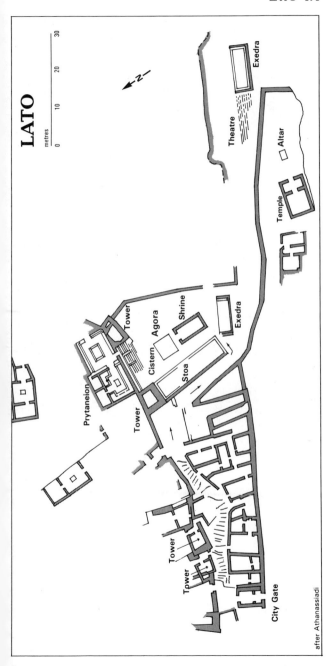

LATO

metres
0   10   20   30

Theatre

Exedra

Altar

Temple

Tower

Cistern

Agora

Shrine

Stoa

Exedra

Prytaneion

Tower

Tower

Tower

City Gate

after Athanassiadi

below the temple terrace, there are traces of a semi-circular area facing N, understood as a small theatre, and beside it is another exédra similar to that on the edge of the agorá.

To Dréros and Eloúnda.

A round trip of c 50km (30m) to (16km) Dréros, a classical city-state with an important early temple (20 minutes on foot from road), returning by (37km) Eloúnda and the site of ancient Oloús. Eloúnda is only 11km along the coast from Ayios Nikólaos, but the recommended drive down from the hills provides a spectacular *panorama of the Bay of Mirabéllo.

Seven buses a day between Ayios Nikólaos and Eloúnda. Frequent service to Neápolis (Herákleion schedule) for a walk to Dréros.

Leave Ayios Nikólaos along the road past the museum, to join the N Coast Highway running W towards Herákleion. At 13km the exit for *Neápolis* is signposted right. For the town, the slip-road describes a circle to cross above the highway, but just before the bridge there is a turning uphill (left) for the site of Dréros, signposted also to Kouroúnes. After 2km keep right at a fork and 1km further the road ends at the start of the path to the site.

On foot, from the centre of Neápolis leave the big plateía at its N end. At the T-junction turn left and immediately right, following signs for the New Road. Cross the bridge over the highway and turn uphill right. (See above; from the plateía to start of path up to site, 3km.)

A well-worn stony path first climbs the S flank of the hill and then levels out along the contour to reach (15 minutes) the saddle between two peaks where the centre of the city lay. Cross the saddle keeping to the W (left) slope. The temple excavation, now protected by a stone-built shed, lies just over the crest.

The city's ancient name is known from an inscription of c 220 BC vividly detailing an oath of loyalty taken by the young men of Dréros. Other inscriptions found include an early code of constitutional law and an important text in Greek script but in the older Eteocretan language (see Praisós, Rte 10B). The city was flourishing by the Geometric period.

The city plan is to some extent comparable with that of Lató: an agorá with retaining wall and bordered by a flight of steps, cistern, temple and nearby

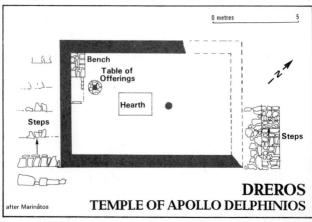

DREROS
TEMPLE OF APOLLO DELPHINIOS
after Marinátos

public building (perhaps a prytaneíon) to the S of the agorá, but here all is much less well preserved. There are house remains down the N slope.

The majority of finds from the site date to the Geometric and Archaic periods, but the huge *cistern* below the temple was constructed in the Hellenistic period (3C BC). Two of its walls were rock-cut and two were built; all were faced with plaster. The city declined in importance before the end of the 2C. It flourished again during the Second Byzantine period, and there are traces of Byzantine and Venetian occupation on the E acropolis hill which takes its name from the chapel of Ayios Antónios on the summit.

The **Temple of Apollo Delphinios**, dated to the second quarter of the 8C, is one of the earliest temples known in all Greece. It was approached from the SW corner of the *agorá* by a flight of steps. The temple, orientated NE–SW, consists of a simple cella (see plan) with entrance probably in the N Wall. (The N corner was destroyed by the construction of a kiln.) On the long axis is a central rectangular sunken *hearth* lined with stone slabs, and a base for a wooden column; it is believed that there were originally two columns. On a ledge in the SW corner were an early 6C gorgoneion, vases and terra-cotta figurines, and in front of this on the floor a stone 'table for offerings'. Three important bronze statuettes (c 650 BC) found in the temple would probably have stood on the ledge. They are made by the sphyrelaton technique—hammering bronze plates over a wooden core—and are thought to represent Apollo, Artemis and Leto (Herákleion Museum, Gallery XIX). Beside the ledge was a later addition, a low altar in the form of a stone box filled with the horns of young goats, recalling the horn altar at Delos around which Theseus and the Delian maidens performed the crane dance after his triumphant return there from Crete.

On a walking expedition it is possible to make your way down the N slope of the hill, but the going is rough in places. One path joins the dirt road below at a large water trough, and a right turn will bring you out on the Eloúnda–Neápolis road at Kastélli, 5km from Neápolis; or you can make a short cut round the base of the E acropolis onto the same road.

By car you return as you came, and cross the bridge over the highway towards the centre of Neápolis, but instead of turning into the square keep straight ahead (signposted for Ayios Nikólaos by the Old Road). After 1.5km, in *Nikithianó*, watch for the left turn for Eloúnda. From Nikithianó the road climbs steeply, and the site of Dréros is above left where the little church of Ayios Antónios can be seen on the hill top. The rural scenery is interspersed with unspoilt villages until suddenly the **Bay of Mirabéllo** fills the view, with the island of *Pseíra* and the hills of E Crete in the distance.

18km from Neápolis, you descend to the coast at *Eloúnda* (Skhísma) and turn right. There are pleasant tavernas on the waterfront.

500m towards Ayios Nikólaos a left fork is signposted to Oloús. The track leads along the shore, past salt-pans dating from the Venetian period, to the isthmus of Póros which joins the Spinalónga peninsula to the mainland. This is the site of the Greco-Roman city-state of **Oloús**. During the occupation of Crete by the Great Powers at the turn of the century, a narrow channel was cut through the isthmus by French sailors, thus opening up the S end of the natural harbour of Eloúnda to the open sea.

The track crosses the channel by a bridge near a restored windmill. The sea level has risen and structures can be seen in the water on either side of the isthmus, and along the shore to the right (E), level with a white chapel. Just NW of this chapel, and reached by a path beside a taverna, is an excavated Early Christian *basilica*; its exact date is uncertain. It may be a two-phase building, as the 4C black and white *mosaic floor* appears to belong to a smaller church. The unusual asymmetric design of geometric and natural motifs includes panels of lively dolphins and two inscriptions naming the donors. The mosaic was dated from the style of the writing.

This is all that has been excavated and all that remains visible above ground of a city that is known to have had great temples to Zeus Talaios and Britomartis. In the Hellenistic period Oloús maintained close relations with Rhodes, and an inscription of 200 BC gives details of an agreement by which Rhodes could use anchorages here for her drive against piracy.

Outside the summer season this isthmus is a tranquil place, and a walk out along the peninsula of Spinalónga (recommended to bird-watchers) offers fine coastal views.

On the E coast of the peninsula opposite the little island of Kolokýthia was a small Hellenistic and Roman settlement, and there are remains of another basilica at what is now the water's edge. An ancient road, of Roman or possibly Hellenistic date, can be picked up crossing the rise between the two sites.

The road from Eloúnda runs S along the Mirabéllo bay. At *Elliniká* in 1937 the French School excavated a 2C temple dedicated to Aphrodite and Ares; this became a 'border temple' in settlement of a dispute between Lató and Oloús. (Nothing remains to visit.)

You keep left along the coast into Ayios Nikólaos.

8   Ayios Nikólaos to Ierápetra and the South Coast

This itinerary follows the N coast (Rte 9) towards Siteía as far as (21km) Pakhyámmos, and then crosses the island at its narrowest point to 35km (21 miles) Ierápetra. There is an alternative route (c 36km) through the hills via Kalamávka. From Ierápetra you can turn E to Siteía (Rte 10B) or continue W to (17km) Mýrtos, (42km) Viánnos, and on to Herákleion (Rte 3C). An (unfinished) stretch of the projected S Coast Highway—from Viánnos to Pýrgos on the Mesará plain (37km)—makes it possible to cut across to Phaistós and SW Crete.

Good bus service from Ayios Nikólaos to Ierápetra. Twice daily (except Sundays) Ierápetra to Viánnos.

Leaving Ayios Nikólaos you join the bypass and turn E towards Siteía (as for Rte 9). After 9.5km a minor road (right), signed Kaló Khorió and Kalamávka, offers a recommended alternative route (c 25km) through the hills to the S coast at Ierápetra (for Kalamávka see below).

At 18.5km the important archaeological site of *Gourniá* (p 182) is spread over a low hill to the right, and soon after, at 21.5km, beyond the village of Pakhyámmos you turn away from the coast to cross the island to Ierápetra.

This is the narrowest part of the island, 14km coast to coast, and the valley road is dominated to the E by the massive Thryptí range cut by a dramatic cleft, the gorge of Monastiráki.

Opposite the cleft, at 24km, is a right turn for (300m) **Vasilikí**, an

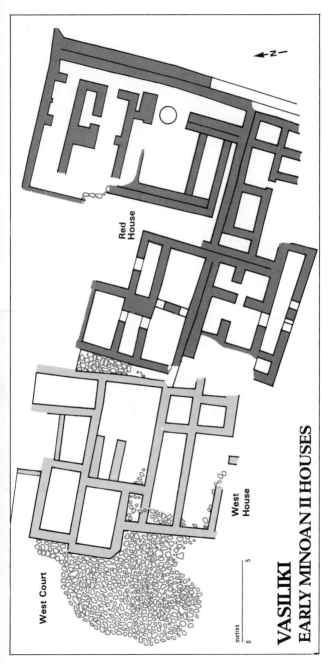

VASILIKI
EARLY MINOAN II HOUSES

West Court

West House

Red House

metres
0   5

important EMII settlement (c 2600–2200 BC). The guardian's hut is a landmark from the approach road and there is a sign at the start of the path to the left (3 minutes up the rise). Vasilikí is renowned for its profusion of wild flowers in spring.

The site was investigated in 1904 by the American archaeologist E. Hall, and further explored in 1906 by her compatriot R. Seager. During the last decade A. Zoïs has been re-examining Vasilikí for the Archaeological Society of Athens.

The path along the flank of the hill (leaving the hut on your right) brings you first to the level ground of recent work. Up the slope behind this is an area easily identified from the depth of the excavated (basement) rooms; the house walls still stand in places to near a man's height. This complex, named by Seager 'The House on the Hill', and dated to EMII, was generally regarded as the most luxurious building of this early date that had so far been excavated, and as an important step towards the splendid architecture of later Minoan times.

Erosion of the N slope of the hillside confused the picture, and it was thought that only the SW and SE wings of the House on the Hill, with a paved West Court, were preserved. These two wings have now been shown by Zoïs to be two separate buildings, the Red House and the slightly later West House (see plan), both of which have been dated within EMIIB. The W Court paving was used for both buildings.

The deep basement rooms belong to the Red House. The rough construction of the walls was concealed by a hard red lime plaster, which at other sites in later periods was to provide an ideal ground for Minoan fresco painting. Small patches of this red stucco are still preserved, as are channels for structural timbers.

The original excavations brought to light many distinctive clay vases with mottled decoration; the site gives its name to this EMII Vasilikí ware. The specialised firing technique achieved a semi-lustrous surface, with mottled patches from red through orange and brown to black. The unusual shapes of these hand-made pots, often with beak spouts or elongated horizontal ones (the so-called 'teapot' shape) are well illustrated in the first two rooms of the Ayios Nikólaos museum.

28km In the middle of the village of *Episkopí*, below the road (left) is an interesting medieval church with a double dedication to Ayios Yeóryios and Ayios Kharálambos (key with village priest but access is often difficult). The 19 blind arches round the drum below the dome are outlined with an elaborate decoration of tiles set upright in mortar and fringed with a band of rosettes, a scheme rarely found on the Byzantine churches of Greece. (Similar decoration on mainland churches, including two at Mistra in the Peloponnese, uses a glazed fabric.) The closest parallels occur in Bulgaria dating from the end of the 12C, and in conjunction with the complete absence of Venetian influence here at Episkopí, they help to date this church to the 12–13C, the years just preceding or at the beginning of Venetian rule.

This was not the bishop's church of medieval Episkopí. A bishopric (of Ierápetra) is recorded as early as 343, but the episcopal church, only finally destroyed in 1897, stood in the same position as the conspicuous modern one, just above the through road. Decorative marble fragments of the episcopal basilica are preserved in Ayios Yeóryios and Ayios Kharálambos.

The unusual ground plan of the little church consists of a S nave (Ayios Kharálambos) which was added to an earlier domed church (Ayios Yeóryios) with conch-shaped E and W cross-arms and a small, strictly rectangular, N aisle or inner room, now reached only from the main body of the church. There are two altars in the E conch or apse, but originally there was no W portal opposite. The existing doorway in the W conch was opened up during the Venetian period. The conch plan suggests that the church may have been designed as a martyrion. Recent examination (1981) by the Service for Byzantine

Antiquities under M. Borboudákis led to the further intriguing suggestion that a martyrion may have been associated with a system of Early Christian catacombs perhaps reached through the N inner room.

During road building, LMIII chamber tombs with larnax burials (c 1300 BC) were found under the village street. One outstanding clay larnax is decorated with scenes of hunting, a chariot procession and a stylised octopus, in 12 painted panels.

At the end of Episkopí a left turn leads to *Káto Khorió* just off the main road, and the start of a 12km dirt road into the mountains to the hamlet of *Thriptí.*

35km **Ierápetra**, the only sizeable town (pop. 10,750) on the S coast of Crete, is the centre of a district lately made prosperous by horticulture. Its warm dry climate and long beach have made it a favoured summer resort, and there is plenty of accommodation, mainly at the economical end of the market, geared to holidaymakers who enjoy lively tavernas, bars and discotheques.

The small archaeological museum was closed indefinitely in 1987, and the collection was put into store pending refurbishment of larger premises. The star exhibit of the museum used to be the Episkopí larnax described above, but it also housed antiquities from the Greco-Roman city of Ierápytna, which destroyed neighbouring Praisós c 155 BC to become the main rival to Itanos at this extreme E end of the island.

Ierápytna put up strong resistance to the Romans in 67 BC, but flourished later in the Roman period as a seaport well placed for trade with Africa. The ancient city covered a larger area than the modern one, but little has yet been excavated and nothing remains above ground of the amphitheatre, two theatres, temples, baths and aqueducts mentioned by earlier travellers.

There has been a *fortress* guarding the harbour at least since the early years of Venetian rule. It was twice rebuilt: in 1626 (after earthquake damage) by Francesco Morosini to counter the Turkish threat, and again during the Turkish occupation. It has recently been fully restored.

From Ierápetra to Mýrtos and Viánnos. The road runs W along the coast; distances are calculated from Ierápetra.

At the edge of the built-up area a minor road leads off (right) into the hills to (12km) Kalamávka, at the start of a recommended alternative route across the island to Kaló Khorió and (c 25km) Istro on the N coast. *Kalamávka* is dramatically sited in a cleft on the spine of the island; from a watershed beyond it there is a fine view encompassing both coastlines. In spring a great variety of orchids flourishes in this hilly terrain.

The main road, part of the projected S Coast Highway, stays close to the shore. After 4.5km, in *Gra Lygiá*, there is a turning inland (signed Anatolí) for a side-road to (c 22km) *Málles.*

This village clings to the well-watered slopes of Mount Díkte at 580m, and is a recommended starting-point for a walk into the mountains. To return to the coast, continue to the far end of the village and then turn sharp left onto a dirt road (signed Mýthi). The road is rough in places and needs to be taken slowly, but it descends to one of the most beautiful valleys on Crete, and the Mýrtos river. 10km from Málles you come to *Mýthi* and 2km further, in *Mourniés,* there is a crossroads where you can turn left for Mýrtos and the return to Ierápetra, or keep straight on to rejoin very shortly the main road (4.5km NW of Mýrtos) and proceed W towards Viánnos.

Staying on the coast road at Gra Lygiá you come to *Néa Mýrtos* where, 14km from Ierápetra, there is a domed chapel on a knoll behind the beach. Opposite, on the hill beyond the bridge, is the first of two interesting excavations in the neighbourhood of the modern village of Mýrtos (which is 3km further W); this Early Bronze Age settlement is known as *Phournoú Koriphí* after the summit on which it stands.

The site was excavated by the British School (P. Warren) in 1967–68, when c 90 rooms were uncovered. These represent two periods of urban occupation of EMII date, c 2500 and c 2170 BC. Much evidence was found for the manufacture of pottery and textiles, and a room on the SW corner of the site proved to be the oldest known Minoan domestic shrine. The clay goddess figurine and some of the 700 clay vases and other objects of daily life are displayed in the Ayios Nikólaos museum.

The path to the site is easiest from the W side of the hill (15 minutes).

16.5km Overlooking the Mýrtos river is a second Minoan site; it stands on the summit of a hill called *Pýrgos* (Greek for tower) from the watchtower which stood here during the Turkish occupation, and the Minoan site is therefore known as **Mýrtos Pýrgos**. The path starts just E of the bridge (10 minutes).

This site too was excavated by the British School (G. Cadogan, 1970–75). It proved to be a Minoan settlement of long duration. There was EMII occupation contemporary with Phournoú Koriphí, and also a destruction by fire at the same time (c 2200 BC) but, unlike Phournoú Koriphí, Pýrgos was reoccupied and a Minoan town continued to develop on the slopes of the hill.

Visible today from the early phase is a stretch of fine paved road on the NW side of the hill (not on plan) which led to a built communal

MYRTOS PYRGOS
Minoan Villa

0 metres   5

after Cadogan

tomb. At its S end was a pit used as an ossuary in which was found a large jar of bones surrounded by neatly stacked skulls.

By the time of the New Palaces (MMIII–LMI, c 1600 BC) the settlement was dominated by a large *country house* standing on the very top of the hill and facing across a court to the sea. This house, which produced a quantity of finds consistent with the elegance of its architecture, was built on two or possibly three floors, and the lower floor cut into the rock of the hilltop is what you see today.

A *stepped street* (1 on plan) leads up from the town on the E side of the hill to the paved *courtyard* (2). The plaster-lined *cistern* (3) dates from the Old Palace period, and when the house was built it was filled with 22 tonnes of river pebbles, perhaps as an ornamental soak-away for storm water. A *raised walk* (4) of flagstones bordered in purple limestone ran along the front of a gypsum-floored *verandah* (5) which had two wooden columns on purple limestone bases either side of a pillar. The building (6), of uncertain use, completed an L-shaped façade for the courtyard. The main *entrance* (7) at the W end of the verandah opened into a passage which led to a staircase (8) with a *light-well* (9) beyond, and opposite that a bench (10). Both staircase and bench are of gypsum and have had to be covered over for protection from the weather. The staircase, which showed no signs of wear, had a stepped parapet with traces of wooden columns, recalling in a modest form the Grand Staircase at Knossós. The floor of the light-well, of purple limestone set in white plaster, sloped to a central basin. The bench had gypsum back panels, and triglyph decoration, perhaps imitating legs, below the seat. Beside it a rock-cut *pantry* (11) held a large tub and a quantity of plain cups.

In the E wing a passage (12) led to storerooms (13 and 14) which contained large pithoi; clay and stone vessels, found in the street among the debris resulting from the fire, suggested the existence of a grander room above. The fire which destroyed the house (c 1450 BC) was so fierce that it splintered the ashlar masonry, vitrified pottery and fired mud bricks (as well as a Linear A tablet), and yet it did not touch the houses of the surrounding town.

If you walk round the hill starting down the stepped street (1), and then left along the contour of the E slope, you pass a deep *cistern* dating from the Old Palace period, the largest of its kind known from Minoan Crete. When it burst over the N edge of the hill it was not repaired, so that from then on all water had to be carried up to the big house from the valley below. Above the path are terrace walls and the lower courses of what may have been a defensive tower. The path leads to the EMIII–MMIA paved street and tomb mentioned above, and then on down the hillside back to the road.

At 17km the coastal village of *Mýrtos* has tavernas and simple accommodation. The dirt road along the shore (negotiable—slowly— by car) runs W past banana groves through the hamlet of *Tértsa* to *Arví* (see below), *Keratókambos* and *Tsoútsouros*. The track is recommended to walkers, as are the hills up the Mýrtos river valley.

The new road climbs inland, passing outcrops of serpentine rock. At 31.5km there is a right turn to (2km) *Káto Sými*. High above the village (1200m) an important *sanctuary of Hermes and Aphrodite* has been excavated in recent years by K. Lembéssis for the Greek Archaeological Service. The road into the mountains is unsuitable for normal cars but is recommended as a strenuous walk (6km from Káto Sými). Keep left at the fork beyond the village.

The right fork leads (2km) to the church of Ayios Yeóryios, Epáno Sými, with frescoes, dated by inscription to 1453, by Manuel Phokás (cf. Embaros and Avdoú). The church key used to be held in Káto Sými, but in 1987 it was not obtainable. Enquire in the hope that there is a new arrangement.

The track to the left at the fork climbs very steeply and eventually passes in front of the sanctuary (fenced) which occupies a series of platforms on the mountainside. This was a place of worship from the Middle Minoan period to the 3C AD, and provides a rare example of continuity of religious practice from Minoan to Postminoan times; Hermes and Aphrodite are seen as a transformation of the Minoan goddess and her young consort. Great quantities of votive offerings were brought to the sanctuary over the centuries, and some of the more remarkable finds are a recent addition to Herákleion Museum, Gallery XII.

At 34.5km on the main road a left turn leads through *Amirás* (keeping left at the fork at the end of the village) for the descent to (13km) *Arvi* on the coast. The village caters for visitors; there is a small hotel as well as rent rooms and tavernas behind a narrow beach. You can walk (15 minutes) to the Monastery of Arvi at the bottom of the gorge in the hills back from the shore.
    42km Viánnos (Rte 3C).

From Viánnos to Pýrgos. This 37km stretch of the projected S Coast Highway is unfinished and is very rough indeed in places for a distance of about 10km; some short patches may have to be taken at little more than walking pace. However in 1987 work was in progess again after a lull, and directions are given because the only alternative route between the E and W regions of the island involves returning to Herákleion.
    From Viánnos follow the main Arkalokhóri road (Rte 3C) for 10.5km, and then take the second of the roads signposted (left) to Mártha. (In recent years there has been at the junction a large notice board explaining in Greek the New Road project.) The route leads SW down a river valley towards the Asteroúsia mountains. It is 7.5km to *Skiniás*, now on a good asphalt surface all the way. After this the road is difficult for 6km through *Demáti* and on to *Káto Kastelliná* where you cross the road to Tsoútsouros (12km left, on the coast). You continue along the S edge of the Mesará plain, through *Mesokhorió*, and regaining an asphalt surface reach *Pýrgos* 37km from Viánnos.
    From Pýrgos (see p 140) the main road runs N 50km to Herákleion. 5km along it there is a left turn for (20km) Ayii Déka, to link up with the main road to Phaistós (Rte 4).

9   Ayios Nikólaos to Siteía

70km (43 miles) on the North Coast Highway. 18.5km, the excavated Minoan town of Gourniá; at 39.5km a detour to Mókhlos on the sea. The new kilometre posts on this section of the highway are calculated from the centre of Ayios Nikólaos.

Buses five times a day to Siteía; Gourniá is also served by the Ierápetra bus.

Leave Ayios Nikólaos as for Kritsá, and at the bypass turn left. At the

2km post you pass a reed-fringed beach. The road winds close to the shore around the Bay of Mirabéllo, through some of the finest coastal scenery on Crete. On the first stretch there is a steady increase in villa developments enjoying beautiful views.

After 9.5km you come down to the bay at *Istro*. (Until recently this area was known as Vrókastro, and was officially part of Kaló Khorió.) At the new bridge there are two roads to the right: the first for Pýrgos, and the second for (2km) Kaló Khorió and (13km) Kalamávka (see Rte 8).

Above Istro is *Vrókastro*, a refuge site of the Early Iron Age on a steep limestone spur 300m above the sea. The site was excavated (1910–12) by Edith Hall of the University of Pennsylvania. The plan of the settlement is hard to make out, but the remains of houses clinging to the hilltop are evocative, and the view from the summit is superb.

As you approach the bridge on the way into the village, the site is on the left or seaward summit of the hills ahead, with a terraced gully pointing up to it. There is a choice of routes to reach the site. At the far end of the straggling village (c 12km) a track to the gully (a stiff 20-minute climb to the top) starts just before the road bends right around the next bay. Once the climb begins you are aiming, with the help only of goat tracks, for the saddle which connects the highest peak on your left with the hills behind. For the alternative approach (longer but by an easier gradient) on a path which starts 500m further alng the road, see below.

From the saddle an easy path leads left to the peak, around which is a tangle of house walls, the irregular plan reflecting the nature of the terrain. The rooms are huddled together, and separate houses are difficult to distinguish. All the floors were of trodden earth; column bases were found in three presumably grander areas. The excavator speculated that the choice of such an uncomfortable refuge suggested danger from seaward, and the site has obvious advantages as a look-out post. There is Bronze Age occupation over a long period in the neighbourhood: Early Minoan (3rd millenium) cave burials in the hills behind, and a settlement site on the shore below; also traces of Middle Minoan on the hill-top itself. The pottery from Vrókastro shows continuity from the end of the Bronze Age (LMIII) through Protogeometric to the Geometric settlement, 11–8C BC.

At the far end of the village of Istro, opposite two large tavernas, is a sandy bay with good swimming.

Just before the 13km post is the start of the alternative route up to Vrókastro. At a big concrete culvert over a gully (with a wide parking space on the seaward side) you can see the path following the gully into the hills to approach from the E the saddle behind the site.

At 16.5km a track is signposted right for Moní Phaneroméni. A steep climb (about 5km of careful driving) brings the reward of the austere convent buildings on a rock ledge looking out over the Bay of Mirabéllo. In the foreground of the view is the Vrókastro site. The convent church, dedicated to the Panayía (Assumption of the Virgin, Feast Day, 15 August) is built around a hermit's grotto.

To enjoy further the sense of isolation, walk on past the main door and the modern church hostel; a dirt road brings you out onto the uplands behind the convent.

Immediately opposite the turning to the convent from the main road is the approach to a long-established camping site. Good swimming from rocks.

In March the roadside for the next few kilometres is covered with the brilliant yellow *Ranunculus asiaticus*; the yellow form is notably localised in its distribution. Orchids also abound in the uncultivated areas.

18.5km **Gourniá**. This excavated Minoan town lies on a low hill to the right of the road. (Entrance 150m along a track, signposted. Open (summer 1987): 08.45–15.00, Sunday 09.30–14.30; admission free.) The town, ancient name unknown, looks out over a sheltered cove of the Bay of Mirabéllo. A glance at the map of Crete will underline the geographical advantages of the position for trade and communication with the S coast; the alternative in ancient times to a hazardous sea voyage around the eastern capes was a mere 12km journey across gently undulating terrain, now the isthmus of Ierápetra.

The site was extensively excavated (1901–04) by Harriet Boyd Hawes, a member of a team of American archaeologists in the area at that time. There is evidence for occupation from the Early Bronze Age (3rd millenium), and there were houses on the site in the Middle Minoan period, but most of the existing remains are of the LMI town contemporary with the New Palaces. Like so many other Minoan sites Gourniá was destroyed by fire c 1450 BC. There was very limited reoccupation in LMIII, the period of Mycenaean rule at Knossós.

The street plan of the Minoan town, and the ground floors or basements of houses are well preserved. The narrow streets, which are wide enough for pack animals but not for wheeled transport, are cobbled, and where necessary stepped, and they have an efficient drainage system. In places the houses still stand to a man's height and there were certainly second storeys, because five stone staircases were found as well as evidence for wooden steps. Stone was used in the building, but also mudbrick, often faced with plaster. The doorways were carefully constructed, with limestone thresholds level with the street. If the visitor is already impressed by the grand scale of the Palaces, it is here at Gourniá that the everyday domestic life of the Minoan civilisation becomes a reality.

The street around the outside of the houses leads up from both directions to the top of the hill, where there are *Palatial quarters* on a miniature scale (bold outline on plan). At this site you are required by the guardian to stay on the paths to avoid damaging the walls. If you keep left inside the entrance gate you arrive at a large open space which the excavator called the *Town Court* (1); it has been compared to an agorá or market place. At its N end the arrangement of the steps (2) recalls the *Theatral Area* at Knossós, and beside them the circular stone with hollows (perhaps for ritual offerings) may serve the same function as the Mállia kernos. It is not certain whether the main area with alternate pillar and column bases (3) was an open court or a large room like the Hall of the Double Axes (King's Megaron) at Knossós. To the N were storerooms (4), and there were others behind the W Façade. There is a small cobbled *W Court* (5) in front of the façade, which is of imposing ashlar construction and is recessed for windows on a floor above. It is speculation to call this complex the Governor's, or Ruler's, quarters, but its existence certainly implies hierarchy of some sort.

The finds from the LMI town increased understanding of economic and industrial aspects of Minoan life: of particular interest was the evidence for stone vase-making, also the set of carpenter's tools (found at 8), the workshop of a potter (9) and of a bronze-smith (10). Near the modern entrance a press was found with other equipment for the production of olive oil or wine.

To the SW of the Town Court are houses (6) of the LMIII reoccupation period. These show an architectural scheme influenced by the Mycenaean megaron of mainland Greece.

Contemporary with these houses is a small **Shrine** (7), reached by the cobbled street running N from the W Court. Off this, right, a sloping path is carefully paved with a central pattern of evenly matched cobbles. The shrine, up three steps, is a simple room (3m by 4m) with a ledge for cult objects. The finds (now in Herákleion Museum, Gallery X) included a low tripod altar in clay, goddesses with raised arms and bell-shaped skirt, clay tubes with snakes modelled in relief, a sherd with a double axe in relief, terracotta bird figurines and serpents' heads. At the NE corner of the site (11) are remains of a MMI house.

In 1910 the American archaeologist, R. Seager, excavated a cemetery on *Sphoungarás*, the hill-slope near the sea just to the E of Gourniá. 150 pithos burials were found, the majority LMI, contemporary with the town.

As the road climbs away to the E of the site there is a fine general view of the ruins of Gourniá. On foot a rocky mule path shortens the route to *Pakhyámmos*. At 20km the road descends sharply through several bends to this coastal village. To the right on the hillside is a single-storey stone house built by Seager early this century.

In 1914 he excavated, at the back of the wide beach, a large Minoan cemetery which had been uncovered by a severe storm. Apart from six chests, or larnakes, the remains were in upwards of 200 clay jars. These *pithos burials* mostly dated from the MMIII–LMI period, but a few were EMIII (c 2100 BC). The body was folded head down into the jar, which was then buried with the base uppermost. Seager found many jars below the present water level, and because of the labour required to sink jars into wet sand, took this as confirmation of a rise in sea level on this coast since the Bronze Age.

Pakhyámmos has accommodation and good tavernas. The name means 'deep sand', but adverse currents carry debris into this bay and unless a major effort is made to clean up the beach, the swimming here cannot be recommended.

Beyond the village (21.5km) is the parting of the ways to Ierápetra (Rte 8) and Siteía.

For Siteía keep straight on. At about 23km an angular knob is conspicuous jutting out from the wall of the Thriptí mountains that runs parallel to the road. This marks the Kástro refuge site above (at 25km) the village of *Kavoúsi*.

Several sites inland of the village were excavated in two short seasons at the beginning of the century by the young American archaeologist Harriet Boyd Hawes; her discoveries included the two principal sites of Vrónda and Kástro, and she excavated the completely preserved (but looted) tholos tomb of Skouriasménos. In 1901 she undertook the exploration of the Minoan town of Gourniá, and Kavoúsi returned to relative obscurity. Since 1981 the area has been subjected to a systematic re-examination by a team from the American School of Classical Studies in Athens (W. Coulson, L. Day and G. Gesell). There was some MM activity in the area, but no settlement has yet been found, and study is concentrated on the Early Iron Age sites along the old road up to the Thriptí plain, to arrive at as accurate as possible an understanding of the ancient habitation.

On the top of the hill called *Vrónda* (thunder) there is a sizeable settlement (c 60m by 40m) with cemeteries at the periphery. This was inhabited from LMIIIC (c 1200 BC), and parts of it continued in use into the Protogeometric period (c 875 BC); later (Geometric period) activity in the area appears to have been connected with funeral ceremonies. On the summit of Vrónda stands a house with a paved court on its S side; this (Boyd's 'House on the Summit' and now known as Building A) was constructed in LMIIIC but there is evidence of occupation only until the succeeding Subminoan period. Its size and dominant position suggest that it belonged to a prominent individual, or perhaps served some public function. In the N part of the court a flat kernos-stone has 24 small circular depressions set in an oval ring. Similar objects at other sites (Gourniá, Mállia) have usually been interpreted as cult-related offering tables, but it has been suggested that some were used for gaming. Erosion has unfortunately affected a lot of the hilltop, but it is clear that a cobbled street ran W from the court. Structures on its SE side are interpreted as (basement) storerooms with one area for the preparation of meals. The massive wall on the E is thought to be a terrace wall rather than one for defensive purposes.

On the N slope of the site are a number of stone-built tholos tombs with chambers approached by a short trench or abbreviated dromos. Boyd excavated eight, not all of which have been identified, and two more have since been cleared. The burial practice was solely inhumation, and, in contrast to the transition at neighbouring Vrókastro, cremation was not adopted during the later phase. The American team is considering the possibility of a true Eteocretan period of conservatism, in which developments occur independently from changes in central Crete.

Above Vrónda the inaccessible refuge site known as the *Kástro* (noticed from the road) is built on top of a jutting pinnacle which commands one of the passes into the hills behind. The pottery dates this site to slightly later in the Geometric period than Vrónda, giving rise to curiosity about the (no doubt compelling) reasons that led to this move up to such a precipitous position. The houses, which occupy at least seven narrow terraces around the summit, are fewer in number than at Vrókastro but of much more regular construction. Each complex is carefully rectangular, and large blocks are employed in foundations and doorways; there were stone benches outside the houses either in the streets or in small private courts.

The view from the pinnacle is stunning, and the strenuous walk (90 minutes–2 hours from the village) is highly recommended, regardless of archaeological interest.

A new track leaves the main road just before the bridge at the end of Kavoúsi, and climbs as far as Vrónda, but in its 1987 condition it is not recommended for normal hire cars. From the village a roughly paved path, a Turkish kalderími, marked by occasional splashes of red paint, passes between the two archaeological sites on its way over to the upland valley of Thriptí. It is cut in places by the new track.

In the middle of Kavoúsi turn right off the main road at the crossroads beyond the big modern church (kapheneíon on corner). By a kiosk (250m) turn left and continue uphill, then right into the picturesque ΟΔΟΣ ΔΕΡΜΙΤΖΑΚΗΣ (Odós Dermitzákis). At the end of the houses, passing (left) the old village school and a cemetery church, the kalderími sets off into the hills. At the second road crossing there is the choice of following the kalderími (which strikes left) or taking the easier footpath ahead beside the water channel. (In this case, at the road again, turn left and in 200m take another footpath right which will rejoin the old paved way.) The Panayía Kardiótissa (on the new road) is now in view above left, with the Kástro pinnacle towering behind it. Watch for a split in the path; the red-splashed kalderími continues ahead, but for Vrónda take the right fork uphill. In 5 minutes the church of Ayía Paraskeví, with a ruined building adjoining it, comes into view, and the old cottages of the summer-pasturage village of Vrónda appear on the sky-line (right). A path between them leads over the hill (5 minutes) to the excavated site and cemetery (see above).

From Vrónda the path to the Kástro passes in front of Ayía Paraskeví and rejoins the paved path, climbing steadily. When this reaches the head of a cultivated valley it turns right, away from the site, and on to Thriptí. Leave the kalderími, cross the head of the valley, left, on a terraced path and make for the saddle behind the pinnacle. From here the easiest approach to the site on the summit is round the further flank.

The highway climbs from the coast. 4km beyond Kavoúsi, at (31km) Plátanos, a well-sited café (left) commands a fine view across to the island of Pseíra. Seager (see Sphoungarás and Pakhyámmos) excavated on the island in 1906–07, uncovering a prosperous Minoan settlement founded in EMI and continuously occupied until its final destruction in LMIB (finds in Herákleion and Siteía museums). In 1985 archaeologists returned to the island, in a Greek–American collaboration headed by P. Betancourt and C. Daváras, to clean and re-examine Seager's settlement, and to seek answers to questions that his report and plans had left unanswered. A start has been made on several important buildings including the Shrine. The settlement's streets and lanes, not plotted by Seager, were traced and plotted, contributing interesting information on settlement organisation and access. It is possible (but expensive) to arrange to visit the island from Mókhlos or Ayios Nikólaos.

39.5km Spháka offers the easiest of several signposted roads for the detour to (6.5km) Mókhlos on the sea (also the most convenient bus stop).

On the descent keep right at a fork after 1km, and the coastal plain soon comes into view with a large hotel on the shore. The tiny island of **Mókhlos** is at the far end of the bay opposite the modern hamlet, which is still unspoilt and is recommended for very simple accommodation and waterfront tavernas. (Two modest hotels, also rooms for rent.)

This was an important settlement in Minoan times. The island, now 150m offshore, is believed to have been attached to the mainland by a narrow isthmus, thus creating a harbour sheltered from the prevailing NW winds. The settlement on the S slopes of the island facing the modern village was excavated by Seager in 1908. It proved to date from the Middle Minoan and Late Minoan I periods, with traces of Early Minoan occupation. But the most exciting Mókhlos finds came from tombs nearby, recently reinvestigated by the Greek archaeologist C. Daváras. At the W end of the island, Early Minoan rectangular chamber tombs resembling house structures were built against the cliff. Some of the tombs have doorways which could be closed with large stone slabs; one group opened onto a roughly paved court. The tombs would have had flat roofs of reeds and clay. The rich burial gifts included spectacular *jewellery* and *sealstones* as well as one of the finest collections of *stone vases* known from Minoan Crete. The materials include rock-crystal, marble, steatite and brecchia (Ayios Nikólaos Museum, Room II, and Mókhlos case in Siteía Museum).

There is often rough water in the strait, but in calm weather a local boatman will ferry you to the island, or strong swimmers can cross unaided (footwear desirable on landing.) The chamber-tombs are easily reached by a path from the S shore that hugs the W slope of the island. As well as the Minoan excavations, there are Roman fortifications above the northern cliff, with traces of a tower behind an E–W curtain wall. It has been suggested that they were a defence against 8C AD Arab raids. There was an extensive town in the area of modern Mókhlos up to the Second Byzantine period.

Beyond Spháka the highway, attractively planted with cypress and oleanders, continues past a number of villages along the foothills of Mount Ornon.

43.5km The road skirts *Myrsíni*, but it is worth stopping to walk up into the village. The terrace of the well-restored church enjoys a good view of this stretch of the coast. To the left, the village of *Tourlotí* is prominent; there was a LMIII cemetery on the hillside below. On the Aspropiliá hill near the sea N of Myrsíni, 12 rock-cut chamber tombs of the same Postpalatial period, excavated by N. Pláton in 1960, yielded a rich variety of vases, weapons and utensils, now on show in the Ayios Nikólaos museum.

Also below Myrsíni a much earlier circular tomb, the first of the Mesará type to be found in E Crete, contained over 60 burials dated by associated finds to the EMIII and MMI periods.

The road crosses a high spur to (50km) *Mésa Moulianá*. Nearby in the place known as Selládis, two tholos tombs were excavated in 1903 by S. Xanthoudídes. These were LMIII tombs re-used during the Protogeometric period; it is interesting that at this time of transition from interment to cremation, there was evidence for both burial rites within the same tomb. The rich LMIII grave offerings included a gold mask, bronze vessels and a sword reflecting the Mycenaean influence. Particularly remarkable is a Protogeometric bell-krater (10C BC), with on one side a hunting scene with two wild goats (probably the 'agrími' or Cretan ibex), on the other a man on horseback, the first such representation known from Crete (Herákleion Museum, Gallery XI).

The wine from the Moulianá region is highly regarded.

At 56km stone windmills are a striking landmark on the last crest before the Bay of Siteía. Here a track leaves the road (right), signposted for **Khamaízi**, a Minoan site which rewards a detour (1.5km). On the track take the second turning right, the one just beyond the windmills (possible by car, or a 15 minute walk).

Khamaízi is interesting because it is the only Minoan building so far discovered that is roughly oval in plan. The site, visible for some distance on top of a conical hill, was first excavated in 1903 by S. Xanthoudídes. After controversy in the archaeological world it was reinvestigated in 1971 by C. Daváras.

There is a paved entrance at the SE (1 on plan). The rooms are set around a small courtyard also paved (2), an arrangement which no doubt offered some protection from the fierce winds which sweep across this eastern tip of the

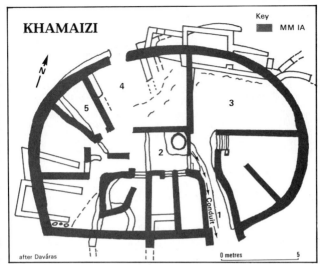

KHAMAIZI

Key
MM IA

4

5

3

2

Conduit

1

after Daváras

0 metres 5

island. Raised in the NE corner of the court is a deep circular cistern, or well, lined with masonry. The conduit system can still be traced.

A find of figurines now in Herákleion Museum, Gallery II, had led to the suggestion that the building was a peak sanctuary rather than a dwelling, with the cistern interpreted as a votive pit, but the discovery of the conduit made this hypothesis less convincing and it is now agreed that the three figurines probably furnished a small household shrine; the area (3) to the NE of the court contained a movable hearth and fragments of a clay altar. In 1979 a second entrance was found, and this lessened speculation about the fortress-like aspect of the building. The walls of the room (4) into which the entrance leads were faced with schist and limestone, and adjacent (5) was a staircase to an upper floor.

There had been discussion whether the choice of a curved exterior wall was a deliberate architectural decision or was determined by the shape of the hill-top. The 1971 excavation found earlier (EM) rectangular buildings, discernible now on the site (unshaded on plan), which suggest that the curved walls of the MMI house were a new and presumably deliberate design.

In the village of *Khamaízi*, the *Folk Museum preserves some of Crete's rapidly vanishing past, including a rare type of loom. (Open: 09.00–13.00 and 17.00–20.00. Small admission fee.) Park on the main road and follow the signs on foot.

After (c 60km) the large village of *Skopí*, two turnings 4km apart are signposted to Moní Phaneroméni (Φανερωμένη), a former monastery near the coast with a dramatically sited chapel.

The second turning (3km from Siteía, 6km on a track to the chapel) is recommended to walkers—good bus service along the main road. At the coast the track runs W (c 2km) below white cliffs along the Bay of Trakhíla. The monastery (signed) lies a short distance inland. The frescoed church (graffito date 1465), built over a grotto associated with the miraculous appearance of an icon of Mary, is dedicated to the Panayía Phaneroméni (the Virgin made manifest). Perched on the edge of a ravine, the church became the nucleus of an important monastery (now spoiled by modern buildings); the grotto is still revered today.

The main road runs down into **Siteía**, a small harbour town (pop. 8000) and a convenient base for exploring E Crete. Though crowded at the height of the summer season, for the rest of the year the town is well-equipped to welcome visitors, and deserves a greater share of them than it currently receives. The Siteía Archaeological Museum opened in 1984, and there is a new airport 10 minutes from the town centre with regular flights to Kásos, Kárpathos and Rhodes. The tree-shaded waterfront (at one end of a long beach) is lined with good cafés and tavernas, and the attractively colour-washed modern houses rise steeply, tier on tier, behind. A conspicuous red-domed church is the seat of the local bishop. Cretan raisins are exported through Siteía and a lively 'Sultana Festival' takes place in August.

There was settlement on the bay both in Minoan and in Greco-Roman times (probably the Eteía mentioned by Stephanos of Byzantium as the birthplace of Myson, one of the Seven Sages of Classical Greece), but the exact location is still disputed. There has been a town on the present site since the First Byzantine period, before the 9C Arab conquest. During their brief stay on the island (early 13C) the Genoese strengthened existing fortifications, and under Venetian rule Siteía flourished as a fully walled city; above the harbour, one of the forts of the wall has been restored and is used as a theatre in summer. The Venetian city was twice damaged by earthquake, and frequently by Turkish raids until, in 1539, it was sacked by the renowned Turkish pirate, Barbarossa. When, in 1648, the Turks blockaded the city, the Venetians forcibly evacuated the reluctant population to safety inland. The Kástro held out for three years, but the town was utterly destroyed and lay in ruins for two centuries. Not until 1870 did the Turkish authorities decide to build a new administrative centre here. The new town was laid out, but unfortunately little more than the regular street plan survives.

Siteía is proud of its association with the Hellenised Venetian family of Kornáros, distinguished in the spheres of art and learning. Vintzétzos Kornáros, author of the great epic poem, 'Erotókritos', is thought to have been born here.

Hotels: Siteía has a number of pleasant, well-equipped Class C establishments, some right on the harbour front, and many houses offering rooms to rent.

Youth Hostel: 4 Odós Therissoú on the road into town from Ayios Nikólaos. Tel. 22 693.

Tourist Information office run by the municipality in a caravan on the quay, E of the harbour and in front of the Hotel Itanos.

National Bank: across Plateía Iróon Polytekhníou from the Tourist Information office.

OTE: Odós Kondiláki. Area code 0843.

Post Office: in Odós Therissoú near the Hotel Alice on the road in from Ayios Nikólaos.

Bus station off Odós Praisoú, part of the dual-carriageway running down to the harbour.

Ferry services regularly connect Siteía with Kásos, Kárpathos and Rhodes, and with various islands in the Cyclades en route to Piraeus. The schedule alters each spring. NTO offices should have details, or check direct with the Tzortzákis travel agency (tel. 28 900), whose office is on the quay by the inner pier.

Olympic Airways: 56 Odós El. Venizélou, almost opposite the National Bank, tel.22 270. Services at present only to Kásos, Kárpathos and Rhodes.

From near the inner pier, broad steps lead up to the episcopal church of Ayía Aikateríni. The *Folklore Museum* is on the same level, in Odós Gabr. Arkadíou, three houses from the church. Open daily, 10.00–13.00 and 17.30–20.00 (winter, mornings only); small admission fee. The collection concentrates on domestic crafts and equipment; the antique bed-hangings are particularly fine.

The same street leads out to the restored *Fort*, known locally as the 'Kazárma' (Casa di Arma); it provides, especially in the evening light, a superb view of the bay, and the hills of E Crete.

On the seafront beyond the Port Authority building, rock-cut *Roman fish-tanks* have been recognised just below the present water-level. They are comparable to those at Khersónisos (Rte 5), but less easy to make out. The water-front walk diverts a few paces inland to avoid old buildings, and the fish-tanks are just beyond them, level with the Star hotel.

A lively evening 'volta' (the traditional hour of strolling and chatting) takes place along the harbour quays.

The **Archaeological Museum** is back from the seafront, inland of the bus station, at the junction with the road S across the island, signposted Lithínes. The museum was opened in the summer of 1984. The building, attractively designed around a courtyard, displays finds from the extreme eastern end of the island.

Open (1987): 09.00–15.00 (Sundays 09.30–14.30), closed Tuesdays. Admission Drs 200.

The collection is in four sections, each introduced by explanatory notes and a relief map.

Just inside the main room is a free-standing case with finds from the important Neolithic site of Pelekitá, a cave on the seaward slope of Mount Traóstalos, N of Zákros; also an impressive exhibit of Neolithic stone axes.

Left of the entrance are two cases of finds from the cemetery of Ayía Photiá, 5km E along the coast, where more than 250 tombs (EMI/II, c 3000–2500 BC) were excavated. The material is interesting because of the strong Cycladic character of some of the finds in a clear Early Minoan context; the 'frying pans' are a local variation of a type characteristic of the Early Bronze Age in the Cyclades and on the Greek mainland. There is also a good exhibit of obsidian pressure blades.

Next come Minoan votive terracottas from various Peak Sanctuaries, the majority from Petsophás above Palaíkastro. A large proportion of the known sites of this type are found in E Crete.

The adjacent central case contains material from the off-shore islet of Mókhlos. Note the lamp on the lower shelf, and the high quality stone vases from EM/MM tombs. Next, in the centre, are finds from the Minoan settlement on the island of Pseíra, including a fine stirrup-jar in the Marine Style, probably a product of a Knossós workshop. Along the wall are cases of Early and Middle Minoan material from various sites in the Siteía region, and nearby an exhibit of bronze objects. Finds from the Minoan town of Palaíkastro have a wall-case to themselves. Note the horns of consecration in stone, and the same motif used to decorate a pottery rhyton; also two multiple vases or kernoi, one in clay (four cups) and one in stone (two). Then comes a case of Late Minoan (Neopalatial) finds from the region.

In the *Zákros section* the first wall-case contains a large bronze saw from the Palace, also finds from the Minoan town. In the corner is a well-preserved *Wine-press from the Minoan villa at Ano Zákros (LMI, contemporary with the New Palaces). The nearby central case holds large pots with signs of burning from the great fire which destroyed the Palace c 1450 BC. Along the wall more large pots and also giant pithoi emphasise the importance of storage in a Minoan palace. The nearby *Exhibit of Linear A script is a reminder of the Palace's administrative function, and, between the two largest pithoi, a selection of Minoan cooking pots illustrates one of the domestic aspects of Minoan life. These exhibits are followed by cases of finer wares from the Palace, including a good display of spouted jars. In the corner are stone offering tables and lamps.

In the *Geometric and Archaic section*, note especially the display of Daidalic heads and figurines; this important deposit of terracottas was found in the centre of Siteía during road-works near the present post office.

The last section is devoted to material from the *Hellenistic and Roman* periods. Most interesting are the finds from the small island of Kouphonísi off the SE corner of Crete, with fishing equipment and objects connected with the preparation of purple (or deep crimson) dye from a gland extracted from the shell *Murex trunculus.*

Finally, a large stone block with Greek inscription comes from a Roman-period building at Itanos.

For touring from Siteía see also Rtes 10A and B. Obtainable locally is 'Sitia' by the Greek archaeologist N. Papadákis (translated by J.M. Kaphetzáki), a detailed guidebook to the region which is highly recommended.

10 Excursions from Siteía

A. To the East Coast

Direct road to the Minoan Palace of Zákros 50km. The recommended route (c 70km to the Palace) includes: (16km) the Monastery of Toploú; (25km) the palm-fringed beach at Vái; (27km) ancient Itanos; (c 40km) the archaeological site of Palaíkastro with the opportunity of a walk up to the peak sanctuary of Petsophás.

One bus a day to Vái, two a day to the village of Ano Zákros and then a further hour on foot to the Palace.

The Zákros road runs E out of Siteía along the edge of the bay. At 5km is the village of *Ayía Photiá*, site of an important EMI–II cemetery excavated in 1971 by the Greek archaeologist, C. Daváras. There were more than 250 tombs, with multiple burials and a rich variety of grave offerings; the outstanding finds of pottery, with bronze and stone artefacts, tools and weapons are exhibited both in the new museum in Siteía and in Ayios Nikólaos Museum (Room I). Some graves were simple shallow pits but there was also a primitive form of chamber-tomb. The cemetery, recently re-examined and restored, lies on the low hill near the sea, just W of the Mare Sol bungalows. The rock-cut tombs were closed with an upright blocking slab, and outside there was a small paved antechamber for the cult of the dead; many of the big pedestalled cups displayed in the museums were found on these paved areas. On the next hill to the W excavations in 1984 began to uncover what may be the settlement associated with the cemetery.

At 12.5km the direct road to Palaíkastro and Zákros runs straight on, but the recommended route takes the left turn to (3.5km) the fortified *monastery of Toploú*, a striking sight standing out from the barren upland. The Turkish name has replaced the earlier Panayía Akrotiriáni, the Virgin of the Cape. A 14C church (torch useful for icons) is the original nucleus of later (much restored) Venetian buildings; the monastery was fortified at the end of the 16C.

Toploú has a chequered history. It acquired great power and wealth, with dependent churches and monastic foundations scattered across the island (including a nunnery on the site of the present church of Ayía Triáda in Herákleion) and even today is a major landowner in E Crete. The monastery endured many acts of destruction and plunder by among others the Knights of St. John of Malta in 1530 and by the Turks in 1646, as well as severe earthquake damage in 1612. The monks maintained a tradition of support for the Cretan national cause, and suffered accordingly. During the 1940–45 war they operated an underground radio transmitter, and for this the Abbot Silignákis was executed in the notorious Ayiá jail near Khaniá.

Only three monks remain in residence; one should be on duty at reasonable hours to open the church, but persistence may be required. A major programme of repairs has been under way for some time and there is a plan to restore the monastery workshops as a museum of the practical aspects of the monastic life.

The main entrance is through the *Loggia Gate* into a reception and workshop area, and then by an easily defended double doorway into the monastery proper. The small *court* with patterned cobbles is surrounded by three levels of cells, as well as the abbot's quarters and a big refectory; above are the battlemented walls and tall Italianate *bell-tower*. The ancient *well* opposite the church door was in use until very recently.

On the façade of the church, to the left of the doorway, four stone slabs are let into the wall. One is a relief of the Virgin with Child, Our Lady of the Cape. The two central inscriptions record the pious labours of the Abbot Gabriel Pandogalos, who restored the monastery after the 1612 earthquake with financial help from the Venetian Senate.

The inscribed slab at door level is part of the 'Arbitration of the Magnesions', 132 BC. Two copies of this inscription have been found. One, from the Temple of Artemis at Magnesia itself, preserves lines 27–140. This fragment at Toploú overlaps with lines 1–86. Maqnesia, a city of the Roman Empire in Asia Minor, was called to arbitrate in a complicated series of territorial disputes, first between Praisós and Itanos, and then after the destruction of Praisós, between Itanos and Ierápytna (modern Ierápetra). A central issue in the dispute was the control of the Temple of Zeus Diktaios at Palaíkastro. This fragment was brought to Toploú from Itanos to serve first as a tombstone and then as an altar table in the beautiful little cemetery chapel of Tímios Stavrós (the Holy Cross) outside the monastery. In 1834 it was noticed by the English scholar and traveller, R. Pashley, who suggested its present setting.

The two-aisled church has, as is usual, a double dedication: the northern and older aisle, of the Panayía Akrotiriáni, to the Nativity of the Virgin, and the southern to Ayios Ioánnis Theológos (the Evangelist)—Feast Days respectively 8 and 26 September. *Frescoes* of scenes from the gospels recently uncovered in the N aisle are dated stylistically to the 14C. An *icon stand* painted with designs from bird and plant life bears the signature Stamation and the date 1770; such antique pieces are now very rare on Crete. Alongside this N aisle is a small room used in the past by women at the services.

There are several fine *icons* in the church. The outstanding one, displayed between the two aisles, is entitled 'Lord, Thou art Great.' There are two inscriptions at the foot of the icon establishing the artist: Ioánnis Kornáros, the date: 1770, and the donor: Demétrios, with his wife and children. The work portrays 61 densely painted scenes each inspired by a phrase from the prayer of the Orthodox Liturgy used on the Feast of the Epiphany. This icon is one of the great masterpieces of Cretan art.

The road continues for 6km across moorland to (22km) a T-junction. Turn left and (after 1.5km) right, for the beach at *Vái* set in a remarkable grove of tall palm trees.

Phoenix theophrasti greuter, a distinct species closely related to the date palm though its fruit is smaller, dry and inedible, is restricted solely to E Crete. The trunk may grow to a height of 10m. The grove's existence is attested since Classical times.

There is especially fine swimming here from a sandy beach with theatrically placed off-shore rocks, but because of its exotic reputation Vái in summer can be very busy indeed.

If the crowds and noise are intolerable you are advised to continue a further 3km—back to the coast road and turn right—to the site of ancient Itanos, where there is a choice of attractive bays, the one S of the archaeological site being particularly recommended.

The road comes to an end at the site. Beyond is *Cape Síderos*, the extreme NE point of Crete, but entry is restricted because of a Greek naval establishment. The small island of Elása to the E has ancient remains, and is still used as a sheltered anchorage.

The area is known locally as Erimoúpolis, 'the deserted place'. There was sufficient exploration here at the turn of the century to identify the ruins with **Itanos**, one of the most influential ruling cities of E Crete, with territory stretching to the S coast including the island of Kouphonísi. The French excavated in 1950 but the results have not yet been published.

A LMI villa to the S of the Greco-Roman site is evidence of Bronze Age occupation in the area. It is not known when the city was founded, but according to a story in Herodotus (IV.151) it was flourishing by the 7C BC. There is a fine 5C silver coinage, and this prosperity continued through to the Early Byzantine period. Around 260 BC Itanos asked for Ptolemaic support against neighbouring Praisós, and an Egyptian garrison was established here, apparently without prejudice to the city's independence. Until the end of that century, and briefly again 50 years later, Egypt seems to have welcomed the opportunity to influence Aegean affairs, and E Crete was a convenient base for the vital recruitment of mercenaries. With the defeat of Praisós by Ierápytna (modern Ierápetra) c 155 BC, that city became the chief rival of Itanos, especially over the control of the important Temple of Zeus Diktaios at Palaíkastro. It took 20 years to settle this frontier dispute. The *Arbitration of Magnesia* (132 BC; see Toploú) is proof that by this time the Roman Empire was interested in the fate of Crete.

At least four temples are recorded here from Classical times, but the remains intelligible today are mostly from the First Byzantine period. Itanos was a double acropolis site on two low hills and the land between. The E hill rises sheer out of the sea; the W one has incongruous dwellings beside the ancient watch-tower and fine Hellenistic terrace walling. Traces of the city spread on to the rise beyond the bay to the S. The cemetery area is up the coast in the opposite direction.

On the inland slope of the main E acropolis are the excavated remains of a 5–6C *basilica* which stood on the site of, and perhaps was converted from an earlier temple to Athena Polias. The plan shows side aisles extended to the limit of the main raised apse, and the central aisle has unusual small apse-like niches in its long walls. The church was built partly of re-used material, and the floors were paved with stone slabs. Several incomplete marble columns survive. One large block has carved decoration of circles filled with rosettes (one with a Greek cross).

There are traces of two other basilicas on the slope behind the bay to the S.

Back at the T-junction beyond the Vái turn (with Toploú and Siteía right) keep straight ahead for Palaíkastro. The ancient site comes into view after 2.5km; the prominent flat-topped hill is Kastrí, and the Minoan town lay on the coastal plain to the S of it. The modern

The Bay of Palaíkastro (from Spratt, Travels and Researches in Crete, *1865)*

village of Palaíkastro has two small hotels and simple rooms to rent. When you reach the plateía, turn left towards Zákros.

After 150m, on a right-hand bend, a by-road to the left (signed Marina Village) leads in 2km to the *archaeological site*. On the by-road ignore a fork right, continue to the new bridge over the stream-bed and across it turn left skirting the hamlet of Angáthia. Then follow the dirt road heading for the sea, keeping left again at a fork, until you emerge from the olive trees at the base of the flat-topped hill, Kastrí. (Popular beach tavernas in summer and good swimming all along this coast.)

The scramble up *Kastrí* is worthwhile for the view (path behind the taverna on the edge of the sea). Off-shore are the Grándes Islands. On a clear day you may make out Kásos and Kárpathos, 'stepping stone' islands to the E towards Rhodes. This was the notorious Kásos channel through which the British Mediterranean Fleet so often had to risk its warships during the 1941 Battle of Crete; Stuka dive-bombers were based at the German-held airfield on Kárpathos.

Excavations on Kastrí in 1962 revealed walls, still visible, dating to EMIII and LMIIIC, that is early in the Bronze Age and at the very end of it, periods when the defensive potential of this hill apparently assumed considerable importance.

Palaíkastro was first investigated by R.C. Bosanquet and R.M. Dawkins (1902–06). In 1962 a team from the British School at Athens returned to the site two years running under the direction of L.H. Sackett and M.R. Popham. Excavation on a major scale produced evidence for occupation in the area from the Neolithic to the end of the Late Minoan period, with a continuing cult of Zeus Diktaios from Geometric down to Hellenistic and Roman times. Most of the excavation has been back-filled, but part of the *main street* is uncovered, and along it are the ground-floor plans of several LMI houses. This is enough to demonstrate that Palaíkastro was a town on a grander scale and architecturally more elegant than Gourniá. If, as seems likely, there were palatial quarters at Palaíkastro comparable with those at Gourniá they have yet to be discovered.

In 1983, at the invitation of the Greek government, the British School (L.H. Sackett and J.A. MacGillivray) returned once more to the site to carry out a topographical survey of the whole area, and to begin a new programme of excavations to try to define more exactly the nature of the town and its limits.

The Minoan town lay to the S of Kastrí, in the centre of the bay a little back from the salt-flats of the present shore line, on a stretch of land known locally as Roussolákkos (the red pit). A broad path (signed) at right-angles to the coastal track along the salt-flats leads (100m) to the site.

You come first to the fenced area of the newest excavations, which have uncovered the foundations of a large LMI public building destroyed in LMIB and succeeded by a less impressive structure of LMIII date (possibly a bench sanctuary of the type known at Knossós).

In 1987 fragments of an ivory statuette were found in an open area adjacent to the LMI building. They comprise the torso, which had been at least partially adorned with gold leaf, of a young male with arms bent and clenched hands held to his breast, in the pose familiar from numerous terracotta figurines. It is tempting to speculate, in the light of the discovery of this (presumably) cult figure, on the ritual practices here at Palaíkastro which may have preceded those of the Greco-Roman temple of Zeus Diktaíos. It is hoped that forthcoming seasons of excavation will throw further light on such matters.

Leading E from the LMI building was a walled route, named by the excavators 'Harbour Road' because it runs down to the likely location of the Minoan harbour in the hollow with vineyards between the excavation and the salt-flats. The sea level is higher than in antiquity, but at the same time the silting process has raised the level of the valley floor.

About 40m to the E of the harbour was found part of a LMI house with paved court and a cupboard containing LMIA pottery, indicating that the house was destroyed at a time roughly contemporary with the volcanic destruction of Théra (c 100km to the N), perhaps 50 years before the widespread LMIB destructions on Crete.

Inland of the new Roussolákkos excavations (at the Kastrí end of the site) there is a separate excavation (1962 vintage) of a LMIB house known as House N. The entrance to the house from the street is on the N side. (The off-shore Grándes Islands lie roughly NE.) The broad entrance passage leads to an inner *hall* (which had a staircase, left, to an upper storey) and then to a large *main room* at the back. In one corner of this room, a small *pantry* produced nearly 400 cups, many stacked inside each other as they had fallen from shelves; there were also large jars and a tripod cooking pot that were taken as evidence that the adjacent main room was a dining room. In the Inner Hall were two pyramidal double-axe stands like those in the 'Corridor of the Magazines' at Knossós, and nearby miniature horns of consecration, all of which had fallen from above, suggesting a *shrine* on the upper floor.

The uncovered stretch of the *main street* starts just to the E. It is paved with irregular blocks of limestone and schist, and is bordered by drains. On the right, *House Δ* has a grand ashlar façade, 40m long. Behind the wide doorway midway along the façade is the megaron, marked by four column bases round a large slab. Further on, beyond the evergreen oak tree, a major crossroads has been left visible. Beyond it *House B* (MMIII–LMI) is on the seaward side of the street; the entrance is at the far end of the façade across a large thresh-old block, with evidence for a staircase to an upper storey just inside the doorway. The large porticoed court ahead may have been a walled garden. It leads left into a *Peristyle Hall* with central impluvium, and adjacent lustral basin. The finds from this house were in keeping with the standard of the architecture and further emphasised the prosperity of its owner. Many of these objects are on show in Herakléion Museum, Gallery IX, including superb Marine Style vases almost certainly from a Knossós workshop. There is also a good display in the first section of the Siteía museum. On the opposite side of the street is *House* Γ. It too has a wide entrance (under an olive tree). Four column bases distinguish the megaron, and next to it to the W is a bathroom. The house lay in the angle of two town streets. From this point on, the excavation is back-filled.

In this area, just beyond these two houses where the main street now disappears under the fill, R.C. Bosanquet's excavation identified the site of the *Temple of Zeus Diktaios*; it was already known that control of this sanctuary was disputed between the city-states of E Crete in the 3C BC and was one of the main subjects of the Arbitration of the Magnesians in 132 BC (see Toploú and Itanos). The temple building had been completely destroyed. Not even the plan could be made out, but architectural fragments dated from the 6C BC, including a clay 'sima' or waterspout with relief of a warrior mounting a chariot drawn by two horses, and a dog running below. The most important find was the scattered fragments of a limestone slab (3C AD) inscribed with part of the Hymn to Zeus Diktaios, an invocation used in re-enacting the dance of the Kouretes around the infant Zeus (see the Idaian cave, Rte 3A). Both this and the 'sima' are in Herákleion Museum, Gallery XIX. The inscription is dated to the 3C AD, and is taken as evidence that a cult of Zeus Diktaios persisted here for nearly a millenium.

On top of the steep hill of *Petsophás* (215m), conspicuous to the S of Roussolákkos, was an open-air Minoan Peak Sanctuary. First explored by the British in 1903, this was fully excavated in the 1970s by the Greek archaeologist C. Daváras. Tucked against the rocks on the summit, the walled precinct contained a small *shrine* with plaster benches. A great quantity of votive offerings was found, mainly human and animal figurines in clay, and examples are shown in the Ayios Nikólaos and Siteía museums. Offering tables were inscribed in Linear A.

There are two routes by which you can approach Petsophás. The new track (marked with paint splashes) starts from the little promontary S of the salt-flats, striking diagonally inland, and keeps to the coastal plain until, when level with the peak, it turns towards it. (You can take a car along behind the shore until you are level with the peak, and then join this path for the climb following a wire fence.)
    For the time-honoured route (or on the return), there is a path along the hillside from the direction of Angáthia. From the lowland, 200m SE of Roussolákkos, you can see, in the red earth up the valley inland, a tin roof on posts that covers a well. To the left of this a ridge runs inland and where it merges with the hillside you can turn left on a well-worn path. Steadily gaining height this becomes a built path (kalderími) that skirts the summit of Petsophás by the S flank. At the highest point strike out to the right, less than 5 minutes to the peak. The sanctuary site overlooks the sea.

From Palaíkastro village the Zákros road leaves the sea and winds (for 20km) across windswept hills and through several villages. At 57km, just before the village of *Adravásti*, a minor road (right) offers an alternative return route to Siteía (see below).
    60km *Ano* (upper) *Zákros.*

Originally the settlement must have prospered because of the plentiful spring water, but now the village caters for visitors to the remote Minoan Palace. There is a simple hotel, also a number of rooms for rent, and several tourist-orientated tavernas. This is the end of the bus route.

The way to the site on foot (c 1 hour) is down a spectacular gorge carved by the river which flows into the bay at Káto (lower) Zákros. The path is marked at intervals by red paint. The gorge is subject to flash floods early in the year and after storms. Ask at one of the kapheneíons to be shown the start of the path, and if in doubt check for safety. Caves in the gorge were used for burials during the Early and Middle Minoan periods, hence the local name, the Ravine of the Dead (Pháranga ton Nekrón).

The car road (9km) to the Palace of Zákros is signposted (past the hotel) to the right from the central plateía. Just out of the village it cuts through a LMI villa where in 1965 a wine press and a pithos inscribed in Linear A were found; the wine-making equipment is well displayed in the new Siteía museum, and the pithos is in Herákleion Museum, Gallery VIII.

Within the last decade the road has been radically realigned so that it now makes the final aproach to the Palace along the coast from the S.

On the coastal stretch two islets further S mark Xerókambos, and beyond is the island of Kouphonísi (see below).

With the Bay of Zákros and the bottom of the gorge in view, the Palace excavation lies a little back from the far end of the beach. The mountain to the N is Traóstalos, site of a Minoan Peak Sanctuary. *Káto Zákros*, inhabited only from April to October, is a cluster of houses with tavernas, a shop, and a number of simple rooms for rent. Swimming is from a shingle beach.

The Palace and town of ****ZAKROS** lie on the N side of a small enclosed bay which provides the best sheltered harbour on this coast. It was ideally placed for trade with Egypt and the Levant, and valuable imports found here show that the Minoan civilisation recognised and exploited this advantage.

The town site at Zákros was investigated by the British under D.G. Hogarth at the beginning of the century. But the spectacular nature of the finds, including gold objects, unearthed locally, gave grounds for suspecting an undiscovered Palace, and in 1962 the eminent Greek archaeologist N. Pláton began an excavation for the Greek Archaeological Society (with the help of American money) which immediately met with success. Work on the Palace has continued each year since then but only preliminary reports have been published. The Siteía museum devotes a whole section to finds from Zákros.

The Zákros site consists of a terraced town with narrow streets, stepped and cobbled as at Gourniá, and overlain by larger villas or palace dependencies; sheltered on the flat land below is a Palace of LMI period. The sea level has risen here since Minoan times and the Palace is often partly under water. It is similar in plan to the other Minoan palaces, though smaller, and itself covers earlier remains (also probably Palatial). The Palace, like so many other Minoan sites, seems to have suffered a sudden and terrible catastrophe c 1450 BC which caused the buildings to collapse and burn. The inhabitants had had time to collect their most valuable portable belongings and escape, but though there was rebuilding in the town area, the Palace was left largely undisturbed. It was neither restored nor looted (possibly placed under a 'taboo') and yielded to the excavators an almost full range of antiquities. Dr Pláton links the destruction (not entirely plausibly) with the eruption of the island of Théra.

The Palace is open daily 09.00–17.00 (1987 hours), admission Drs 200.

You approach the site at the NE corner along a paved Minoan road (1 on plan) which came up from the harbour. The paving had a con-

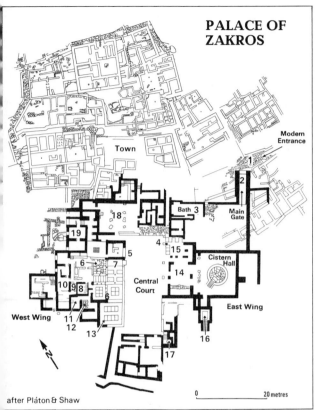

PALACE OF ZAKROS

Modern Entrance

Town

Bath 3

Main Gate

18

19

4

15

Cistern Hall

5

6 7

14

Central Court

10 9 8

6

East Wing

West Wing

11

12

13

16

17

after Pláton & Shaw

0   20 metres

trasting pattern of blue and white stones. On the left, Old Palace period excavations brought to light evidence for a *bronze foundry*: a horseshoe-shaped smelting chamber with four air ducts and remnants of the ore still in situ. This apparently went out of use in 1600 BC.

The street continues ahead into the town, but the Entrance (2) to the Palace is obliquely left through what was a *covered gateway*, now marked by a large limestone threshold block. You descend to the NE Court by a *stepped ramp* where the excavator compares the regular central slabs to a strip of ceremonial carpet. Some original fragments remain. The roofed area is a bath (3) which had columns on its N and W sides, and also a bench. Its proximity to the entrance suggests comparisons with the N Lustral Basin near the N Entrance at Knossós, where visitors to the Palace may have taken part in cleansing and purification rituals.

In front of the roofed area you pass between two pillars (4) into the Central Court, on a NE–SW alignment differing very slightly from that found at the other three Palace sites. At 30.30m by 12.15m this court is only about a third the size of that of Knossós. There is the base of a square altar in the N–W quadrant. The façades of the surrounding buildings were in ashlar masonry incorporating vertical and horizontal timber beams as in the other palaces. The squared blocks came from a quarry at Pelekitá, 5km to the N along the coast.

Behind the façade of the WEST WING is a large Hall, a series of connecting areas with distinguishing floor patterns, and behind this, away from the Courtyard, is a shrine and its associated rooms. There was a second storey reached by a staircase near the triple entrance to the wing which was at the N end of the Hall.

The entrance (5), with massive threshold block level with the altar in the Court, led through an anteroom which had a slender central column, into a square room characterised as a reception lobby, and distinguished by a floor with a central square of red tiles. Then to the left was a paved and colonnaded light-well (6) which also lit the N end of the Hall (7). The light-well with a drain at the NE corner had crazy paving with interstices of red plaster. Here were found in pieces the chlorite *bull's head rhyton* and the *mountain shrine rhyton*. The latter is not only a finely worked stone vase which had originally been covered in gold leaf, but also pictorial evidence of the greatest importance for an understanding of the Minoan Peak Sanctuaries (Herákleion Museum, Gallery VIII).

As was usual in Minoan architecture, the hall space was made versatile by pier-and-door systems. The main area had central columns, there were traces of wall paintings, and decorative panelling in the floor was framed by narrow strips of stucco originally painted red. These frames survived but the material they outlined unfortunately did not. There was no trace of stone, nor archaeological evidence for wood, so it is hoped that soil analysis may suggest the substance that disappeared in the final conflagration.

Immediately S and W of the light-well (6) is a Lustral Basin (8) with eight steps down into it; it is reminiscent of those at Knossós. Next to this (W), at the heart of the complex was the Central Shrine (9), a small *sanctuary* with a ledge built into a niche across from a low bench. Nothing was found on the ledge, but on the floor were fine clay rhytons and pedestalled cups. Integral with the Shrine was a labyrinthine arrangement of workshops and pot stores, also an Archives Room (10) where record tablets had been kept on wooden shelves. Most had been crushed but 13 were recovered, some inscribed in Linear A. Immediately S of the Shrine, and accessible only from the Hall, was the **Treasury** (11), equipped with eight clay chests, now restored. This room was found undisturbed, the chests tightly packed with fine vases, larger pots on the floor and probably on the chest lids as well; more pots had fallen from an upper floor. Here were some of the finest Minoan stone vases yet known. They included chalice shapes and jugs, and the exquisite *rock crystal rhyton* with bead handle and collar, which had been crushed into more than 300 fragments. A vase of porphoritic rock from Egypt had been adapted for pouring by the addition of a Minoan bridge-spout. These, with the finest pottery, are now exhibited in the Zákros room of Herákleion Museum (Gallery VIII). There are also bronze double axes, fine stone mace-heads, artefacts in ivory and faience, and (found fallen from the upper storey) six bronze ingots and three large elephant tusks. All these illustrate the great richness of the trappings of a Minoan ruler's Palace. Next to the Treasury is the Workshop (12) the grouped flat stones perhaps a support for a craftsmen's bench and in the storeroom to the S were 15 pithoi.

Returning to the Central Court you pass the room (13) which the excavator called the Banqueting Hall because a large number of drinking vessels were found here; it was decorated with a frieze of painted stucco and was connected by a triple doorway with the Main Hall to the N.

Across the Court the EAST WING, unfortunately damaged by flooding and by cultivation, is designated by the excavator as the *royal living quarters*, to correspond with the two-storeyed private apartments found in the other Palaces. Behind a pillared and colonnaded verandah are two main rooms (14 and 15), connecting by multiple doors. The N room opened onto a light-well on the E side, but uniquely interesting behind the big S room is the **Cistern Hall**, a large area with a central basin or pool, built to retain spring water at a standard level. The substantial wall of the cistern was lined with plaster, and eight steps led down to it. The Hall floor slopes inward for drainage, and column bases suggested that the area may have been at least partially roofed. The water supply came from the *Spring Chamber* (16) immediately to the S with its adjacent built *Well of the Fountain*, which formed the main water supply for the Palace. For much of the year these structures are now themselves under water.

At the SE angle of the Central Court is another stone-lined *well* (17). From this in 1964 came a conical cup containing olives perfectly preserved in the water for more than 3000 years. On exposure to air they shrivelled in a very few minutes.

Back up the Central Court towards the excavation of the town on the hillside, the kitchen area (18) of the Palace is to the N of the W Wing. The six rugged column bases may have supported a Dining Room above. A staircase is on the E side, and on the W a storeroom area (19) which would also have had grander rooms above.

It is worth walking up the stepped streets to the upper levels of the town for the splendid bird's-eye view of the Palace excavation. 500m inland from the site gate is the bottom of the Zákros gorge.

On the return drive along the coast from the Palace, the low-lying and now deserted island of Kouphonísi is in view (4km off-shore) on the horizon to the S.

On this island (2km by 4km) there is evidence for settlement dating from the Early Bronze Age, and remains of a prosperous Roman town include a small stone-built theatre. Kouphonísi is known to have been a port-of-call on the trade routes from Rome to Egypt and Asia Minor. The Greek Archaeological Service has excavated here each year since 1976 under the direction of N. Papadákis, Ephor of Antiquities for E Crete. During the Roman period the island played an important part in the mediterranean textile industry known as the 'purple trade', which was based on the murex shell (*Murex trunculus*). A gland in this spiny sea-snail yielded a red dye prized by Phoenicians, Greeks and Romans. (The colour purple associated with Roman Emperors was more exactly a deep crimson.) The excavation uncovered vast numbers of murex shells and interesting evidence for dying installations. The murex was first exploited during the Minoan period—by the simple process of crushing the shells. The Romans developed more sophisticated methods of harvesting the shells and processing the precious fluid from the glands (from each of which only a few drops of dye were obtained) in order to produce strikingly bright colours. (See exhibit in the Siteía museum.)

From Ano Zákros a dirt road leads in 9km to *Xerókambos*. It is well signed thanks to local initiative. There is a long beach and another striking gorge, with micro-environment less disturbed by visitors than that of Zákros.

An alternative return route to Siteía from Ano Zákros (30km by minor roads) runs through deserted country that is a rich hunting ground for wild-flower enthusiasts. Part of the route is not asphalted but has a good hard-packed dirt surface.

Retrace the Siteía road for 3km to *Adravaśti* (noted on the approach to Zákros). Through the village a minor road left (signposted Karýdi and Sítanos) climbs to a plateau where in March you may find the distinctive *Tulipa cretica*. At 11km *Karýdi* is the centre of a network of upland roads (including those to Khandrás and Zíros, or across to the Siteía–Ierápetra main road, Rte 10B).

Turn right for (14.5km) *Mitáto*, (16km) *Krionéri*, (22.5km) *Roússa Eklissía* and a descent, especially beautiful in the evening light, to the coast 3km E of Siteía.

B.   To Praisós and the South Coast

Direct to Ierápetra 64km (40 miles). Suggested itinerary c 70km via (18.5km) Praisós. Using minor roads from (4km) Piskoképhalo, there are alternative round-trip excursions from Siteía to the Akhládia valley (also recommended to walkers), or to Zoú and Karýdi.

Buses: eight a day to Ierápetra, one service to Néa Praisós.

The route to the S coast, signposted Lithínes, leaves Siteía from the junction in front of the museum. After 2km at *Manáres* the road cuts through the site of a Minoan villa (sign). This large LMI country house, contemporary with the New Palaces, was terraced into the hillside and looked out to the E over a fertile river valley. There is a well-preserved staircase at the N end of the site, with an entrance to the upper level. The lower level, which includes storerooms, is protected by massive stone blocks, possibly as an embankment against flood water or a wider river below.

A detour leads in less than 5km to another excavated LMI villa at Zoú. Just beyond the Manáres site a dirt road slips off left at a sharp angle (signposted Zoú). This first follows the river-bed, then crosses it and climbs into a side valley. The site is on the bank to the right of the road, and again the house looked out over the fertile and cultivated land on which its economy would have depended. Beside the well-preserved entrance at the S or far end of the façade is a small room with a stone bench. Two deep pits, right of entrance, suggest storage of grain. This Minoan farm had its own pottery kiln.

Just beyond the site is the village of Zoú, noted for its plentiful spring water which now supplies Siteía. A recommended minor road across uplands continues through Stavroménos and Sítanos to Karýdi (17km from Zoú, see end of Rte 10A), for a leisurely return drive to the coast near Roússa Eklissía.

4km down the main road from Siteía, in *Piskoképhalo*, a minor road branches right, signed Khrysopiyí and Stavrokhóri; this is the start of a detour to (5km) the *Akhládia valley* for the excavated site of a Minoan villa, and a well-preserved example of a LMIII tholos tomb. After 3km, at a culvert, take a track to the left. In 150m this forks, and on the uphill slope right are the villa's massive foundations.

N. Pláton excavated the Akhládia villa site in 1952, and found two phases of a building contemporary with the New Palaces, its destruction dated to c 1450 BC. The house was approximately rectangular, with 12 rooms and a main entrance in the centre of the SE façade. Left of the entrance passage, through double doors, was the main hall; it had three column bases along its axis, and was open onto an area with a stone bench in the S and W angle. Beyond this against the NW façade, was a small room where utensils and cupboard sug gested a kitchen. On the other side of the entrance passage was a group of storerooms.

The tholos tomb is 1km nearer Akhládia. On a right-angle bend before the village a rough track diverges to the left uphill, and climbs, round an awkward hairpin bend left, to (1km from the road) a T-junction. Turn left between concrete pillars carrying a modern aqueduct system, pass almost immediately a track to the left, and 30m beyond it take a footpath (right) through an olive grove to a gap in a wall. Turn left and follow the terrace contour till it peters out on an upward slope. Just ahead in a vineyard is the tomb, hard to see until you are right upon it, but marked by a notice, ΘΟΛΩΤΟΣ ΤΑΦΟΣ ΑΧΛΑΔΙΩΝ (Tholotós táphos, tholos tomb).

The tomb dates from c 1300 BC during the period of Mycenaean control of the island. At the end of the 'dromos', or sloping approach, the low rectangular doorway has two uprights supporting a massive lintel, and the circular chamber is built of large stones in horizontal courses, corbelled inwards to a keystone at the centre of the roof. Opposite the entrance is a small doorway against the natural rock. When found it was blocked by two walls and has been compared to the false door in Egyptian tombs, through which the owner's spirit came and went. When excavated in 1952 the tomb was found to have been robbed—the hole in the roof is the robbers' entry—but three larnakes remained. One was decorated with the double axe, horns of consecration and a griffin. Another had a lid shaped like the back of a bull, including head and tail at the gables. The finds, which included pots and a stone lamp, were destroyed during the war.

Back on the road, and 150m on towards the village of Akhládia, a good dirt road turns right along the valley, and in less than 4km joins the main N coast road 6km from Siteía. You pass *Kimouriótis*, with its chapel and a cluster of traditional stone-built houses with cobbled yards near a spring and a stream shaded by plane trees. Only a few houses are now occupied.

From Piskoképhalo the main Ierápetra road continues S to (11.5km) *Epáno Episkopí*, so called because it became the seat of the bishop of Siteía during the 16C, when raiders such as the Turkish pirate Barbarossa were a constant threat to the coast. At the beginning of the village there is a left fork, signed Zíros, which leads to the site of the Hellenistic city-state of **Praisós**. The road descends into the fertile valley of the River Pantélis (ancient Didymos) below the site, and then climbs through *Ayios Spirídon* high above the valley to (18.5km) *Néa Praisós*.
  From the village plateía a dirt road (rough) is signposted downhill left to the archaeological site. After 1km, at a hairpin bend, keep on downhill to the right. After a further 800m you pass a low rocky hill just left of the track (the city's Third Acropolis; see below), and half left ahead is the First Acropolis, distinguished by a network of terrace walling. Continue (200m) to ruined buildings (remains of a Venetian village) beside the track; they are just before a gate and signed footpath (left) to the centre of the site.

The site was first investigated by the Italian F. Halbherr in 1884, and the main excavations by the British School under R.C. Bosanquet began in 1901. The city spread across three hills designated as First, Second and Third Acropoleis; the third is also referred to as the Altar Hill. Praisós was the capital of the Eteocretans who were probably survivors of Minoan stock; their inscriptions using the Greek alphabet but for a non-Greek language form one of the most intriguing finds from the site. Bosanquet looked for continuity from a Bronze Age settlement, but found that the city of the Eteocretans was built mostly on the natural rock, and had no earlier remains below it.
  Cemeteries were excavated, including a number of chamber-tombs, two of

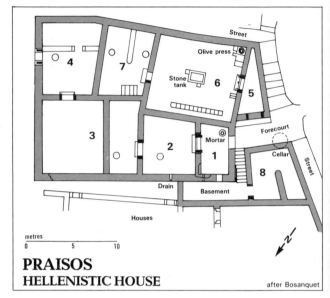

PRAISOS
HELLENISTIC HOUSE

after Bosanquet

which produced indications of Bronze Age habitation in the neighbourhood. The material found in the cemeteries dates from LMIII, at the end of the Bronze Age, to the Hellenistic period.

Despite their ethnic origins, the Praisians had many contacts (both peaceful and warlike) with the neighbouring Greek cities of Ierápytna (modern Ierápetra) and Itanos, and their culture seems to have been purely Greek. A major cause of dispute with Itanos was the question of control of the important temple of Diktaian Zeus at Palaíkastro. At one stage in the Hellenistic period, the Praisians even shared citizenship with Ierápytna, but about 155 BC (Strabo X, 479,12) their city was destroyed by Ierápytna, and was never reoccupied.

An easy path leads round the W flank of the *First Acropolis* to the saddle between two peaks where the ancient city lay. On the summit of this acropolis the foundations of a temple can be made out, and on the S side of the *Second Acropolis* (at the further end of the saddle) rectangular cuttings in the rock show where houses were cut back into the slope. The defensive wall which enclosed these two hills can still be traced in places. Across a broad gully the *Third Acropolis*, investigated by both Halbherr (who found the first inscriptions) and Bosanquet, is a flat-topped wedge formation, approachable with ease only from this direction. A primitive altar was found on the summit of this hill at the site of a sanctuary frequented, as the offerings prove, from the 8–5C BC. In the late 5C–early 4C the temenos wall perhaps enclosed a small temple. Some of the finds, including figurines, are displayed in Herákleion Museum, Gallery XVIII.

Where the path meets the saddle, just uphill right on the slopes of the First Acropolis and looking across to the Second, are the excavated remains of a Hellenistic house (see plan) dating from the 3C BC. The outer walls are of ashlar masonry with carefully exact joints, though lime mortar has also been used. The house is built on a terrace on the steep hillside, the upper wall making use of the native rock and the lower being carried down as a strong retaining wall. There are water spouts for drainage through this lower wall. Traces of cobble paving remained but the usual flooring was native rock or hard clay. The roof was tiled.

The house, designed to fit into an existing street plan, is entered from a shallow-stepped street. A forecourt leads to a vestibule (1) and the main front door into the living quarters (2–4); wide doorways and substantial stone jambs are a feature of the architecture. The doors turned on pivots as did the windows which were fitted with wooden shutters.

The principal living-room seems to have been on the NE corner, enjoying the coolest aspect of the house. (The unshaded walls are part of alterations to the original design.)

From the forecourt there is also an entance to three rooms of a different nature at the back of the house. A triangular vestibule (5) led to a large room (6) with an olive press in one corner, and in the centre a stone vat presumably for the storage of oil; it is fitted to take a wooden lid, and could have been lined with lead. There are the remains of a stone platform that ran round the walls of this room. Next door was a storeroom (7) which contained numerous pithoi, one with a projecting spout flush with the base for the drainage of liquids. The stone stairs are part of the lower flight of a staircase to the upper floor; the upper flight was of wood.

From the forecourt 11 steps lead down to a basement room (8) with a small rock-cut cellar in the rear wall. There may have been a room above with a door from the forecourt.

This building has always been known as the Almond-tree House, for the tree which hung over it at the time of the excavation. There are still many almond trees on this hillside, though few visitors can enjoy the January blossom. Praisós is a site strongly recommended in spring to wild-flower enthusiasts.

From Néa Praisós the road continues towards the Zíros plateau. After 5km, just before Khandrás, the romantic ruins of the medieval village of *Voilá* are spread along the hillside to the left of the road. A by-road (left and right before you are abreast of the village) leads to a Turkish fountain at the start of the former village street. The ruins are dominated by the 15C double-aisled church of Ayios Yeóryios, and a tower of the Turkish period; the decorative carving on the doorway includes an inscription dated 1742. The track leads on into *Khandrás*.

Here one road keeps left to *Ziros* where the church of Ayía Paraskeví (left of the village street) preserves in the arch above the door the latest dated fresco painting on the island (1565).

A right turn in Khandrás leads through *Arméni* back to the main Siteía–Ierápetra route. You pass at *Etiá* the remains of a 15C •Villa, highly praised at the turn of this century by G. Gerola in his study of the island's Venetian monuments; he attributes the building of the villa to a member of the Venetian De Mezzo family. Very few examples survive on Crete of the country houses of the Venetian period.

Writing an account of his travels on the island in 1856 Captain Spratt describes a castellated Venetian villa combining strength, luxury and taste. 'It has a vaulted basement, like a fortified tower, with well-constructed second and third stories above, and displays some architectural effect throughout. In the upper part were five windows in front, and in the lower, one on either side of a handsome entrance, approached by a flight of steps ascending from a paved courtyard, around which were the servants' dwellings and outhouses.' The house, by then Turkish property, was severely damaged during the 1828 Revolt, and fell into ruin before it was rescued and restored by the Greek archaeological service. Spratt's 'vaulted basement like a fortified tower' is what remains today.

In 2km you arrive at *Pappayianádes*, 20km from Siteía on the main road. This now climbs gradually SW to the watershed and then descends, passing (23km from Siteía) the village of *Lithínes*; in the grotto church of the Panayía a number of old icons are preserved. Soon the Libyan sea is in view and the Siteía mountains extend to the W, rising to the heights of Thriptí.

About 10km E along the coast is the Monastery of *Kapsás*. There are two signposts to it on the main road. The first is 4.5km from Lithínes, but the easier route is by the dirt road along the coast; this second sign is 4km beyond the first, not far short of Makryialós.

The monastery is built into the cliffs above the sea at the mouth of a gorge. According to tradition it was founded in Venetian times, but the present buildings (apart from modern intrusions) mostly date from the mid-19C when the much earlier grotto church—the present N aisle dedicated to Ayios Ioánnis Prodrómos (the Baptist)—was enlarged by the addition of a second aisle dedicated to the Holy Trinity. The wooden iconostasis was installed at the same period. All this was achieved by an eccentric (some say saintly) character, a monk named Gerondoyiánnis, whose remains are displayed (and revered) in the church.

The coastal track continues 4km to *Goúdouras*.

On the main road, 2km beyond the Kapsás turn, in *Makryialós* there is a road, right, for Ayios Stéphanos; 500m further on (across a dried-up watercourse towards the end of the village) is the Minoan villa, excavated by C. Daváras in the 1970s, which produced a series of high-quality finds, some of which are on display in Room III of the Ayios Nikólaos museum. This country house is comparable to those described at the beginning of this itinerary, and to that at Mýrtos–Pýrgos (Rte 8).

The site (signed up a track) lies 200m inland of the road. The ground plan can be seen to resemble in miniature those of the Minoan Palaces. The villa is constructed round a central court; it has a monumental W façade, and a W court from which a passage leads into the central court. The main entrance was probably on the N side of the villa, but the central court also has an entrance from the E, and there may have been a walled E court. In the central court the excavator identified an altar, and a bench on the W side thought to have been associated with it.

From Makryialós the road follows the coast for 24km. Easy access to this stretch of shore is relatively recent, but the area has rapidly become popular with tourists. At first the road passes a number of rocky coves, such as Ayía Photiá, where in spring the streams run down to the sea. Then the coastal plain opens out behind a long beach as you approach the town of *Ierápetra* (see Rte 8).

III KHANIA AND WESTERN CRETE

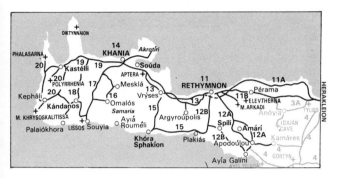

11 Herákleion to Réthymnon

A. Direct route 78km (48.5 miles) by N Coast Highway or 'New Road': 15km Ayía Pelayía; 22km Phódele; 54.5km Pánormos. No direct exit for the Monastery of Arkádi, so a short diversion is necessary onto the last stretch of the Old Road.

B. The Old Road, 79km (49 miles), is recommended for excursions or as part of a leisurely round trip: 20km Márathos, for the walk to Phódele; 55km Pérama for detour to ancient Elévtherna; 75km Plataniás, for (17km) Arkádi.

There is a good minor road (7km) between Pánormos and Pérama. Beware of other cross-country links suggested by signposts or maps; some are still very rough.

Frequent bus service by the New Road; two or three times a day (non-Express) on the Old Road. Note that Réthymnon (and Khaniá) buses leave from the bus station W of the harbour, near the Historical Museum.

A. The New Road

The North Coast Highway, which bypasses Herákleion, may be reached either from the Knossós road or 3km out along the Old Road which leaves town for the W through the Khaniá gate—both junctions clearly signposted for the New Road. (Distances given below are from the W junction; the new kilometre posts operate in the reverse direction, calculated from Khaniá.)

The highway runs W passing oil-storage tanks and cement works. At 8.5km, beside the Pandanassa Bridge there is an Orthodox seminary, and soon after, at Palaiókastro, remains of a medieval fort (1573) stand to seaward of Rogdiá, a village clinging to the hillside high up on the left. Goats roam this territory, as they did long before the new road was built, and herds or stragglers are an attraction, but also a potential hazard to the fast-moving traffic. You climb out of the Bay of Herákleion, and almost immediately over the crest (13km) a dirt road leads off (right) to *Ligariá*, with tavernas and good swimming, a practical alternative to the town beaches after a morning's sightseeing in Herákleion.

This is the first of several independent by-roads leading to the sea around *Ayía Pelayía*. In the mid 1970s a large hotel was built on a headland here, on the site of the ancient city-state of Apollónia. More recently, development of a rather charmless kind has followed the hotel. However, the coastline is still attractive, and there is a wide choice of beach tavernas. At 14.5km an asphalt road (left and then under the highway), signposted for Ayía Pelayía, leads down to the main development, with a branch right by the chapel on the headland to the bay of Ligariá mentioned above. Ideally avoid Sundays at the height of the summer, for the family outing to the sea is a popular Cretan pastime and the crowds may be excessive.

Recent excavations have revealed extensive remains of the Classical–Hellenistic city of Apollónia, which was destroyed in 171 BC by the people of Kydonía (Khaniá), in what came to be regarded as the most treacherous attack on record on a friendly city-state. The Apollonians went down to the harbour to welcome their allies who came streaming out of the boats to slaughter them. After this destruction the site was fought over by Górtyn and Knossós, and these squabbles led to one of the earliest diplomatic interventions by the Romans in a Cretan border dispute.

Excavated remains of the city are still preserved, scattered among the terraces and gardens of the hotel complex; they include what is probably the ancient prytaneíon.

Archaeologists also uncovered a LMI villa, one of the increasing number of country houses and estates of the Minoan period that have been examined in recent years; the finds are displayed in the Herákleion museum.

22km from Heráleion on the main road, *Phódele* lies a short distance inland amid orange groves. There are pleasant shady kapheneíons beside a stream where water runs for most of the year, and paths around the village offer escape from the ubiquitous souvenir shops, though not always from the black-shrouded grandmother offering her macramé or crochet work.

Traditionally, Phódele was accepted as the birthplace of the painter El Greco (Doménikos Theotokópoulos, c 1541–1614), but it is now thought more probable that he was born in Herákleion. However, in 1934, the University of Valladolid in Spain erected, under the plane and chestnut trees at the top of the village, a bilingual inscription in his honour carved on slate from Toledo.

On the drive into the village the domed Byzantine church of the Panayía (Virgin Mary) can be seen across the valley to the right. Paths through the orange groves, stunning at blossom time around Easter, lead to the church, or there is a track that starts from the larger bridge in the village.

The cross-in-square pillared church, with dome supported on a drum lit by 11 narrow windows, is built into the central nave of a 8C (pre-Arab) basilica; traces of the basilica apses can be seen. Remains of several layers of frescoes have been uncovered, in contrasting styles. The older paintings date back to the early years of the Venetian occupation (13C); those in the S cross-arm include a donor inscription of 1323. The ruins of the medieval village lie round about the church.

At 44km is the exit (left) for *Balí* (Μπαλί). Set in a particularly beautiful bay, sheltered from the prevailing summer wind or 'meltémi', the tiny village of Balí, frequented until recently only by fishermen, is growing each year to accommodate holiday visitors. There is a modern Class B hotel and a considerable choice of rent rooms and tavernas.

In Classical times this was the site of Astále, sea-port of Axós, and on Venetian maps the bay keeps that name. (Balí is derived from the Turkish word for honey.) In this region, myrrh used to be extracted from the wild cistus plant.

At 45km, just above the highway, and with a fine view of the coast-line below, lies the *Monastery of Ayios Ioánnis*, dedicated to St. John the Baptist (Feast Days, 24 June and 29 August).

This was founded (1635) by a descendant of one of the 12 noble families, the 'Arkhontópouli', sent from Constantinople in the 12C to strengthen the Christ-ian ruling class after the ravages of the Arab occupation. The monastery escaped destruction by the Turks, perhaps because of its remote position which was further exploited in two particular ways. From other parts of the island valuable church possessions were hidden here; if Turkish forces were in the neighbourhood these were swiftly taken out to sea until the danger passed. Equally, the sheltered but remote bay below was suitable for disembarking weapons and ammunition for use in the struggle for independence, and there was a regular arms traffic through the hills to Arkádi. A mule track inland led to Melidóni and the centre of the island; the path is still usable, and indeed walked by the monks today. 400m up through the gate behind the church is a fountain dating from 1791.
  The monastery fell into decay earlier this century and had stood empty for 54 years until 1983, when the abbot and monks started to bring it to life again.
  On the terrace in front of the church, a fine bell struck in Trieste dates from 1884.

10km beyond Balí, at the junction for Pérama and the Old Road, the highway bypasses *Pánormos* on the coast. (Tavernas and a small hotel.) This is now a relatively unspoilt backwater for most of the year, but traces of substantial buildings where the village meets the sea bear witness to its former importance from Venetian times till the turn of the century as a port and trading centre for the surrounding area. As road communication developed between Herákleion and Réthymnon, commercial traffic moved to these two ports and inland to Pérama on the Old Road.

The ancient site of Pánormos, of which very little is known, extends over the low ridge to the SW, inland of the highway and above the narrow coastal plain. Coins from here in the Herákleion museum date from 1C BC–9C AD. Worth visiting are the excavated remains of the Early Christian *basilica* of Ayía Sophía on the crest of this ridge (10 minutes from the village on foot, possible by car), with extensive views S across the island. From the highway, the road bends left behind the centre of the village. At a fork near the W end of the village keep to

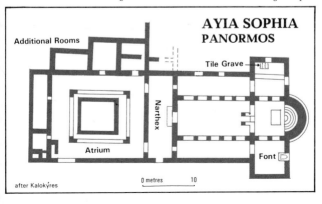

AYIA SOPHIA
PANORMOS

Additional Rooms

Tile Grave

Narthex

Atrium

Font

after Kalokýres

0 metres   10

the left or upper road which soon passes under the highway. The site is straight
ahead, 150m uphill. Or slip off the main road onto a dirt track (left), 400m W of
the turning for Pérama, and proceed uphill.

The *basilica* was excavated by K. Kalokýris and N. Pláton in 1948. Clearly
preserved are the foundations of the three-aisled church, with triple transept
and single apse (see plan). The nave was divided by stylobates of four Ionic
columns. There are no mosaics, and the floors are of slabs or pebbles, but architectural fragments such as capitals are of high quality. At the W end of the
church is an *atrium*, which originally had a Corinthian colonnade around the
central cistern. There were rooms along two sides of the atrium; their function is
uncertain but the one nearest the narthex may have been the original baptistry.
Under the chancel floor there was a small container filled with bones, presumably a foundation offering. The tile grave in the N pastophorion is known
from inscription as the tomb of a minor cleric, Theodoros.

60km Just before the Ieropótamos bridge on the highway, the White
Mountains come into view. The Bay of Réthymnon opens out ahead,
a coastal plain with a long sandy beach attracting a number of large
hotels. (There are also long-established camping facilities.)

The airstrip here (just beyond the bridge) was one of the major
objectives of the German airborne invasion which in 1941 launched
the Battle of Crete. The sector was successfully defended by Australian forces, with skill and bravery, in the face of great odds against
them in men and equipment. During the first wave of attack over this
beach, 161 German transport planes were counted in the sky at one
time.

5km beyond the Ieropótamos bridge, the highway is raised to cross
the Old Road, visible immediately below on the right. There are slip-
roads, at present unsignposted, on both sides. To visit the monastery
of Arkádi, leave the highway here, and follow the parallel coast road
to Plataniás (p 212).

At 73.5km this stretch of the New Road has until recently ended at
a T-junction, but in 1987 work began on the planned Réthymnon
bypass which will continue straight ahead. Left at this point leads up
into the beautiful Amári valley. (This junction is the start of Rte 12A.)
Turning right, and soon joined from the right by the Old Road
(alternative approach to Plataniás and Arkádi), you proceed through
the extensive outskirts to the centre of Réthymnon (see p 213).

B.   The Old Road

The road leaves Herákleion by the Khaniá gate, and at 3km passes
the junction for the New Road (N Coast Highway) and also for
Phaistós and the Mesará plain.

1km further on, a right fork keeps parallel to the sea, with easy access at several
points to a long beach for swimming or an evening walk—simple tavernas at
the town end. (Binoculars recommended for bird-watchers.)
    This area may be reached on some of the No. 6 town buses, which serve a
clutch of large hotels at the far end of the beach. (See Herákleion bus
information.)

The Old Road continues through *Gázi*, site of the LMIII shrine from
which came impressive clay figures now on show in Herákleion
Museum, Gallery X. One goddess, 75cm tall, in the familiar position
with arms raised, has three poppy-heads in her crown.

Just after Gázi you pass under the highway and, with urban sprawl
left behind, can look forward to spectacular views of Mount Ida; in

the high crevasses the snow lies until June. At c 8km a by-road to the right is signposted to Rogdiá.

This village, 17km from Herákleion, clings to the hillside 300m above the sea with magnificent coastal views, and taverna terraces from which to enjoy them. Rogdiá was part of a Venetian feudal estate, and the ruined façade of a grand house can still be seen near the church. You can continue 5km NW into the hills (signed) to the Savvathianí monastery founded during the Venetian period, now flourishing as a nunnery. The monastery church, dating from 1635, is dedicated to the Panayía (the birth of the Virgin, festival 8 September). About 200m W of the monastery an earlier (grotto) church is reached across the stream-bed in the valley by an old bridge; the date 1535 is carved on its arch. For a short round-trip, the Rogdiá road continues to the N Coast Highway, opposite one of the turnings to Ayía Pelagía (see above).

At 11km on the Old Road to Réthymnon, you pass the left fork for Týlissos and Anóyia (Rte 3A) to climb high round the seaward flank of the conical Mount Stroúmboulas (800m). The domed building in ruins on the right of the road (known by the name Koumbédes) was in Turkish times an inn for travellers unable to reach the city before the gates were closed at nightfall; it probably succeeded a similar Venetian esablishment. It is recorded that in 1670 this hillside was covered with cypress trees. Viewed from here, the shape of Júktas (the isoloated peak behind Knossós which can be seen as a reclining bearded god) goes some way to explaining the tradition that here was the burial place of the Cretan Zeus.

On a left-handed hairpin bend, you pass (on the right) the so-called Voulisméno Alóni, or sunken threshing floor; there is a better view over this curious geological feature round the next corner.

Near the 15km post, a cleft (right) between two outcrops of rock briefly affords a dramatic view of the Bay of Herákleion. The landscape is wild and strewn with boulders. Very soon a small taverna poised (right) over the valley is convenient for a pause to enjoy the view.

A little way beyond (20km) *Márathos*, just at the 21.5km post, a rough road descends to the right for *Phódele*. This offers a splendid opportunity for middle-distance walkers.

Arrange to take a bus on the Old Road route to Réthymnon, and alight at the turn for Phódele. On the gradual 7km descent to the village (see p 206) you pass (left) the abandoned monastery of Ayios Pandeleímon. The afternoon bus from Phódele may leave inconveniently early, but a further 3km on a minor road through orange groves brings you to the highway, and a choice of Khaniá and Réthymnon buses for the return to Herákleion. The bus stop is 500m E of the junction, at the other end of the bay.

Past the Phódele turn, the Old Road continues through the Ida foothills and a number of small villages, where memorial stones are a reminder of the sufferings of the population during the 1940–45 war. At 30km you enter the nome (province) of Réthymnon, and descend gradually amid vineyards. *Drosiá* is a pleasant shady village, one of many along the twisting road. After (45.5km) the junction with the road from Axós and Anóyia (Rte 3A), you follow the E–W Mylopótamos valley.

At 55km in the middle of *Pérama* (pop. c 1000) is the turning for (7km) Pánormos and the N Coast Highway.

Immediately across the bridge over the Ieropótamos, a branch from the Pánormos road keeps straight on for (4km) Melidóni. In summer charcoal-burners are often at work in this region. Keeping left through the unspoilt village, you ascend 2km to the *Melidóni cave* which has been frequented intermittently since Neolithic times, and was the site of a Classical sanctuary dedicated to Hermes Tallaios. It is now revered, and a place of pilgrimage for Cretans, because of an atrocity in 1824, when 370 Christians, most of them women and children, who had taken refuge in the cave, were trapped by a Turkish force under the ruling Pasha of the time. When the Christians refused to surrender, the entrance was blocked up and a great fire lit so that they were suffocated.

There is easy access just above the church; the cave has some fine stalactites. (Torch and sensible shoes.) From the church platform there is a good view S across the Mylopótamos valley to the Psiloritís mountain range.

2km on the Réthymnon side of Pérama, on the Old Road, is the turning left for a recommended detour to (5km) Margarítes, and on to Prinés for Elévtherna. (Keep right at an unmarked fork after 1km.) *Margarítes* is a village of potters where during the summer months all stages of the manufacture of clay vessels can be studied. At the far end of the village on the left is a workshop specialising in the traditional large storage jars or pitharia, which have altered little since Minoan times. This is a pleasant village with extensive views, and cafés from which to enjoy them. The ruins across the valley are the deserted village of Káto Tripódos.

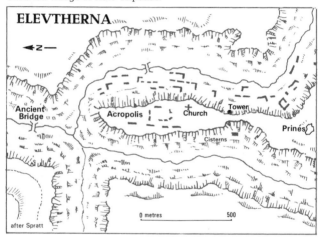

after Spratt

From Margarítes the minor road continues to Prinés. After *Kinigianá* you pass a turning for Tripódos, and at the top of the village of *Prinés* opposite a fountain take the narrow paved way to the right, which in 200m leads to parking under a spreading oak tree, and the start of a path ahead (5 minutes) to ancient *Elévtherna.

Ελεύθερνα (also transliterated Eleútherna and Eléftherna), one of the most important of the Dorian city-states, was inhabited from the 9C BC to medieval times. It put up strong resistance against Quintus Metellus during the Roman campaign of 67 BC. The British archaeologist H. Payne excavated here (1929), and noted massive walls from the Classical period repaired in Roman times, since when little has been done in the way of archaeological investigation. But the site is well worth visiting because of its spectacular position, and for the opportunity of a walk in exhilarating scenery, the objective being a bridge of the Hellenistic period which is one of the architectural delights of Crete. In spring the site is covered with wild flowers.

Ancient Elévtherna stood on a promontory between two streams (see Spratt's sketch), and was easily defensible, as is at once apparent on the main approach to the site along a rock-cut road to a saddle which forms a natural causeway. The surface here is worked, perhaps to imitate paving stones, and the road has drains at the side. At the acropolis end of the saddle are the ruins of a massive *tower* still standing to a height of 8m, dating either from the late Roman or early medieval period. The ancient road keeps to the left or W of the acropolis, under the little chapel of Ayía Eiríne (probably on the site of an earlier church), and bends round left to a remarkable complex of rock-cut *cisterns* supplied by an aqueduct thought to be Roman, though the cisterns are probably earlier.

To walk to the Hellenistic *bridge* (c 20 minutes), retrace your steps a short way from the cisterns to the first sharp bend in the ancient paved road. At this point a well-trodden path strikes off N along the W flank of the hill. At the NW corner of the acropolis it descends steeply, keeping left, to the westerly of the two streams; turn right and follow the stream-bed a little way to find the bridge. This was one of the ancient cemetery areas with tombs cut into the cliffs below the acropolis. On the return to Prinés, keep to the path along the stream (in early spring carpeted with cyclamen), until this path ascends by a gentler gradient to rejoin the ancient road below the cistern complex. On a walking tour you can continue across the other side of the old bridge, and climb up to the road at the modern village of Elévtherna (see below).

Hellenistic bridge near Elévtherna (from Spratt, Travels and Researches in Crete, *1865)*

Boys from Prinés are sometimes waiting near the entrance to the site, and are willing to act as unofficial guides—a small tip is appropriate. A longer visit could include the E side of the acropolis hill, where there is a second bridge, and a water system of smaller cisterns with connecting conduit which can be explored (torch advised).

An important Archaic statue from Elévtherna (a female torso in the Daidalic style) is on show in Herákleion Museum, Gallery XIX.

From Prinés it is possible to continue (past the village fountain) to

modern Elévtherna and on, either to the Monastery of Arkádi or to
rejoin the Herákleion–Réthymnon Old Road. This route soon affords
a fine retrospective view across the valley to the ancient site. After
the village of Elévtherna, you pass a turn (left) for a dirt road to
Arkádi (see below). If you continue ahead towards the coast, you
reach the Old Road either in or a little to the E of *Virán Episkopí*,
depending on which fork you take at *Skouloúthia*.

Medieval (Ano) Virán Episkopí lies 1km S of the main road. From the modern
village take the side-road signed for Elévtherna, and then the second dirt road
right. Ayía Eiríne, partly hidden (left) by old houses (and a few ugly modern
additions), is built into the ruins of a 10–11C basilica. There was another earlier
church on the site which replaced a temple thought to be dedicated to the goddess Díktynna, because an associated milestone records road repairs paid for
under her aegis. The basilica may have succeeded Sýbrita (modern Thrónos) as
the seat of the bishopric of Agrion after Sýbrita was destroyed by the Saracens.
The medieval village was surrounded by a wall, part of which is still standing,
as are many contemporary dwellings now often used for livestock. Continue
through the village down the hill to a T-junction and turn left. After 1km you
come to a bridge over a stream and the romantic ruined church of *Ayios
Demétrios*. Note the re-used (early Roman) Ionic capital. Returning in the reverse direction by the same track, you can keep straight on along it, to rejoin the
main road.

The Old Road nears the coast at *Stavroménos*, passing (left) an
Australian war memorial. For the monastery of Arkádi it is important
here to remain on the Old Road, which for 300m runs parallel to the
highway on the side away from the sea, and then passes under the
highway bridge. From the bridge to the Arkádi turn on the Old Road
is 7km.

The junction (4km outside Réthymnon) is in *Plataniás*. The road
leads inland through great groves of ancient olive trees to *Amnátos*,
and up a gorge to (17km from the coast) the handsome *'Moní
Arkadíou*, venerated in Crete as a symbol of freedom. This stems
from a heroic episode during the 1866–69 revolt against the Turks.
Besieged by overwhelming Turkish forces, the defenders of the
monastery, under the leadership of the Abbot Gabriel and together
with many women and children, chose death rather than capture or
surrender. They waited till the enemy broke in, and then blew up the
gunpowder magazine, killing themselves and at the same time many
hundreds of Turks.

In the little museum, where a guidebook is on sale, relics of this holocaust are
preserved. 60m to the W outside the main gate is the cemetery of those who
died, with the skulls displayed as is the custom. (Annual festival of commemoration 9 November.)
    There is also a small tourist pavilion café (summer only).

Much of the monastery that you see today dates from the 17C, though
the main *gateway* into the courtyard was rebuilt to the original
design after the 1866 destruction. The chief architectural interest lies in the ornate 16C *west façade* of the double-nave church.
(The naves are dedicated to the Transfiguration of Christ and to
Saints Constantine and Helen.) This two-aisled design is reflected in
the twin pediments of the façade, which are unified by a tall bellcote
(with an inscription dated 1587). In the colonnade below, the pairs of
Corinthian columns are evenly spaced, forming three equal bays in
which the two doors serve the aisles, and the conventional central
doorway is converted into a niche.
    On the N side of the courtyard the *Old Refectory*, pitted with bullet
holes, and the roofless *gunpowder storeroom*, scene of the historic

explosion, are melancholy places. There is a fine view from the adjacent E gate, and from the walls above.

300m below the monastery, just on the left of the modern road to Réthymnon, is a well-preserved ancient *bridge* (1685).

The dirt road NE from Arkádi starts near the café and leads (c 6km) to the road between Virán Episkopí and ̄Elévtherna (see above). This is good walking country—Arkádi to Elévtherna c 2 hours.

For Réthymnon direct, retrace your steps from the monastery to Plataniás and turn left to follow the Old Road 6km into the centre of town.

RETHYMNON (PEΘYMNON), a pleasant town (pop. 20,000) and capital of its nome as it formerly was of a Venetian province, is widely considered to be the intellectual capital of the island. It houses two departments of the new University of Crete, and in the old part of the town the relics of its medieval past have begun to be appreciated and restored.

The town stands behind a long sandy beach, with at the W end the picturesque Venetian harbour and a splendid lighthouse; the massive walls of the fort dominate the harbour from the hill above. There is a wide variety of hotel accommodation, as well as rooms for rent, self-catering holiday flats and a youth hostel. The harbour, crowded with caiques, is lined by tavernas that are popular for expeditions from elsewhere on the island. As an important market centre, the town is connected by bus with most of the villages of the province, which reaches to the S coast. Herákleion (for the Archaeological museum and the Palace of Knossós) is only an hour away by the New Road, but the comparatively relaxed environment of Réthymnon helps the town to offer an attractive as well as comfortable base for exploring this part of the island.

The *Tourist Information Bureau* (NTO) is centrally placed on the road behind the beach (see town plan).

Bus station on the inland side of the main through road.

Wine Festival in the last week of July.

Minoan occupation is attested by LMIII tombs at Mastambás, now a residential area at the back of the town. There is little doubt that Réthymnon occupies the site of Greco-Roman Rhíthymna, well known from ancient texts and inscriptions and from its coinage, but the physical remains must lie hidden under later buildings, most probably under the castle hill. Despite the many harsh privations of Venetian rule, the town flourished during that time, a period of artistic and literary distinction. The Venetians surrounded their sea-port with walls and built the great fortress above the harbour, but in 1645, after a siege of 23 days, Réthymnon surrendered to the Turks and became one of the three seats of government set up under the Turkish rule.

The City Park or municipal garden, which was laid out over the former Turkish cemetery, is a convenient landmark for the start of a walk through the old part of town. It stands on the main thoroughfare, ΛΕΩΦ. ΚΟΥΝΤΟΥΡΙΩΤΗ (Leophóros Koundourióti), at the junction with the road S across the island (signposted for Ayía Galíni). This is the venue of the annual Wine Festival.

From the NE corner of the public gardens (see plan), cross the main road and walk downhill under the arch of the Venetian 'Porta Cuora' into an atmosphere far removed from modern commercial Réthymnon. Charming Venetian house façades and doorways are preserved, while the minarets and overhanging wooden balconies with iron supports are a reminder of Turkish times. The street, crowded with colourful shops, eventually curves left and widens into ΠΛΑΤ. ΤΙΤΟΥ ΠΕΤΙΧΑΚΗ (Plateía Títou Petikháki).

On the left the 'Odeion', or concert hall, has a 17C *doorway* in the style of Sebastiano Serlio from its Venetian days as the Latin church (Santa Maria) of a religious house. The Turks converted the church into a mosque, replacing the timber roof with cupolas and the bell-tower with a *minaret*, but the original doorway remains. It has an arched entrance flanked by pairs of Corinthian half-columns on tall pedestal bases; each pair of columns is separated by a moulded impost with two levels of rounded niches. The Italian architect Serlio (1475–1554) was renowned for his treatise, 'Archittetura' (Venice, 1527), and this doorway has been shown to follow very closely one of his designs.

In summer the plateía is a pleasant open-air café. At the far end of it, just ahead on the left, is the *Arimóndi fountain* (1629), with Corinthian columns and lion-head waterspouts. A Venetian engineer, assessing the city's defences against the Turks, expressed more confidence in Réthymnon's water supply through this fountain than in its fortifications or harbour.

From the plateía a street (right) leads towards the harbour, passing the 16C Venetian *Loggia* which now houses the **Archaeological Museum**. Open (summer 1987): 08.45–15.00, Sunday 09.30–14.30, closed Tuesday. Admission Drs 200.

The exhibits, from sites all over the province of Réthymnon, are arranged as nearly as possible chronologically, clockwise. On the left as you enter are two cases of Late Neolithic material from the Yeráni cave; this is one of the most comprehensive exhibits of finds from the period in any of Crete's museums, and includes clay and stone idols, obsidian and bone *tools. In the next wall case are finds from the LMIII (1400–1200 BC) cemetery at Arméni which produced the remarkable series of clay sarcophagi (lárnakes), some of which are now on show in the Khaniá museum. Then comes material from the LMIII and succeeding Subminoan periods, including figurines of the 'psi' and 'phi' types, so-called because their stylised shapes recall these letters of the Greek alphabet; widely scattered at this period across the E Mediterranean, these idols always indicate a Mycenaean presence. In the same case two bell-skirted goddess figurines with raised arms are from Sakhouriá in the S of the province. The nearby free-standing case contains seals and jewellery from the Bronze Age, but also from the Archaic (from Axós), Hellenistic and Roman periods. Along the wall are two cases of terracottas: the first has Archaic heads and animal figurines, again from Axós (note the moulds used in the manufacturing process); the second affords a comparison between figurines from the Late Classical (5C BC) and Hellenistic (late 4–mid 1C) periods, and the bottom shelf also has marble heads and part of a Roman bronze statuette from a shipwreck off Ayía Galíni. Lastly, in the corner, a free-standing case displays bronzes, including axes from the Amári district, mirrors and a large tray from the Idaian cave.

Within the central columns, between cases of LMIII pottery from Mastambás (Réthymnon), and both local and imported red-figure vases from various sites, is an outstanding exhibit of silver and bronze *coins, Classical to very late Imperial, from various mints both on Crete and the mainland. The LMIII larnakes with octopus decoration are from Mastambás.

Against a column towards the back of the room is an unfinished statue of Aphrodite, half-worked and still showing the chisel marks (labelled ΜΙΣΟΤΕΛΕΙΩΜΕΝΟ ΑΓΑΛΜΑ ΑΦΡΟΔΙΤΗΣ). On the wall opposite the door is a tympanum of 1531 in a debased style, also statuary and Greek, Roman and Byzantine inscriptions, and these continue along the right-hand wall.

On the same side of the room are three cases. In the first are Egyptian statuettes, cartouches and scarabs, a gift to the museum. Next is a good exhibit of Hellenistic and Roman glass, including a mould-blown flask and three superb core-formed amphoriskoi. On a metal rod the glassmaker shaped a core (of clay or sand with an organic binder) to fit the inside of the body of a vessel, and then wound a trail of glass around this core; sometimes the core may have been dipped in molten glass. In the same case, among the vases and lamps, note the marble pyxides. The last case displays bronzes of the Hellenistic and Roman periods from various sites, as well as the finds from the Ayía Galíni shipwreck.

The Venetian Fort, known as the Phroúrion (stronghold) or Fortétsa (usually open only Tuesday–Friday: 08.00–20.00, winter 09.00–16.00—small admission fee) is well worth visiting, both for its imposing fortifications and for the vantage point they afford for views over this part of the island. Leaving the museum gate, turn left into the street and walk one block N towards the open sea. Left again leads to the sloping approach to the formidable *main gate*.

Begun in 1573, the fort was a response both to damaging pirate raids which had pillaged the town a number of times during the middle years of the century, and to the growing threat of Turkish intervention in the seas around Crete. The architect was the Venetian engineer Pallavicini, and the building took ten years to complete; the cost was enormous, and islanders from a wide surrounding area were dragooned into forced labour. The immense ramparts still stand, with their intriguing loopholed battlements and six great bastions. But in imagination we can fill the area within the walls with the governor's palatial quarters, with buildings of the administration, barracks, a hospital, churches, storerooms, cisterns, with artillery and perhaps squadrons of Albanian and Croatian cavalry, as well as with the mixed Cretan and Venetian population that all this implies.

Visible now in the *lower ward* (left near the main entrance) is a deep well reached by a sloping subterranean passage. In the main *enceinte* are a small church, and a *mosque* with a huge dome, which is thought to have been converted from a Venetian building; nearby there is a lone date palm. The Venetian *governor's quarters*, partially restored, stand near the main gate.

As the Turkish menace increased in the 17C, there were misgivings that the ramparts should have been surrounded by a moat and fears lest the limitations of the harbour below would prevent reinforcement in times of emergency. In 1645, after the town had been overrun by a large Turkish force, the great fort held out for only 23 days.

12 Réthymnon to the South Coast

A. Via the Amári Valley

65km (40 miles) to Ayía Galíni on the S coast. Recommended
round-trip excursion (c 120km; 75 miles) from Réthymnon: 25km
Apóstoli at the head of the Amári valley; then a circuit of the valley
down the main road to (48km) Apodoúlou, returning by the minor
road up the W side to (92km) Apóstoli, and thence back to
Réthymnon. This beautiful area has many frescoed Byzantine
churches within easy reach of the road.

There are bus services to the villages of the valley, but the
expedition needs careful planning.

On a touring holiday there is the alternative of turning E at
Apodoúlou to (c 60km) Kamáres, to link up with Rte 4 to (c 120km)
Herákleion.

This route starts S from the junction 3km E of the centre of
Réthymnon, where the Herákleion–Réthymnon stretch of the N
Coast Highway meets the Réthymnon bypass currently under con-
struction (see Rte 11, p 208). The road S is signed for Amári.

Immediately there is a right turn for a detour to (7km) *Khromonastíri*, and a
walk (c 30 minutes) to Ayios Evtíkhios, an architecturally important Byzantine
church with scant remains of 11C frescoes that are among the earliest yet uncovered on the island.

After 4.5km, the deserted village of *Milí* clings to the wall of a narrow valley
down on the left. As you approach *Khromonastíri* the road runs straight
with the village and its modern church in view ahead; 50m beyond a concrete
culvert is the track (left) to Ayios Evtíkhios. It is now possible to drive (rough
and very narrow) down into the valley, but many will prefer the walk—less
than 2km. There is no problem about access to the abandoned church which lies
below the track (right) with a small-holding close by it.

Inside, a magnificent Christ looks down on a building strongly evoking
former glories. The long nave consists of five bays (no parallel on the island),
with the central one enlarged to form the cross-arm surmounted by the dome.
The 11C frescoes, preserved only in the bema, are in a flat linear style. Christ is
flanked by the Virgin and St. John the Baptist; the standing figures include
St. Peter. Very few examples of frescoes from the Second Byzantine period
(961–1204) have survived on Crete.

From the highway junction the Amári valley road soon begins to
climb into the hills through groves of huge old olive trees. At 6km
there is a fine view (right) of the church of Ayios Evtíkhios on the
wooded hillside across the valley. In the distance to the SW, the highest peak, with a white chapel on its summit, is Mount Vrýsinas
(860m), site of one of the richest Minoan Peak Sanctuaries. *Prasés*
(8km) is attractively situated, and some buildings are preserved from
its Venetian past. On the through road, the cemetery church of the
Panayía (Virgin Mary) has remains of 14C frescoes (key at
kapheneíon near turning into the village centre).

Above the village the road crosses a ridge, and a wide valley opens
out ahead. The rare Bonelli's eagle may sometimes be sighted in
these hills.

At 11.5km is a turning for (3km) Mýrthios on a cross-country road to join, in c
11km, the main Réthymnon–S coast route near Arméni (Rte 12B). 4km beyond
Mýrthios is *Goulediana*, above which, on an isolated upland plateau, are the
excavated remains of a 5–6C basilica (p 221). The plateau is also the probable
site of ancient Phálanna.

14.5km You cross a tributary stream and enter the eparchy, or district, of Amári, and, as the valley closes in, the road runs alongside the main river, the Stavromána.

17km A road (still rough in places) sets off to the right for (9km) *Patsós* and on to Lambíni, near Spíli on Rte 12B. The cave of Ayios Antónios W of Patsós was intermittently an important sanctuary from the Middle Minoan period to Roman times, with a cult of Hermes Kranaíos.

26.5km *Apóstoli*, with its 14–15C church, stands at the head of the Amári valley, which lies between the Psilorítis range on the E and Mount Kédros on the W. Steps (right) lead to the church terrace, with views of Ida and (further left, with telecommunications mast) the site of the Greco-Roman city-state of Sýbrita. At a T-junction, less than 1km further on, there is a full view of the valley from the hamlet of *Ayía Photiní*; the recommended circuit will bring you back to this point.

This valley is one of the natural routes between the N and S coasts, and yet historically it has often served as a remote refuge, especially after the Venetian conquest and during the Nazi occupation, though the number of war memorials show that the refuge was not always secure. It is a region of unspoilt natural beauty, and there is a strong sense of community among the 40 villages of the eparchy of Amári.

The major road keeps left at the Ayía Photiní fork. At the first bend a left turn uphill is signposted for (1km) *Thrónos* (ancient Sýbrita). In the middle of the village the frescoed church of the Panayía (dedicated to the Assumption of the Virgin) is built into the foundations of an Early Christian basilica, with remnants of mosaic floor (possibly 4C and if so re-used from a previous building). The frescoes (very dark, torch useful) are of two periods, dated stylistically to the early 14C and the late 14–early 15C. The paintings of the first period survive only in the bema. An interesting comparison is possible because the scene of the Presentation of the Virgin has survived from both periods: on the N side of the bema, and on the N side of the vault of the nave (W bay, lower register). The Transfiguration (S side of the vault) has a graffito date 1491.

The village occupies part of the site of Greco-Roman Sýbrita, which flourished at least from the 5C BC into the first Byzantine period. The city spread over the hill with a cemetery at Yéna in the valley below; probably the basilica site was always one of its focal areas. Its harbour was at Soulía, the modern Ayía Galíni.

The notably fine coinage portrays, among others, Dionysos and Hermes; dedications to Hermes also suggest an undiscovered temple here, perhaps related to the cult of Hermes Kranaíos at the cave sanctuary near Patsós (see above).

An easy 10-minute walk leads up the acropolis above the village, a strongly recommended climb which at suitable seasons will reward wild-flower enthusiasts.

Continue E down the main street from the church, and after 50m a ridged concrete slope (left) leads up to an ancient stone path visible from the village street. The path starts to climb, and then briefly levels out along the flank of the hill before it forks left to climb again. At this point (before the path joins a dirt track) on the right is a well-preserved stretch of the ancient *city wall*. From here the built path leads to the summit.

There are traces of Classical or Hellenistic walls along the crest, and of a gateway on the E ascent, but little archaeological investigation has yet been undertaken. The climb is worthwhile for the *view alone. Sýbrita commanded all this fertile, wooded and well-watered Amári valley, and must have owed its prosperity at least in part to its apparently unchallenged position on this important trade route.

The next recommended objective is *Ayios Ioánnis Theológos (St. John the Evangelist), a little frescoed church below a hermit's cave near *Kalógeros*, but best reached by a footpath (10 minutes) from the main valley road.

Less than 1km after the Thrónos turning you pass a left turn to Kalógeros. Continue 800m on the main road, watching carefully for a well-trodden but narrow path that climbs the bank to the left. The path ascends (5 minutes) to a gate, in front of which you turn uphill left. The way levels out along the hillside, with a wall on your left, and as you pass the hermit's grotto, the church comes into view ahead. The frescoes are dated by inscription 1347. In the bema Christ is flanked by the Virgin Mary and St. John, and the scene was repeated on the S wall of the nave.

500m further along the road, you will notice in a field (right) the tiny 15C domed and cruciform church of Ayía Paraskeví.

At 31.5km the former *Moní Asomáton* has since 1931 housed an agricultural school. This wealthy monastery had a long tradition of Greek learning and education—the Abbot ran a neighbourhood school during the Turkish occupation—and also a stirring history of support for the Cretan cause. Buildings from the monastery's Venetian past stand alongside those of the modern farming complex, and a huge ancient plane tree provides summer shade. A considerable range of rich liturgical furnishings from the chapel is preserved in the Historical Museum in Herákleion.

The monastery stands in the angle of two roads. The branch to the right leads through Monastiráki to (4.5km) the village of Amári. In April the fields are colourful with wild tulips and lupins. Below *Monastiráki* a Minoan settlement is being excavated by the Greek Archaeological Service.

Downhill from the memorial in the village plateía you can see the bell of the church of the Arkhistrátigos (St. Michael the Archangel). Only one frescoed scene remains (the Assumption of the Virgin), but it is of high quality. There is also an interesting doorway. The church of Ayios Yeóryios at the top of the village has a well-preserved 'Platytéra' (Virgin with Child, symbolising the Incarnation) in the apse, which is said to have been influenced by the art of portable icons.

Outside *Amári*, the little 'capital' of the district, the church of Ayía Anna preserves the earliest frescoes dated by inscription yet known on Crete (1225). The paintings are worn and perhaps of interest only to specialists, but the chapel occupies a fine position in wooded countryside.

Through the hamlet of Opsigiás, just before Amári, is a solitary church (right) and 150m beyond this on the left the District Police Station. Opposite, at an acute angle, a good track leads in less than 1km to Ayía Anna. Originally a monastery church, Ayía Anna had two naves, which explains the walled-up arches along the S side.

On the way back to the valley road, in Monastiráki, a narrow turning right leads (3.5km) to *Lambiótes*; at the far end of the village a path (left) will bring you in less than 1km to the chapel of the Panayía, with elegant frescoes dated to the second half of the 14C, and said to be influenced by the style of the Palaiologan Revival. (Enquire for the key at the houses by the start of the path.)

The main valley road continues S from the Asómatos monastery through *Aphratés* to (37.5km) *Vizári*. Here, 1km W of the village, on the site of a large Roman town, are the ruins of an Early Christian basilica, one of the best preserved on the island.

Opposite the post office in the middle of the village take the side road right. Out in the country this bends sharply right then left and levels out between stony remains of the ancient town. 250m from the second bend an inconspicuous path, right, crosses the ditch and soon runs between walls—5 minutes to the basilica site.

The church, excavated by K. Kalokýris, is tentatively dated to the late 8C, not long before the Arab conquest. Two Saracen coins were found in the destruction debris.

The plan is unusual in that the side aisles end in small apses of their own. In the S aisle in front of the apse is a stepped font built of tile and cement. The church floors are also tiled. Not many architectural fragments were found, but there is evidence for a screen mounted between columns dividing the central aisle into a spacious chancel and nave. In spring the site is overgrown and exploration may be difficult.

The building of this large church reflects the wealth of the Amári valley at the end of the First Byzantine period, at a troubled time in the E Mediterranean when the island's coastline was frequently harassed by foreign raiders.

40km *Phourphourás* is a starting point for walking in the Ida range. By a fountain at the entrance to the village is a left turn for **(4km)** *Platánia*. The church of the Panayía, with remains (lowest register only) of 14–15C frescoes, lies on the right of the main street near the middle of the village. (Ask for key at kapheneíon opposite church gate.)

Soon after Phourphourás the Libyan sea comes into view, with distant views of the Mesará plain and the Asteroúsia mountains. Through *Kouroutés* and *Níthavris* you reach (51km) *Apodoúlou*.

On the last bend before the village is a LMIII tholos tomb (sign on the left, beside steps up the bank). A dromos, or passage, cut into the hillside leads to the entrance, with the lintel still in situ. The tomb, excavated by C. Daváras, had been plundered, but four disturbed clay larnakes remained; one with a scene of lamenting figures is now in the Khaniá museum.

Across the road, just before the tomb, is a signpost for the footpath (10 minutes) to Ayios Yeóryios (mid 14C frescoes by Ieréas Anastásios).

On the far side of Apodoúlou the road divides. The left fork follows the S slopes of Ida to (63km) Kamáres, and on to Zarós, Ayía Varvára and Herákleion (see Rte 4, p 139). The right fork runs down to the S coast at (65km) Ayía Galíni (Rte 12B).

For the circuit of the valley, follow this road S for 5km to the meeting of the two Amári valley roads, where you turn sharp right and begin to climb N again. There are fine tall olive trees as far as the eye can see. After 4.5km, in *Ayía Paraskeví*, the old church of the Panayía stands on a rise (right) in the centre of the village just before the large modern church. (Key at kapheneíon back down the street.) Elegant frescoes dated by inscription 1516.

After (60km) *Ayios Ioánnis* the scenery becomes grander. You cross the River Plátys which runs into the sea near Ayía Galíni. The old bridge is preserved to the right of the modern one. Now the road climbs above the olive-tree zone to a series of high villages along the slopes of Mount Kédros: *Khordáki, Ano Méros, Drigiés, Vrýses*. Between the first two there are fine retrospective views of the southern coastline, and across the valley the dramatic wall of the Psilorítis mountains. The memorials are a reminder that these villages suffered severe reprisals for the activities of the Cretan Resistance during the 1940–45 war.

At 82km *Kardáki*. Less than 1km beyond this village, opposite a spreading oak tree, you pass the ruined monastery church of *Ayios Ioánnis Theológos, Phóti*. The unusual architectural scheme can still be appreciated, though the building is open to the elements and the frescoes have suffered accordingly. A rare feature is the domed narthex. Remains of frescoes: late 13C in the chapel, 14–15C in the narthex. The old stone road on which the monastery lay still runs behind the church.

Through *Yerakári*, which was razed to the ground in 1944, you come to (88.5km) *Méronas*, where the church of the Panayía lies on the right of the road towards the end of the village. The soft pink, three-aisled church shows Venetian influence in its architecture. Some of the frescoes have been uncovered; they are known to have been painted between 1339 and 1341. In the bema, the Hierarchs officiate appropriately, but the portrayal of the Christ child lying on the altar, representing the elements of the Eucharist, is very rare on Crete. In addition, the icon of the Panayía (late 14C) is one of the earliet known on the island. (Key with the village priest—enquire across the road.)

A further 3km brings you back to the T-junction at Ayía Photiní, where you turn left for the last 30km back to Réthymnon.

B. Réthymnon to the South Coast via Spíli

62km (38m) direct to Ayía Galíni. Convenient bus service.
    A branch road right to Selliá for (36km) the resort of Plakiás links up with Rte 15 along the S Coast to Sphakiá. A second branch leads to the Préveli monastery near the sea, 35km from Réthymnon.

This itinerary starts from the crossroads by the public gardens in the centre of Réthymnon. The road, signposted for Ayía Galíni, climbs inland with the town spread out below. *View of the fort.

At 8km, the LMIII *cemetery* of Arméni, with elaborate rock-cut tombs, lies to the right of the road. At the crest of a long hill, a turning is signed for Somatá, and the cemetery is in the grove of holm-oaks 100m back from the main road. Excavated in the early 1970s by the Greek archaeologist Y. Tzedákis, the tombs have yielded an important series of decorated clay lárnakes (sarcophagi), now among the chief attractions of the Khaniá museum. Among a variety of gifts accompanying the burials—decorated vases, bronze weapons, tools and ornaments, sealstones and beads—one find was uncommon on Crete. There were 60 boar's tusk plates from the covering of a helmet of a type described by Homer. A similar helmet is displayed in Herákleion Museum, Gallery VI.

The broad main road continues through a forest conservation area of pine, cypress and oak. 2km beyond the cemetery is the pleasant village of *Arméni*. At 12km, a cross-country road (signed, left, for Karé) leads over gentle wooded hills to join (11km) the Réthymnon–Amári valley route (12A). High above the village of Gouledianá (after 4.5km) is the probable site of the city-state of Phálanna; two houses investigated were found to belong to the Archaic period. On the same plateau are the excavated remains of a 5–6C basilica, one of the most remotely situated in the whole island.

2.5km *Karé*; 4.5km *Goulediáná*. At the beginning of the village take a dirt road left which climbs ahead at an acute angle behind the houses, and gains height up a fertile and well-watered valley. After 1km you pass a fountain, and 500m further on, emerge on the rocky upland plateau at the ruins of the village of Onythé—an increasingly rare glimpse of the old vernacular architecture of the island. In the middle of the little plateau turn left and follow the track N, past a sheep-fold. It is less than 1km to the basilica; keep right where the track forks, and then follow it as it curves left (gate) to end at the site. The mountain to the N is Vrýsinas (Minoan Peak Sanctuary, see Rte 12A).

The basilica, excavated by N. Pláton in the 1950s but not yet fully published, is built on a downward slope from S to N. The narthex, entered down three steps from a porch, has rooms at its N end, probably for a baptistry, and at the S (uphill) end there may have been an atrium. Three doors lead into the aisles; one needs a step on account of the slope, and the two side-aisles are of unequal width. Polychrome mosaics (no longer visible) of elaborate geometric designs in the apse, chancel, nave and narthex helped to date the building to the late 5–early 6C. Much of the chancel and apse had been destroyed by a later chapel, but a collection of small bones deposited in a pit sunk into the chancel floor is interpreted as a foundation offering, similar to that found at Pánormos (Rte 11A).

The main road to the S coast climbs gently into a broad valley growing cereal crops which are harvested in June.

At 18.5km a secondary road diverges right beside a cemetery with a modern chapel. This is the turn for Plakiás and also for Selliá (14km from this junction) where you link up with Rte 15 in the direction of Rodákino, Frangokástello and the district of Sphakiá. (This section of Rte 15 is described in the reverse direction from Khóra Sphakíon—see p 242.)

This minor road at first follows a valley running W through a landscape of meandering streams lined with plane trees. There are several small villages, including *Áyios Vasílios*, before (26.5km) *Áyios Ioánnis*; then the road turns S through the Kotsiphós gorge, to emerge above the wide bay of Plakiás.

At 29km the road forks. Ahead (c 2km) is Selliá (see above). For Plakiás keep left downhill, continue a kilometre or so through *Mýrthios* (tavernas with view) and just beyond the village turn right, signposted 3km to Plakiás. (You pass a turnng left for a road along the coast to Levkóyia and the Préveli monastery.) Until recently **Plakiás** was only a cluster of houses around the tiny quay at one end of a long tamarisk-shaded beach, but it has grown rapidly into a small resort. (Seven hotels heavily booked from abroad, many rooms to rent and a number of tavernas.) This is still an especially fine beach and there is also good swimming from coves along the coast to the E. The walk to the Préveli monastery (see below) is highly recommended (c 2 hours), and the country inland is beautiful and unspoilt.

The main Réthymnon–Ayía Galíni road continues in a south-easterly direction. 20km from Réthymnon (1.5km beyond the turning for the first detour above) a second branch road to the right leads to Moní Préveli, signposted from the Ayía Galíni direction for Plakiás. Beyond *Koxaré* this road enters the Kourtaliótis gorge of the Megapótomos (megálos pótamos, the great river) which flows into the sea near Préveli.

7km from the main road is *Asómatos* where for Préveli you turn left (downhill beside a kapheneíon) towards Levkóyia. (Ahead would lead to Mýrthios and Plakiás.) After 1.5km, just short of Levkóyia, you turn left again onto a dirt road signposted (5.5km) to the monastery.

Walkers from Plakiás can make use of coastal tracks which shorten the distance. The dirt road from Plakiás to Levkóyia passes a number of rocky coves and the occasional beach taverna.

From Levkóyia the Préveli road drops down to the Megapótamos, one of the few rivers on Crete which flows all the year round. After

2km you pass a steeply arched early 19C bridge, and 500m further on are the deserted ruins of the original 16C monastery, Káto (lower) Préveli, set on a slope above the river; its church was dedicated to St. John the Baptist.

In the 17C the Abbot Prévelis built a second monastery, hidden in relative safety in the hills nearby, to which he moved the monastery's valuable library. He dedicated the new church to Ayios Ioánnis Theológos, St. John the Evangelist, and for a time this new foundation was referred to as Píso Moní Préveli (píso, meaning behind). The road climbs up to this second monastery.

Round the last corner the splendid buildings, now always known simply as **Moní Préveli**, come suddenly into view. The 19C traveller Captain Spratt enthused over 'this paradise of Crete, in one of the most happily chosen spots for a retreat from the cares and responsibilities of life!' Today the monastery is no longer allowed to accommodate overnight visitors looking for such a retreat.

Open: 08.00–13.00 and 17.00–20.00. The rules on decorous clothing are strictly observed.

Only the abbot and two or three monks are now in residence at Préveli, but there is a guardian who opens the church and the small museum (guidebooks on sale). After the Battle of Crete (1941) the abbot and monks of Préveli organised an escape route for Allied soldiers stranded after the evacuation; there is a commemorative plaque in the courtyard, and a gift of silver candlesticks from Britain is exhibited in the museum.

The present relatively modern church (1836) is surrounded on three sides by picturesque buildings which include the original bakery with a huge oven capable of turning out 800 loaves a day. The terrace commands an extensive *view down to the Libyan sea. In the lower courtyard there is a fountain with an inscription dated 1701; on either side of it are a long stable and a workshop for making beeswax candles, and behind is an underground chamber, a naturally insulated cold store.

Early in the period of Turkish occupation (1669–1898) Abbot Prévelis's monastery was granted a privileged position subject directly to the Patriarchate in Constantinople. It acquired great wealth for Cretan money was thereby protected from seizure by the Turks. It became a focus of Greek learning and education, and the monks ran many secret schools. The monastery became known as a strong ally of Cretan nationalism. During the 1866 Rebellion the fast steamship, the 'Arkádi' (purchased in Liverpool) made several sorties from the free Greek mainland along the S coast of the island, running in guns and ammunition (and boot-leather, among other necessities) for the insurgents, and taking off women and children as well as the Cretan wounded. J.E. Hilary Skinner, a reporter for the London *Daily News*, sailed in the 'Arkádi', and gave a fascinating account of the experience in his book 'Roughing it in Crete'. Préveli was an important link in this chain of relief operations.
 The tradition of support for Cretan independence persisted through the 1940–45 war and then, as before, the monastic community suffered because of its involvement.

To walk to the palm-fringed Préveli beach, return 1.5km along the approach road. The broad path can be clearly seen starting across a flat expanse of clifftop towards the sea (15 minutes from the road). You can also drive to the sea down the river valley (see below).

For the frescoed chapel of Ayía Photiní continue 1km further. The road bends left and right, and (at 2km from the monastery) crosses a culvert. 100m beyond this the little church is in view among olive trees in the valley below, but for the easiest path continue 300m (across a second culvert) to a left bend where there is room to park.

From here (10 minutes to the chapel) first follow the water pipe S, and then at the ridge strike downhill. The path is making for the river, so it is necessary to branch right just above the chapel.

The frescoes date from the late 14/early 15C. Ayía Photiní is among the female saints (named as Paraskeví, Marína, Kyriakí and Eiríne) who, with the Archangel, line the S wall. (The chapel was not locked in 1987 but check first with the guardian at the monastery.)

To drive to the sea (5.5km detour) at the mouth of the Megapótamos near Préveli beach, you cross the river at the 19C bridge near the ruined monastery, and immediately turn right along the river. Soon you recross it by another picturesque and earlier bridge and continue the descent down the valley. There has been a taverna at the cove in recent years. A walk (scramble) of 10 minutes W along the rocks brings you to the Préveli beach fringed with palm trees.

From the Koxaré junction (see above) the main Réthymnon–Ayía Galíni road continues SE in the direction of Spíli. After 3km, in the middle of *Mixórrouma*, a side-road left signed Karínes leads (1km) to the domed cruciform church of the Panayía at *Lambíni*, in a fine situation overlooking the valley. In plan this church is developing towards cross-in-square, but externally the arms are still visible; an unusual feature is that the E arm is longer than the W. The dome is supported on a blind-arcaded drum.

A plaque left of the doorway commemorates a Turkish atrocity in 1827 when the congregation was burnt to death in the church. The key is held at one of the houses nearby. Fragments of two layers of frescoes (14–15C) have been uncovered.

The minor road, still slow in places, continues E through the hills to Patsós and (c 25km between the two main roads) to the Amári valley (Rte 12A).

Spíli, on the main S road 30km from Réthymnon, lies on a steep hillside, well-watered and fertile all the year round. In the plateía, one of the most delightful on the island, is a picturesque tree-shaded fountain with a long row of 19 lions' head spouts. (Tavernas and a small hotel.)

Beyond Spíli you follow a valley between Mount Kédros (1777m) to the N and Sidérotas (1136m) to the S. Great efforts have been made to improve this road and stretches have been realigned, but the terrain is liable to subsidence, and it is wise to anticipate potholes or broken road edges. Beside the broad river bed of the Plátys the road nears the coast. The Amári valley, Timbáki and Phaistós are to the left. Turn right to run down (3km) into *Ayía Galíni*.

Around a tiny harbour this village has developed into the principal resort on the S coast. It caters particularly for the inexpensive end of the package holiday market, and in summer its charms attract more people than it can comfortably absorb. The rocky beach at the mouth of the Plátys has a long-established camping site.

13 Réthymnon to Khaniá

Direct route by North Coast Highway 59km (37 miles): 21.5km Yeoryioúpolis; 26km Vrýses; c 50km Aptéra above Soúda Bay. The Old Road is superseded as a through route, but a suggested detour from Yeoryioúpolis to (16km) Argyroúpolis follows it as far as Episkopí.

Frequent bus service. The twice-daily Old Road bus goes through
Episkopí.

The highway or New Road runs W along the coast, with the kilometre posts giving distances from Khaniá. 3km from the centre of
town the Old Road diverges left, but the building of the Réthymnon
bypass now under way will eventually affect this junction.

At 6.5km on the highway, below the *Yeráni bridge*, is a cave (not
open to the public) which was a sanctuary during the Neolithic
period. A series of finely worked Late Neolithic bone and obsidian
tools from here is exhibited in the Réthymnon museum. Also of interest from the excavation was a find in pleistocene levels of bones of
the curiously named dwarf giant deer. The cave was only discovered
in 1967 during construction work on the New Road.

Now the Levká Ori (White Mountains) are in view ahead. The road
runs for 10km parallel with a fine sandy shore; there are frequent
access points, and the beach is relatively deserted. The bay is not
always as innocent as it appears in calm weather, and even strong
swimmers should be wary of unexpected currents. Midway along the
beach is a long-established camping site.

13.5km A recently improved road sweeps up to (3km) Episkopí. This can be
used as a short-cut to the detour from Yeoryioúpolis (see below), and may particularly help those using buses.

21.5km *Yeoryioúpolis*, 5 minutes off the highway at the end of the
bay, can be reached by a slip-road to the right, 400m beyond an
overhead bridge, but as this is technically an infringement of
highway traffic law; by car it is wiser to continue 4.5km to the
approved exit; here a very pretty minor road leads back to the village
along the river valley.

Yeoryioúpolis is named after Prince George, High Commissioner
of Crete (1898–1906), who had a shooting lodge here. It has developed rapidly in the last five years, but is still a beguiling place
shaded by eucalyptus trees, at the mouth of the Vrýsanos river, with
a quay for one or two fishing boats at the end of the long beach.
Egrets, on migration in April, are among the many birds which
appreciate the marshy land nearby, known as the almyró. There is a
Class C hotel on the beach, and a considerable choice of rooms for
rent, and tavernas, in the village.

Yeoryioúpolis stands on the site of Amphímalla, port of ancient Láppa, one of
the more powerful Greco-Roman cities of W Crete. The Dorian city of Láppa
was destroyed during the Roman invasion in 67 BC but later flourished again
until the Arab occupation.

A recommended detour inland leads to (16km) *Argyroúpolis*, the
modern village on the site of Láppa, of which little is therefore preserved. The village retains hints of its medieval past, and occupies a
fine position above the Mouséllas river valley, looking back to the
sea from the wooded E foothills of the White Mountains. The return
route drops down to the only freshwater lake on the island.

From Yeoryioúpolis take the road S (signposted Kournás) and cross
the highway on a bridge. After 2km keep straight ahead when the
Kournás road leads off to the right. At 8km there is a second turn for
Kournás, the way to the lake on the return journey. 10km *Episkopí*,
and towards the end of the village fork right to *Argyroúpolis*. On the
approach to the village (c 14.5km), where Así Goniá is signed to the
right, keep straight ahead to arrive by the upper road at a plateía in
front of a large church and a war memorial (1912–18, a reminder of

Greece's Balkan War). The plateía gives a bird's eye view of the the pitched roofs typical of a W Crete village; from here you can explore downhill on foot. The architecture of one or two of the old buildings reflects the style of the Cretan aristocracy who made this an important centre during the period of Venetian rule.

The country around Argyroúpolis is a little-known part of Crete, but it repays exploration. The road through the village continues S, 12km to *Myrioképhala*, where the monastery church of the Panayía (a foundation of the 10C evangelist Ayios Ioánnis Xénos) has Second Byzantine period frescoes that are among the earliest on the island. Fragments (early 11C) are preserved in the dome, bema and S cross-arm, as well as four scenes from the Passion of Christ in the W cross-arm, which are later (end of 12C) but still pre-Venetian.

6km to the W into the White Mountains from Argyroúpolis (see above for the turning) is *Así Goniá*, home village of the author of 'The Cretan Runner' (see Bibliography). A great festival, the blessing of the sheep, is celebrated here on 23 April (St. George's Day).

To return to the coast by way of *Lake Kournás*, at first retrace the route from Argyroúpolis. Before Episkopí, across the valley (left) the ruins of another medieval village, Arkhontikí, can be seen rising above the modern houses. 2km beyond Episkopí, turn left on a fair dirt road to (4km) *Kournás*. The surface is asphalt from there on. After the village you descend steeply with a *view over the only freshwater lake on Crete (160 acres, 65 hectares). Despite holiday activity in summer and the efforts of local sportsmen, the lake is frequented by waterfowl. There is a footpath all round the shore (leisurely circuit, c 1 hour).

Passing the lake, continue until you meet (3km) the direct road from Episkopí to the coast. Turn left for Yeoryioúpolis, and, back in the big plateía at the centre of the village, take the minor road to the left along the river. After 4km you rejoin the N Coast Highway. This (26km direct from Réthymnon) is also the junction for Vrýses (Rte 15).

The highway, beautifully planted with cypress, tamarisk, mimosa and oleander, cuts across the peninsula of Vámos, and beyond the Kiliáres river nears the sea at the entrance to *Soúda Bay*.

Before this, at 40.5km, a detour right leads (1km) to *Kalýves*. This pleasantly old-fashioned village resort is strung out along the waterfront at the E end of a sandy beach looking across Soúda Bay to the hills of the Akrotíri, which provide shelter from the strong summer winds (meltémi). The coast road continues 5km to Kalámi where it rejoins the highway. You cross the mouth of the Kiliáres river, often a rewarding area for bird-watchers.

On the promontory above Kalámi, the highway passes a massive Venetian fort, now a prison known by its Turkish name, 'Itzedín'. A little way beyond it there is a *view of the entrance to the superb natural harbour of Soúda, one of the largest in the Mediterranean. The Venetian fortress, on the island of Soúda towards the far shore, was built to guard the narrows, and did not surrender to the Turks till 1715, 46 years after the fall of Candia (Herákleion). In 1941 the anchorage played an important role, first during the evacuation of the Allied Expeditionary Force from the mainland of Greece, and then in supplying the garrison during preparations for the Battle of Crete, though by this time all shipping was at the mercy of the Luftwaffe which had undisputed command of the air. Now the area is a Greek and Nato naval base, so photography is strictly forbidden.

At 46.5km is a left turn for a detour to (3km) the site of ancient **Aptéra**, which is said to take its name (Wingless Ones) from the

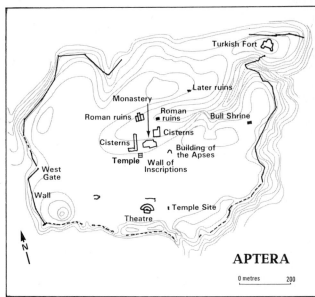

APTERA

0 metres 200

Sirens who, defeated in a musical contest by the Muses, plucked off their wings and, drowning in the bay below, formed the islets there.

From its vantage point at the mouth of the island's safest harbour, Aptéra, already flourishing by the 7C BC, was one of the largest and most powerful of the Greco-Roman city-states of W Crete. The impressive Early Hellenistic city walls and the huge Roman cisterns indicate the scale and strength of the city at those times. Aptéra was destroyed by the Arabs, but flourished again in the Second Byzantine period when it was the seat of a bishop.

From the main road you ascend to the site, keeping left in (1km) *Megála Khoráphia.* 1km beyond this village, where the road bends left, there is (right) a fine stretch of defensive *wall* in polygonal masonry. Straight ahead in the ruins of the overlapping walls are traces of the *main gate* with towers (see plan). At the top of the hill the road divides: left for a deserted Turkish fort (*view), and right for the recently restored monastery of Ayios Ioánnis Theológos (at the centre of the site, fenced). The rare Eleonora's falcon sometimes hunts across this upland, perhaps from breeding grounds on the offshore islands further W.

Aptéra is a vast site, with remains scattered on a plateau surrounded by 4km of defensive walls still standing to 3m high in places.

In the angle of the paths in front of the monastery a small *double-cella temple* (2C BC) built of clamped ashlar blocks was excavated by German archaeologists in 1942. The temple, without central communicating door, would have been dedicated to a pair of divinities. Across the path to the E a *Wall of Inscriptions*, probably part of an important public building, was seen by the English scholar R. Pashley (1834); excavated in the mid 19C, it was later destroyed.

The large L-shaped building, of concrete faced with brick, is one of two Roman *cistern complexes.* The remains of a small theatre are now little more than a hollow in the ground with traces of seating preserved. Two further temples are recorded from this site; one, excavated, is known as the *Bull Shrine* from figurines found nearby, and one has been identified only by its preserved Doric column fragments. In spring the undergrowth may make exploration of the outlying parts of the site difficult or impossible.

From Megála Khoráphia, a minor road inland (S) leads (5km) to *Stýlos*, passing (left, c 2km) a sign for the Minoan site of that name just above the road. The well-preserved LMIII tholos tomb has a stone-lined dromos and vaulted chamber; evidence for a settlement was found nearby.

As the road descends the hill before the village there is a fine view of a solitary Byzantine church (domed and cruciform) in the cultivated valley ahead. The partly-ruined church of the Panayía Serviótissa is all that remains of a monastery founded in 1088 by monks from the monastery of St. John the Evangelist on Patmos. For the easiest path, continue to the bridge across the river (Kiliáres) where a track runs back to the church (15 minutes on foot).

8km beyond Stýlos, on a rough road, is *Kyriakosélia* where the beautiful domed church of Ayios Nikóloas (11–12C, with modern addition at the W end) has an important set of early frescoes dated 1230–36. These paintings are said to show the influence of the Comnene artistic tradition, which emanated from Constantinople during the previous century.

The New Road continues W from the Aptéra turning, high above Soúda Bay, with splendid views across to the *Akrotiri peninsula*. At 51.5km a road diverges right signed for the Soúda ferry.

Take this road if you intend to visit the *Commonwealth War Cemetery*. You come down to the waterfront in Soúda at a plateía with cafés (by the Piraeus ferry quay). Continue towards Khaniá, and in less than 1km turn right (signed for the airport); the road follows the shore for c 2km.

The cemetery, beautifully planted and tended, occupies a superb position at the head of the bay. It contains the graves of 1527 men (862 British, 446 New Zealanders, 197 Australians, 22 from other Commonwealth countries) who were killed in the last ten days of May 1941 during the Battle of Crete. There is a brief account of the campaign just inside the cemetery gate (see also p 27).

In 1963, 19 First World War graves were transferred here from the Consular Cemetery, as were 51 others dating back to 1897.

Among the graves (10E) is that of John Pendlebury, the English archaeologist, shot by the Germans on 22 May 1941 as a member of British Intelligence. From 1929 Pendlebury continued the work of Sir Arthur Evans at the Palace of Knossós. He is remembered for a legendary series of travels on foot throughout even the wildest parts of the island, searching for hidden evidence of Crete's past; he published the results in 'The Archaeology of Crete', still in print. On his travels he won the friendship and respect of very many Cretans. Pendlebury joined the army in 1939, and was sent to Crete to coordinate preparations for the defence. He was captured and killed during the German attack on Herákleion. After the war the people of Herákleion held a memorial service for him; an address given by the eminent Greek archaeologist Dr N. Pláton included the eulogy: 'Dear friend, Crete will preserve your memory among her most sacred treasures. The soil which you excavated with the archaeologist's pick and enriched with a warrior's blood will shelter you with eternal gratitude.'

Staying on the New Road you come to the start of the Khaniá bypass which is only completed as far as the Mourniés junction, and does not yet (1987) lead to the coast road W of Khaniá. The slip-road is signposted for (3km) Soúda. (There is also a sign for Khaniá, ahead by bypass, 8km). The centre of Khaniá is more easily negotiated if you leave the highway here.

At Nerokoúrou, on the hillside just S of the bypass, a joint Greek–Italian excavation (1977–80) uncovered the foundations of a MMIII–LMI villa, including a large rectangular room with access between two columns to a small closed courtyard. The excavation was of particular interest because comparatively little is known about the western part of the island during the Bronze Age. Unfortunately the site (just N of the partly ruined Venetian farmhouse visible from the bypass) cannot be properly seen from outside the protective fence, but some of the finds are on display in the Khaniá museum (Case 7).

Leave the highway at the start of the bypass, and at the end of the slip road (joined from the right by the road from Soúda) turn left and continue, along an avenue of eucalyptus trees, until compelled to fork right down a one-way street system. This leads (signed high up on lamp posts) straight ahead through a suburb of faded elegance to Odós Stratigoú Tzanakáki, at the bottom of which is the bustle of the E–W road in front of the cruciform covered market in the centre of Khaniá.

14 Khaniá

KHANIA (XANIA), officially plural, Ta Khaniá (pop. 50,000), is the administrative capital of its 'nome' or province, and the second city of Crete. The old town preserves many features of its Venetian and Turkish past. Khaniá makes an agreeable base for exploring W Crete, and as a tourist centre is still geared to the independent visitor rather than the mass market. The Archaeological Museum housed in a restored Venetian church is an added attraction.

Travellers at the planning stage are urged elsewhere in this Guide to consider the possiblity of starting their holiday in Khaniá, to enjoy the leisurely pace of this end of the island before embarking on the bustle of Herákleion, and the more demanding major Minoan sites.

Tourist Information: the National Tourist Organisation (EOT) has for many years had its office in the Janissaries Mosque on the Outer Harbour. In 1987 restoration work began on that building, and the NTO moved to premises in the Pantheon, a new corner block in Plateía 1866, with an entrance round the corner at 40 Odós Kriári (tel. 26 426). When work on the mosque is completed, it may house a new municipal bureau of information; in the meantime directions to the NTO are posted outside the mosque.

Tourist Police: enquire at the NTO.

Airport at Sternés, 13km E of the city on the Akrotíri peninsula. Olympic Airways summer schedule: four flights a day from Athens (and daily connection with London Heathrow). Airport bus to and from Olympic Terminal opposite the public gardens in Odós Tzanakáki. Many charter companies now operate direct to Khaniá (see Practical Information: Travel to Crete).

Directions for leaving the airport in a hired car: bear left round the end of the runway, and (1km) turn right onto the main Sternés–Khaniá road. 5km along this road, a fork left to Soúda is the route to (c 7km) the North Coast Highway for destinations E of Khaniá. The main road continues straight ahead, and descends, with views of the Bay of Khaniá, to a T-junction with the coast road. Here turn left, almost in front of the Dóma hotel, and soon cross a main dual-carriageway to arrive (13km) in the centre of Khaniá in front of the covered market. For destinations further W keep on the main road through town. Khaniá is clearly signed; look for directions high up on lamp standards or electricity pylons.

Car Ferry services from Athens (Piraeus) dock at Soúda (6.5km E). Year-round nightly service by ANEK and sailings three nights a week by Minoan Lines. ANEK office: Plateía Soph. Venizélou, opposite the covered market, almost next to the National Bank, tel. 23 636. Minoan Lines: 8 Odós Khálidon, near the harbour, tel. 24 352. Buses (frequent) to Soúda stop on the main road in front of the market.

For Car Ferry service to the Peloponnese (Greek mainland) see Kastélli Kisámou (Rte 19).

Hotel accommodation, provided at all price levels, is most desirable with harbour or sea views. Khaniá offers a great number of easily located Rent Rooms and Pensions; the Kastélli and Topaná quarters around the harbour (see below) are suggested as good places to start enquiries. Advance booking of hotel rooms is advisable in the high season and essential during Battle of Crete Week.

Commemoration of the Battle of Crete, with many organised festivities, takes place during the last week of May.

Youth Hostel: 33 Odós Drakonianoú (not on plan; Ayios Ioánnis bus from in front of the covered market).

Tavernas on or near the Outer Harbour.

Post Offices: the main post office is at the market end of Odós Tzanakáki. A second office, for mailing and currency exchange, now operates in Plateía Mitrópolis, in front of the cathedral.

OTE (Telephone Company headquarters) next door to main post office. Khaniá area code 0821.

Bus station for out-of-town services on the edge of Plateía 1866; these buses are green. Town buses are blue; their stops are on the main through road opposite the market, and in Plateía 1866.

Swimming: 20 minutes W on foot from centre to Néa Khóra beach. Buses (blue) from Plat. 1866, marked Kalamáki or Galatás (ΚΑΛΑΜΑΚΗ or ΓΑΛΑΤΑΣ). Kastélli Kisámou buses (green) will drop you further along this coast (see Rte 19). On the Akrotíri peninsula, Stavrós and the bay of Kalathás are popular.

Guided tours. A great number of agencies operate successfully in this field; the following are well-established and can be contacted by telephone if necessary: Canea Travel, 28 Tzanakáki, near the main post office (tel. 24 780); Kydonia Travel, 10 Karaiskáki, between the market and Plateía 1866 (tel. 57 412); Aptera Travel, 11 Ktistáki, near the municipal gardens (tel. 52 666).

Car Parking near the waterfront is not easy. The harbour quays are closed to cars from the end of March till October (except from 07.00–11.00), and strict controls are enforced, under penalty of the removal of number plates and a substantial fine. Tourist status does not provide immunity. There are meter bays in Plateía 1866 opposite the main taxi rank, and on the E side of the covered market. There the street beside the minaret (Odós Daskaloyiánni, signed at the junction with the main road 'to the Old Town') leads to an area centred on Odós Kaneváro where unrestricted parking may be found.

Mountain climbing: contact the Secretary of the Alpine Club at 90 Odós Tzanakáki (tel. 24 647). The club maintains the Kallérgis and Volikás refuge huts in the Levká Ori (White Mountains).

RC Church on Odós Khálidon near the Archaeological Museum.

Hospital: Οδός Δραγούμι (Odós Dragoúmi).

History. Khaniá lies on the site of ancient Kydonía, founded according to legend by Kydon, a grandson of King Minos; the place-name (ku-do-ni-ja) occurs in the Linear B tablets of Knossós, and is familiar from many ancient literary sources. Since the 1960s, extensive excavations on the Kastélli hill above the harbour have confirmed the existence of a Bronze Age settlement from EMII–LMIIIB (c 2600–c 1200 BC). Despite partial destruction by fire in LMI, this site continued to flourish after the final destruction of Knossós (c 1380 BC), and it seems likely that the centre of Mycenaean power was transferred here. Modern occupation makes it difficult to prove the existence of the presumed Palace, but the architecture so far uncovered, and the range and quality of the finds, demonstrate that the culture was undoubtedly Palatial in style.

There was Geometric period occupation on the Kastélli, and Kydonía was prominent in the politics of the Classical and Hellenistic city-states. It minted coinage from the 5C BC, and by the 2C was the leading city in W Crete. It fell to Metellus early in the campaign of 69 BC but went on to flourish throughout the Roman period, and in the first Byzantine period became the seat of a bishop.

The etymology of the name Khaniá is uncertain, but it may have derived from the place-name Alkania, known from an ancient inscription. During the Venetian occupation it was rendered as La Canea. In 1266, the Genoese, frustrated in their ambition to control the whole island, took the city from the Venetians and held it till 1290. When Venetian rule was restored, the new buildings included a Cathedral, a Rector's Palace and a theatre on the Kastélli hill, which, as the Venetians' Castel Vecchio, had a wall around it by the mid 14C, perhaps on the line of earlier Byzantine fortifications. La Canea prospered both materially and culturally at this time. But in 1537 the raids of the Turkish corsair, Barbarossa,

Khaniá in the early years of Turkish rule, by (?Claude) Aubriet

compelled Venice to fortify the whole town. The wall had four bastions and a great moat nearly 50m wide, which ran along the line of what are now the streets Skalídi and Khátzi Mikháli Yiánnari. The architect of the fortifications was the Italian Michele Sanmicheli who was also responsible for the great walls of Candia (Herákleion), but these at La Canea were less successful, for in 1645 the city held out against the Turks for only two months. It became the seat of a Pashalik and in the 19C the island was governed from the Kastélli hill. The English scholar Robert Pashley landed at Khaniá in 1834 and was impressed by its peaceable nature for by this time over three-quarters of its population was Moslem. However from the viewpoint of the movement for Cretan independence, it was from this city that the heroic uprisings originating in the mountainous hinterland were ruthlessly repressed.

The Turkish occupation ended in 1898. The Great Powers (Britain, France, Italy and Russia) installed the Greek Prince George as High Commissioner, and Khaniá was made the capital of an independent Crete. It remained the capital city after 1913 when Crete became part of Greece, until in 1971 this title was transferred to Herákleion, the geographical centre of the island. Khaniá retains the island's highest judicial authority, the Court of Appeal, and houses the Art and Architecture departments of the new University of Crete.

A useful starting point for a walk around the town is the open space in front (S) of the cruciform *Covered Market* (see plan), constructed in 1911, which is itself one of the sights of Khaniá. Across the dual-carriageway main road is the National Bank, and just into OΔÓΣ TZANAKAKH (Odós Tzanakáki), leading away from you, the Post Office is next door to the Telephone and Telegraph office (OTE). Along this busy commercial street are tour agencies, car-hire firms and Olympic Airways, but also the *Municipal Gardens* with a pleasant shaded café. One block beyond the gardens turn left for the **Historical Museum and Archives** (open Monday–Friday only: 09.00–13.00, admission free) at 20 Odós Sphakianáki in an area of 19C villas and fashionable apartments. The collection of historical records held here is considered second in importance in all Greece only to those of Athens.

The museum exhibits are arranged on two floors. The first room to the right of the entrance is devoted to the politician and statesman Elevthérios Venizélos (1864–1936), Khaniá's most distinguished citizen of modern times; here and in the hall are exhibits connected with the penultimate stage (1896-98) of the struggle for independence in which he played a leading part. A Greek force was sent to support the Cretan Revolutionary Assembly, and despite the initial ambivalence of the Great Powers, the Turks were finally compelled to withdraw from the island. But not until 1913 did the flag of Greece at last fly from the Firkás overlooking the harbour of Khaniá.

Upstairs there are Venetian maps, and at the foot of the staircase a 16C cupboard elaborately carved with hunting scenes; its three sets of doors conceal drawers. It is remarkably rare for Venetian furniture of this quality to have survived on the island to the present day. However the majority of the exhibits are related to the long struggle against the Turks for Cretan independence, and they illuminate the spirit of those engaged in it, as much as the events themselves. A portrait of Daskaloyiánnis, leader of the 1770 Sphakiot rebellion, hangs in the upstairs corridor, one of a long row of portraits of regional chiefs; their proud bearing and their formidable weaponry proclaim their deadly earnest.

On the landing at the top of the stairs, the theme of resistance to invaders is extended to resistance to the Germans during the Second World War. The New Zealander General Bernard Freyberg VC was Supreme Commander of the forces defending the island in 1941 during the Battle of Crete.

The museum's folklore collection includes traditional costume (already well illustrated in the many 19C portraits), Cretan weaving and embroideries, and some pieces of gold embroidery and metalwork.

Most visitors will now retrace their steps to the Municipal Gardens (see above), but beyond the Historical Museum on the E edge of the town is the faded elegance (increasingly encroached upon by modern buildings) of the Khalépa quarter, where at the turn of the century social and political life revolved around the villa of the High Commissioner, Prince George. A minor road along the waterfront starting to the E of the Dóma hotel (in 1912 the British Embassy to independent Crete and in 1942 the German Commandant's house) leads to a waterside village with tanneries.

On the E side of the covered market a graceful *minaret* is conspicuous. The busy main road (Khátzi Mikháli Yiánnari, a famous name in the district of Kydonía during the struggle for independence) leads W past a little square commemorating the Battle of Crete to the central Plateía 1866, green with trees and shrubs. (Main taxi rank and some metered car parking.) On the E side is the NTO information office (see above), and to the S of the square is the regional *bus station.*

The old *walled city* of the Venetians lies back across the main road (N), and around the harbour, and from the big Plateía 1866 ΟΔΟΣ ΧΑΛΗΔΩΝ (Odós Khálidon) leads down to the waterfront, passing (right) the modern cathedral of Ayía Triáda. Dedicated shoppers will notice the two side-streets concentrating on the local leather goods. In the cathedral square is one of the new Post Office caravans (with currency exchange). A multi-domed building on the next corner was once a Turkish bath. Across the street is the restored Venetian church of St. Francis, now housing the *Archaeological Museum* (see below) which displays the antiquities of this western province of Crete.

The *Outer Harbour* has been deserted by shipping, but its quays, lined with picturesque houses and tavernas, are the focus of social life, especially for the evening 'volta'.

Odós Khálidon reaches the waterfront at Plateía Venizélou. To the right is the Plaza hotel, where an external staircase and canvas awnings conceal the Venetian Santrivani fountain, and beyõnd is the *Mosque of the Janissaries* constructed in 1645, the year in which the Turks captured the town. The mosque, severely damaged by bombing during the last war, was partially restored soon afterwards, but recently further work has become necessary. Above the mosque, the *Kastélli hill*, site of the earliest settlement, overlooks the harbour.

Walking round the foot of the Kastélli, where the Venetian wall is still formidable above on the hillside, you come to the *Inner Harbour* protected by a Venetian mole, with a ruined fort (in process of restoration) half way along it. The mole is probably built on the foundations of an earlier one. The original Venetian *lighthouse* was restored by the Egyptians during their brief occupation of the island (1832–40); it offers a fine viewpoint. On the E and S sides of the inner harbour a number of *Arsenals* remain from the Venetian dockyard. Here the galleys were built or repaired, each vaulted structure holding one ship. Nine survive, in two groups, comparable with those at Herákleion but better preserved. Beside the first group, a street running inland offers a view of the unconventional twin towers of the big Venetian church of Ayios Nikólaos.

Guarding the harbour from the NE (on the edge of the sea) is the *Sabbianara Bastion*. If you follow the E Wall along the shore from the bastion and then make your way towards Ayios Nikólaos (see plan), you will discover the maze of narrow streets which is one of the most picturesque corners of Khaniá.

Ayios Nikólaos, a Dominican church of the Venetians, was transformed by the Turks into the Imperial Mosque of Sultan Ibrahim, and still retains both bell-tower and minaret; it did not become an Orthodox church until 1918. The tall galleried nave has a fine coffered ceiling.

In front of the church is Plateía 1821 with convenient pavement cafés. (Excavations here in 1987 were examining the levels of the Venetian and Turkish periods of the city.) The plaque in the middle of the square records that an Orthodox bishop was executed by hanging from the plane tree during the 1821 revolt. At the W end of the square the little Venetian church of San Rocco, no longer in use, has a bold Latin inscription of 1630. A block further S, 16C Ayii Anárgyri (the Holy Poor) contrived to remain an Orthodox church under both Venetians and Turks.

Stretches of the *Inner Wall* are best seen along ΟΔΟΣ ΣΗΦΑΚΑ (Odós Síphaka), where the Venetians incorporated into their 14C rampart numerous column drums from earlier Greco-Roman buildings. The Kastélli suffered much damage during the last war, and modern houses are often built into the remains of old structures. ΟΔΟΣ ΚΑΝΕΒΑΡΟ (Odós Kaneváro, parallel to Síphaka) was the Venetian 'Corso', with the Arcade of St. Mark at its eastern end. Across the top of ΟΔΟΣ ΛΙΘΙΝΩΝ (Odós Lithínon, harbour end of Kaneváro) the doorway of the Venetian Archives (No. 45) has an inscription of 1623.

There are signs of archaeological activity all over this area. Half way along Odós Kaneváro, on the left walking up from Plateía Venizélou, the largest and most important excavation can be seen. This is Plateía Ayía Aikateríni, a site which helped to establish the chronological sequence of Minoan Kydonía. Many of the finest exhibits in the museum come from here.

Parallel to the S quay of the Outer Harbour is ΟΔΟΣ ΖΑΜΠΕΛΙΟΥ (Odós Zambelíou), which leads to the Topaná area, well worth exploring. Past the first crossroads, walking away from the Kastélli, is the shell of a Venetian palazzo with, high up on the façade, a crest and Latin inscription. Just as this street starts to climb some steps, a right turn leads to the *Renieri Gate*, with the family coat of arms and a 1608 inscription. Through the gate is an elegant little Venetian chapel, overdue for restoration; it is now locked. Beyond it, on the left, the vaults of the Venetian Armoury have been restored and put to use. The steps in Odós Zambelíou lead to the attractive ΟΔΟΣ ΘΕΟΤΟΚΟΠΟΥΛΟΥ (Odós Theotokopoúlou). Visitors looking for higher quality, specifically Khaniot souvenirs will enjoy this area which is becoming a marketplace for local craftsmen. When you reach the waterfront, the Xenía hotel is to the left, and above it there is a good view of the outer fortifications and moat. The athletically inclined can follow the western wall to the Bastions of San Demetrio and Schiavo-Lando (mid 16C).

On the harbour point is the Bastion of San Salvatore, reached through a passage beside the abandoned Venetian church of the same name. Below, in the restored Venetian building known as the Firkás, is the *Naval Museum of Crete* (open daily: 10.00–14.00, Tuesday, Thursday, Saturday 19.00–21.00, closed Monday; small admission fee). Episodes of Greek naval history are illustrated by ship models and photographs. There is an open-air theatre here for summer drama productions. At the Firkás the Greek flag was for the first time officially hoisted on the island in 1913 to celebrate Crete's union with Greece; the ceremony is repeated on Sundays and festivals to this day.

The **ᐧArchaeological Museum** (open daily: 08.00–19.00, Sunday 09.00–18.00, closed Tuesday; 1987 admission Drs 200) is in Odós Khálidon, opposite the modern cathedral. It is housed in the restored monastery church of St. Francis, one of the largest Venetian churches on the island. The building is crudely constructed with a vaulted nave and narrow side-aisles; a peculiarity is its reverse ecclesiastical orientation, the additional side-chapels being off the N aisle. In the adjoining garden a Turkish fountain and the base of a minaret survive from the church's days as the Mosque of Yusuf Pasha.

The exhibits, from sites all over W Crete, are displayed in chronological order, beginning to the left of the entrance with finds of the Late Neolithic period from the cave of Platyvolá. The labels (Greek and English) in the show-cases are clear and informative; they date the exhibits and give details of their provenance, sometimes with photographs of the site. There is comment where appropriate on the most important objects, and these are comparable to items starred in this Guide at other museums. The display is zealously kept up-to-date, and cases may be rearranged as the results of recent work become available. It has been considered superfluous to repeat the museum's information.

The collection falls into five broad categories: artefacts of the Neolithic, Bronze and Early Iron Ages, in cases along the left wall as you enter, and continued in the side-chapel behind the ticket desk; the larnakes (coffins) prominent in the centre; the later material (Archaic–Roman) associated with the city-states of W Crete, in cases in the rear side-chapels; statuary and stelai; mosaics.

Case 7 has material from a Minoan site at Nerokoúrou on the rising ground S of Soúda bay; this is the first excavation in this part of Crete of a Minoan villa or country house of the type familiar further E on the island. Case 11 displays vases from the local Khaniá workshop; Plateía Ayía Aikateríni, from which many of the exhibits come, is on the Kastélli hill above the harbour. Note also the remarkable seal impression of a Minoan god or king on a great building topped by horns of consecration. Case 12 builds up a picture of relations between Kydonía and other parts of the Aegean world. The LMIIIA–B cases (1420–1200 BC) are particularly important as pottery of this quality from this period has not been found in the centre and E of the island.

The material in the side-chapel to the right of the entrance is from cemeteries of this period in and around Khaniá; outstanding is the extraordinary pyxis (mus. no. 2308), which portrays a man playing a lyre to birds; it is from a tomb at Kalámi beyond Soúda.

The collection of Minoan clay *Larnakes includes magnificent polychrome examples from the cemetery near Arméni, S of Réthymnon; among the animal and plant decorative motifs are the religious symbols of the double axe and horns of consecration.

Among the statuary (at the far end from the entrance): the 'Philosopher of Elyros', a heroic Roman copy of a Greek orator; from Lissós, an Asklepios, a head of Hygieia, and a Youth with delicate features; from the Diktýnnaion sanctuary on Cape Spátha, Díktynna with hound (head missing).

To the Akrotíri: a round trip of c 40km. This is the limestone peninsula NE of Khaniá that protects the anchorage of Soúda bay. The recommended excursion includes two important monasteries (closed 14.00–17.00), with the possibility of a walk to a cave near the superbly sited ruins of one of the earliest monastic foundations on the island.

The bus service to Khordáki (ΧΩΡΔΑΚΙ) passes close to the Monastery of Ayía Triáda, but the recent timetable has not been very convenient.

Leave Khaniá on Odós Elev. Venizélou, signposted for the airport and Akrotíri. After 4.5km a left turn leads to the hill of *Prophítis Ilías* and the graves of the eminent Cretan-born statesman Elevthérios Venizélos and his son Sophoklés. The tomb is impressive in its simplicity.

Born in Khaniá in 1864, Elevthérios Venizélos was prominent in European politics for nearly four decades (see p 25), and is honoured as one of the architects of the modern Greek state.

On this hill in 1897, while the Turks were nominally still in control of the island, the Greek flag was raised by Cretan insurgents in the teeth of an international naval bombardment ostensibly designed to defuse a tense situation between the Greek and Turkish nations.

Popular summer tavernas on the hill, with a fine view over the Bay of Khaniá to the distant Cape Spátha.

The Monastery of Ayía Triáda can be reached directly by the main road to the airport, c 15km from Khaniá by this route. However, a relatively peaceful minor road across the Akrotíri peninsula is very little longer, and is especially recommended in spring to wild-flower enthusiasts.

For the direct route, continue on the well-signed airport road until you pass (right) the end of the runway. Then turn left at the T-junction within sight of the airport buildings, and almost immediately right and left again, signed by now for the monastery.

For the cross-country route continue from the Venizélos graves on the airport road. Soon Soúda Bay comes into view ahead. Both here, around *Korakiés* and Moní Kalograión, and on the road along the shore of the bay, there are areas to explore for tavernas on summer evenings, or for live Cretan music. After 2km you pass a main turning, right, for Soúda (4.5km from this junction to the Commonwealth War Cemetery, see Rte 13).

Very shortly watch for a minor road left, signed Kounoupidianá and Stavrós. Less than 2km along it, at a T-junction, bear right and very soon at a fork in *Kounoupidianá* keep right again. Pass the left-turn to Stavrós, and continue through *Kambáni*. The uncultivated areas along the way shelter many species of wild flowers. After another 2km bear left, following signs for the monastery of Ayía Triáda. Almost immediately after the junction with the road from the airport, turn left again. (This corner is the most convenient bus stop.) In 1km a long tree-lined avenue marks the approach to the monastery.

*Moní Ayías Triádas (the Holy Trinity) was founded in the first years of the 17C by two brothers, Venetians from the Zangaróli family who had adopted the Orthodox faith. The monastery is still sometimes known by their name. The massive multi-domed church (1632), its façade reinforced by Doric columns, reflects the Venetian influence as do the elaborate entrance and the mid 17C campanile. This is a rich and influential foundation with a fine library. There was a religious college here in the 19C and the abbot is still responsible for a school in Khaniá. On Trinity Sunday the monastery is a place of pilgrimage from far around.

From Ayía Triáda it is 4km on to the second, more isolated, Venetian monastery, the **Gouvernéto**. At first the road has a hard-packed dirt surface, but from the point where it starts to climb into the wild NE corner of the Akrotíri it is asphalted.

The monastery is thought to date back at least to the first years of the Venetian occupation, and perhaps to the 11C when pirates were ravaging the coast of Crete and an inland position offered relative safety. The history of the Gouvernéto is bound up with that of its predecesor in this region, the monastery of Ayios Ioánnis Xénos known as the Katholikó, certainly one of the earliest religious foundations on the island; its ruins are hidden in a ravine to the NE, near the sea (see below).

The plain exterior wall of the Gouvernéto quadrangle, with towers at the four corners, hides a richly decorated church dedicated to the Presentation of the Virgin, Η Κυρία των Αγγέλων (Our Lady of the Angels), which was started in 1548 (but not at that time completed), and reconstructed after damage during the 1821 Revolt.

The relief carving of the bases of the six columns set into the church façade is highly unusual for Crete, as is the circular plan of the church. One of the side-chapels is dedicated to the Ayii Déka, (Crete's ten martyrs under the Persecution of Decius in 250), and the other to the renowned local saint, Ayios Ioánnis Xénos, St. John the Stranger, an 11C hermit who died in the cave down at the Katholikó.

The ruins of the **Katholikó** are the objective of a recommended walk (40 minutes) which starts from the Gouvernéto. The well-built path drops away over the right-hand side of the rise beyond the monastery.

After ten minutes you pass a first cave with a chapel at its entrance, and inside a stalagmite said to resemble a bear. The cave, excavated by C. Daváras, was originally sacred to Artemis, venerated here in the form of a bear (Αρκούδα in

The Katholikó monastery on the Akrotíri near Khaniá
(from Pashley, Travels in Crete, *1837)*

Greek). The chapel is now dedicated to the Panayía (Our Lady) Arkoudiótissa.

The ancient path continues downhill and becomes a long flight of rock-cut steps; on a bend the Katholikó is suddenly in view. The ruined buildings lie on either side of a wide bridge across the bed of a dried-up stream, between cliffs from which the unmistakable notes of the blue rock thrush can often be heard.

St. John's Feast Day is 7 October, and the vigil for this, traditionally one of the great religious festivals of W Crete, begins here on the previous evening. Although known as 'Ermítis', the hermit, St. John was an influential evangelist in the early 11C, devoted to the task of re-establishing the Christian faith after the army of the Byzantine Empire had recovered the island (in 961) from the Saracens. His grave is at the end of a spectacular cave on the left at the bottom of the rock staircase. (The cave is perilously slippery underfoot and is considered unsafe in places.)

A 10-minute walk down the river-bed leads to the rocky shore. It is possible to swim from an ancient rock-cut slipway.

15   Khaniá or Réthymnon to Khóra Sphakíon and the South Coast

About 70km (43 miles) to Khóra Sphakíon. The road crosses the island from Vrýses which is roughly equidistant (c 30km) from Khaniá and Réthymnon. Khóra Sphakíon, one of the principal harbours for the S coast boat service, can be used as a base for exploring the region.

The coast road is described E as far as Selliá where it joins the route S from Réthymnon.

Buses to Khóra Sphakíon (via Vrýses) from Réthymnon, about three

a day; from Khaniá guaranteed connections at Vrýses. Daily bus
along the S coast in summer (probably Easter to mid October).

The first part of this route uses the North Coast Highway (Rte 13). At
30km from Khaniá, immediately after a bridge over the road, an
insignificant turning leads (right, across the stream, and then left)
into Vrýses from the W. The main highway junction is 3km to the E,
26km from Réthymnon. Distances on the road across the island are
calculated from Vrýses.

Vrýses is generally agreed to be one of the most beguiling villages
on Crete. Two rivers, the Vrysanós and the Boútakas, meet at a
shallow cascade frequented by ducks. Local yoghurt with honey is a
speciality of the tavernas under the plane trees beside the stream. A
monument commemorates the Constitutional Commission set up in
the wake of the 1897 Revolt which was to lead to autonomy for Crete.

It is possible to spend a night here, but for most travellers the
village is the start of the road through the district of Apokóronas to
Sphakiá.

5km out of Vrýses is a left turn for *Alíkambos*. The *church of the
Panayía (Virgin Mary) is one of the most delightful of the frescoed
churches of Crete.

1km along the narrow lane, on a wide hairpin bend right, you see
ahead a Venetian fountain, still used to water flocks. Below left, an
old path leads past the church, hidden in a graveyard shaded by an
oak and a bay tree and looking out over orange groves in the valley.
The interior is dark but the church is well cared for and the frescoes
are in a good state of preservation. The paintings in the nave are the
work of Ioánnis Pagoménos (see Rte 18, p 252), dated by inscription
to 1315.

On the N wall next to the iconostasis the Virgin with Child (Odiyítria), with the
Baptism above. Ayios Demétrios, mounted left of Ayios Yeóryios. Opposite:
Ayios Konstantínos. Rather indistinct on the upper register of the vault (S) is a
fine Nativity.
The frescoes in the bema, by a different artist, date from the later 14C.

The main road climbs steadily into the increasingly rocky scrub of
these E ranges of the Levká Ori (White Mountains). It gains height up
a valley, often crossing the older more direct track, and reaches at
10km the little upland plain of Krápi. (Lekanopédio on the sign is
literally a basin plain.) The only natural route into Sphakiá from this
direction ran through the ravine of Katré, which opens out of this
plain, and Cretan folk-memory enshrines many heroic ambushes
and rearguard actions against Turkish armies here at the frontier of
the Sphakiot stronghold. 3km beyond Krápi the pass of Katré is noted
on signposts.

16km At a ridge, the *plain of Askýphou* (730m) comes into view.
The 19C traveller Robert Pashley described the plain as 'so surrounded by lofty mountain-summits that it has somewhat the
appearance of an large amphitheatre'. The villages occupy the raised
ground around the patchwork field-system dominated by a ruined
Turkish fort on a conical hill. To walk to the fort stop on this ridge; the
old road is immediately to the left, and you can see the route ahead of
you. On this plain one of the major pitched battles of the 1821 Cretan
insurrection was fought between the Turks and bands of mountain
warriors; it resulted in a resounding and bloody victory for the Sphakiot forces which is still related in poetry and song.

The road follows the W edge of the plain, and then climbs again. At the top of the pass (22km) a narrow side-road turns off left to (8km) *Asphéndou*, offering a chance to get a car off the beaten track; very soon there is a glimpse (right) of the sea. This is country recommended for walking, both to long-distance walkers and to bird-watchers and naturalists who would like to find the wild solitude of the Cretan mountainside. The traditional mule-paths out of the Askýphou plain climbed W into the Levká Ori, SW to Anópolis and E over to Asi Goniá (see Rte 13); the tracks (still used by shepherds) can be spotted from the plain as scars on the hillsides.

For Khóra Sphakíon the main road continues S to (23km) *Imbros*, and the descent begins. The traditional route kept to the E wall of the ravine down to Komitádes, and this track too might apeal to some serious walkers. Now the road twists high (to the W) above the spectacular *Nímbros gorge*.

Along this route, during four days and nights at the end of May 1941, 12,000 weary troops, survivors of the Battle of Crete (see p 29), withdrew to the coast under constant attack, the majority to be embarked by the Royal Navy for Egypt.

The road emerges high above the Libyan sea, with superb views of the coast. The large island directly S is Gávdos, the most southerly inhabited point in Europe (see Rte 18). To the E you can make out the Venetian fortress of Frangokástello down by the shore, and beyond it are the Paximádia islands in the Bay of Mesará, backed by the Asteroúsia range of mountains. At the foot of the vertiginous (850m)

View of Khóra Sphakíon in 1615, by Francesco Basilicata

descent, 36km from Vrýses, the road divides; the right branch leads in 4km to *Khóra Sphakíon*.

In the 18C this was a substantial town defended by a castle (ruins on the hill as you descend to the harbour), and the centre, as its name implies, of the fiercely independent district of Sphakiá; its coastline sheltered a fleet of 40 merchant ships. After the 1770 rebellion under Daskaloyiánnis, Sphakiá was savagely repressed by the Turks, and although its people took a leading part in the struggle for freedom all through the 19C, the area never regained the same economic strength. The traditional Sphakiot costume of black shirt and trousers or breeches with tall leather boots is still habitually worn at least by the older generation of men of this region.

Today the tiny harbour's prosperity is closely related to the great number of foreign tourists brought here by the renowned attractions of the walk down the Gorge of Samariá.

Khóra Sphakíon is still an enjoyable place to spend a few days unless you insist on complete tranquillity. In the early evening the boats return from Ayiá Rouméli at the bottom of the gorge, and from May–October (the months when the walk is permitted) the village is sometimes overwhelmed by people and coaches. However the coaches leave for the N coast resorts, and then the diminutive harbour regains its charm. The waterfront is packed with the tables of prosperous fish tavernas. There is a small hotel (well-situated though rather ambitiously listed as Class B), but visitors often prefer the well-equipped rooms for rent above these tavernas. There are also pleasant and quieter rooms in the village behind, some with views (W) along the rocky coast.

South Coast Boat Service. Khóra Sphakíon is at one end of the route now served by these boats which operate a complicated but reliable schedule between this harbour and Palaiókhora to the W. The service grew up as a rather haphazard affair based on the traditional fishing boats or caiques, but it is now thoroughly organised, subject always of course to weather conditions. A new and larger breed of ferry (Samariá I began operating in 1987) will no doubt alter its character once again.

The primary aim is daily transport to and from Ayiá Rouméli at the bottom of the gorge of Samariá, but the boats also put in to Loutró and Soúyia, and several times a week it is possible to travel the whole route in either direction. An innovation is the day-trip to the island of Gávdos, 2 hours away. The new schedule is issued every March (and is available at tourist information offices), so no exact times are given here, but the 1987 service from Khóra Sphakíon would lead you to expect: in April, a morning boat daily to the bottom of the gorge with evening return, and three days a week travel along the whole route; May–September, the full service to and from the gorge, with at least three boats a week continuing to Palaiókhora; in addition from June, trips to Gávdos three times a week (Friday, Saturday and Sunday in 1987; see also under Palaiókhora, Rte 18); in October a limited service to and from the gorge and along the coast, including always a late afternoon return from Ayiá Rouméli.

Suggested excursions from Khóra Sphakíon.

A. To Ayiá Rouméli. The boat journey (see above) along the coast to *Ayiá Rouméli* via *Loutró* takes c 75 minutes, and the timetable allows at least five hours for exploring the lower part of the Gorge of Samariá (see also Rte 16). You can walk (c 1 hour) to the dramatic narrow pass known as the 'Iron Gates', in the relative peace before, in the high season, the worst crowds begin to arrive from the top. Ayiá Rouméli (on the site of ancient Tárra) is well provided with tavernas and there is good swimming.

There are organised tours from the N Coast centres, known as 'Samariá the Lazy Way', though it should be said that there is nothing especially lazy about a stiff 2–3-hour climb up the gorge. If you are staying locally and have any choice, you might like to make enquiries to try to avoid these tour days.

Another recommended expedition from Ayiá Rouméli is a walk E along the coast (in a little over an hour on a well-marked path) to the 10/11C Ayios Pávlos, a Byzantine cruciform and domed church, the origins of which are associated with Ayios Ioánnis Xénos. Remains of frescoes are tentatively dated to the 13C.

Tradition links the sweet-water spring beside the church with baptisms by St. Paul who sailed along this coast on his way to Rome.

It is possible for long-distance walkers, properly equipped, to take the first boat to Ayiá Rouméli from Khóra Sphakíon and walk back in the day over the S flank of the Levká Ori. From Ayios Pávlos you climb, on a mule-path, up the river gorge c 3 hours to the village of Ayios Ioánnis at a height of 750m (two frescoed churches), then a good hour E to Arádena on a newly-widened track, and a 3.5km stage on to Anópolis, about 6 hours in all to this point. (See excursion C. below.) From here it is 12km on an asphalt road to Khóra Sphakíon. If desired taxis are available; ask at any kapheneíon. (The 1987 fare was c Drs 1000.) In April and October, when temperatures are most agreeable for this type of walk, the boat schedule probably does not allow an early start, and a taxi or an overnight stay in Anópolis may be unavoidable.

B. To Loutró. This walk (c 2 hours) may be combined with the boat trip to or from Loutró. (When the last boat back from Ayiá Rouméli to Khóra Sphakíon is full, it does not call at Loutró.)

The footpath along the cliffs is properly built and maintained on the line of an 'ancient way'; it is well marked with splashes of red paint, but they not infrequently indicate a diversion after a rock fall and this is an expedition for reasonably agile walkers; it should not be attempted in bad weather.

Set out along the road to Anópolis. At 3km on the first hairpin bend (easy parking if required) the path drops down from the road and leads W along the coast. The second chapel in sight is your destination. The first beach (less than half an hour) offers especially fine swimming; here the cliffs are perpendicular, creating a narrow coastal strip sheltered and calm in all weathers except a strong S wind. You pass a number of caves, one the refuge of the legendary 18C Sphakiot leader Daskaloyiánnis who came from Anópolis.

Loutró, in the shelter of a promontory and an island, is the only natural year-round harbour on Crete's S coast. On the promontory between two anchorages are scanty remains of the ancient city of Phoínix, port of Greco-Roman Anópolis in the hills above. More recently this was the winter harbour of Sphakiá, and the home port of vessels large enough to trade as far as Smyrna and Alexandria. The only route inland is a near-vertical ascent, on a well-built footpath, of more than 700m to Anópolis, and perhaps for this reason Loutró was gradually abandoned in favour of Khóra Sphakíon.

A decade ago Loutró was virtually deserted, but then there was a move to reinvigorate the harbour. As a result of the prosperity derived from tourism in this region, the quay has been rebuilt and the houses behind the shingle have been resettled. The word has got about, and this exceptionally beautiful little bay, still accessible only by boat or on foot, is gaining renown as an escapist paradise. There are now rent rooms and tavernas attempting to meet the demand.

C. To Anópolis. Daily bus, but in the late afternoon with early morning return. A fine asphalt road sweeps up from Khóra Sphakíon to (12km) Anópolis in a high E–W valley of the White Mountains; this and the plain of Askýphou are the traditional heartlands of Sphakiá. The straggling modern village has kapheneíons and (increasingly) rooms to rent. Above it, to seaward, are the unexcavated remains of one of the foremost Greco-Roman city-states of the area. As you enter the village you can distinguish on the skyline the church of Ayía Aikateríni, which, with the adjacent tower, is at the centre of the site.

Anópolis was the birthplace of Ioánnis Daskaloyiánnis who was martyred by the Turks for his part as leader of the 1770 rebellion; his statue stands in the plateía at the end of the village, and this is the starting-point for the walk (20 minutes) to the ancient site. The lane S from the plateía led until recently to the traditional stone-built path for the climb up the hill, but now the bulldozer has carved out a (rough) track so that vehicles can reach Ayía Aikateríni; the scars of the operation will take some time to heal. The church is just above the crest and immediately to the W is the large but still unexplored site. Great quantities of stones mark collapsed buildings and strong fortification walls can be made out in places. The city commanded the route between the upland plain and its harbour, Phoínix, at modern Loutró; the ancient way to the coast, still a well-worn path, zigzags down the near-vertical slope to the sea below. Clearly this is a very stiff climb uphill, but in the downhill direction it is a highly recommended (c 30 minutes) walk. For the return to Khóra Sphakíon see the alternatives (of coast path or boat) in excursion B. above.

From the plateía in the centre of Anópolis, the road (unsurfaced in 1987) now continues across the plain to (3.5km) Arádena and Ayios Ioánnis. Leave the statue of Daskaloyiánnis to the left, and just out of the plateía fork left in front of a kapheneíon.

The right fork leads c 14km into the Levká Ori. The surface is not suitable for ordinary hire cars, but this is a route into the mountains for serious walkers. Anópolis is one of the established starting-points for the climb to the summit of Pákhnes (2452m); the climb takes 8 hours and as there is no refuge hut on the way it involves a night camping out on the mountain. Anyone intending to make the climb should first consult the Greek Alpine Club—see introductory information for Khaniá (Rte 14).

About 2km after you leave Anópolis, *Arádena* comes into view, with the mellow Byzantine church of Mikhaíl Arkhángelos tranquil on the edge of one of Crete's most dramatic gorges. At this point for many centuries travellers have descended by the steep path into the ravine to arrive at the church on the far side, but in 1986 the gorge was spanned by a great steel bridge, financed by the internationally successful Vardinoyiannís family. The bridge was built as a gift to the village of Ayios Ioánnis from which the family came, and is welcomed locally as a move towards economic viability for these isolated communities.

Romantics may like to take the old path down into the gorge; it is strongly recommended to botanists. Strike off the modern road 600m short of the bridge to pick up the old track before the stepped descent, which is a fascinating example of the obsolescent road system of Sphakiá.

Modern Arádena occupies the site of the Greco-Roman city-state of Aradén, and Mikhaíl Arkhángelos is built into the central nave and apse of an Early Christian basilica. The 14C frescoes include scenes from the Christ cycle in the vaulting, and the donors with the archangel in the N cross-arm. The church key is kept at one of the houses on the edge of the village furthest away from the gorge.

The new road continues on the far side of the bridge almost to *Ayios Ioánnis*; it is very rough in places for cars but offers a highly recommended walk (c 1 hour 15 minutes). In 1823 Egyptian troops, called in to reinforce the Turks, were pursuing along this route the women and children of patriots of the region who had taken refuge in the gorge of Samariá. At Ayios Ioánnis, in an heroic stand, the army's path was blocked by a mere 32 Cretan rebels; all perished but they gained enough time for the women and children to reach the safety of Samariá.

On the approach to the village there are (left of the road) two frescoed churches, Ayios Ioánnis and the Panayía, both painted in the 14C. (Ask for the keys in the village.)

Serious walkers can cover the distance between Anópolis and Ayiá Rouméli in one day—see excursion A. above.

The S Coast road to Frangokástello, and on to (38km) Selliá to link up (c 50km) with the Réthymnon–Ayía Galíni route (Rte 12B).

There is at present one daily bus each way during the summer season only (May–mid October). Check beforehand in Réthymnon or Khaniá if plans depend on it.

The road has been widened and its surface greatly improved in recent years; the last 4km was scheduled for asphalt in 1987. Care may be needed after bad weather, and the road edges are still unstable in places, but this is now a highly recommended scenic drive.

Return from Khóra Sphakíon to the start of the road inland for the Nímbros gorge and Askýphou, but continue E along the coast. Just past the junction the church of the Panayía (below the road to the right), all that remains of the Thymianí monastery, is important in Cretan history because here on the 29 May 1821 1500 Sphakiots met to proclaim the revolt against the Turks in sympathy with the struggle for freedom on the Greek mainland.

5km from Khóra Sphakíon is *Komitádes*, where the chapel of Ayios Yeóryios has the earliest known frescoes (1313) by Ioánnis Pagoménos.

The road bends left in front of the village church. Someone from the kapheneíon opposite will guide you, but to find Ayios Yeóryios (10 minutes below the village) unaided, start down the path from the church which bends left round the church wall and then keeps straight ahead downhill. Three or four minutes from the main street you pass (right) a small white chapel. 30 paces further turn left through a break in the wall onto a side path, and follow it as it bends right downhill towards the sea. Continue until the path seems as if it must plunge into the ravine below, but persevere, and there half hidden to the left is the arched doorway of the ruined narthex in front of Ayios Yeóryios. The chapel has been sadly neglected, but the frescoes are sufficiently preserved to reward the enthusiast.

The road along the edge of the coastal plain at the foot of steep hills links a series of villages. At 12km a broad track is signed right to (3km) **Frangokástello** on the sea, but in a car it is better to continue through *Patsianós* and *Kapsodásos* 4km to the second signed turn (asphalt surface, 2.5km).

On foot the first turning is the most direct route to the fortress, and there is, at the time of writing, a beach at the end of the track. (The movement of sand between one year and the next is disconcertingly unpredictable along this coast.) This approach to the fort is not visually improved by new concrete buildings, but they do offer tavernas and very simple rooms for rent. There is a fine beach (with taverna) dominated by the castle. The bay is shallow for a long way out, giving noticeably higher sea temperatures in spring, and making this one of the best beaches on Crete for children.

In the mid 14C a petition urged Venice to protect this coast from pirate raids. Frangokástello was built in 1371 and appears always to have been an isolated fort without a nearby settlement. It must have served a dual purpose, also strengthening the Venetian hand against the rebellious stronghold of Sphakiá. The fortress is rectangular, with square towers at the corners; the SW tower is larger than the rest and forms a guardhouse for the main gate facing the sea, watched over by the Lion of St. Mark. The interior now preserves only the skeleton of the original plan.

The castle was at first called by the name of the nearby Venetian church of Ayios Nikítas, but it became known to the Cretans as Frangokástello. ('Frankish' is still used as a generic term for all West Europeans.) In 1770 the Sphakiot leader, Ioánnis Daskaloyiánnis, gave himself up to the Turks here, and was later brutally executed in Khaniá. In 1828 the adventurer Khátzi Mikhális Daliánis made a heroic last stand at the fort with 385 men against vastly superior Turkish forces. The Cretans were massacred, but it is claimed that in the dawn mist on the anniversary (17 May) each year, a phantom army known locally as the 'drossoulites', the 'dew shades', returns to dance on the plain.

400m NE of the fort on the way back to the main road is the chapel of Ayios Nikítas; it is built on the bema of the smallest Early Christian basilica yet known on the island. There are remains of a polychrome mosaic.

Continuing E on the main road the coastal plain peters out, and the road runs high above the sea, with narrow strips of cultivated land and the occasional glimpse of a beach far below. After (18km) *Skalotí* a 2km stretch of rough road was scheduled for surfacing in 1987.

27km *Rodákino* is a delightful village still little affected by organised tourism. There are a few simple rooms for rent. A turning in the village leads down the river valley (recommended to bird enthusiasts in spring) c 2km to the shore and access to swimming from isolated beaches or rocks; there is a car track W as far as some tavernas.

The main road climbs out of Rodákino. Tracks into the hills (for example at 1.5km and 4km from the village) offer opportunities for walks. At the watershed (32.5km), on a bend where the road is still high above the sea, the view extends E to the Mesará and Mount Ida, and the White Mountains are left behind. In the foreground is the beautiful Bay of Plakiás.

38km *Selliá*. 2km further, after the coves and beaches have been enticingly spread out below like a large-scale map, you reach an oblique T-junction where Plakiás and the Préveli monastery are to the right. To the left the main Ayía Galíni–Réthymnon road is reached (in c 12km) through the *Kotsiphós gorge* and the village of *Ayios Ioánnis*. On this main road you are then 18.5km from Réthymnon. For these alternatives turn to Rte 12B, p 221.

16 Khaniá to Omalós and the Gorge of Samariá

This can be treated as a simple excursion, 44km (27 miles) by car or bus to the Omalós plateau to spend a day among Crete's most impressive mountain range, the Levká Ori (White Mountains).

Alternatively the trek to the S coast through the Gorge of Samariá, which can also be undertaken as part of a day's round-trip from the N coast centres, is a major expedition that needs careful planning (see below).

Mesklá is a short drive (20km from Khaniá). A recommended 5km walk up the valley to this attractively situated village uses the Omalós bus service as far as Phournés.

There are several buses a day on the Omalós route, including one in the early morning. One bus a day to Mesklá.

The road leaves Khaniá along the coast to the W in the direction of Kastélli, but after 1.5km turns left for Omalós up an avenue of eucalyptus trees. These soon give way to groves of orange trees behind reed windbreaks; in spring the scent of orange blossom is overpowering.

This broad and fertile river valley was nicknamed 'prison valley' during the Battle of Crete, on account of the Ayiá prison which still exists. German paratroops were landed here in strength as part of a pincer movement in the planned attack on Khaniá, then the capital of the island; they met with fierce resistance, not least from the local population.

At c 9km a flash of water (right) is a glimpse of the Ayiá reservoir, which, with the adjacent reed-beds, has proved consistently rewarding for bird-watchers, especially during the spring migration. The open water can be viewed from the dam at the S end.

At the beginning of the village of *Ayiá* (9.5km from Khaniá), there is a possible detour to the ruins of an episcopal church of the Second Byzantine period built over one dating from Early Christian times.

Turn off the main road at the sign for Kyrtomádos, but after 100m fork left. After a further 300m turn right, and 150m along this narrow track the ivy-clad walls are in view ahead to the right, opposite well-tended orange groves. The area is known locally as Episkopí.

When the Arabs were driven from the island (in 961) by the forces of Byzantium under Nikephóros Phokás, a great building programme was required to replace the churches which had been destroyed during more than a century of Saracen occupation, and for the new episcopal churches the sites of the pre-Arab ones were naturally, as in this case, favoured.

The Early Christian church here has not been excavated, but it seems to have been a substantial structure with narthex and atrium. The 10/11C episcopal church is in ruins but the walls, which incorporate material from its predecessor (see lower courses of N wall), still stand to above window height in places, preserving some of the brickwork round the arches. It can be seen from the remains that this was a three-aisled basilica divided by two colonnades, each of three columns, the pair at the W end marble, the others granite. The tall (50cm) column bases may have facilitated the re-use of the columns of the Early Christian basilica for its loftier successor.

The church is dedicated to the Panayía, though there is an old tradition of association with Konstantínos and Eléni, the first Christian Emperor and his mother. In the Second Byzantine period and throughout the Venetian rule this was the seat of the Orthodox bishop of Kydonía (Khaniá).

At 12km on the main road, opposite a memorial to partisans killed by the Germans, the Soúyia road (Rte 17) diverges right; it crosses the river into Alikianós—see p 248 for a detour to two churches of interest.

The Omalós road continues ahead past the memorial until at

15.5km, in the middle of the village of *Phournés*, it swings right. Here a left fork offers a recommended detour to (5km) *Mesklá*, lying in the fertile tree-lined Kerítis valley and surrounded by orange groves. On foot it is more pleasant to follow the old track which keeps to the river-bed; fork right downhill 100m after leaving the main road.

On the edge of Mesklá, just across a bridge and on a long right-hand bend, a track on the left leads uphill (100m) to the frescoed church of the Metamórphosis Sotírou (Transfiguration of the Saviour); its gate is overhung by a mimosa tree. The frescoes, very worn in the bema, are well-preserved in the nave, and include a fine Transfiguration in the arch on the S wall. Right of this is the donor inscription dated 1303; the artists are named as Theódoros Daniél and his nephew Mikhaíl Venéris. Below the inscription Leontios, the patron saint of the donor, is depicted. The paintings in the narthex are by a different hand (graffito 1471 on S wall).

The houses of Mesklá are strung out up one side of the street beside the river. The war memorial of this small village carries a long list of names, including those of a group of about 30 'missing' in Germany.

It is known that there was a city on the slopes above the valley in the Greco-Roman period, but its name is still disputed. At the top of the village stands the big modern church of the Panayía, and, beside it, the old 14C chapel with the same dedication (the Assumption of the Virgin) is built into the foundations of a 5–6C basilica, from which fragments of a mosaic floor could be seen until recently. It is thought that there was an earlier building on the site, a temple of Aphrodite.

The terrace below these churches overhangs a meeting of streams and there is the constant sound of running water, a rare delight during the Cretan summer. The track leads on invitingly into the hills, towards Thériso.

To the W there is a steep footpath (less than 1 hour) up to Lákki (see below). Ask for the kalderími 'stous Lákkous'.

The Omalós road crosses the Kerítis and leaves the valley, climbing in great zigzags. The land is terraced for olives and the view increases in grandeur. At 24.5km *Lákki*, a superbly sited mountain village, has trim red-roofed houses widely dispersed over the hillside. The climb continues across bleak stony uplands and the air is scented by aromatic rock-plants. For a while the Levká Ori appear in the distance to the left. Then, across a saddle, the road turns towards them, and (33km) reaches a pass. Less than 1km further on, a plaque 'from your comrades in the national resistance 1941–45', records the death in an ambush on 28 February 1944 of the New Zealander, Dudley Perkins, and a Greek partisan companion. Perkins, known to the Resistance as Vasilí or 'Kiwi', escaped from the island in 1942 and then returned from the Middle East as an undercover agent. His guerilla exploits are legendary.

The road climbs yet higher. The fir trees are stunted, but in season they shelter a profusion of mountain flowers. At the crest the **Omalós** plateau comes into view.

The mountain plain (average height 1100m) is roughly triangular, with the distance along each side about an hour's walk. At each of its three corners a pass leads out of the plain, which thus forms the focal point of the routes through the White Mountains. Snow lies till March, leaving behind as it recedes a cloud of the crocus, *C. sieberi*, *Tulipa bakeri* and other rareties. The land drains slowly by a swallow hole, and remains green during the early part of the summer. It is too high for the olive, but cereals and potatoes are cultivated by people from the villages of Lákki and Ayía Eiríne (Rte 17).

The Cretan leaders met here in May 1866, and protested to the ruling Sultan against new taxation; their approaches to foreign consuls and the declaration by Sphakiá of union with Greece, precipitated the ill-fated 1866–67 Cretan revolt. Where the road comes down to the plain, on a knoll to the left is the house and grave of Khátzi Mikhális Yiánnaris, one of the great rebel leaders of 19C Crete, who survived to become president of the Cretan Assembly which in 1912 at last achieved the long-desired union with Greece. He built the chapel of Ayios Pandeleímon as an act of gratitude after his deliverance from a Turkish prison where he had prayed to the saint for help.

At the edge of the plain a group of tavernas has rooms to rent, useful for an early start on the walk through the gorge. Telephone bookings may be possible; enquire at NTO in Khaniá.

Crossing the plain, as you near the rising ground at the end, you pass, left, a track to (5km; c 75 minutes on foot) the Kallérgis mountain refuge (1680m, 30 beds); from the hut it is a climb of 7 hours to the summit of Pákhnes, (2452m). Psilorítis (Mount Ida) is higher at 2456m, but the Levká Ori are a formidable range, with ten peaks over 2000m. The Kallérgis hut is run by the Greek Alpine Club (see Khaniá information, Rte 14).

Almost opposite the turning to the refuge, a dirt road branches off to the western climb out of the Omalós. Through wild and beautiful country this eventually connects (c 15km) with the asphalted Khaniá–Soúyia road (Rte 17).

At 44km you reach the pass of *Xylóskalo* where a Tourist Pavilion (café; seven beds, no telephone bookings) is dramatically sited, 1227m above sea level, at the head of the Samariá gorge. This is now a Regional Park, in which animals and plants alike are strictly protected. At uncrowded times it is possible to descend into the gorge for the first 2km or so; otherwise it can be difficult to make your way back up the steep steps. Alternatively, to avoid the crowds, there is a recommended path (starting beside the Tourist Pavilion) which climbs W on the slopes of Mount Gíngilos.

The **Gorge of Samariá.

Though many tens of thousands make the 17km trek each year from the Omalós plain to Ayiá Rouméli on the Libyan sea, this ought to be treated as an expedition for experienced and fit walkers. Fatal casualties are not unknown, usually caused by unpreparedness or foolish disregard for regulations, and many tourists ruin several days of their holiday by walking the gorge in unsuitable footwear or insufficiently protected from the sun.

The gorge is closed until the beginning of May. The exact date depends on the volume of water coming down from the mountains and is at the discretion of the rangers (enquire at NTO in Khaniá). It is foolhardy to embark on this walk when the river, which has to be crossed many times, may be above knee height and affected by sudden flash floods. The gorge is closed again at the end of October and the boat service from Ayiá Rouméli ceases then too.

This said, the expedition properly planned and prepared for is one of the major tourist adventures Crete has to offer. There are a number of ways of tackling it. The all-inclusive round-trip conducted coach tour from places as far afield as Ayios Nikólaos will suit many people. The guides iron out all logistic problems. For those who prefer an independent, less regimented approach, a car is no help unless a party happens to include a willing 'chauffeur'. A taxi (Khaniá to Omalós) is one possibility. The ordinary bus service offers an early start from Khaniá (also possible from Herákleion and Kastélli Kisámou). If you reach the Omalós the previous evening you must be prepared to rough it, for there are very few beds at the tourist pavilion and tavernas. Thursdays and Sundays are usually the most crowded days in the gorge.

You should allow 5 or 6 hours to enjoy the walk. Ayiá Rouméli has welcoming tavernas and many rooms for rent, and also good swimming. Three days a week at present there is a boat to Palaiokhóra (Rte 18). After walking the gorge most people will leave by boat for Khóra Sphakíon (Rte 15). The service is very efficient, though the last boat may often be crowded. For departure time, according to season, enquire at NTO in Khaniá. The practice has been for the 17.00 boat to connect with the 18.00 bus to Réthymnon; guaranteed connection at Vrýses for Khaniá.

Sideróportes, the 'Iron Gates' pass, the narrowest point in the Gorge of Samariá (from Pashley, Travels in Crete, 1837)

Everyone who undertakes this formidable walk remembers the excitement of the first precipitous descent down the Xylóskalo (the 'Wooden Staircase', originally constructed of tree trunks), and the drama of the scenery dominated by the rock face of Gíngilos. Far down at the bottom, the path joins the river-bed of the Tarraíos, named after the Greco-Roman city-state of Tárrha on the present site of Ayiá Rouméli. There are two springs on the way down: Neroútsiko and Ríza Sykiás. From the E, from the region of the Kallérgis mountain refuge (see above) a tributary joins the Tarraíos. After this, stages along the route are defined by: the little church of Ayios Nikólaos amid giant cypresses; the deserted village of Samariá; the church of Osía (Blessed) María—with the date 1379 above the door; and the so-called 'Iron Gates', where the pass narrows to a few metres. The whole route is very well cared for, and clearly marked. Botanists will appreciate the distinct micro-environment of the gorge and bird-watchers will be on the look-out for the bearded vulture or lammergeier. The White Mountains are the last region where the 'agrími' (Cretan ibex) is still to be found in its natural habitat, but these wild creatures usually take care to keep well away from the frequented trail.

17 Khaniá to Soúyia

A scenic road, 70km (42 miles) through the western foothills of the White Mountains to a remote village on the Libyan sea. The itinerary includes a suggested expedition on foot or by boat to the site of the Greco-Roman city-state of Lissós.
The bus service to Soúyia enforces an overnight stay.

Leave Khaniá following Rte 16. After 12km, opposite the war memorial, the Soúyia road diverges right, signed for Alikianós 1km, to cross the Kerítis river with the distant wall of the Levká Ori (the White Mountains) upstream left. It skirts Alikianós and, passing the turn into the village, makes a left bend, and heads for the mountains.

To visit the 14C church of Ayios Ioánnis (1.5km off the road) it is necessary to detour into the village. Almost immediately keep right at a fork following the sign for Kouphós. 300m from the fork you pass, right, the tiny cruciform chapel of Ayios Yeóryios, dating from the early part of the Venetian period. The chapel has been restored after war damage which destroyed its fine frescoes.
    Continue on this road 1.3km and you will find the church of *Ayios Ioánnis* hidden in an orange grove (right) 50m back from the road. Despite partial restoration in 1951, the church is abandoned (and has lost its dome).

In the First Byzantine period there was a basilica here, dated to the 6C; there are records of a mosaic floor depicting deer, peacocks and vases similar to that of the basilica at Soúyia (see below). Ayios Ioánnis replaced a church probably destroyed in the severe earthquake of 1303; that church, dedicated to the Panayía (Zoodókhos Piyí, the Virgin as the source of life) is thought to have been founded in 1004 by the evangelist Ayios Ioánnis Xénos, and the tradition survives in the name given to the existing early 14C building.
    Ayios Ioánnis is cross-in-square in plan with the W cross-arm wider than that of the E end (the narthex is later); the design of the apse is most unusual for Crete, and is said to show the influence of Constantinople. The dome was supported on three columns (the SW one now restored) and a single square unadorned pillar. The capitals of the two northern columns are of an early 6C type, probably re-used from the Early Christian basilica.
    The surviving frescoes, tentatively dated to the 15C, are valued as illustrations of an early phase of the Cretan School of painting. The best-preserved scenes are: in the apse the Platytéra with the Ascension and Pentecost; in the S cross-arm (W wall) Ayios Pandeleímon, and in the same position in the N cross-arm Demétrios; opposite, in a niche, Ayía Paraskeví. Left of the main W door is a worn portrayal of the Archangel Michael.

The main Soúyia road continues S to (16km) *Skinés*, a pleasant village along a wide·street, and one of the main centres for the citrus trade of the region. Soon after (17km) *Khliaró* the orange groves come to an end, and the road begins to gain height following a narrow **river valley** into the well-watered and wooded foothills of the White Mountains. It crosses the river at 21.5km, and at 24km you reach a watershed. Through (26.5km) *Néa Roúmata* .and (30km) *Prasés*, and on past *Sémbronas* (at 620m), the long climb continues.

The afforested hillsides are particularly beautiful as their colours change in the autumn to red and gold.

Finally at 37.5km the road reaches the pass, with extensive views ahead as well as back to Khaniá and the N coast.

A turning to the left, along the spine of the island, is signposted to Omalós (10km). This dramatic road, still rough in places, runs through wild country to the western pass out of the Omalós plain, and then down to join the main road across it (Rte 16). The pass is marked by a white church. At the fork near houses down on the plain, keep right (the better road) for the Samariá gorge, left for the Omalós tavernas and Khaniá, (also for the swallow-hole draining the plateau, which is a worthwhile stop for bird-watchers).

The Soúyia road follows the Ayía Eiríne valley, above a ravine. For centuries the people of *Ayía Eiríne* have spent the winters in their village here, and cultivated their land on the Omalós, or pastured their flocks above it, in the summer months.

The descent to the S coast begins. At 45km, by a chapel on a ridge above *Epanokhóri*, comes the first sight of the Libyan sea. The road drops down through *Prinés* and *Tsiskianá* to (52km) *Kambanós*. There is evidence of malachite mining in antiquity in this region. *Marália* clings to the hillside in tiered rows below the road, and can be seen if you look back from the corner at the end of the village. 1km beyond this, after a long bend, a big modern church with clerestory is conspicuous on a saddle far ahead. This marks the site of Elyros, one of the largest and most powerful Greco-Roman city-states of SW Crete.

57km At a T-junction just below the church the Soúyia road turns left.

The right turn at this junction leads into the village of *Rodováni* and then through Teménia to Anisaráki and (c 17.5km) Kándanos on the main Khaniá–Palaiókhora road. Much of this cross-country road (see Rte 18) had been widened and where necessary realigned in 1987, and work was still in progress; when the asphalt surface is completed it will offer an alternative main route from Khaniá to Palaiókhora.

The site of *Elyros* was rediscovered in the early 19C by the English scholar and traveller, Robert Pashley. The modern church of the Panayía is built on the site of a 6C basilica near the centre of the ancient city, which controlled the valley running down to one of its harbours at Syía (modern Soúyia); the other was at Lissós. In the first Byzantine period the basilica was the seat of a bishop, and the city flourished until the Saracen invasion. The site has not been excavated and scant traces of walls remain above ground, but a detour to the church is recommended for the *view.

A large Roman statue of 'the Philosopher of Elyros' is prominent in the museum at Khaniá.

From the junction the new broad road sweeps down the river valley, 10km to Soúyia.

Halfway to the coast, outside (62km) *Moní*, is the church of Ayios Nikólaos with remains of frescoes by Ioánnis Pagoménos (see Rte 18), dated by the donor inscription to 1315; they include (S wall) an unusually large portrayal of the patron saint.

At the entrance to the village there is a fountain (left) and the house beyond it keeps the church key. There is a driveable track that starts 800m back along the road, but the footpath from here is recommended (15 minutes). The main church has at its W end a later addition that is not a conventional narthex, because originally it could only be entered from the church nave. Unique on

Crete is the campanile a lttle to the SE, which is thought to be contemporary
with the main church.

2km beyond Moní a good dirt road crosses the river and climbs E,
8km into the mountains to *Koustoyérako*.

Here in 1943 ten men of the village shot and destroyed a German platoon which
was preparing to execute the womenfolk for concealing a British wireless transmitter. The stirring episode is vividly described in George Psychoundákis's
'The Cretan Runner' (see Bibliography). Thereafter the village suffered accordingly, but it has since been rebuilt.
    From the top of the plateía a paved path, or kalderími, leads E into the White
Mountains (c 2 hours) to the village's summer pastures on Mount Akhláda.

The improved road has brought visitors to Soúyia, for centuries no
more than a haven for the fishing boats of the people of
Koustoyérako, and has lessened the isolation of its remote position
tucked away under the SW flank of the White Mountains. Until recently it used to be a tiny cluster of houses sought out for its back-of-
beyond air, but, inevitably, prosperity (and the consequent building boom) has removed this particular charm, and it is too early to
tell what will replace it.
    Soúyia has one of the best beaches on the S coast (which attracts a
fairly constant population living outdoors), and the country inland is
superb for walkers and entirely unspoilt. There is a small hotel, many
rooms to rent, and tavernas on the tamarisk-shaded beach. The tiny
harbour at the extreme W end of the bay is a regular port of call for
the S coast boat service (see Rte 18) for excursions to the Samariá
gorge and the island of Gávdos.

The modern village is on the site of ancient Syía, the port of Elyros. The sea
level was higher in antiquity, and the harbour lay to the W of the river mouth,
protected by a mole. To the E of the stream-bed, traces of tile- or stone-faced
concrete remains of the Roman city can be made out. On the raised beach on
the W side of the village, a modern church stands on the site of a 6C basilica.
The polychrome mosaics from the basilica are considered the finest of this date
yet known on the island; the design includes kanthoroi, tendrils of ivy leaves,
deer and peacocks, these birds being symbols of immortality. (The mosaic,
which until 1986 could be seen both inside and outside the modern chapel, has
been removed to the Khaniá museum for conservation.)

A highly recommended walk of one and a half hours (or 15 minutes
by boat to the W of Soúyia) is to ancient **Lissós**, which was prominent
in the 3C BC in the League of the Oreíi (the People of the
Mountains), and flourished until it was abandoned during the 9C
Saracen occupation. The city had a temple of Asklepios, the god of
healing, and in antiquity the sanctuary was visited from afar by pilgrims in search of cures.

The path to Lissós (well marked all the way with paint splashes) strikes inland
from the harbour, 500m W of Soúyia, where a narrow gorge leads into the
mountains. At first you pick your own way up the stream-bed, but after c 20
minutes keep to the left side and watch for a cairn and arrows indicating the
path which, built at first and afterwards where necessary, snakes straight up the
cliff (W), and then continues to climb through trees on the pine-scented hillside.
From the crest you cross a broad stony upland, from the far side of which the
little Bay of Ayios Kýrkos is visible far below, with a roughly triangular valley
behind in which the ancient city lay. There remains a precipitous descent on a
skilfully built path with an increasingly detailed view of the site.
    There are two chapels: Ayía Panayía near the shore, and, inland, towards the
apex of the triangle, Ayios Kýrkos (built into the remains of an Early Christian
basilica) which is a useful landmark near the centre of the site. The outline of
the theatre can be distinguished, just on the seaward side of it.
    The marked path leads down the steep hillside at the NE of the site to the

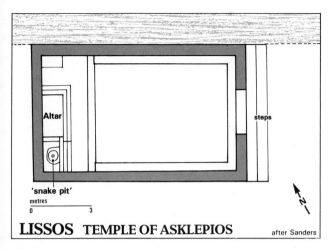

Altar

steps

'snake pit'

metres

0   3

LISSOS TEMPLE OF ASKLEPIOS

after Sanders

temple of Asklepios built against the cliff at the place where the required sacred spring flows out of the rock; the sanctuary is fenced but can be fairly well viewed from the slope to the SE.

The remains of a small Doric temple of the Hellenistic period (4–3C BC) have been excavated; it is built of ashlar blocks except for the E wall where the rougher masonry may be earlier, or may be designed for added strength against the thrust of the hillside. The cella has a S doorway up two steps and on the opposite wall is a marble podium for the cult statue. In the NW angle a stepped bench with a hole in it could be a libation channel, or a pit for the sacred snake. A low bench or kerb surrounds the remains of a good-quality mosaic floor of later date (1C AD); panels of black and white geometric designs include the remains of a large maze inlaid with polychrome birds, one a quail. The excavation uncovered a pit, dug through the mosaic, which contained about 20 fragmentary statues, including the (headless) Asklepios now on display in the Khaniá museum; perhaps this was the work of the fanatical Christians who destroyed the temple and defaced its walls with their symbols.

There was a stoa on the W (downhill) side of the temple, from which a flight of steps leads past the sturdily constructed fountain of the medicinal spring.

Less than 100m W is Ayios Kýrkos and S of this the indistinct outline of the theatre. On the terraces up the W slopes of the valley are a great number of built, barrel-vaulted tombs, a type so far known on Crete only from three sites in this locality. (The other two are Lasaía and Soúyia.) There are traces of Roman ruins among the cultivated plots on the way down to Ayía Panayía on the shore; built into the church wall is a fragment of an Asiatic sarcophagus with Medusa head.

18 Khaniá to Palaiókhora

This route (77km; 48 miles) follows the North Coast Road W (to c 20km) Tavronítis, then climbs into the hills to (59km) Kándanos, and descends to Palaiókhora, through the district of Sélinos, a part of the island rich in frescoed Byzantine churches.

Much of this road across to the S coast has recently been widened, but where narrow stretches remain they require care. There is a major programme of roadworks under way on the Khaniá–Soúyia road (Rte 17), including the branch W to Kándanos, and when this is completed it is likely that Khaniá–Palaiókhora via Alikianós and Rodováni will become an established alternative route.

Palaiókhora is a convenient base for exploring this extreme SW corner of the island, and its harbour lies at one end of the S coast boat service with a schedule to the Gorge of Samariá and Khora Sphakíon, and also the island of Gávdos.

Buses three times daily, duration of trip 2 hours.

The coast road (see Rte 19) runs W from Khaniá to (20.5km) *Tavronítis*. In the middle of the village you turn inland for Kándanos and follow the W bank of the broad river-bed up a fertile valley. At 26km *Voukoliés* is a market centre with a large plateía around plane trees. The road climbs out of the valley, for a while running along a ridge with views on either side and back to the sea near Máleme. In the vicinity of *Kakópetros* (c 40km) the hillsides are densely wooded, but soon the landscape becomes wilder. Above the village is a monument to a patriot hanged by the Germans in 1944, and beyond there is a final glimpse (right) of the N coast near Kastélli. Passing through a cut, the road continues above a deep narrow valley and climbs to a pass before the descent to Kándanos.

A stretch of the old road leads down (left) into a gorge, scene of an heroic delaying action, in May 1941, by the local population against a German force pushing S after the capture of the Máleme airfield. In retribution for the death of 25 German soldiers, Kándanos was utterly destroyed. On the outskirts of the town (left) are the waterworks given by a German group after the war, as an act of atonement.

58km *Kándanos* is the administrative centre of the 'eparchy', or district of Sélinos.

A detour here to (2km) **Anisaráki** offers a chance to visit a group of easily accessible frescoed churches.

Before the big plateía, the Teménia road turns left. It is 14.5km across country to the Rodováni junction below Elyros on the Khaniá–Soúyia road (Rte 17). Roadworks have been in progress for some time, and when completed will link Palaiókhora to Khaniá on a major road through Rodováni.

For Anisaráki turn at the sign for Teménia (11km). On the outskirts of Kándanos you pass through the hamlet of *Kouphalotós* and 300m further on is Ayios Mikhaíl Arkhángelos, Kavalarianá. The landmark here is a square house with a flat roof, on the left below the level of the road. On the bend just before it a track descends (5 minutes) to the cemetery church visible across a stream. Frescoes of 1327–28 (unfortunately somewhat clouded by chalky film) by Ioánnis Pagoménos. Work of this artist dated by inscription between 1315 and 1347 can be found in several areas of W Crete; outstanding examples include the church of Ayios Yeóryios, Anýdri (near Palaiókhora, see below), Ayios Nikólaos, Moní, near Soúyia, and the

Panayía, Alíkambos (Rte 15). His style is said to show the influence of the Palaiologan revival while retaining conservative elements.

Anisaráki has four churches with well-preserved frescoes. At the entrance to the village the first of these, *Ayía Anna* (signposted left and in sight from the road), is built over an earlier church, probably of the First Byzantine period (see column fragments outside). The frescoes, dated 1462, depict scenes from the life of St. Anne, the mother of the Virgin; the donor is depicted on the S wall (W), with the donor inscription opposite. A very rare feature is the stone iconostasis; it is fully decorated, with the two main scenes depicting St. Anne with the baby Mary and Christ Pantokrátor.

These small Byzantine churches very often lie along the medieval road network of the Cretan countryside, which the modern realigned roads have only partially superseded. Children on their way to school, villagers going to work in their fields, shepherds, women gathering herbs, as well as donkeys and goats, use these tracks and paths, still known by the Turkish word, kalderímia.

200m further along the road, a track for *Ayios Yeóryios* leads left past a group of houses set at an oblique angle to both road and track. It is 5 minutes on foot to the chapel, keeping left at the fork beyond the houses. Late 13–early 14C frescoes: scenes from the life of St. George on the S side of the vault (martyrdom on the N side), and on the S wall (W) the saint mounted on his horse, between the Virgin (left) and Ayía Marína.

At the top of the village the street bends right and just after this, signposted left, is the church of the *Panayía* (Virgin Mary), visible on a terrace immediately above the road. The architecture of this church shows strong Venetian influence. The original doorway was in the S wall, and the graffito 1614 may be associated with the alterations. The late 14C *frescoes are particularly well preserved, with the Communion of the Apostles below the Platytéra in the bema, and the barrel-vaulting densely painted with scenes from the life of Christ.

On the adjacent higher terrace is the church of *Ayía Paraskeví*, with frescoes dated stylistically to the first half of the 14C. The saint is depicted on the N wall, with Ayía Varvára.

The road turns S, with a wide view over Kándanos, and climbs steadily through (6.5km) *Vamvakádes*, and then a further 2km to the crest. At 11km *Teménia* is delightfully situated at 700m in a sheltered valley. A new pension has opened here (May–September), and if successful this would be an alternative, in the heat of summer, to the crowded coastal villages.

Above Teménia is the site of the city-state of Hyrtakína, which flourished in the Hellenistic period. There are traces of walls in polygonal masonry, probably of a late-Classical or early-Hellenistic date, and Hellenistic houses have been excavated, as well as a 4–3C sanctuary of Pan. A 1C AD statue of the god is in the Khaniá museum.

Just outside the village keep left for the Khaniá–Soúyia road; right at this fork would take you back to Palaiókhora (c 15km) via Anýdri (Ayios Yeóryios, see p 256). Continue through *Máza* to (16km) *Rodováni* and, just out of the village, the junction with the main road (Rte 17), 10km from Soúyia. (Site of ancient Elyros above right; see p 249.)

From Kándanos the main Palaiókhora road continues S, and in less than 2km crosses at *Plemeni'aná* the little river Kandanós, which runs for most of the year. Immediately before the bridge (right of the road) is the path (5 minutes) to the frescoed church of Ayios Yeóryios; walk under a pergola to the right of the last house to pick up the paved path. The frescoes here are dated by inscription 1409–10. One of the archangels is shown mounted on a horse, a rare scene although there is a similar one in the Astrátigos church; see below.

Just beyond the bridge is a turning for (10km) Strovlés, near the head of the Yíphlos valley; this turning leads across country to the newly-improved roads described in Rte 20, and makes possible a circular drive from Palaiókhora with the return through Sklavopoúla.

To visit two frescoed churches above *Kakodíki*, continue 8km further on the main road. At 64.5km from Khaniá, on a bend towards the end of the long village, there is a sharp turn left onto a track signposted 'Ay. Triás' (kapheneíon above the turn). The track leads steeply uphill and then through olive groves, 1km to the large modern church (Ayía Triáda, Astratigós) and beside it the old frescoed *church of Mikhaíl Arkhángelos.

The key is held by the priest (papás) whose house is 250m further up the hill. Pass the church gate, (leave a car at the fork just beyond), and take the left track uphill until it ends at the papás's house. He or his wife will open the church. (Short-cut: from the fork, follow the concrete water channel straight uphill to the spring, where the path veers left out onto the last stretch of the track.)

Mikhaíl Arkhángelos, with frescoes from the first half of the 14C and a beautiful old wooden iconostasis, is a single-naved church, but the nave is divided by pilasters into four bays (rather than the usual two or three). The original Byzantine chapel was altered and elaborated by the Venetians; a new door and window have damaged the frescoes on the S wall. Scenes preserved include the Apostle Communion below the Pantokrátor in the apse, and on the N wall, next to the iconostasis, a rare portrayal of the Archangel mounted on a horse (see Plemeniána, above).

A little further S, at Tselenianá, is the church of Ayios Isídoros, with elegant frescoes dated by inscription 1420–21. From Astratigós, keep right at the fork by the houses (see above), and less than 1km along the hillside, just across a stream-bed—in spring a ford—the keyholder's house is in view down a track to the right; he will accompany you (700m further along the road) to the church.

These are the only frescoes on Crete dealing with themes from the life of St. Isídoros, who was martyred for his faith on the island of Chios during the reign of the Emperor Decius, notorious for his persecution of the Christians. The upper registers of the vault are devoted to the Christ cycle, but in the lower registers are: on the S side scenes of the baptism, imprisonment (behind a grill) and beheading of Isídoros, and opposite, his avowal of the faith before Numerius, the commander of the Roman fleet, and the saint being dragged behind two arab horses.

The dirt road continues (less than 2km) to the church of the Panayía, Kádros, which can also be approached from the main valley road (see below). Using the Khaniá bus from Palaiókhora, it is possible to spend a day walking on this peaceful hillside; the tracks connecting the hamlets are high above the valley with wide views across it.

From Kakodíki on the main road, continue 1km S and then (at 68km from Khaniá) turn left for *Kádros*. Near the top of the village (more than 1km from the turn), 80m beyond the last shop-cum-kapheneíon, a path leads downhill right (5 minutes) to the church of the Panayía dedicated to the Nativity of the Virgin (Feast Day, 8 September). The key is kept at the nearby house (over a stile beside a gate). This church has a well-preserved and complete set of *frescoes dated to the second half of the 14C; in the apse is the Panayía Eléousa (the Virgin of Mercy).

Less than 10 minutes on foot above the village enthusiasts can find the frescoed Ayios Ioánnis Theológos (the Evangelist). Keep right where the road forks; the little church is hidden below a group of old houses downhill to the right.

Castel Selino, the Venetian fort at Palaiókhora (from
Gerola, Monumenti Veneti nell'Isola di Creta, *1905–32)*

77km Palaiókhora is the 'Castel Selino' of the Venetians who in 1279 built a fort on the promontory here. The modern village, which owes its popularity more to its idyllic setting than to any intrinsic charm, now straddles the base of the peninsula, with to the W a fine long sandy beach backed by tamarisk trees. Small boats moor at a quay on the E beach, but the main harbour is out on the point, 500m beyond the fort. Palaiókhora has become popular with young foreigners who live here all the year round. However this big village, with shops, accommodation and tavernas, can be a useful base for tourists wanting to explore the many Sélinos churches, or the unspoilt hill country back from the coast (for example, see Kakodíki and Kádros described above) and it is a logical stop on a journey using the scheduled S coast boats. There is a modern Class B hotel (heavily booked Easter–September), several smaller ones and many rooms for rent.

The entrance to the 'Phroúrion' or fort is near the church; the enceinte provides good mountain views to the E but a better idea of the walls is obtained from the beach below.

Palaiókhora to (5km) Anýdri, where the church of Ayios Yeóryios has *frescoes (1323) by Ioánnis Pagoménos (see above). The road runs E along the coast before climbing in a wooded valley; the two-aisled church is in the middle of the village. The N nave is densely painted by Pagoménos with scenes from the Christ cycle and of the miraculous deeds and martyrdom of St. George. (Some chalky film.) The patron saint is one of the supplicant figures beside Christ in the vaulting of the apse, and the portrayal on a white horse is found on the N wall of the cross-vaulted bay. (The frescoes in the S nave, which is dedicated to Ayios Nikólaos, are by a different painter and of inferior quality.)

Palaiókhora to (20km) Sklavopoúla, on newly-improved roads which have opened up this remote SW corner of the island. Leave Palaiókhora on the road running parallel with the W beach, and after 1km watch for a turning right, signed for Voutás. The first 3km stretch may still be rough, but it is worth persevering; work is in progress.

At 9km, by a bridge below the village of Kondokinígi, there is a short detour, right, to (3km) the little frescoed church of Mikhaíl Arkhángelos, Sarakína. The side-road climbs beside the stream-bed, passing a monument (erected in 1986) to commemorate a battle in 1897, the last year of the Turkish occupation, in which 150 Turks were killed by Christian forces. After 3km, at the meeting of two streams, the church is hidden in undergrowth at the end of a paved path, ahead right. The frescoes are dated stylistically to the second half of the 14C; the stone iconostasis (a rare feature) is painted with icons of Christ and the Panayía Eléousa (The Virgin of Mercy).

For Sklavopoúla the road continues to (13.5km) Voutás where you keep left. Just out of the village the old bridge still remains, to the right of the modern one. The road, narrow but surfaced for most of the way, starts to climb and the valley opens out. At 17.5km, still climbing, you pass Kalamiós, and at 20.5km reach Sklavopoúla at 640m looking out across cultivated hillsides to the distant sea. The name reflects the origins of the village, which was founded by Slav mercenaries of the army of the Byzantine Emperor Nikephóros Phokás when they settled on Crete after the reconquest of the island for Christendom in 961.

There are three much-admired frescoed churches in the village. Left of the road on the way in is Ayios Yeóryios, an unusually tall church beside a school playground. Remains of frescoes in two different styles; the earlier work, chiefly in the apse, has an inscription of 1290–91 above the window. The key is kept at the house downhill beside the playground—or enquire at the café-bar in the plateía, opposite the big modern domed church.

The other two frescoed churches are close together lower down the hill. From the plateía, continue downhill 400m to a rough track (left) which leads to the lower village. Walk straight on into the village, up some steps and through a roofed passage, past a partly-ruined tower of the Venetian period (key, see below). Where the houses stop, the kalderími runs on ahead but the two chapels are above the path (left). The first you come to (recently not locked) is dedicated to Sotíros Khristós, Our Saviour Christ. The remains of 14C frescoes include the portrait (defaced) of the donor, Partzális, on the N wall.

with trees and the chapel in the background. (On the S wall with the
military saints are graffiti of 1422 and 1514; on the N wall some
scraps of earlier painting.)

Straight up the hillside (30m) is the chapel of the *Panayía* (Virgin
Mary); the key is held at one of the village houses near the old tower.
Densely painted, and well-preserved set of gospel scenes, and on the
N wall the donor with a model of his church. The frescoes are dated
stylistically to the late 14–early 15C (graffito 1518); experts value
them as an important link in the development of the Cretan School of
painting.

South Coast Boat Service. Palaiókhora is at the W end of the route to
Soúyia, Ayiá Rouméli and Khóra Sphakíon. (See also Rte 15.) In
recent years the reliability of the schedule has greatly improved, as
has the frequency though this varies according to season. The timetable is published each spring, before Easter, and is available from all
tourist information offices. During the high season (May–September)
there is at least a daily service from Palaiókhora to Ayiá Rouméli at
the bottom of the Samariá gorge (duration of trip c 2 hours), with a
connection on to Khóra Sphakíon if required. In April and October
the service is reduced.

Boats run twice a week in summer to the almost deserted island of
Gavdos, 24 nautical miles S of Khóra Sphakíon, and the most southerly point of Europe. With archaeological evidence for occupation
dating back to the Neolithic period, the island was in Greco-Roman
times a dependency of the city of Górtyn, and it seems to have flourished as the seat of a bishop during the last years before the Arab
conquest. Now it has four small settlements and less than 100 inhabitants, mostly sheep farmers.

The boat trip takes c 4 hours depending on whether there is a call
at Soúyia, and allows c 4 hours on the island. From the little harbour
(with a few rent roms for the adventurous) it is a half-hour walk to
swim off the beautiful sandy bay of Sarakíniko (tavernas).

There are now high-season day-trips to Gávdos from Khóra Sphakíon, and the
shorter journey time (2 hours) may allow longer on the island.

19 Khaniá to Kastélli Kisámou

43km (27 miles) to Kastélli Kisámou (officially renamed Kísamos
but still known locally as Kastélli), which may be used as a base for
exploring extreme W Crete. 24km Kolymbári for the Goniá
monastery and the Rodopós peninsula. Excursion from Kastélli:
7km to site of ancient Polyrrhénia.
Until recently this road W of Khaniá was a main route, but not of
highway standard; however the Kolymbári–Kastélli section of the N
Coast Highway, the so-called New Road, was building in 1987.
There is a good bus service from Khaniá to Kastélli.

The road leaves Khaniá to the W, and passes at 1.5km the turning for
Omalós and the Gorge of Samariá. Ahead is the stretch of coast
which in 1941 was the scene of the German airborne invasion from
bases in Attica which launched what came to be known as the Battle
of Crete. Left of the road (2.5km) on the outskirts of town, the
German monument to their 2nd Parachute Regiment takes the
aggressive form of a diving eagle.

At 3km a beach convenient for Khaniá is signed by the NTO.

(Town buses to Kalamáki and Galatás, see Rte 14.) A turning (at 4km) leads to Galatás where New Zealand troops fought a heroic rearguard action in 1941.

The road runs close to the shore along the Bay of Khaniá. The beach here is not wide, but long stretches of good sand alternate with rocky outcrops. As far as Plataniás there is fairly continuous development on a small scale, offering rooms for rent, bungalows, and beach taverna meals, with the occasional larger hotel geared to package holidays. The prominent off-shore island of *Ayii Theódori* is one of several reserves for the Cretan ibex, the 'agrími'.

11km *Plataniás* is a pleasant, large village which has spread from its flat-topped hill down to the shore. Beyond, the scene remains more rural, with less tourist development.

Where (13km) the road crosses the river (also Plataniás) a side-road along the W bank cuts across to Ayiá (Rte 16). This minor road is signed for Vrýses, but keep left at a fork to follow the river.

The main road winds through groves of orange and tangerine trees, which are sheltered by the windbreaks of growing bamboo sometimes laced together for greater strength. Around Easter the scent of blossom is overpowering. You are approaching (16km) *Máleme*; the airfield here (right of road beyond the village) played a decisive part in the German airborne attack in 1941. Before the airfield, now a military base, there is (at 17.5km) a left turn for the German war cemetery (signposted in Greek and German, 1.5km inland on the rising ground). A schematic wall map illustrates the sombre facts of the Battle of Crete, 20 May–1 June 1941. 6580 Germans were killed, including those missing at sea, and there are 4465 well-tended graves on the hillside. (Of the total Commonwealth force on the island some 2000 were killed; 1527 are buried in the cemetery at the head of Soúda bay.)

The Máleme cemetery lies at the end of a N–S ridge running out from the White Mountains. This was the notorious Hill 107, a vital tactical position in the battle for the airfield that in pre-war days had been the aerodrome for Khaniá, then the capital of the island. The bird's-eye view of the coast from here is the best-possible illustration of accounts of the battle (see Bibliography and p 27).

The Late Minoan (LMIIIB) chamber-tomb of Máleme is just below the military cemetery. Return 200m down the road to the first left bend, and walk 100m E along the terraced hillside; the tomb lies on the right of the path.

An exceptionally long (13.8m) lined dromos leads to a rectangular chamber with corbelled roof; the doorway is built with a relieving triangle behind the upright slab above the heavy lintel. The tomb, which had been robbed, was excavated in 1966 by the Greek archaeologist, C. Daváras. Two interesting seals are recorded; one in bronze, perhaps originally covered with gold leaf (a rare find), showed a cow suckling her calf, and the other in agate was carved with agrímia.

The main road continues past the airfield to (19km) the bridge over the broad stony river-bed of the Tavronítis; this replaced the wartime Bailey bridges (right) that had done service for 30 years.

You can walk or drive (1km) out to the estuary down the W bank (first circumnavigating the works buildings); when the river is fed by the melting snows there is enough water to form a small lagoon which often shelters wading birds on migration.

The Goniá monastery (from Pashley, Travels in Crete, *1837)*

In the village of *Tavronítis*, a centre for melon-growing, Rte 18 to Kándanos and (c 55km) Palaiókhora on the S coast diverges left. As you approach the Rodopós peninsula, which forms the W boundary of the Bay of Khaniá, the red-painted dome of the *Moní Kerá Goniás* (Γωνία, meaning corner), stands out ahead above the shore.

24km At the Kolymbári crossroads the main road bears left uphill for Kastélli, but a 1km detour to the right leads to *Kolymbári* and the monastery just beyond. The village only recently began to develop its tourist potential, and the atmosphere is correspondingly agreeable. The main street backs onto the diminutive harbour, at the end of a long pebble beach sheltered from the summer wind, the meltémi. There are good fish tavernas (popular for an evening outing from Khaniá in the height of summer), a new small hotel that is heavily booked from abroad in the season, and many pleasant rooms for rent, the best overlooking the harbour.

The existing monastery of Our Lady Goniás, also known as the Odiyítria, Our Lady Guide, was founded in 1618 by the monk Blaise (who came from Cyprus) with the help of the Zangaróli family, Venetians who had adopted the Orthodox faith. The first (1634) cruciform church was severely damaged by the Turks, whose forces disembarked nearby in the Bay of Khaniá at the start of their assault on Crete (1645). However when the monastery obtained a charter which put it under the direct authority and protection of the Patriarch in Constantinople, the church was rebuilt (1662); the side-chapels and narthex are 19C additions. Although the monastery escaped relatively unscathed during the Turkish rule, its rich library was burned at the time of the 1866 Rebellion; a few treasures including a 17C codex were saved.

There is a tradition that links the origins of the monastery, at least by the early years of the Second Byzantine period if not before, with the church of Ayios Yeóryios in the vicinity of the ancient sanctuary of Díktynna, N along the coast near the tip of the Rodopós peninsula. The monks are thought to have moved from that remote spot to the greater safety of Kolymbári, where there are the ruins of a monastery dating from the 13C on the hillside above the main buildings.

The Odiyítria (Feast Day, 15 August) possesses one of the most important collections of icons on Crete. A monk is on duty to open the church and museum (both closed 13.30–15.30). A leaflet lists the icons in the church; in the N side-chapel an icon of Ayios Nikólaos (1637), by the greatly admired Cretan painter Konstantínos Palaiókapas, adheres strictly to the artistic conventions of the painters of the Cretan School.

The small museum (SE corner of the quadrangle) displays vestments and ecclesiastical valuables, some interesting historical documents, and a number of precious icons. These include a superb Crucifixion by Palaiókapas, and in contrast to the Ayios Nikólaos icon in the church, this painting shows the influence of Italian art in the background buildings and landscape, and in the realistic anatomical treatment.

At the NE corner of the quadrangle is the refectory, its classical doorway embellished with baroque volutes. From the terrace at the E end of the church there is a *view of Khaniá bay and the White Mountains; a cannonball preserved in the wall of the S apse is a memento of the Turkish bombardment.

Outside the handsome W gate is a fountain (1708). Its inscription translated reads: Most delicious Spring of water bubbling up for me, Water, for all creation, is the sweetest element in life.

Steps beside the fountain lead to a steep path (5 minutes) up the herb-scented hillside to the old (13C) monastery church with remains of frescoes.

The modern building on the road beyond the monastery is the Orthodox Academy of Crete. This road continues a short distance N along the coast of the peninsula which ends at Cape Spátha; after 1.5km you pass a turn for a Cretan war memorial, and in a further 3km reach *Aphráta*. For the beach (1.5km) keep right in the village; the track is rough for the last stretch through a ravine before the narrow rocky bay. (After 600m a fork left leads out onto wild scrubby hillside, the typical maquis or *phrýgana* of much of the Cretan countryside.) N along the coast is a cave known as Ellinóspilios, an important Neolithic habitation and burial site, where sherds were found at the back of the 100m-deep chamber.

To the Diktýnnaion. Boats may be hired from Kolymbári for the excursion to the cove, near the NE tip of Cape Spátha, that was the site of the ancient sanctuary of Díktynna; ask at the kapheneíon next to the OTE in the narrow part of the tamarisk-shaded main street. Expect to pay from Drs 5000 depending on the size of the boat. (Duration of the trip also variable—between one and two hours. You pass the Ellinóspilios, see above.) In high season the larger caiques make the trip with parties of tourists. Almost nothing remains of the great temple to Díktynna (see reconstruction), but the site is evocative. There is excellent swimming at the (uninhabited) cove.

The alternative is to drive (taxi possible) to Rodopoú and then walk. Take the road to *Aphráta* (see above). Turn left for (7km) *Astrátigos* and climb (good dirt surface) across the peninsula, with views ever deeper into the Levká Ori. 9km from Kolymbári you join the asphalt road from Khaniá, and turn right for (11km) *Rodopoú*.

Beyond the long village the newly improved road climbs again towards the spine of the peninsula. (Until very recently only a mule-track, this is the route of an annual pilgrimage on 29 August to the church of Ayios Ioánnis, Yioní, for the baptism of babies with the name John who are brought from all over W Crete.) There is now a road of sorts, roughly levelled by bulldozer, all the way to the Diktýnnaion (17km from Rodopoú to the sanctuary site), but in its present (1987) condition—a hard-packed red earth interrupted by sections of dangerously uneven rock—it is not suitable for the normal hired car. It is, however, highly recommended to long-distance walkers. If a car is available it may be taken at least 3km beyond Rodopoú, and perhaps eventually the surface for the rest of the way will be improved. At 6km a stony track branches left to Ayios Ioánnis, a further hour on foot.

At c 12km the main track runs for some distance along a flat valley floor; at the end of this stretch it veers left, and shows up as a scar on the rock wall. At this point raised stretches of the ancient paved road continue straight ahead. The new track continues N until, nearing the sanctuary, it makes a long bend right to come down to the E shore of the cape. You can see, in a hollow (right), the old church of Ayios Yeóryios Meniés, beside a medieval tower which was perhaps part of the monastery traditionally associated with the Goniá foundation (see above). The track comes to an end just above the bay and the sanctuary site.

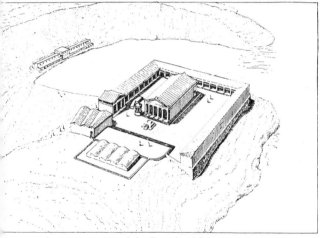

A reconstruction of the Temple of Díktynna on Cape Spátha

The *Diktýnnaion*, mentioned with admiration by many writers in antiquity, was the most important religious sanctuary of W Crete in the Greco-Roman period. The prestige derived from control over it is well documented, and this was fiercely contested among the powerful city-states of the region, in particular Kydonía and Polyrrhénia. The accumulated wealth of the sanctuary was sometimes used to finance public works programmes.

The cult of the Cretan goddess Díktynna, closely related to that of Britomártis (an old Minoan name known to mean 'sweet maiden'), was to some extent a survival of the worship of the Minoan mother goddess. Although there were cult centres in Athens and the Peloponnese, and as far away as Marseilles, Díktynna seems to have been especially venerated in western Crete. The name may perhaps

be related to Mount Díkte or (the Greek historian Strabo's version) to
the word δίκτυον (díktyon), the fishermen's net which is supposed to
have saved the goddess when, in flight from the unwelcome atten-
tions of Mínos, she leapt into the sea. Díktynna had many of the
attributes of the Greek goddess Artemis; she was a huntress, and the
deity of nature, the wild countryside and mountains, and her sanctuary on Cape Spátha was guarded by hounds which the Cretans
claimed to be as strong as bears.

The sanctuary site occupied the sheltered SE-facing cove where
the boats now land, and lay on either side of the water-course. There
are remains of Roman buildings on the N side of the beach (the statue
of Hadrian now in Khaniá museum came from one of them), and
traces on the S side of the stream-bed of the bridge which crossed it;
this may have served also as an aqueduct. The temple, no doubt
visible from a great distance, stood on the high promontory to the S of
the cove. The foundations of the Roman cisterns are preserved, but of
the courtyard temple, unique on Crete, only some ashlar blocks of
the terrace and a few architectural fragments survive.

The temple was excavated by German archaeologists in 1942, but some uncer-
tainties remain because it had been systematically looted and robbed. The
temple terrace measured 55m by 50m. The peripteral temple, the only one
known on Crete, was built of limestone, with marble paving. The columns on its
E side were of the Ionic order in blue marble, and the remainder were white
marble Corinthian columns. The temple stood in a paved court surrounded on
three sides by stoas. S of the terrace were four cisterns; their total capacity has
been estimated at 400 cubic metres. Between the temple and the cisterns stood
a stepped altar of white marble. At the SW corner of the temple there was a
small circular building which may perhaps have been a treasury; the statue of
Díktynna with hound, now in Khaniá museum, was found here.

The excavated temple is tentatively dated to the 2C AD. There was certainly
an earlier building on the site, and there were traces of a Doric predecessor to
the W of the Roman temple.

To Spiliá and Episkopí. From the Kolymbári crossroads on the
Khaniá–Kastélli route, take the minor road S. Pass the turn for
Marathokephála to (3km) *Spiliá* (frescoed church of the Panayía),
one of the most delightful villages in this part of the island. It is
agreeable to walk (5 minutes) from the prominent modern church
(bearing left at the bottom of the flight of steps up to it and following
clear signs), past a fountain and out to the edge of the village, to the
tree-shaded old church dedicated to the Presentation and Assumption of the Virgin. The frescoes (torch useful), dated stylistically to the
14C, with graffito of 1401, are cited as an early example on the island
of the style of painting which is referred to as 'Cretan', though it was
not confined to and probably did not originate on Crete.

Above Spiliá is a cave which is a popular place for Cretan outings. It can be
reached through Marathokephála (see above), or from the centre of the
village—signed from the modern church.
A church in the cave is dedicated to Ayios Ioánnis Xénos, the hermit saint
who founded the 11C monastery of the Katholikó on the Akrotíri near Khaniá
(Feast Day, 7 October).

The minor road continues S from Spiliá towards Episkopí. After 2km
Ayios Stéphanos is signed right. A path (5 minutes) follows a bank,
that in spring is smothered in cyclamen, to the tiny chapel, dating
(10C) from the time of the restoration of the Christian faith after the
Arab occupation.

1km further, turn right for a (beautifully situated) church of particular architectural interest, *Mikhaíl Arkhángelos, Episkopí*. This church is a rotonda, with a stepped dome consisting of five concentric rings, a design unique on Crete, and with few exact parallels in Byzantine architecture. (The only comparable building on the Greek mainland is Ayios Yeóryios, Thessaloníki.) The present church is built over the foundations of an Early Christian (6C) basilica, from which part of the mosaic floor is preserved.

The exact sequence of the architectural development of Mikhaíl Arkhángelos has, until now, been imperfectly understood, but a three-month study of the church building and the surrounding structures, conducted in 1987 by the Service for Byzantine Antiquities (Khaniá), is expected to resolve many of the problems.

The guardian (phýlakas) who holds the key lives near the first corner in the village, 500m further up the hillside. Frescoes have been uncovered from three periods, the earliest dating back at least to the 12C.

Continuing towards Kastélli from the Kolymbári crossroads, you pass (right) the turning for Rodopoú. The old road is narrow and winding as it crosses the neck of the peninsula, but major work is in progress to realign it to highway standard. Through a natural gap in the hills the plain of Kastélli and the Kísamos bay, sheltered by two long capes, are suddenly in view below. The road descends steeply in a series of bends. To the S, craggy dolomitic mountains fill the sky, and ahead is the Gramboúsa promontory, the extreme NW of Crete; the plain is densely planted with olive trees. There is a long-established camping site on the coast.

At 40km in *Kaloudianá* a minor road sets off inland up the Yíphlos valley towards (8km) the attractive village of Topólia, and the SW corner of the island (see Rte 20).

43km Kastélli Kisámou was so named for its Venetian castle, but to avoid confusion, in particular with Kastélli in the Pediáda district, it officially reverted in 1966 to Kísamos (after the Greco-Roman city-state at this place). However, locally, the traditional name persists.

Kastélli is a convenient stop on a touring holiday. It lies to seaward of the road, a long straggle of buildings set back from a fine sandy beach (tavernas). The little town (pop. 2800) is not yet much affected by international tourism, and has an air of preoccupation with regional business rather than with visiting foreigners, but a road-building programme down the W coast, and a regular car-ferry service (via the island of Kýthera) from the Greek mainland, have recently increased its popularity with tourists. There are several small hotels, also many simple rooms for rent.

The harbour is 3km W of the town (Rte 20). Agent for ferry service to the Peloponnese: M. Kheroukhákis in the main plateía; tel: (0822) 22 655.

In summer there are day-trips by caique to the Venetian fortress of Gramboúsa (see Rte 20).

Ancient Kísamos, a port of Polyrrhénia, became an independent city only in the 3C AD, but then gradually superseded Polyrrhénia. It was the seat of a bishop till the Saracen occupation (9C), and later a thriving Venetian town, fortified in the 16C. There are eye-witness accounts from early travellers of ancient remains, but, as at Khaniá, the modern town impedes archaeological investigation of the site. Recent excavations have explored part of the theatre, a bath complex, and a 3C AD house with fine mosaic floors, also a short length of an aqueduct from the SW. The small museum in the main square contains local finds but unfortunately, in recent years, it has not been open to the public.

To Polyrrhénia, 7km inland. The bus leaves Kastélli for the once-a-day return journey in the early afternoon. (Taxi rank in the plateía.)

At the Khaniá end of the Kastélli ring-road is a junction with central triangle planted with oleanders. 250m W along the main road take the first turn left signed only in Greek (ΠΡΟΣ ΠΟΛΥΡΡΗΝΙΑ). The road climbs inland through olive groves with a view of dramatic rock formations ahead, and ends, near a ruined tower, at the foot of the village formerly known as Ano Palaiókastro.

Both cobbled streets ahead lead to the ancient site (10 minutes). To the left (steep only briefly), after 150 paces at a meeting of tracks take the upper one to the left. At the top of the village turn left onto a dirt track which winds round to the right to level ground. Here the church of the Ninety-nine Martyrs is built over the foundations of a large Hellenistic building, probably a temple. The lower courses of massive walling now support the cemetery. A clear Roman inscription is built into the wall of the church.

The ancient city of *Polyrrhénia* lay on the slopes around the church and down to the village, with the acropolis and its secondary spur above to the NE. Sherds indicate occupation from the Archaic (6C) to the Roman periods. The site was reoccupied in the late 10C and became a Venetian stronghold. Although its position was almost impregnable, on a steep hill surrounded by ravines, the city was also walled. The remains of the fortifications, including the towers, date from the Second Byzantine and the Venetian periods (best preserved on the N spur), but lie in part on earlier foundations, probably of Hellenistic walls repaired in Roman times. Water was supplied by rock-cut aqueducts.

There are few remains within the acropolis walls, but the walk (c 30 minutes) to the top is highly recommended. There is a steep path up the W (left) side of the hill, but the easier way sets off from the church, and gains height round the right flank, with views spectacular even by Cretan standards. This path is marked occasionally with red paint splashes. The site of Polyrrhénia is renowned for its spring flowers.

For the walk to the tip of the Gramboúsa peninsula, see Rte 20.

20　Kastélli to the West Coast

A circuit of c 100km (60 miles); 16km ancient Phalásarna; 34km Sphinári; 54km Kepháli; 62km Monastery of Khrysoskalítissa, and return to the N coast from Kepháli by the Yiphlós valley.

An alternative is to turn S after Kepháli and Elos, towards the coast at Palaiókhora, on the recently improved roads of this SW corner of the island.

Buses to Kepháli from Kastélli (via Sphinári) and Khaniá (on to Váthi for the monastery), but the timetable probably enforces an overnight stay.

The road runs W along the coast past a small fishing harbour (tavernas), to (3km) the quay for the car-ferry to the Peloponnese—see Rte 19. (Café-bar on the quay, and taxis meet the ferries.)

Soon the road turns inland to cross the base of the *Gramboúsa peninsula* that stretches away to the N sheltering the Kísamos bay. Off its NW tip is a rock on which (1579) the Venetians built a fortress that held out against the Turks till 1692, 23 years after the surrender of Herákleion. Gramboúsa later became a stronghold of piracy. In the 19C the Turks exploited its position to harass the short sea-crossing between rebellious Crete and the island of Antikýthera, by then a part of independent Greece. (For boat trips to Gramboúsa, see Rte 19.)

At 5km an insignificant right turning leads to (c 2km) Kalyvianí. From a little beyond the village there is the opportunity of a long walk on the peninsula, 2–3 hours out to Tigáni bay, a spectacular beach of white sand on the W side of the cape opposite the Gramboúsa fortress.

The unmarked turning is beside a cement works, and immediately (100m) you fork left. In Kalyvianí the road bends left, but at the corner keep straight ahead to the end of the village street where at a kapheneíon (left, opposite a tree) a broad track branches off downhill to the right; the track is rough but driveable with care for c 3km. From this point allow about 2½ hours for the walk to Tigáni bay.

The path is marked spasmodically with paint splashes; it keeps to the E side of the spine of the peninsula, and gains height gradually to pass the head of several small water-courses. Long stretches of this walk are across bare hillside, but at a little over half way a large clump of oleanders marks a welcome spring, and conceals the weathered blocks and pointed arch of the old Ayía Eiríni fountain. A long slow climb brings you on to a plateau; bear left across it, cutting off the narrow tip of the peninsula. Before the path begins the steep descent to the bay on the W coast, walk out to the edge of the perpendicular cliff; one island is linked to the beach by a sandy spit, but just to the N is the island of Gramboúsa. The rock is flat-topped except for a knob at its seaward end on which the Venetians built their fortress; the turreted walls of this isolated outpost still stand.

On the main road W from Kastélli you pass at 6km the turn for the village of Gramboúsa at the base of the peninsula, and at 10km reach a fork at the beginning of *Plátanos*. To visit the Greco-Roman harbour site of Phalásarna keep right at the fork on the new road which (when finished) will avoid the village centre. After 100m take a narrow turning right, and in 1km keep to the right round a red-roofed church.

Road-works W of the village in 1970 uncovered a chamber tomb containing Protogeometric pottery, the first time that evidence for the Early Iron Age had been found this far W.

From the church the road drops downhill 6km to Phalásarna; the surface is asphalt except for the last km or so. The panoramic *view of the Bay of Livádi includes a dense olive grove, and plastic-sheeted greenhouses glinting behind a long sandy beach; the Gramboúsa peninsula stretches away to the N. Halfway down the hillside, at a junction, follow a hairpin bend right to head N towards the site, which is below Cape Kutrí, at the end of the bay.

The asphalt ends 4.5km from the church at a taverna and a new block of rent rooms. The long sandy beach 500m to the S is one of the finest on Crete.

The last stretch of track ahead takes you right onto the site, near the so-called 'rock-cut throne' which has been the subject of much speculation. It remains an enigma.

Phalásarna, the most westerly city-state of Crete, was at the height of its power in the Hellenistic period (4–3C BC) though sherds from the 6C testify to earlier occupation. For a time it was the W coast port of Polyrrhénia (Rte 19). It was mentioned by ancient geographers especially for its 'enclosed harbour'. The Englishman Captain T.A.B. Spratt, on a Royal Naval survey expedition in the mid 19C, was the first to realise that owing to a 6–7m drop in the sea-level, this enclosed harbour was high and dry c 100m inland (see Spratt's map).

The *acropolis* is on the headland, dropping sheer into the sea with a rough path up from the E, above the chapel of Ayios Yeóryios.

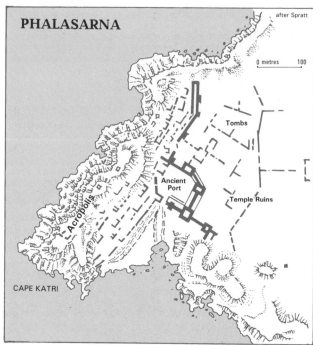

PHALASARNA

after Spratt

0 metres 100

Tombs

Ancient
Port

Temple Ruins

Acropolis

CAPE KATRI

Remains on the higher summit may belong to a temple, perhaps to
Diktynnaion Artemis; the other known temple (to Apollo) was probably down by the harbour. The city spread onto the slope below the
headland. The NE–SW orientated promontory was crossed in the
Hellenistic period by a fortification wall with rectangular towers;
600m of wall have been traced, with four square towers.

The artificially excavated *harbour*, 100m by 75m, now a flat area
filled with earth, opens to the S into an enlarged rock fissure 10m
wide which served as an entrance channel. The rectangular harbour
is encircled by the city wall, and protected by four round towers and
a mole. The SE tower was excavated in 1985 (by archaeologists from
the Khaniá museum led by E. Marder), and study of the site continues. The tower's massive foundations are built with ashlar blocks of
sandstone (eight courses preserved with a moulding above the third
course).

The city's cemeteries were on the rising ground inland, with at least 32 cist
graves (4C) on the SE side of the town. From 6C tombs came imported black-
figure Corinthian pottery now on display in the Khaniá museum.

Back in the village of Plátanos turn right towards the Bay of Sphinári.
After 2km you pass (left) a turn for Lusakiés. The coast road, built
during the last ten years, winds high above the sea, with a fine view
over the bay to Phalásarna. There are plenty of opportunities for
short walks off the road; tracks (signed) lead to chapels in the hills or
down to the sea. At 32.5km a broad track, an old drover's road,
climbs into the hills beside a stream.

34km *Sphinári*, a small village on a pebble beach, has a few rooms for rent. The road turns inland to (41.5km) *Kámbos*, strung out along a wooded stream; here also are rooms for rent. A kalderími following the stream into the hills leads over the watershed to Sirikári. At 45km you pass above the pitched red-tiled roofs of *Keramóti* clinging to the hillside at the head of a valley. Soon after there is a fine view from the road down the coast to the SW corner of Crete, over the narrow plain behind Stómio bay, with Moní Khrysoskalítissa perched on a rock, the roof of its church a brilliant blue.

At 47km a dirt road descends c 5km to the coast to join the (driveable) track that runs close to the shore all the way from below Kámbos to Stómio and the monastery.

47.5km *Amigdalokepháli*. **54km** *Kepháli* (simple tavernas and a few rooms to rent) is beautifully situated high up above a wooded valley, looking down to the distant Bay of Stómio. A church on the S edge of the village, Metamórphosis tou Sotírou (the Transfiguration of the Saviour), has frescoes (1320). Ask for directions and key at the kapheneíon.

This remote region of Crete was in fairly serious economic decline until very recently. Road communications were poor. Secondary schooling involved weekly boarding with family or friends in Kastélli or Khaniá. In a vicious circle of depopulation and hardship the younger generation was leaving for work in Athens. Now there are welcome signs of prosperity based on the tourism encouraged by the new W coast road.

At the end of the village is an acute right turn onto a minor road, widened and improved but not yet surfaced, to (11km) **Moní Khrysoskalítissa** on the coast. 2km down the hill you come to *Váthi* (formerly Koúneni). There are two frescoed churches here for enthusiasts; both are locked, and the village priest (whose house is 100m S of the plateía, straight ahead where the road bends left)) has the keys. In case of difficulty ask at the kapheneíon.

The church of Ayios Yeóryios (in the village, to the right of the road at the plateía), has frescoes dated by inscription 1284. (Some of the scenes in the upper register of the vault were inexpertly reassembled during repairs to the roof.) The original sketches in the apse form an interesting comparison with the frescoes themselves—the narrow jaws contrasted with the fully painted heads.

In the fields below the road, a few minutes S of the village (path left) the church of Mikhaíl Arkhángelos has early 14C frescoes, notably the Fall of Jericho and the Presentation in the Temple. The paintings in the bema are later 14C work.

The road continues beside a stream overhung by sweet chestnut trees; chestnuts are a commercially important crop in this part of the island. Walkers would enjoy exploring the tracks off the road to the unspoilt villages of this valley. About 7km from the turn in Kepháli there is a new bridge over the stream, and when there is much water coming down from the hills it is advisable to cross to the other bank here. Otherwise you can keep straight ahead (signed for Stómio) to emerge on the bay. To the right are the ruins of the village of Stómio and a gypsum quarry.

Turn left towards the blue roofs of the monastery, nowadays a convent though few nuns remain. The first church here was built inside a grotto. The double-naved church is dedicated to the Panayía Khrysoskalítissa (Our Lady of the Golden Stair—χρυσός means gold, plus σκαλί, a stair). Ninety steps lead down to the sheltered cove S of the pinnacle on which the church is built, and it is said that only those without sin can tell which is the stair that is made of gold. The present buildings are of no great age, but the panoramic *view from the terrace is worth the climb.

MM and LM sherds in the area of the monastery indicate a Minoan coastal settlement.

Scattered concrete buildings (tavernas and bars with rooms to rent) have not increased the romance of this remote spot. 5km further along a dirt road, the *Elaphonísi* islands just off-shore protect a long sandy beach coloured pink by fragments of coral, a good spot for a lazy afternoon.

On the return journey retrace the route only as far as Kepháli and there turn right (signpost for Khaniá). After 5km you pass through the long tree-shaded village of *Elos*, one of the most attractive in the region; there is a Chestnut Festival held here every October. 4km beyond this, just before Milí, is the junction for a cross-country route (right) on newly-improved roads to Kándanos and Palaiókhora (Rte 18).

The road, signed for Strovlés, sets off up the Yiphlós valley following the stream. After 2km, in *Strovlés*, turn left at a T-junction. At 3.5km you can turn left again to cut across (7km) to Plemenianá, just S of Kándanos, on the main Khaniá–Palaiókhora road. Ahead the broad new road (well-engineered though not asphalted all the way in 1987) climbs into the wild and unspoilt hill country of the SW corner of the island, to Voutás and Sklavopoúla (described as part of an excursion from Palaiókhora, see p 256). After 2km a dirt road branches left down into the valley 7km to Sarakína (see Rte 18), but the major road continues to climb to the watershed (6.5km from Strovlés), before the gradual descent (10km), with extensive views, to a fertile valley of orange groves, and *Voutás*.

Continuing through *Milí* on the circular itinerary, the road runs back towards the N coast through chestnut woods along the valley of the Yiphlós. At 87km, above the dramatic *Gorge of Topólia*, the cave of Ayía Sophía (with stalactites) has a chapel at its entrance; the cave was frequented from Neolithic to Roman times. *Topólia* is a pleasant village in a fine setting. The road continues down the river valley to the coast where you turn left for the last 5km to (104km) Kastélli-Kisámou.

INDEX

Topographical names are printed in **bold** type, personal names in *italics*, other entries in Roman type. Churches are indexed alphabetically by the name of their Saint.

ATLAS SECTION

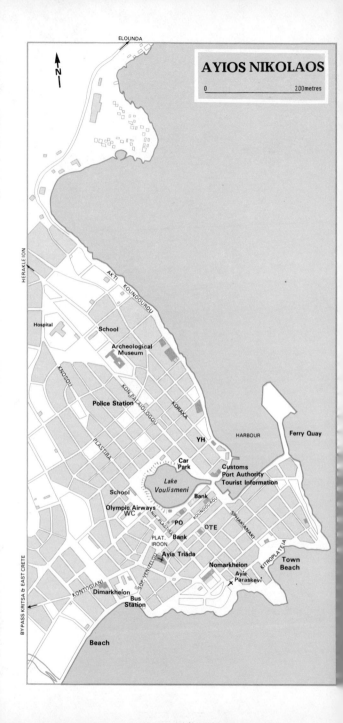

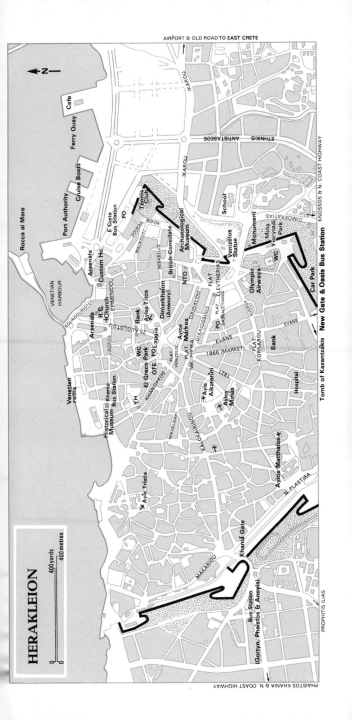

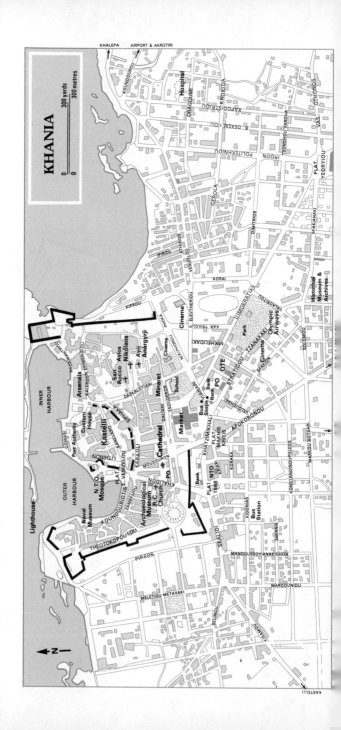

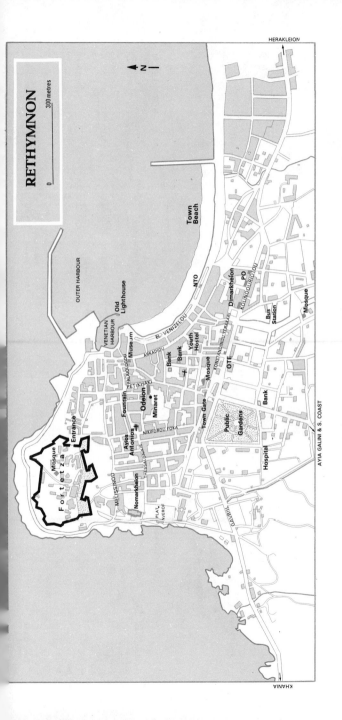

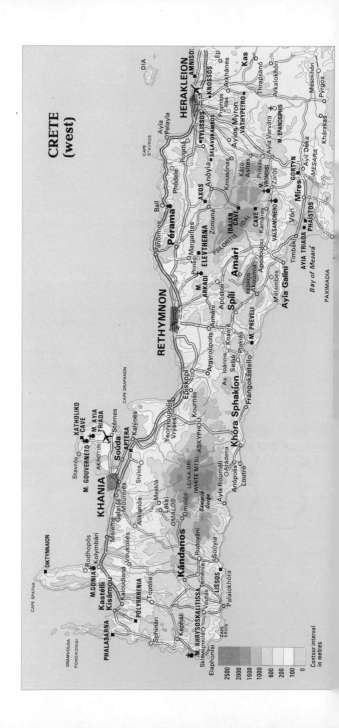

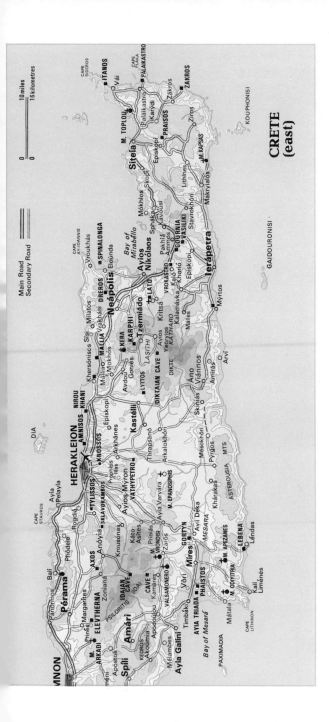